The Urbana Free Library

To renew materials call
217-367-4057

Richard's 21st-Century
Bicycle Book

D1366896

Richard's 21st-Century Bicycle Book

Richard Ballantine

Illustrations by John Batchelor, David Eccles, Peter Williams

THE OVERLOOK PRESS
Woodstock & New York

This book is dedicated to Samuel Joseph Melville, hero.

This edition first published in the United States in 2001 by
The Overlook Press, Peter Mayer Publishers, Inc.
Lewis Hollow Road
Woodstock, New York 12498
www.overlookpress.com

Library of Congress Cataloging-in-Publication Data

Ballantine, Richard.
Richard's 21st-century bicycle book / Richard Ballantine.
p. cm.
Rev. ed. of: Richard's bicycle book. 1972.
Includes index.
1. Cycling. 2. Bicycles. I. Title: Richard's twenty-first-century bicycle book.
II. Title: Bicycle book. III. Ballantine, Richard. Richard's bicycle book. IV. Title.
GV1041 .B32 2001   629.227'2—dc21   00-051510

Book design and type formatting by Bernard Schleifer
Manufactured in the United States of America
1 3 5 7 9 8 6 4 2
ISBN 1-58567-112-6

Contents

Introduction

– – – – – – – – – – – – – – – – – – – –

DEAR READER,

WHEN THIS BOOK WAS FIRST PUBLISHED IN 1972, there were just three kinds of bikes: single-speed paperboy with wide tires; roadster with 3-speed hub gears; and sport with derailleur gears, popularly known as a "10-speed". Typically built in a road racing pattern with downswept handlebars, a narrow saddle, and high, closely-spaced gear ratios, the 10-speed formed the leading edge of a massive boom in bikes throughout the 1970s that swelled to see, in one year alone, sales of nearly 20 million bikes in Britain and America.

A few quality lightweight racing and touring bikes were made by specialist builders and small firms, but most 10-speed bikes were mass-produced. The limitations of the steels then available meant that the bikes had heavy frames, and basic models had the further burden of steel components. New owners out on Sunday rides to celebrate the joys of cycling earned aching muscles from trying to push heavy bikes with oversize gears, and if they were luckless enough to be on steel wheels in wet conditions, suffered from heart convulsions caused by terrifyingly ineffective brakes. After a few such experiences, many "boom" bikes were put aside and forgotten;

they linger still by the millions and millions in basements, stairwells, sheds and garages, quietly gathering dust and visited only by spiders.

The 10-speed was often crude, but it gave a taste of what was possible and thereby set in motion a true and lasting renaissance of the bike. In a common pattern, many owners upgraded to better machines with quality frames and alloy components. A new bike culture arose, flowering with colorful new cycling magazines and books by the score, and bike technology rapidly advanced. By the start of the 1980s, new metals and materials suitable for mass production of true lightweight bikes became available, and firms run by people for whom cycling was a personally important lifestyle activity began producing quality bikes at affordable prices. Then came the seminal advent of the mountain bike, and an explosion of fresh designs and energy that is still growing in magnitude.

We are now spoilt for choice, for the new firmament glitters with cycles and components of every description. Today is as golden an age of cycling as has ever been. Never before has there been so much variety, nor better quality, nor better value! The questions are no longer "Should I have a bike?" and "How do I get a good bike?" but rather, "How many bikes?" and "What kinds?" Bikes are so wonderful, so much fun, so useful, it makes perfect sense to have several.

Modern lightweight bikes equipped with the latest components are a treat almost without comparison, but even a heavy old 10-speed, or a rusty roadster dredged out of a canal and restored with liberal applications of elbow grease and lubricants, can be useful and endearing machines. Bikes have a lot of range, all of them work to one degree or another, and thus speak very well for themselves. Yesterday, today, and tomorrow, I guarantee: Get a bike, any bike, start going with the thing and using it as it suits you, and it will get better and better and better.

RICHARD BALLANTINE
New York City
November 2000

Measurements used in this book

Please be advised, there is no single system of measurements for bicycles. Rather than burden the text with conversions, as in "24-inch (60.96 cm) mountain bike handlebars and 105 cm (41⁄8-inch) stem," I've simply followed common usage, trusting that like me, you are familiar with both systems.

Get A Bike!

Bicycle as ideal personal vehicle • Biological and biochemical efficiency • Quickness as transport • Advantages to personal health, happiness, and wealth, and to society, the economy, and the environment

MOTION AND FREEDOM ARE SYNONYMOUS. As kids, we play with toy bikes and cars, boats and ships, airplanes and rockets, and dream of flight and liberation. Our toys somehow represent a means of breaking the restrictions of everyday life, of having our fantasies come true – and it happens! As we grow and age, our play becomes real: we race across the land, sail the ocean, fly in the air, and even journey into space. Alone among the creatures of Earth, humans are transport engineers, designers, and builders of devices and machines that enhance or even completely transform our ability to get around. And yet, of all the incredible means of accelerated motion and transport that we have ever devised, from simple wood boards or pieces of metal attached to the feet, to immense, awesomely powerful machines comprised of literally millions of parts, there is still nothing to beat the bicycle. It is the most efficient means of transport on Earth, and in many cases, the quickest.

EFFICIENCY

Most of life's daily journeys are short in distance, but long in duration. In urban and suburban areas, traffic congestion is the rule rather than the exception. It's a matter of space. There are more cars on the roads than ever before, reducing room in which to move and slowing the speed of traffic to a crawl. At peak travel times in cities, cars average 8 to 12 mph as against 10 to 15 mph for bikes. Cars and buses go fast at times, but because of their size and lack of maneuverability, are often at a standstill. Bikes post higher average speeds because they are able to wiggle through traffic and keep on moving.

Bikes are also fast because they go door to door. Use public transport, and you've got to walk to the local stop or station, wait for your bus or train to show up, travel (possibly in segments, with more waiting time at each stage), and then walk to your destination. Use a car, and you've got to walk to where it is parked, travel, and then find a parking space – in many places, an increasingly difficult task that usually involves another walk. Go by bike and there's no idling around: you simply step out the door, take off, and go until you are there. A bike makes the best use of the most important thing in the world: your time.

Of all trips in the US, about 90 percent are by motor vehicle. Of these, about 80 percent are within eight miles from home. Most are a lot less. At these distances, in urban and suburban areas, a bike is the quickest thing going.

And a bike is freedom. You can go where you want, when you want. Worries about things like bus and train schedules, periods of peak traffic congestion, having enough money for public transport, or coping with a car that won't work, are not part of your consciousness. If you want to see a film, try out a new restaurant, dash off to buy a kite, or whatever, you just go. There's nothing to think about except doing it. What's more, you'll always be able to get back home. At night, taxis, trains, and buses can be elusive, but a bike is always ready to go. In fact, the wee hours are one of the nicest times to ride. In cities, the streets are quiet and calm, the air is cleaner, and you glide along with smooth grace. If it is night you might have the moon and stars for company; if it is early morning, the rising dawn and energy of a new day.

Travelling by bike is punctual. It does not take much experience to make the timing of most journeys predictable within a minute or two. When buses and trains do not arrive on schedule or fail to show up at all, you are helpless. When a car becomes mired in traffic, you're stuck. You can't even abandon the thing. On a bike you are in charge: if you're running late you can literally step on it and go faster, and conversely, if you have time to spare you can dawdle or take a detour to check out something you've not seen before. Reliability? A bike kept in decent condition is going to work. Once you have mastered a few mechanical basics, any problem that does arise can usually be solved within minutes. A bike gives you time, freedom, and control – your life is truly your own.

ECONOMICS

Can you afford not to have a bike? In terms of cost per mile, cycling even beats walking. Bikes pay for themselves. If you use a bike instead of public transport or a car to get to work and back, you are looking at saving some serious money; the cost of a decent bike is usually recovered within a few months. Commuting is just one application. Bikes are great for general moving around: going to shops, attending classes, visiting friends, going to theater and movies, and so on. There are savings every time, and over a year the total can amount

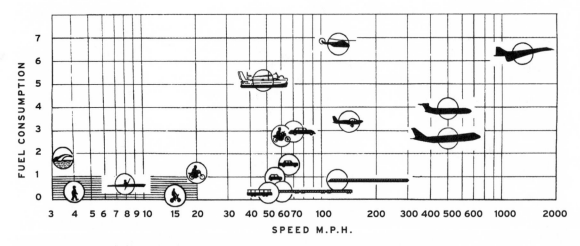

Energy Efficiency of Different Kinds of Transport – Courtesy Alex Moulton.

to enough for a holiday, an addition to the house, perhaps even a nice boat – take your pick.

Ha, some car owners might say, sure bikes are cheap, but time is money. Perhaps a bike is quicker at distances of up to six or even eight or nine miles, but I've got to travel 12 miles to work and by car the journey usually takes 30 to 35 minutes. Going by bike would take at least an hour. So both ways, using a car instead of a bike saves an hour. Yes – but an average car owner devotes four to five hours a day to his or her vehicle, either using it, looking after it in various ways, or earning the money to support it. Even if a car does manage a 12 mile journey in half the time of a bike (likely only on open roads), the saving in time might in the end be no saving at all. The price of a basic small car is roughly ten times more than that of a decent bike and accessories, and over a five year period the annual running cost for a small car is at least 20 times greater than for a bike. Looked at this way, the hour the car "saves" is at a stiff price.

As for the cost of cycling versus motoring, if you own, or are thinking about owning a car, try this: add up all your car-related expenses for the year, plus your annual expenditure for all other transport. Next, add the costs of bikes and accessories for each family member (say, a generous $1,000 per person, though you can restore a bike rescued from a rubbish heap for $50 or less); renting cars for weekends, holidays, and special events; and all other transport, including a sizeable allowance for taxis.

Unless you drive many miles a year, or have a large family, using bikes and hiring taxis and renting cars when required will probably show a savings within a year, two years at most – and you will have a better life style, too. You'll still be able to use a car if and when you want, but without any of the hassles or stresses of ownership. Increasingly, for many people it is both cheaper, more convenient, and lots more fun not to own a car.

An option that works well for infrequent, short journeys are car share programs. These started in Europe and are now rapidly growing in popularity in cities across the US. Members have access, via special keys and smart cards, to a fleet of vehicles, including special purpose models such as vans and pickups. All a member has to do with a car is use it. There's no car washing, maintenance, parking, or any of the other hassles that typically go with owning a car. Plus, so long as annual miles driven are 5,000 or fewer, there's a considerable cost savings.

Some people are more or less forced to use cars because they live in places where distances are long and public transport services are inadequate. Stations or stops are far from trip origins or destinations, services are erratic, and/or routes are such that it can take hours to travel a distance that is but a few miles as the crow flies. There's hope in some cases here, too, because by using mixed mode transport – bikes combined with public transport – the time for many journeys can often be substantially reduced. See Chapter 13 on urban commuting for more on this subject.

LIVING IT UP

Cycling is economic, but it does not have to be cheap. In fact, one of the nicest things about bikes is that going first class is affordable. As a leisure activity and sport, the cost of cycling is competitive with other outdoor pursuits, but this is only partially relevant, because individual preferences and priorities vary. If you are nuts about scuba diving, or horses, or whatever, then spending your money on what you love most will give a good return. However, it is worth noting that bikes are a tremendous value. You can have the pride and pleasure of owning and using a brilliant bicycle for less than the cost of a year's worth of gasoline for a mid-size car, and if you want to own and use a state-of-the-art, ultimate machine, you can still do so without breaking the bank.

Finally, and by no means least, the basic economy of a bike can be about a lot more than money. If you are stuck supporting a car, then you might take some guff from your boss that otherwise you would not stand for. Or pass up a beckoning adventure. Or endure a numbing dumb school. In life, one trap tends to lead to another – and equally, freedom is habit forming!

You owe it to yourself to have a bicycle.

FITNESS

Riding a bike makes you feel better. As animals we have relatively big brains and are much given to thinking and cogitating on the substance and meaning of complex ideas and issues, but physically we are not much different from the time when we first dropped out of the trees to compete for food and territory with saber-tooth tigers and other rival predators. We're made for action, physically and mentally, and riding bikes makes us more fit, quicker and more accurate thinkers, and best of all, more glad to be around.

When you do physical work you take in oxygen and use it to burn the fuel stored in your body. The important measure of fitness is not strength, but efficiency in breathing, and in circulating oxygen to the body tissues while simultaneously clearing away the waste by-products of muscle activity. Exercise increases your fitness and makes all your activities – from changing nappies to thinking through chess problems – easier to do. Riding a bike is a particularly good form of exercise, because it can be done at the pace that suits you best, and with no stress to joints – a nice, general workout that leaves your lungs, heart, and blood circulation system in better shape. How much better? Put it this way: if you are now fairly sedentary and take up riding a bike with reasonable regularity, your life span will increase by about five years. Plus, all your years will benefit, because you will enjoy a fitness level equal to that of a person ten years younger.

By exercising your lungs and heart you make them more efficient and keep them cleaned out, so they work better, and for longer. Cardiovascular problems account for over 50 percent of all deaths each year and are basically due either to muscle atrophy or to one form or another of clogging. When you are at rest, your heart pumps five quarts of blood per minute. When you are in motion, the rate reaches up to 30 quarts per minute. That's some performance, and to appreciate it, turn on a water tap fast enough to fill a quart container in the time it takes you to say "One-and two-and". That's the work your heart does running at open stretch. It is an amazing muscle, and to be healthy and strong and perform as it should, it needs real work to do.

Blood moves inside your body through arteries, veins, and other circulation mechanisms that are essentially tubes. If the flow is typically slow, the walls of the system calcify and harden, and fatty deposits accumulate. The bores of the tubes decrease and to cope, the heart pumps harder, resulting in higher blood pressure and in turn, greater risk of a stroke or rupture of the brain blood vessels. Or, one of those fatty deposits gets stuck at a critical point like the heart or brain – heart attack or brain stroke. Exercise stimulates the blood flow, thereby reducing the rate of calcification (arteriosclerosis) and helping to prevent fatty deposits (atherosclerosis).

Cycling is a complete exercise. The legs, the body's largest accessory blood pumping mechanism, are used extensively, and depending on the kind of bike you use and where and how you ride, the arm, shoulder, back, and diaphragm muscles also come into play. A critical factor is that you set the pace. This is one of the prime features of riding a bike. Regular vigorous exercise is great, but we all have good days and bad days. Sometimes when you ride, the buzz is on, and you whirl along out on the edge with all systems go. Other times, you are happy to ride well within capacity and enjoy your thoughts or the scenery. You can relax and let it come. Cycling has natural bite: the more you do it, the better you become, and the more inclined you are to do it.

Cycling is fairly unique in that it allows you to combine healthy exercise with things you have to do anyway, such as commuting to and from work, delivering and picking up the kids from school, and other daily routines. Skiing, swimming, sailing, sky diving, and a zillion other activities are great fun as sports, but only rarely can work as a means of transport to the bank.

Riding a bike clears the mind. At one level, this is because riding a bike is physical. At a deeper level, how you ride reflects your thinking and thoughts. You are with yourself. You might laze along with your own dreams and memories, or delight in butterflies and flowers, or get up on the stick and charge to make the next set of traffic lights, or pick a race with another cyclist. It's your call, your moment. You can be as you want. I reckon this is the most precious thing about riding a bike.

Over the years, I've had many a time of having someplace to go, but feeling so-so for one reason or another, or looking at marginal weather conditions, and wondering, should I take the bike, or leave it? I've learnt that when in doubt, mount up. If I'm a bit down and ride, then just about always I wind up feeling better. As for marginal weather, the tonic effect of regular exercise pushes back the boundaries. The more you ride, the more you want to ride, and the more you cope with a bit of mist, cold, or wind, the more you are alive. As I said, we're built for action.

A word about weight control. Cycling or other exercise will help your body's tone and figure, but it is not a gobble licence. Cycling burns off anywhere from 300 to 800 calories per hour, depending on the extent of effort. Your body uses up about 150 calories per hour just hanging around, so for regular cycling the extra burn is only about 150 per hour. At 3,600 calories per pound of body weight, it would take 24 hours of riding to lose this amount. There are easier ways.

$$E = mc^2$$

Of course, nutrition and health are more than a matter of calories. Exercise has a great effect on how the body uses food. You need both to exercise and to eat foods that burn well in your particular system. If you are overweight because of inappropriate eating habits then cycling or other exercise will probably help balance your metabolism and appetite, and give you a push in the direction of eating foods that are right for you, in the quantities you actually need.

ENVIRONMENT

Air pollution is a major problem, in America and throughout the world. It's worst of all in cities, where most people live and work, and where cars are the source of up to 85 percent of all air pollution. Cars are also especially noxious: the effluents from gasoline engines hang in the air and chemically interact with other substances and sunlight to form even deadlier poisons.

Living in a major city is dangerous to your health. The damage from air pollution is as bad, if not worse, than smoking two packs of cigarettes a day, and will eventually turn your lungs black. None of this should be news. Turn on the TV, consult a newspaper, and you'll find daily indexes of air pollution. When certain specific weather conditions exist, air pollution intensifies, and warnings are posted. Sometimes people are told to stay indoors and avoid non-essential journeys. And in direct proportion to the amount and intensity of air pollution, people die – particularly the vulnerable new born, the elderly, and those frail in health. On a worldwide scale, the World Health Organization estimates that urban air pollution kills at least three million people each year.

We know all this stuff, if only instinctively. Public surveys show that people rate air pollution the No. 1 health hazard and problem. What is hard to appreciate is how much better things could be.

Many, many years ago, I got one of the all time surprises of my life. A friend and I drove into New York City late at night after a skiing vacation in Canada. To my amazement, the air was perfectly clear. The lights of the city shone like jewels, each building standing sharp and distinct. Looking across the Hudson River from New Jersey I could for the first (and so far only) time in my life see Manhattan and the Bronx in perfect detail from beginning to end, and even beyond, to Brooklyn and her bridges. As we crossed the George Washington Bridge into the city, the air was clean and fresh, and the city, usually filthy and smoky, was astoundingly beautiful and iridescent. The explanation was simple: two days earlier there had been a major storm, and enough snow had fallen to effectively eliminate vehicle traffic. No vehicles, no junk in the air. A better world.

You don't have to trek out to the middle of the Sahara Desert, or sail the vast reaches of the Pacific, to experience the freshness and wonder that is plain clean air. All you have to do is shut down the cars. Try going out for a ride or a long walk on some occasion when most of the cars are off the road, and the difference will literally be clear.

Of course, it is now increasingly fashionable to say we must now do something to restrict or eliminate cars. There are articles in newspapers, and films on TV with close up pictures of smoking exhaust pipes. There's a real problem: since 1969, the number of motor vehicles in the US has grown six times faster than the human popula-

tion, and at twice the rate of new drivers. Even the motoring organizations are saying we should back off a little. But when push comes to shove, such ideas are resisted as idealistic and impractical – society is built around cars, their time saving characteristics are essential, and if they go, the economy will fail and all will be lost. Bilge! In fact, in US metropolitan areas alone, the cost of traffic congestion in wasted fuel and lost productivity is reckoned at $74 billion. There sure is no savings in time. Even pedestrians often drone past urban traffic, and bikes of course do much better. Cars are said to spare physical effort, but this is misleading. Of all road users, motorists are the most vulnerable to air pollution. It's extraordinary, but motorists seated in their cars have higher blood levels of carbon monoxide and other poisons than cyclists pedalling through the same soup.

Cars are wasteful. In America, transportation accounts for over 25 percent of all energy consumed, and uses over 65 percent of the oil supply. We have enough cars so that if every person in the country got into one at the same time, no one would have to ride in a back seat. Yet they wouldn't get anyplace. The open roads and brisk speeds shown in TV advertisements for cars are a myth; in fact, the majority of motor journeys are short and local, use up a lot of gas, take forever, and stink. For most journeys, walking, roller blading or skating, and cycling, are often faster, and without question, hugely more energy efficient. It is conservatively reckoned that a cyclist can do 1,600 miles on the food energy equivalent of a gallon of gasoline, which will move a car some 10 to 30 miles. Put another way, per mile it takes about 35 calories to move a cyclist, as against 1,860 calories to move a car and one person – and the cyclist is faster.

Facts and figures not withstanding, using a 100 horsepower, 5000 pound car to move one 150 pound person a few miles is like using an atomic bomb to kill a canary. We cannot sustain such prodigious waste. Of the six or so billion people on the planet, a third are desperately poor. In impoverished countries, people scrabble for every calorie of food, and are terribly vulnerable to disease – and overpopulation, ignorance, and lack of initiative are symptoms, not the root causes of their problems. The US leads the world in ability to consume and waste, and utilizes a disproportionate amount of the planet's resources. For example, America has five percent of the world's population, yet possesses about 35 percent of the global car fleet. Well, affluence would be fine if it were through our own enterprise and industry, but much of it comes through ripping people off who have no power to resist. For example, in South America the forests are being burnt away to make room for beef herds. Never mind that the ecology of the planet is being irreversibly damaged. Do the people down there get to eat the beef? Nope, it's sent to America, Europe, and elsewhere, to make hamburgers for fast food outlets. Anyone in South America who objects "disappears." And we wonder why people in those parts don't like us.

Using a bicycle is using less, an initial antidote to the horrors of consumerism. Solving the problems of the world is not an easily delineated task, but one thing I know for sure: riding a bike, I go about my business completely self-contained, without harming or exploiting anybody. It's right. In case you feel that riding a bike on your lonesome is insignificant when set against the scale of world events, consider: in 1968, world production of cars and bikes was about equal; today, annual production of bikes is well above 100 million, and outpaces car production by at least three to one. Bikes are on the winning team.

Good for the world is fine, but the most positive series of reasons for using bicycles at every opportunity is that doing so enhances your life, bringing to it an increase in quality of experience which is reflected in everything you do.

Well! You have to expect that I believe cycling is a good idea, but how do I get off expressing the notion that it is philosophically and morally sound? Because it is something you do, not something that is done to you. Increasing alienation is a fact of our lives – the uniform behavior and ideas promoted in schools, the mechanization of work and daily activities, the hardships our industrial society places in the way of loving and fulfilling relationships and family life, the difficulties individuals experience trying to influence political and economic decisions which affect them and others.

What values do you want to incubate? Some people say the world is as it is, and thus they have a "right" to charge around in automobiles, annually killing 850,000 people and injuring 15 million more. This is more a failure of awareness than of logic. The most important negative effect of alienation and the use of destructive technologies is the defeat and inhibition of consciousness. Consciousness, self-awareness, and development are the prerequisites for a life worth living. Now look at what happens to you on a bicycle. It's immediate and direct. *You* pedal. *You* make decisions. *You* experience the tang of the air and the surge of power as you bite into the road. You're vitalized. As you hum along you fully and gloriously experience the day, the sunshine, the clouds, the breezes. You're alive! You are going someplace, and it is *you* who are doing it. Awareness increases, and each day becomes a little more important to you. With increased awareness, you see and notice more, and this further reinforces awareness.

Each time you insert *you* into a situation, each time *you* experience, you fight against alienation and impersonality, and you build consciousness and identity. You try to understand things in the ways that are important to you. And these qualities carry over into everything you do.

An increased value on one's own life is the first step in social consciousness and politics. Because to you life is dear and important and fun, it is much easier to understand why this is also true for others, wherever they live, and whatever their color, language, and culture. Believe it. The salvation of the world is the development of personality and identity for everyone in it. Much work, many lifetimes. But a good start for you is to *get a bicycle!*

The BICYCLE !

What Is A Bike?

Invention of bicycle and evolution from boneshaker to high wheel bike to chain drive safety and beyond • Nature of modern cycle manufacture and high quality bikes

DISCOVERY

THE BICYCLE IS TOO UNIQUE TO HAVE BEEN invented – it must have been a chance discovery. Describing the dynamics of how a bicycle in motion remains upright, say eminent mechanical engineers Chester Kyle and John N. Olson, involves fourth order, non-linear, partial differential equations with variable coefficients, and complex calculations that cause problems even for big computers. Yet it is almost impossible to make a bicycle that will not work. Build a frame, attach two in line wheels, one of them with steering, set the thing in motion, and with someone or something aboard to "steer" (a monkey will do), the vehicle can be made to stay upright – depending on design characteristics, less handily in some cases, more easily in others. In fact, it is possible to build a bicycle that so long as it is rolling will stay upright by itself, without a rider.

Once a bicycle is seen, it all seems incredibly obvious. A bicycle in motion does not fall down because it is constantly moving from out of balance into balance; motion resolves the yes/no issue of balance into dynamic equilibrium. Simple. But the process is physically unique, and there is no way to imagine it in the abstract. No creature in nature, nor any mechanical process, will serve as a model for a bicycle. The principle of jet propulsion, for example, can be observed in primitive invertebrates such as squid. The only analogy for the bicycle I can imagine is life itself. Ecosystems operate just like a bicycle. Responding to environmental change, elements in an ecosystem increase or decrease, constantly moving the entire ecosystem from an out of balance state toward equilibrium.

As with the bicycle, motion keeps the ecosystem stable. Simple, constant ecosystems with few parts can be prolific (for example, a food chain producing large quantities of a single species of fish) but vulnerable; if a component is removed or perishes, the entire system is likely to collapse. Diverse ecosystems, on the other hand, comprised of complex food webs and structures, with various components constantly thriving and fading, are more stable, because they are better able to adapt to change. Motion is fundamental to the operation of a bicycle, and the complexity of the balancing process is probably why it works so well despite many variables. Those "fourth order, non-linear, etc." equations for how a bike stays upright have never in fact been completed, because the permutations are infinite.

Drawings said to be from the studio of Leonardo da Vinci and attributed to one of his students appear to be of a bicycle with chain drive. The drawings are not available for date testing, and most historians regard them as fake. There is no record indicating such a machine was ever built. Even if the drawings are authentic and the device shown is intended to be pedal-propelled, it lacks the crucial feature defining a bicycle: steering.

The vision of a bicycle as a mechanical mirror of life itself is a beautiful metaphor, a great compliment to the bicycle. Still, if one had no knowledge of the bicycle in the first place, then I do not believe that any amount of enlightenment about the functioning of the natural world would lead to the idea of the bike.

So how did it happen? We can only guess. In his new book *Bicycle Design* (Open Road, 2000), Mike Burrows reckons that the forerunner of the bicycle could have been the common wheelbarrow, with a wheel at the front and two legs at the back, used since who knows when for transporting small loads. As distinguished from a barrow, a cart with two wheels on either side, a wheelbarrow is agile and easy to maneuver in twisting, confined places. This would have been especially important in days of yore, when paths and alleyways were often rough and narrow. But there would have been times when it was only necessary to go in a straight line, in which case someone might have thought of adding another in-line wheel. Such a design could bear all the weight when going straight, yet by simply lifting (or pressing) the handles you could still pivot on one wheel, for maneuverability in tight places.

Let's pretend you were someone trying out this

idea and before the basket was mounted, you needed to move the frame from one place to another. One method might be to roll it along while balancing it with your hand. If you then happened to lean on the thing – particularly on a downgrade – you'd get a bit of a skip-step ride. This kinetic revelation might inspire you to throw your leg over the frame and use your feet to scoot along, tilting one way and then the other. You'd go pretty good then, but without steering, would keep finding yourself headed towards trees, rock walls, and so on. You'd have to stop and pick the machine up in order to change direction. Surely the idea would occur of adding steering? Tinker, tinker, and on your next ride – history!

Any script about how the bicycle was originally developed is pure conjecture, but it is interesting to note that if you try to teach people to ride a bike by explaining how to do it and then just send them off, they are likely to go down in a tangle or head straight for the nearest tree. If you remove the pedals and ask them to use their feet to scoot along, they will learn the mystery of balance within seconds. The bicycle is a 100 percent kinetic machine, i.e. its equilibrium depends on motion, and almost certainly was a hands on discovery made in the course of fiddling with some other idea.

EVOLUTION

Credit for the first workable bicycle goes to Baron Karl von Drais of Germany, who in 1817 introduced a running machine. Popularly known as a hobby horse, the vehicle consisted of a body set above two wheels, and was powered by the rider pushing his feet alternately against the ground. Crucially, the front wheel could be steered.

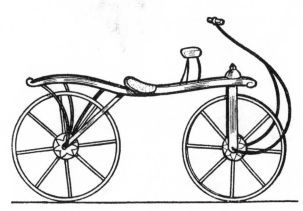

Hobby horse

The hobby horse was crude and uncomfortable, but it was fast; on a good road, a hobby horse rider could beat a horse. This was news in a world in which hay burners had been the fastest means of personal land transport for thousands of years. In one celebrated race in Britain, a hobby horse rider beat a four horse coach from London to Brighton, some 60 miles. In a fashion craze, hobby horses rapidly appeared throughout Europe and even in America, primarily as objects of curiosity for the well-to-do. But the newfangled machines were physically hard on riders, and they were not always liked by the general public – in many places, they were banned. Popular interest in hobby horses ebbed.

Technological improvement was needed, and in subsequent years, a number of backyard inventors devised two wheel machines with pedal drive transmissions. Especially notable was a Scottish blacksmith, Kirkpatrick Macmillan, who around 1839 built a bicycle with rear wheel drive via a treadle transmission. Technically advanced, Macmillan's velocipede (what a bike was called back then) was capable of a sustained average speed of eight mph. Macmillan made no effort to market or manufacture his bike, and the original machine has not survived, although many copies were made. We know about it because an article in the *Glasgow Argus* newspaper reported that while Macmillan was on a 140-mile round trip from his home in Dumfries to Glasgow and – tsk – riding along the sidewalk, he hit a child and was fined for the offence.

Another technically advanced rear wheel drive velocipede similar to Macmillan's was made around 1842 by Alexander Lefèbvre of France. In

Macmillan type bicycle built by McCall c.1860

1860 or 1861 Lefèbvre moved to California, taking his original machine with him; it now survives as the world's oldest existing bicycle.

There were other attempts at pedal drives, but then, as now, achieving widespread popularity for a bicycle design or innovation depended on achieving successful commercial manufacture, marketing, and sales. This was the accomplishment of one Pierre Michaux, a French cabinet maker and locksmith, who, with his son Ernest, organized workshops in Paris and in 1861 launched a bicycle with pedals and cranks attached directly to the front wheel. The first machines were crude and not very comfortable

SOMETHING FOR THE BACK CARRIER —
SUSSEX COAST

By the incomparable Frank Patterson

Lallement velocipede, 1866

WHODUNNIT?

Some historians contend that a Frenchman, Pierre Lallement, is the inventor of the pedal drive bicycle. Supposedly, Lallement came up with the idea while working for Michaux, who stole it. However, Michaux launched his machine in 1861. In an interview with Charles Pratt published in 1883 in *Wheelmen Illustrated*, Lallement, himself, states that he first thought of the pedal drive in 1862 while living in Nancy, France. He moved to Paris and built his first bicycle in 1863 and a second model in 1865, and then emigrated to the United States, where he met Carroll, a local businessman. The pair were granted United States Patent No. 59,915 on November 20, 1866 for a pedal drive bicycle, and set up production of velocipedes in New Haven, Connecticut.

Lallement makes no mention of Michaux. Yet, according to Michaux's son, Henri, Lallement did some development work for Michaux in 1865. Quite possibly this was the counter-weight pedal, which appears to be on both Lallement's 1866 patent and the Michaux 1866 model.

Good ideas or inventions often occur to several people at once. Lallement may well have independently thought of the pedal drive. At that time, crank arms were common on machines and hoisting devices; applying the idea to a bicycle would have been logical. My guess is that Lallement's claim to original concept was made to establish a strong patent, something that turned out to be economically significant – but not for Lallement.

The Lallement/Carroll manufacturing venture was unsuccessful, the patent was sold to one Calvin Witty, of Brooklyn, New York, and Lallement returned to France. Shortly thereafter, interest in velocipedes rose in America, and the patent – tested in court – enabled Witty to force manufacturers to pay high royalty fees for every machine sold. This was one of the factors that caused the American velocipede movement to wither on the vine. A decade later, the advent of the high wheel bicycle made the patent again valuable, and it was taken over by Albert Pope, a major player in the cycle industry. Pope also had the patent upheld by a court. The patent finally expired in 1883 and, in one of life's ironies, that same year Lallement returned to Boston to work as a machinist for the Pope Manufacturing Company.

(the vehicle was known in Britain, more descriptively, as a boneshaker) but in 1866-67 a new model was introduced, with a curving wrought iron frame, a larger front wheel, and various other refinements. Astutely, Pierre supplied French royalty with finely crafted, upmarket versions of the new edition. The aristocracy was entranced, and played with their new toys in the streets of Paris, sparking a vogue for velocipedes. Suddenly, in all the best places, cycling was the thing to do.

As demand for velocipedes soared, an overwhelmed Michaux factory was refinanced and relocated by the Olivier Brothers, who took over the business in 1869–70. The new regime marketed vigorously, advertising top range machines in

"enamelled, polished and damascened steel, polished or engraved aluminium bronze. Wheels of West Indian hardwood, amaranth, makrussa, hickory, ebony or lemon tree. Handlebar grips of sculpted ivory." Until 1867, Michaux had produced a few hundred machines a year; under the Olivier Brothers, production was claimed to be 200 machines a day – and they were only one of some 75 manufacturers of velocipedes in France.

France led the world in bicycle design. In 1869, in a development eventually crucial for the efficiency and performance of all types of machines throughout the world, Jules Suriray patented and produced ball bearings for bicycle wheel hubs. Other innovations featured that same year at the

Michaux velocipede

Paris Velocipede Exhibition were metal spoked wheels, solid rubber tires, a four speed gear, and a freewheel. Ah, fickle fate! In 1870 the Franco-Prussian War broke out, Paris was besieged, and when the cannon smoke cleared all that was left of the world's first bicycle industry was rubble.

Fortunately, the passion for velocipedes had spread throughout Europe and across the Atlantic. In America, the craze, while pronounced, was short lived, but in Britain, the velocipede found an enduring home. Firms in the Midlands counties of England, producing sewing machines, firearms, and other machinery took up the manufacture of velocipedes, first as a sideline and eventually as a principal activity. Coventry, in particular, became the epicenter for the continuing evolution of the bicycle.

With pedals and cranks attached directly to the front wheel, the speed of a boneshaker was a function of wheel size; the larger the diameter of the driving wheel, the faster the rider could go. The limiting factor was rider leg length, and through the 1870s the boneshaker quite literally grew into the famous, elegant high wheel bicycle, a machine that often stood as tall as a man.

I found a high wheel bike once, while rummaging in the back of an antique shop on the Isle of Wight, and on inspecting the machine, was astounded by the quality of materials and construction: hollow tubing frame, double ball bearings for the wheel hub, and a hollow section wheel rim. The bike weighed not much more than 20 pounds – less than many racing bikes you might buy today.

The high wheel bicycle was an athletic sporting machine – extremely fast, and quite dangerous to ride. The large driving wheel gave speed, but since the most effective riding position was almost straight above the wheel, the center of gravity was very high, and finely balanced. This made the bike unstable and when under way, encountering a chance stone, stick, or rut could and often did, cause the bike to cartwheel, pitching the rider over the handlebars in a horrendous forward fall known

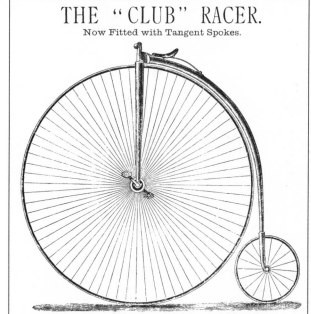

as "coming a cropper." The instability of the bike also prohibited any possibility of serious braking. A spoon brake (which worked by rubbing against the front tire) fitted to many machines was only a wishful hope, because overzealous application of this puny device, or even just backpedaling too hard could also tilt the bike and send the rider flying.

You had to be fit and hardy to ride a high wheeler, and this made bicycling an adventure for young, male middle class sporting bloods. High wheel riders were often frolicsome and daring, and their antics were frequently unappreciated by drivers of horse drawn coaches and wagons, farm-

ers and country oafs, and townspeople who had to dodge out of the way of careening, brakeless bikes. High wheel riders tended to band together in quasi-military clubs that required uniforms and strict riding rules, partly for self-esteem, but more practically for group protection against the frequent abuse, sticks, and stones hurled at them on club runs. Many contemporary racing and touring organizations had their origins in such clubs.

As with the American cowboy, the reign of the high wheeler was colorful but brief; the heyday was around 1880, a period when designers and inventors were experimenting with an enormous variety of pedal powered machines: monocycles, dicycles, tricycles, quadricycles, swimming machines, flying machines, and innumerable cycle-related mechanisms, devices, and accessories. One strong line of investigation was the quest for what would later be called a "safety" bicycle, a machine stable enough to

Hills were dangerous for near-brakeless high wheel bikes. In Britain, an important early contribution of the Cyclists' Touring Club (founded 1878) was the posting of warning signs on wipe-out hills throughout the country. I saw one, while on a meandering ride somewhere in southern England. Later, I understood that I had made a rare sighting of something virtually extinct. I've no idea of where it was; I like to think the sign still stands, brushed by green leaves and sunlight along a forgotten byway that you might, if you were very lucky, still find.

be ridden without the likely possibility of an upset.

To move the rider's weight back toward the rear wheel and thereby improve stability, some designers utilized a treadle drive, as in the Singer 'Xtraordinary of 1878. A different tactic was employed by the famous American Star Machine, which placed the small "rear" wheel at the front.

There were other design variations, but the route to go was rear wheel chain drive and gearing, and

Above, First parade of the League of American Wheelmen, in Boston, 1881. There may have been nearly a thousand bikes. Mass rides with high wheel bikes maintaining formation, three and four abreast, required considerable power and skill on the part of the riders.

Right, Side-by-side "sociable" on Riverside Drive, New York City, c. 1886. Complex tricycles and quadricycles were popular for a time in Europe but only briefly in America. They needed smooth roads, and their large size made them awkward to keep or transport.

Left, From the very start, with Colonel Albert A. Pope's Columbia bicycle, American factories changed the nature of bicycle manufacturing. Instead of each bicycle being handbuilt, parts were produced to standard sizes, so that they were interchangeable.

THE ROVER SAFETY BICYCLE (PATENTED).

Safer than any Tricycle, faster and easier than any Bicycle ever made. Fitted with handles to turn for convenience in storing or shipping. Far and away the best hill-climber in the market.

Rover Safety, 1st model, with indirect steering. Built in 1884, first shown in 1885.

the landmark machine for this evolutionary jump is the second model Rover Safety designed by John Kemp Starley and launched at the Stanley Show in London in 1885. There were earlier chain drive bicycles, quite a few in fact – but it was the Rover that succeeded in commercial production and, as advertised, truly "set the fashion to the world."

The chain drive enabled the use of gearing and hence wheels of a reasonable size, resulting in a stable machine that a rider could mount and dismount easily, and above all, that could use brakes. The smaller wheels reacted more harshly to bumps and holes, but this problem was solved by another invention crucial to the development of cycling: the pneumatic tire, patented by John Boyd Dunlop in 1888. The air filled inner tube provided a cushion against road shock and vibration, greatly improved grip, and most important, dramatically reduced rolling resistance. The

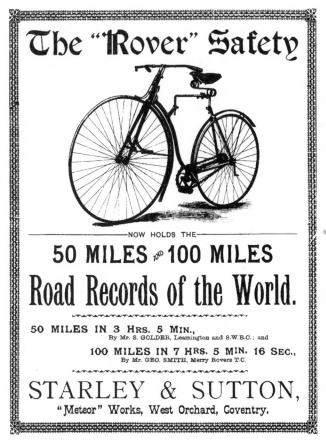

had time for leisure riding. The chain drive bicycle, however, could be mass produced, which made the cost of a bike manageable for an average wage earner.

And people wanted bikes. The scale of usefulness for the bicycle was vast, and ranged through all walks of life: bicycles were instrumental in liberating house bound women from skirts and domestic servitude, and in exploring and opening up such rugged wilderness areas as the Australian Outback and Canadian North-West Territories. Sport, service trades, postal deliveries, gold prospecting, courting, attending classes – bicycles were used in almost every sphere of life. Transport for the people had arrived, and on a global scale.

BIKES IN THE TWENTIETH CENTURY

In the so-called third world where four-fifths of our planet's six billion people live, bicycles and human-powered machines in various of forms are now the staple of personal transport. Eighty percent or more of today's global bike fleet is in developing countries. Rush hour in, say, a principal Chinese city, with hundreds of thousands of bikes moving in constant flowing streams – many carrying entire families or astonishing loads – is an awe-inspiring sight. For ease of manufacture and ongoing maintenance, many of these bikes are technologically little different from those produced around 1910. Simple, strongly made workhorse machines carry the bulk of the world's people and light goods.

In industrialized countries, the bicycle underwent further dramatic technological evolution, but its role in society was affected by two world wars and was profoundly influenced by the rise of the automobile. During the 1914–18 and 1939–45 World Wars general bicycle manufacturing was suspended in favor of producing war materials, although the gasoline and mass transportation shortages served to prove bikes more useful than ever. The effect of the automobile was another story.

geared, chain drive bicycle was already far swifter than the direct drive high bicycle; shod with pneumatic tires, it became the fastest, most energy efficient personal vehicle on Earth.

During the quest for a safety bicycle, the term "ordinary bicycle" came into use to designate a high wheel bicycle, and this later condensed to "ordinary." Once the safety became established, it was called simply a "bicycle." Incidentally, the British term "penny farthing," although commonplace, is slighting; it has the same meaning as "old wreck" for a car, and is inappropriate for the magnificent and often finely built high wheel bike.

The bicycle enhanced individual freedom and mobility and, in the period 1890–1910, its development and spread throughout the world was incandescent. The high wheel bike had been a largely middle class phenomenon, because few working class people could afford to buy one, or

Paperboy bike

In America, the passion for automobiles simply swept away the bicycle. After World War I, enclaves of cycle sport persisted in a few places, but with the onset of the Great Depression in the 1930s the American bicycle industry came to a virtual standstill. Only 194,000 bicycles were sold in 1932. In 1933, Arnold, Schwinn, & Co. introduced a new range of bicycles equipped with low pressure, 2.125-inch wide tires. The bikes were styled like motorcycles and were sturdy but cumbersome. Equipped with massive cowhorn handlebars, a single pedal operated coaster brake, and one low, slow gear, these "paperboy" bikes hit the scales at up to 70 pounds and more. They were used primarily by youngsters not old enough to drive a car.

In Europe and Britain the story was quite different. In the years between the wars the popularity of cycling, both as a recreational activity and as a general means of transport, expanded enormously. In Britain, the year 1935 saw a record 1.6 million bikes sold. The basic bicycle design established by 1910 had been subject to a long evolutionary series of minor improvements, and had split into two distinct types: utility and racing.

Most utility bikes were mass-produced middleweight roadsters with roller lever rim brakes, and 1.5-inch wide tires. Fancier, lighter models had calliper cable actuated rim brakes, hub gears, and 1.25 or 1.5-inch wide tires. Tipping the scales at 45–50 pounds, they were dubbed "English Racers" by Americans because of their startlingly better performance than the domestic product. In Britain, they were just the ordinary ride around bike for local use, to and from work, postal delivery, police work, window cleaning, light touring, and the like.

In the 1920s, the development of "covers" – tires with the casing edges sewn together – helped distinguish the racing bike as a distinct design genre. A tubular tire could be light and thin,

1936 Raleigh Golden Arrow

F. W. Evans (London) frameset, c. 1930

THE CAMPAGNOLO LEGEND

In 1927, while leading a race through the Dolomite Alps in falling snow, Italian rider Tullio Campagnolo's tire punctured. He was unable to loosen the frozen wing nuts on his wheel, which led him to invent and market the hollow-axle, quick-release wheel hub now in universal use, and then in 1933, a derailleur which, later, in 1951, evolved into the parallelo-gram derailleur. By producing components of the highest quality, finish, and – most important to racers – reliability, the firm of Campagnolo set the benchmark. Through the 1970s, the dream machine of virtually every sport rider was an "all-Campy" bike – the best hand-built frame they could afford, equipped with Campagnolo components throughout.

yet hold a high pressure, and could be mounted (with glue) on a thin and therefore light rim. This made sprint wheels dynamic and responsive, especially in those days when ordinary (clincher) tires with wire beads were heavier and bulkier than they are now.

Racing bikes evolved into slim, close clearance (no room for fenders) machines, equipped with compact but effective brakes and, in time, efficient derailleur gear transmissions. In those days, high quality steels were too delicate for mass production building methods, and lightweight frames were hand made by individual builders. Many were artisans of legendary skill, and this was the period when many small, specialist firms producing finely crafted bikes now revered as classics got their start. With the development of well designed and beautifully finished components from firms such as Campagnolo, sport bikes became functional works of art. The racing community was widespread; old time riders and cycle dealers say that nearly every village had a cycle builder, and associated coterie of club riders.

In the 1930s, in a then perhaps little appreciated development, the Union Cycliste Internationale

(UCI), the world governing body of cycle sport, made a decision which froze the evolution of bicycle design. A relatively unknown French cyclist, Francois Faure, riding a new design of bicycle known as a recumbent, smashed several long-standing speed and distance records. His bike, designed and built by Charles Mochet, was a low slung affair in which the rider travelled feet first in a reclining position, as if in a lounge chair. To preserve cycle sport as an athletic contest between riders rather than machines, the UCI decreed that all competition bicycles had to conform to the configuration of the diamond frame safety bike, c.1910.

Meanwhile, in Britain, it was a great time for cycling. In the late 1930s there were over nine million regular cyclists on the roads: racers, tourists, lovers, bakers, whole families. There was a true love and enjoyment of cycling, a culture that today we might experience as paradise. But the end was also at hand; in 1936, 2.5 million motorists killed 1,496 cyclists and injured 71,193 more. Of all road casualties that year, 31 percent were cyclists. Ambulances, called "bloodwagons," did not wait for call outs; they simply

cruised the roads. There was a hue and cry, but no effective action, and the problem was soon eclipsed by the life and death global conflict of World War II.

In the post war period, from 1945 to 1955 the number of cars in Britain tripled. The motoring boom was on, and cycling was ignored or actively discouraged. The country went car crazy, and roads, car parks, petrol stations, and cars, cars, cars proliferated, transforming towns and villages into mazes of one way motordromes. Britain became a world leader in number of cars per mile of road. The bicycle went the way of the dodo. Sales dropped to less than 500,000 a year. Only die hard racers and keepers of the classic faith cycled, or those who could afford no better.

Elsewhere in Europe, the Dutch, the Danes, and eventually the Germans, showed more foresight and embarked on creating transport infrastructures with large scale provisions for bicycles and cycling. The Dutch in particular instituted a nationwide network of cyclepaths that is one of the wonders of the world. Perhaps the thrifty

Dutch recognized that the efficiency of the bicycle would, in the end, gain them more of the better things in life. In the Netherlands, a bank manager who drives a car to work when riding a bike would do as well is viewed as possibly not having good sense. Bikes are welcome at high social functions, and people cycle to the opera while wearing full evening dress. The Netherlands, Denmark, and of course Germany, enjoy some of the highest living standards in the world.

In post World War II America, samples of English Racers and other lightweight European machines brought home by returning soldiers provided the impetus for the development of cycling as an adult recreational activity. Unlike the paperboy bike, the English Racer, despite being a quite heavy all-steel roadster with a fully enclosed chain guard, was a realistic proposition as transportation, in fact fun to ride!

In the 1950s and early 1960s stores devoted mainly to the sale and rental of bicycles developed steadily. Americans began spending more of their leisure time on afternoon rides in the countryside or parks. Bikes appeared in force on university campuses, and hardier souls began using them as all around transportation.

In the 1960s, lightweight 10- and 15-speed derailleur gear, drop handlebar racing and touring bikes entered the scene. The first models came from Europe and were expensive, but just as there was no comparison between the doughty paperboy bike and an English Racer, the new "10-speed" (their generic name) bikes were incomparably lighter and quicker than ordinary bikes. They caught the public fancy, and with the additional stimulus in the early 1970s of a global oil crisis that saw Americans for the first time ever waiting in line at gas station pumps, the cycling revival grew and then positively exploded.

Bike shops were mobbed. If you were buying a bike, you got up early and went with cash in hand, and didn't quibble about such things as color. People bought anything on two wheels, so long as it had drop handlebars, chromed fork blades, quick release hubs, and derailleur gears.

Classic 10-speed: American Columbia with "gut ripper" gear shift lever talons and "suicide" dual brake levers.

To meet demand, small factories in Europe and Asia produced crude machines for the US by the container load. Trading in bicycles was like being first in line at the 1849 California gold rush; individual fortunes were made overnight. Annual sales took a decade to double from 4.4 million in 1960 to 8.9 million in 1971, but only two years to nearly double again at 15.8 million in 1973, with a final crest in 1974–75 at nearly 17 million.

In Britain the bike boom had a later start, but was no less spectacular: in just eight years, annual sales rose from 700,000 in 1972 to 1.6 million in 1980, a match for the halcyon record set in 1935, and then rose still more to an astonishing 2.15 million in 1983. Subsequent sales have floated mostly above the 2 million mark, with occasional rushes such as 2.8 million in 1990. Today, there are some 23 million bikes in Britain.

The bike boom restored the role of the bicycle as a recreation, sport, and utility vehicle for adults. Where once the majority of bikes sold were for children, adult models came to account for the bulk of bike sales. More, the boom reignited the continuing evolution of the bicycle and caused fundamental changes in the cycle industry, including how bikes are made and sold.

Raleigh "look-alike" racer

Cannondale Black Lightning, 1987: oversize aluminium frame tubes; light, stiff, fast, and affordable.

Mountain bike

In America and Europe, the post war years of hard times for cycling saw many small specialist firms and builders of quality bikes engulfed by industry giants or primary manufacturers. In many cases, the names lived on, but not the quality. A distinct double standard developed. Major bicycle manufacturers imaged and marketed their brands on the basis of racing victories won on bikes not of their own manufacture, but rather supplied by custom builders. That was not so terrible – in those days good bikes were still hand made, and even today a "works" bike is apt to be special – but the mass-produced bikes sold to the public were often sinfully poor in quality. In many cases, the "look-alike" models presented in team racing colors and aimed at youths were the crudest of all.

The larger problem was that the big European bike manufacturers had suffered severe losses in export sales, leaving their vast factories idle, and their workforces top heavy with brain dead management. Even after the bike boom was well under way, many large manufacturers persisted in marketing shoddy, cheaply made bikes as performance machines.

The new generation of adult cyclists was not so gullible. They were genuinely keen on cycling and quick to learn about the technicalities of bikes, and they wanted the real thing – quality machines. The rising demand for good bikes triggered the start of new firms in America, Japan, and Taiwan, typically run and staffed by enthusiastic cyclists eager to explore new design ideas and manufacturing techniques. Aided by the availability of new, more production flexible materials such as sophisticated cromo steels, aluminum alloys, and composites, the new firms achieved a vital breakthrough: mass production of exciting, high quality bikes at reduced cost. Today, most quality bikes are created by manufacturers in their own factories, and the bikes that win races are machines that you and I can buy – and do. The broad trend in bike sales continues to move upmarket, toward better and better machines.

Even before the late 1970s, Asian manufacturers had already well undercut for price the old European and American manufacturers, while often beating them hands down for quality. Then came a decisive technological development: in 1980 a pair of rag tag California hippies launched the mountain bike, a mongrel cross of the paperboy bike with technology from BMX and road racing bikes. The lightweight but bomb proof, go anywhere new design was greeted with disdain by the cycle industry's old guard. For many, the ride they missed was their last call.

Enterprising Asian manufacturers eager for new markets including major components manufacturers Shimano and Sun Tour spotted the glint of a mother lode. The first mass-produced mountain bike, the 1981 Specialized Stumpjumper, was the start of a massive shot in the arm for the evolution of the bicycle, and the metamorphosis of the tradition linked bicycle revival into an independent movement standing solidly on its very own two wheels. The mountain bike was a dream come true, a fun to ride machine that at once opened up the great outdoors, yet could also cope with jagged high streets and the rough brawl of urban traffic. It was a people's bike, a freedom machine all the way, just what everyone wanted, and throughout the 1980s and 1990s sales of mountain bikes climbed and climbed, eventually accounting for more than 90 percent of sport bike sales. Unfettered by Union Cycliste Internationale regulations or traditions and guided only by a quest for what works best or better, the continuing technological evolution of the mountain bike has generated innovations and improvements by the score in every area: frame design, brakes, transmissions and, of course, suspension systems.

Although some old guard firms have revived, the manufacturing epicenters of the cycle industry are now firmly in America, Japan, and Taiwan. Of all quality frames made, possibly 50 percent or more come from just one giant Taiwanese factory. The production of components, once the province of European firms, is dominated by Shimano of Japan, which accounts for 85 percent or more of the market. The quality of Shimano equipment can be extremely high, but their success is due more to a fundamental change in the nature of bikes and how they are made and marketed.

Where once top quality bikes were produced one at a time, each hand made frame fitted with the best components one could afford, today top quality bikes are designed and engineered, all of a piece, for mass production. Some modern materials can be produced or worked only with the use of expensive, specialized machines and processes, and engineering for volume production is a requirement to recover high initial capital investment. Bicycle manufacturers save through bulk purchases of components and the total production process is meticulously planned to involve only the necessary number of parts, at exactly the time they are needed, to keep inventories to the minimum. The resulting mass-produced quality bike costs less than the sum of its parts – like an electric drill, it is a complete, production engineered product which sells at a price below that which would accrue if you were to obtain all the individual bits and assemble them yourself.

Although mass-produced bikes are unbeatable value for money and dominate the market, hand made bikes and custom designs are not extinct. Quite the opposite. Today, there are probably more small builders and specialized firms than ever before. Partly this is due to human nature. Whether building or using, many people prefer the ethos of hand made and personal, and a bike is one of the most personal machines there is. The other factor which has given rise to new firms and builders has been the growing development and evolution of a variety of specialized cycles for tasks and interests of all kinds, from transporting babies to breaking speed records.

THE HUMAN POWER MOVEMENT

Back in the 1970s bike boom, a small, eclectic group of academics and backyard tinkerers became interested in creating a "better bicycle", a machine or machines to improve on the classic 1910 design for speed, energy efficiency, cargo and baggage capacity, weather protection, and safety. They focused first on speed, experimenting with low slung, streamlined recumbent designs that were banned by the UCI in the 1930s. Recumbents, also known as human-powered vehicles (HPVs), quickly set new performance standards. Just as the safety bicycle was decisively faster and easier to use than its predecessor, the high wheel bicycle, recumbents are faster and safer than the traditional safety, or "upright."

In recent years the development of cycle designs has widened, embracing such considerations as fast commuting, cargo carrying and light goods delivery, weather protection, special physical needs, and others. The range of new kinds of cycles now available is fantastic and truly exciting. However, these specialized designs augment and complement the upright bicycle rather than replace it. The traditional safety is still a brilliant and highly capable machine, probably about as perfect a design as is possible. There will always, always be a bicycle.

WRAP

Cycle designs cover everything from folding, to converting into a boat, to screaming down rock-strewn trails, to just lazing along and many more. Bicycles and components are made from high tech materials in giant factories, using capital intensive machines and volume production, and bikes are also made in small workshops, using only basic materials and inexpensive tools. You can buy amazing, gleaming superbikes, and you can also build a perfectly useful bike all by yourself.

As with ecosystems, all this diversity is very healthy for cycling. The bicycle is no longer just one species, but many. It lives at all economic levels, and in all places. It is the world's most successful machine, one that will endure for all human time and perhaps longer – and likely it was a chance discovery!

American Star, c. 1880

The Kinds of Cycles

Bike basics: weight, and derailleur vs. hub gear transmissions • Overview of cycle designs and their uses, from roadsters through to streamlined human-powered vehicles

ONCE THERE WERE THREE BASIC KINDS OF bikes: sport bikes with drop handlebars and derailleur gears, roadster bikes with flat handlebars and hub gears, and rugged single speed paperboy bikes. Sport bikes were divided into lightweight racers with no frills, and more strongly built tourers equipped with pannier racks and fenders. Roadsters were heavy and usually featured a chainguard, fenders, carrier rack, and possibly built in lights and a kickstand. Paperboy (now cruiser) bikes were really heavy, and had wide tires and a single pedal-operated coaster brake. Only a glance at a bike was needed to understand its genre and purpose.

Today there are more general categories and sub-types, and distinctions often blur; a mountain bike designed and equipped for touring, for example, may be similar to a road touring bike in all but small details. A roadster city bike with hub gears may be a quality lightweight well able (other things being equal) to show its heels to a sport bike. Cruisers have sprouted alloy frames and wheels, and multi-speed gears. Then there are human-powered vehicles (HPVs), a category covering a range of designs, from sleek, high speed streamliners to large, four wheel quadricycles made to carry freight or passengers.

Despite their many different forms, most cycles have a clear primary purpose, and fit fairly firmly within a category. As a start, this chapter gives a quick overview of the main kinds of bikes and their uses. If you are new to bikes, some of the distinctions and terminology may initially be confusing, but hang in there and it will all sort out. Following chapters go into more detail about the design and construction of bikes, and how well various kinds of machines suit specific purposes such as commuting, off-road riding, and so on. Two things to know something about from the get-go, however, are weight and gears.

WEIGHT

Bike weight is fundamental. If a bike is heavy, it cannot be made to go. The limiting factor is the human power plant. Gifted athletes are capable of churning out up to around one and one-half horsepower, but only for seconds; thereafter, steady output rarely exceeds one-half horsepower, and one-quarter horsepower is more like it. That will still be for a limited duration, maximum effort for an event such as a time trial race, or flight in a human-powered aircraft. In ordinary

riding, the output of most people is around one-tenth to one-eighth horsepower.

Power-to-weight ratio – your body weight plus bike weight, relative to your power output – is the summary determinant of performance. Slim, wiry people benefit the most from lightweight bikes, especially on climbs or when accelerating, but bike weight is significant for all riders. The demarcation line is 30 pounds: bikes at 35 pounds are hard to move, while bikes at 25 pounds seem to glide down the road by themselves. Really fine road racing bikes at 21 pounds and less are joy incarnate.

Heavy bikes are unwieldy and sluggish, light bikes are responsive and quick, and this holds true even if the rider is an ordinary mortal who could do with a little less body weight or a better level of fitness. Champion riders get the most out of good bikes, but the rest of us enjoy them, too. Bike weight is a function of the materials from which the bike is built, which is in turn a function of money; cheap bikes are heavy, more expensive bikes are lightweight. With bikes, the more you pay, the less you get (unless you elect for suspension).

Some people find the idea of spending money on a bike shocking. They believe that the whole point of a bike is that it should be cheap. A machine they can hardly pick up is wonderful, because it is hard work to ride, and such suffering must be good for you. Not so. Slogging away on a heavy bike mostly wears you out while doing little to make you fit. For quality exercise, you need a lightweight machine that moves when you do. The point of a bike is not that it should be cheap, but that it should move!

A heavy bike promotes an inert riding style. Because the bike is unresponsive, it is harder to move with it and, for example, help it to pivot underneath you when going over a bump. Instead, you tend to sit like a sack of oats, which makes bumps more punishing. This leads to counter measures such as using a wide mattress saddle with springs, which only increases weight still more, and further inhibits movement. In contrast, the responsiveness of a lightweight machine encourages you to be active and move with the bike, thereby improving comfort. You can use a slimmer, lighter saddle, which further fosters a dynamic riding style. A bike and rider are a partnership: the bike goes, you go; you go, the bike goes.

Bike weight is also important when you have to carry it up and down stairs, on and off a car, or aboard a train. Carrying a heavy bike at 35 to 40 pounds can be a real chore, but managing a 25 pound lightweight is a breeze. Better yet if the bike is 21 pounds or even less. It may be hard to credit that a mere 10 to 15 pounds makes such a difference, but it does, it does.

As for durability, although heavy, gas pipe bikes can take a lot of casual knocking about (as in, say, pizza delivery service), in terms of absolute strength they are weaker than bikes made from lighter but much stronger materials. In the end, the initial cheapness of a heavy bike is a false economy. A decent basic quality bike with a weight of say 26 to 27 pounds need not cost the earth, and in the long run will prove far better value and miles and miles more fun. You do not have to be Andrés Segovia in order to appreciate, love, and enjoy a good guitar. If you are only going to have one bike, make it the lightest you can afford, because weight in a bike is not just important – it is everything.

GEARS

The transmission converts energy input at the pedals into power at the driving wheel. Different size gear ratios allow the rider to maintain an even match between work rate and terrain. Low gears produce more power but less speed by requiring more turns of the cranks for every turn of the driving wheel; high gears produce more speed but less power by requiring fewer turns of the cranks for every turn of the driving wheel. Thus, if you try to climb a hill with a high (big, large) gear, you will have to push very hard, and if you try to go fast on the flat with a low (small, tiny) gear you will spin out. By keeping your physical pace consistent, gears make riding easier and more efficient.

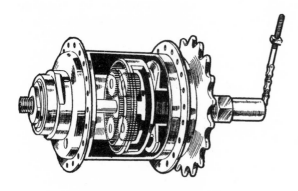

Sturmey-Archer 3-speed hub, 1936

There are two broad kinds of transmissions: internal hub gears and external derailleur gears. In general, hub gears are simple, reliable, and a bit slow; derailleur gears are more complex, need frequent servicing, and are extremely efficient – fast. A choice between the two types depends on what you want from a bike.

Derailleur gears are the route to go if you are interested in cycling as a sporting, dynamic activity, if you want to go quickly or for long distances, or if hills are involved. Hub gears are best if you intend to use a bike only once a month or so, or if you just want a worry free machine that needs minimal care. A no-think bike is quite fun: you can bash it around, loan it to casual friends, and in general never have to think about it.

Derailleur systems change gear by moving the chain, and hence will only accomodate a partial chainguard. Hub gears change internally, so it is easy to fit a fully enclosed chainguard, which will greatly extend chain life as well as protecting clothes from stains.

Although internal hub gears are inherently less efficient than derailleur gears, their simplicity and cleanliness make them appealing for bikes designed for short journeys and everyday use. In addition to the standby 3-speed hub,

more sophisticated 5- and 7-speed hub gears are available, and bike manufacturers now produce quality hub-gear roadster bikes that are true lightweights. These bikes can be a practical and sensible choice for everyday short distance transport.

If the business at hand is cycling, however, consider: Professor David Gordon Wilson of the Massachusetts Institute of Technology has calculated that the energy requirement for maintaining an even 12 mph on a lightweight derailleur gear sport bike is half that for the same speed on a hub gear roadster. Half. This is more than just a matter of the gears, of course, but the basic idea holds: one machine is a lump, the other can move. The efficiency and precision of derailleur gears means you can put more into riding, and get more back in return.

For frequency of servicing, a hub gear has it all over a derailleur system. Aside from an occasional twiddle of the control cable adjustment, all a hub gear will need for years is a monthly shot of lubricant. It's a complex piece of equipment, so if it does go – which is not often – the usual course is to replace rather than repair it. That means a new wheel as well, or a rebuild of the old one. Derailleur gears need regular servicing, but because the parts are fairly simple and readily

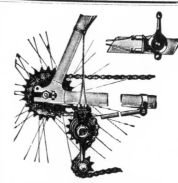

accessible, this is easy to do. Indeed, with a performance bike, fine tuning the transmission and other components so that the bike runs sharp and smooth is part of the fun. If a part does mangle or break, it can be easily replaced.

For more information on gears, see Chapter 10, Fitting and Gearing.

UPRIGHT OR SAFETY BICYCLES

Full size upright or safety bicycles sort out into four basic groups: (1) roadster and style bikes; (2) commuter and city bikes; (3) road sport bikes; and (4) mountain bikes. Keep in mind that these divisions apply more to how bikes are built and look, than to how they are used; many people commute on road sport bikes, and many mountain bikes never touch dirt.

1. Roadster and Style Bikes

• Beach Cruiser

Modern reincarnation of the classic American paperboy bike, a.k.a. the balloon tire bomber. Heavy, robust steel frame, 26-inch steel wheels with hefty 2-inch wide tires, single speed hub with a pedal operated coaster brake, wide handlebars, and mattress saddle. Beach cruisers are about style rather than performance and are usually done up in bright, cheerful colors. They are fine for slowly cruising along a boardwalk, mak-

ing people scenes such as Miami's Ocean Drive, or going a mile or two to the beach. At a weight of up to 50 pounds or more they are hard work on hills; on steep climbs you'll almost certainly have to get off and push.

Cruisers are tough and durable, and are the ubiquitous mount for local deliveries, and rental fleets in parks. Cruisers are simple and need little mechanical care, fitting comfortably with a casual, laid back approach to life. Some models are available with alloy wheels, which greatly improve riding ease and enjoyment. Derailleur gears are sometimes an option, but are a waste of money on so heavy a machine. If you like the idea of combining performance with distinctive style, look at a lightweight roadster or upmarket edition of a cantilever or curve tube frame bike. Specialized do bikes of this type.

• BMX Cruiser

This off-beat category generally features a compact frame, 24-inch wheels with wide, knobby tires, a single speed gear, and straight forks. BMX cruisers are basically BMX for bigger boys and girls, or smaller adults. If the machine is of high quality and very lightweight, it can be quite a bit of fun – simple, like a beach cruiser, but very quick.

BMX Freestyle

BMX freestyle bikes are made and equipped for performing tricks and stunts and have also

Beach cruiser   *BMX Cruiser*

Old Faithful   *Light roadster*

become quite popular as local ride around machines. See the section on BMX bikes in Chapter 6 for more information.

• Heavy Roadster

As seen in 1920. Steel frame and 26- or 28-inch wheels, 1.5-inch wide tires, single speed or 3-speed hub gears. A proper classic version will have 28-inch wheels and roller lever rim brakes. Fully enclosed chainguard, kickstand, stout rear carrier, and built in lights. At around 50 pounds this is the European version of the paperboy bike, sometimes called an "Africa" model because of its popularity in developing countries for transporting heavy loads across deserts, through jungles, and the like. In China, they are the backbone of a national transport system based on pedal power.

Many "Old Faithfuls" are still trundling out decades of service, and new machines continue to be produced by a few manufacturers. Well, cars with two wheel brakes are illegal, and I'm afraid that old bikes with roller lever brakes should also be limited to slow parades. There's just too much chance of running into something. Heavy roadsters with a rear hub brake are imported from the Netherlands from time to time. The bikes are well made and pretty, with rustic charm, and they ride steadily and gracefully as long as the terrain is flat. I like them fine – in the Netherlands. Pedalling a heavy roadster up any kind of a hill is

hard work. The bikes are not cheap either; for the same money you can have a modern roadster that is lots easier to ride.

• Light Roadster

"Light roadster" as a description could embrace several kinds of bikes, including some very upmarket models. A *traditional* light roadster, however, is a more sprightly version of a heavy roadster, and features a steel frame, 26-inch steel wheels with 1.375-inch wide tires, long reach side pull calliper rim brakes, 3-speed hub gears, half chainguard, and steel or plastic fenders. With a weight of around 35 pounds, a light roadster is more than a bit of work to pedal, and steel wheels mean grossly inadequate braking in wet weather. Secondhand or rescued from the dump, a light roadster can serve as a local hack bike, but it is absolutely not worth buying one new; the far better quality commuter, city, and modern roadster models offer much more.

• Modern Roadster Bike

Steel or cro-mo alloy frame. Alloy wheels. Hub gears, fully enclosed chainguard. Hub brake rear, calliper cantilever or V-brake front. Fenders, sturdy carrier rack, and built in lights, kickstand, and lock. Hub gears and fully-enclosed chainguard slant this type toward regular everyday urban use, with a minimum of attention and maintenance – a

Pashley Paramount   *Commuter*

transport machine, but one that goes nicely – a smooth good clothes bike.

A modern roadster is fairly heavy, but handles well and, unlike a traditional light roadster, it has serious brakes. The various built-in features are marvellously convenient when you are shopping and running errands. Steep hills take muscle, though.

Variations and elaborations include models with derailleur gears and part chainguard, and rear or front wheel suspension, or both. Derailleur gears may sometimes be useful, but suspension on a roadster bike adds weight without producing a lot of benefit. If you really need performance as opposed to stately grace, or are faced with steep hills, go for a lighter machine.

If your heart is set on the classic look, Pashley Cycles make modern roadsters with the traditional frame design, but equipped with alloy wheels, 5-speed hub gears, hub brakes, and lots of stylish goodies, including a wicker basket and a bell. At the other end of the spectrum, Pashley also do a curved frame bike fitted out for commuting, the Paramount, with either the Nexus 7-speed hub, or a Sachs 3x7 combined hub/derailleur unit.

2. Commuter and City Bikes

It is at this point that life starts to become semantically tricky, because the distinctions between a commuter bike, a town bike, and a city bike are quite fine, and are readily mixed by manufacturers in their catalogs. The basic concept, though, is a bike which is a proper lightweight with a cro-mo or aluminum frame and full size 26-inch or 700C alloy wheels, fitted with a semi-mattress saddle and flat handlebars for a fully upright riding position. These bikes generally weigh 25 to 30 pounds and have a pleasantly brisk performance, and can cope with day rides and light touring (25 to 35 miles), as well as regular commuting and local utility use.

• Commuter Bike

Derailleur gears, part chainguard, 700C wheels with fairly light 1.125-inch wide tires, calliper V- or cantilever brakes, fenders, carrier rack, and possibly, built in lights. The slant here is towards the performance of a fast road sports bike, and a primary use for regular journeys of some distance, say 7 to 8 miles or more. A good model should be 26 pounds or less. See also the entry for Cross or Hybrid Bike, below.

Some manufacturers have tried producing really high quality commuter models, with a carbon fiber or other high tech lightweight frame and very light wheels, for a weight of 23 pounds and less. Such machines are a real treat, but they are expensive and not enough demand has developed for them to become available on a regular basis. Should you come across one, new or used, my advice is to give it a good look, because they are a lot of fun – clean, very swift, and a snap to handle up and down stairs, and on and off trains.

• City Bike

Similar to the commuter bike, but with 26-inch wheels and 1.5- or 1.75-inch wide tires – a seemingly small but significant difference. Where the commuter bike is kin to the fast road bike, the city bike is clearly derived from the tough, go-anywhere mountain bike, and can cope more ably with the jagged surfaces and deep pot holes of mean urban streets. A city bike has firm, stable handling. On a dark night in town when the weather has suddenly turned nasty, the road has degenerated into a tricky minefield of roadworks and pot holes, and lunatic motorists are breathing down your neck, a bike which is steady and strong is a welcome friend.

A city bike can also be just fine in the countryside. With smooth city tires and close fitting fenders, it cannot cover the same spectrum of rough terrain as a true cross country mountain bike, but it will handily take to paths, trails, and the open countryside and, with a little skill, can be pushed surprisingly far in more extreme conditions.

Weight can be a problem. To keep price down, some manufacturers of city bikes use hi-tensile steel frames – not good enough for a bike to be both light and tough. Seek a model with a cro-mo or aluminum frame, or buy a better grade mountain bike and modify it into a city bike. See Chapter 13 on commuting and Chapter 15 on mountain bikes for more information.

• Cross or Hybrid Bike

A cross between a mountain bike and a road bike, with 700C wheels and flat handlebars. Hybrid bikes are available in many specifications, from plain to full suspension. Some manufacturers offer hybrid city bikes, with fenders, a rack, and lights. Most models, though, lean toward off-road sport and are fairly sparse. The larger 700C wheels are a little faster on the road than 26-inch wheels, a bit of an advantage for longer journeys or touring, but not important over short distances.

A hybrid is a highly flexible all rounder. Depending on the tires and equipment fitted, it can manage, say, 45-mile tours in comfort, tackle all but extreme off-road riding conditions, or serve ably as a quick and durable urban commuting machine. Weight varies according to quality, and can range from around 23 or 24 pounds up to 28 pounds.

3. Road Sport Bikes

• Sport Bike

Modelled after road racing bikes, sport models feature a lightweight frame, steel or alloy components, 700C 25/32 tires, calliper rim brakes, derailleur gears, narrow saddle, and drop bars. Weight around 28 to 30 pounds, sometimes more.

Sport bikes vary a great deal in quality. At the low end, the machine may be nothing more than an ordinary mild steel roadster frame fitted with derailleur gears, drop handlebars, and "go faster" stripes for a racy appearance. At the high end, the machine may be a genuine lightweight with a fairly lively performance. In general, however, most quality sport bikes are function-specific models identified as fast touring, training, triathlon, racing, and so on. Sport bikes have modest performance and easy, predictable handling. All steel models are very sluggish and should be avoided. Better models with alloy components are fine for general riding, commuting, light touring, and moderately hilly terrain.

The sport bike or "10-speed" was the backbone of the 1970s bike boom, mostly because short of going to specialist builders and small firms, it was all you could get. Times have moved on, and if you are interested in a bike with good road performance, then go for a better quality fast touring or fast road model.

• Touring Bike, road version

A full on road touring bike follows the general outline of a sport bike, but the frame geometry or configuration is arranged to provide a more comfortable ride and stable, predictable handling even

Touring   *Fast touring*

when laden with baggage. Panniers are positioned so that they neither foul the rider, nor induce instability in handling because they are too far away from the bike. There are front and rear pannier racks, full-length fenders, and a profusion of mounting points for water bottle cages. The derailleur gearing is wide range, with ample low ratios for easier hill climbing, and the brakes are stout and strong – calliper cantilever or V-brake, or possibly hydraulic calliper. Wheels and tires are 700C or, in some cases, smaller and stronger 26-inch or 650B. Full on touring bikes can be used for commuting and day rides, but their proper activity is daily touring in the 50 to 100 mile range. Some models are claimed to weigh as little as 24 pounds, but, with a comprehensive equipment specification, 27 to 32 pounds is more likely. The market for full on touring bikes is precise and limited, and so most if not all models are well made. See Chapter 16 about touring for more information.

• Fast Touring/Sport Touring

A touring bike tweaked with lighter wheels and narrow 1- or 1-1.25-inch wide tires, and stiffer frame geometry, or a racing bike beefed up with heavier wheels and tires, and a more relaxed frame geometry – either way, a quick machine that can still manage light touring loads. This best of both worlds approach is popular with riders who

want a brisk, snappy bike for general use and commuting, as well as for weekend and holiday touring. Gearing is often what you might call split personality: a group of high, closely spaced ratios for speed, and a handful of low ratios for long climbs. There is provision for mounting slim fenders and a rear carrier rack. Good quality, compact side pull calliper brakes. Weight 23 to 28 pounds.

• Fast Road/Training Bike

Fast touring bikes can be quick, but are still rooted in touring and carrying things. Fast road or training bikes are derived from racing bikes, and the emphasis is on performance. The frame is close clearance, with no room or provision for fenders or a carrier rack, and is designed for quick handling and rapid acceleration. Shod with narrow profile 1- or 1.125-inch wide tires, a fast road bike typically has a stiff ride over rough surfaces. Close ratio gears, compact side pull calliper brakes. Weight 21 to 26 pounds.

Fast road bikes range in quality from a cut or two below medium, to high. Medium high quality models are the most popular, because their performance level is good enough for a fast club run, and is about all that most riders need. Fast road bikes are primarily for sport and fun, but keen, experienced riders also use them for very fast, exciting general transport.

Triathlon   *Giant TCR*

• Triathlon

Bikes made for triathlon (swimming-running-cycling) events are similar to fast road models, but the frame geometry has a tight back end, for fast response to pedal input, while the front end is more relaxed, to help guide tired riders through the bends. Profile bars for an aerodynamic riding position and lots of water bottle mounts are usually standard. Weight 21 to 25 pounds. Quality is usually very good.

• Road Racing

The business: strong, tight, close clearance frame for taut responsiveness and crisp, quick handling. Close ratio gears, and sprint wheels with sew up tubular tires – narrow, fast, and more fragile than the conventional high pressure (HP) clincher type. Mass start road racing in a pack of riders is often rough and tough, and the bikes are made to be light but strong and reliable. Weight is usually 20 to 22 pounds, but can pare down to 18 pounds. With sprint wheels and tubular tires a racing bike is strictly for competition – mending a puncture in a tubular is a hassle, and the condition of today's roads all but guarantees that this will happen. However, easily repaired HP clincher tires have evolved performance levels close, if not equal to that of all but the lightest tubulars. Hence, it is common practice with racing bikes to substitute HP wheels with clincher tires for training and general road riding. A good racing bike is like having wings on your feet. You really do just fly. It's a sport and joy machine, pure and simple.

The trend with road racing bikes is toward compact frames with a sloping top tube, as pioneered by the TCR from Giant. Although I dearly love my 25-year-old F. W. Evans racer, I've been riding a TCR and it is brilliant – very light, yet very stiff. See Chapter 4, What Is A Good Bicycle?, for more information on compact frames.

• Time Trial

A time trial (TT) bike is similar to a road racing bike, but more lightly built. In a time trial, riders race on their own against the clock. The object is to go as fast as possible, and TT machines are set up according to course requirements, for example as a single speed, if the course is flat.

A classic TT bike can be a study in painstaking effort to shed every ounce of excess weight, with cranks, chainrings, and other components drilled with hundreds of holes. A modern TT bike concentrates on aerodynamic efficiency, with a smooth, sculpted frame and profile bars.

• Track Bike

Made for racing on wooden tracks, these are stark greyhounds with a single fixed gear (the

Short distance TT bike by Jack Taylor   *Track*

wheels turn when the cranks turn and vice versa), no brakes, and a weight of 16 to 17 pounds.

4. Mountain Bikes

The mountain bike has changed the definition of what a bicycle is. Mountain bikes began as machines for off-road downhill racing, but then quickly evolved into many different forms covering a broad range of functions. Today, "mountain bikes" account for the vast majority of adult bike sales. Touring bikes, city bikes, trials bikes for negotiating obstacles, freestyle bikes for whatever you fancy, downhill racers, slickrock riders, cross country tourers and racers – the list is almost endless. Today, the term "mountain bike" might be more accurately, just "bicycle."

In essence, mountain bikes represent a fresh, no holds barred approach to bike design, and the use of new materials, to come up with bikes that do what people want. This innovative approach has rewritten the design rules for creating bikes of all kinds, from roadsters through to flat out speed machines. The UCI legal diamond frame road racing bike c.1970, once the consummate, perfect synthesis of design and technology for the goal of speed, is now a classic. Modern racing bikes, built with ideas derived at least in part from mountain bike design and technology, are better and faster.

Mountain bikes have many different forms, and are discussed throughout this book. Here, I'm only going to give a broad overview. There are three primary parameters regarding mountain bikes: technology, quality/price, and function.

Mountain bikes offer a range of options in transmissions, brakes, controls, saddles, and handlebars; how these are mixed and matched has a big effect on the nature of a bike. A feature almost exclusive to mountain bikes, however, is suspension, which can be for the front or the back wheel, or both. Briefly, suspension improves bike control and rider comfort, but adds weight and mechanical complexity. For a downhill racing bike, the benefit of suspension is well worth the extra weight. In the case of a cross country machine that must go up as well as down, weight is a significant performance factor, so there may be front wheel suspension only (a "hardtail" bike), or none at all.

For more technical information, see Chapters 4, What Is A Good Bicycle?, and Chapter 15, Mountain Biking! Very basically, here's what to expect: a lightweight but strong frame; powerful calliper or disc brakes; derailleur gears; 26-inch wheels; semi-narrow saddle, and flat bars.

There are mountain bikes and then there are mountain bikes. Cheap models, like cheap sport bikes, are too heavy and basic to be useful as anything more than general runabouts. Really

Classic: simple and light   *Klein Mantra Pro. Yummy.*

degenerate mountain bikes, the el cheapo gas pipe specials you see in mail order advertisements and in tacky discount outlets, with low-grade components such as long arm side pull brakes, are a menace. If ridden vigorously off-road, such machines can literally break. In mountain bikes, quality is vital, and this is not just a matter of avoiding turkeys. Right up to around the mid-range price point, it is better and more fun to have a mountain bike with a good frame and specification and no suspension, than a bike with suspension but an indifferent frame and specification.

• Mountain Bike, Standard or "Classic"

A simple non-suspension mountain bike of good enough quality to be worth riding off-road is becoming an increasingly rare bird. Most folks want suspension, and so sales of mid-range "classic" design mountain bikes have sagged. However, most manufacturers still produce one or two basic quality, good value models. Bikes of this sort are not for attacking Annapurna or a race course, but are suitable for general transport and moderate off-road riding.

• Mountain Bike, Cross Country

As the name suggests, cross country mountain bikes are designed for both climbing and descending, and in between. There are many different specifications. It's common to have front suspension for comfort but, to save weight, not back suspension (a "hardtail"). On the weight count, many racing mountain bikes do not have any suspension at all. However, as suspension systems steadily become lighter, cross country bikes with dual suspension are becoming more popular.

Cross country mountain bikes are the nearest thing to general, all-round machines. You'll see them variously out for an off-road tour, picking a path down a hairy descent, acing a main street, and competing on a race course. In general, modern designs are more sport orientated, with a frame geometry for responsive handling and quick "kick" for hill climbing. Older designs often featured a more relaxed geometry for more stability on fast descents. This function is now served by specialized downhill models.

• Technical/Trials Mountain Bike

Technical and trials mountain bikes are built for handling extreme terrain and obstacles. The idea with trials is to ride "clean." without the feet touching the ground, and so the bottom bracket is high to provide clearance over obstacles. The frame geometry is tight, for precise control. These are skill bikes and people use them to ride over cars, clamber over 5-foot diameter logs, and perform other incredible stunts. Technical riding is also popular in cities.

Downhill: fast

extreme levels. Like rock climbing and sky diving, downhill bike racing is a sport that should be approached with respect.

• Touring Mountain Bike

A touring mountain bike is similar to a road touring bike, but has 26-inch rather than 700C wheels, and flat instead of drop bars. Otherwise the concept is the same: wide range gears, powerful brakes, pannier racks front and rear, and an abundance of water bottle mounts and other accoutrements for comfortable long distance travelling.

• Freestyle Mountain Bike

At one level, freestyle is about simply messing around – a bit like trials in the sense of attempting stunts to see if they can be done, but with more flash and catching air (jumping). Trials bikes generally do not have suspension, freestyle bikes often do.

At a competitive level, freestyle is wild and woolly. One popular event consists of sending riders off four at a time through a slalom course comprised of berms, dirt mounds, and other obstacles. The action is fast and furious, with lots of air and spills.

• Downhill Mountain Bike

Downhill mountain bikes are made to do just one thing: blast along as fast as possible. Deep travel, dual suspension is a requirement, and as suspension systems become better and speeds rise ever higher, the bikes are becoming bulkier and stronger. A full on downhill racer with a bomb proof frame and massive 3-inch wide tires, resembles a motorcycle more than a bicycle. It's heavy, too; no one ever thinks about pedalling one of these *up* a mountain.

Fast downhill riding and racing is, to say the least, wildly exciting, but the latest advances in suspension systems are pushing speeds to

RECUMBENT CYCLES

Recumbent cycles, where the rider travels feet first, are a major new category, and bring in a whole new bunch of things to understand and think about. On a recumbent you sit in a seat with back support, and extend your legs forward. This lowers the center of gravity, which speeds up handling and allows a recumbent to brake more powerfully than a conventional upright cycle. Depending on the design, and whether or not it has a fairing, the recumbent may also have greater aerodynamic efficiency and speed. Interesting? Sure, but to say any more at this stage would probably be confusing. We've yet to cover all the factors that make a good upright bicycle, which is our reference point, and as for what makes a good recumbent or human-powered vehicle (HPV), this is an open area with a lot of different ideas and possibilities.

Often, the rules for recumbents are completely different than those for safety bikes. So for now I'm going to briefly describe the different kinds of recumbent cycles, to give you an overview of the sort of machines that are available. Chapter 4, What Is A Good Bicycle?, covers in detail how upright safety bikes are designed and made, and Chapter 5, Zzzwwaaaammo!, goes more deeply into the advantages and disadvantages, design and construction details, of recumbents and HPVs. We'll then hopefully be set to talk turkey

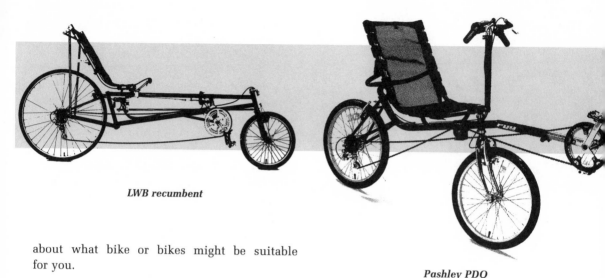

LWB recumbent

Pashley PDQ

about what bike or bikes might be suitable for you.

Types of Recumbent Bicycles

The different kinds of recumbent bikes are distinguished by wheelbase (distance between wheel axles), wheel size, and position of the crankset.

• Long Wheelbase

A long wheelbase (LWB) recumbent bicycle has the crankset behind the front wheel, and a wheelbase of 60 inches or more. The rear wheel is generally full size, 26-inch or 700C, and the front wheel is small, 16- to 20-inches. The riding position is semi reclining; the crankset is below the rider's hips, and the legs extend downward at an angle from horizontal.

LWB recumbents are stable and easy to manage and are popular as touring machines. Their size, about the same as an upright tandem, can make them awkward in traffic. The frontal area is about the same as a regular bicycle, and a LWB recumbent is more about comfort than speed.

• Compact Long Wheelbase

With a compact long wheelbase (CLWB) recumbent bike design, everything tightens up a bit: shorter wheelbase of 50 to 60 inches, crankset nearer to the front wheel, smaller wheels, and an inclined (feet below hips) riding position. The general intention of this design is to make riding a recumbent easy, and performance is again more about comfort.

• Short Wheelbase

On a short wheelbase (SWB) recumbent the wheels are anywhere from 33 to 48 inches apart, with the crankset positioned above and ahead of the front wheel. The big difference with this configuration is that the legs are now horizontal. This reduces the frontal area and hence aerodynamic resistance, for a distinct performance improvement – a good SWB is about 10 percent faster than a conventional upright bike. However, the pedals are farther away from the ground, which means that starting off can be difficult. If you fail to get going on the first turn of the cranks, you have to stop and start all over again. Matters are not helped by the fact that most SWB recumbent bikes have quick handling. In stop-and-go traffic, an inexperienced rider can get into a thorough muddle. Street and touring SWB models typically have a smaller front wheel to slightly lower the crankset and make life easier, whereas the wheels on flat out racing models are usually the same size and may be as large as 700C.

For performance, a SWB recumbent bike is brilliant – fast, smooth, comfortable, and safe. The machine can be banked over forever without grounding, and the braking power is dramatic. As for speed – Zzzwwaaaammo!

• Low-Rider

In a low-rider bike, the rider's seat is close to the ground, the bottom bracket is higher than the hips, and the wheels are usually small, say, 20-inch. Low-rider bikes are primarily for racing, and are the cycling equivalent of a Formula One racing car. Only very adventurous riders use low-rider bikes in traffic.

• Wrap

LWB recumbents are stable and are favored for touring and easy riding, and are a good starting point for new riders. CLWB recumbents are generally most useful as comfortable runabouts. They are easy to ride and many people, who because of age or particular physique are not comfortable on an upright, find that a CLWB is a delight. For performance, SWB recumbents are where it's at, but for the sake of comfort to say nothing of safety, you need to become familiar with the handling characteristics of these machines before taking one out on the open road, much less into traffic.

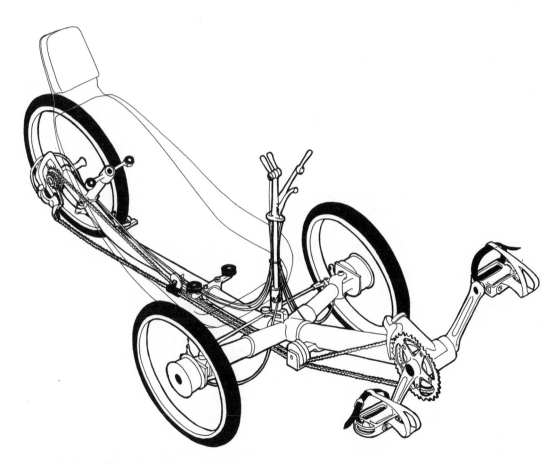

Windcheetah SL Mark IIIA-Series 2

Recumbent Tricycles

Recumbent tricycles are made with two wheels at the rear and one at the front, or with one at the rear and two at the front. Generally, models with two wheels at the rear have a long wheelbase of around 60 inches or more, as an aid to stability when cornering. Usually, the wheels are equal size and small, 16 to 20 inches. Models with two wheels at the front are more stable, and have a shorter wheelbase in the region of 40 inches. The rear wheel is fairly large, 24 inches or more, and the front wheels are small, 16 to 20 inches. Two wheels front, one wheel rear is the most common configuration.

In a recumbent trike the rider sits between the wheels, within a few inches of the ground if the machine is low slung, which places the center of gravity about as low down as it can go. As a result, recumbent trikes can withstand braking forces that have to be experienced to be believed. Cornering ability depends on design: some models are tippy and can lift an inside wheel in a corner if pressed too hard and/or the rider does not know how to counterbalance; other models are solid and can slide through corners.

The stability of a recumbent trike gives rise to what is almost a split personality. On the one hand, a recumbent trike is brilliant for low speed cruising, and idling along in stop-and-go traffic. There's never any problem with balancing; you just sit in armchair comfort and poke the pedals when necessary. On the other hand, at speed a recumbent trike is stable, too! Things that can badly upset a two wheel bike – ice, oil, wet leaves, and other slick surfaces, and sharp cross winds – will hardly faze a trike. Moreover, so long as the machine is well designed, it will be exceptionally agile and responsive.

This combination of maneuverability and stability makes pressing to the edge fun rather than unnerving – recumbent trike riders are known for riding with zest, with wide grins on their faces.

For flat out speed, a SWB recumbent bike is faster than a recumbent trike. However, many is the race where I've seen a SWB recumbent bike go down, while a trike survived. As all-around road vehicles, recumbent trikes have a good deal going for them. They are confidence inspiring, safe, and easy to operate, and hence very suitable for folks who are not comfortable with regular bikes, or who need to take it easy. They are also machines where you can let it all hang out. Do I like them? You bet. If I had to have just one machine, while intellectually I would say it should be a versatile mountain bike, I'd probably choose a recumbent trike because they are so much fun. You only live once.

Probably the greatest liability of a trike is sheer size. They're not the sort of thing you can easily pick up and tuck under your arm, or park in your average building hallway.

Recumbent Quality

The quality of recumbent cycles varies from basic to very high. Many designs are fairly easy to cobble together. Obtain a length of aluminum tubing, hang wheels on either end, perch a seat on top, work out steering and transmission, and you've got a recumbent. However, weight and quality, and refinements of design, are just as important for recumbents as for other kinds of cycles. Engineering in particular can be significant, and two machines that look very similar can have very different performance levels. More about this in Chapter 5, Zzzwwaaaammo!

What Is A Good Bicycle?

Human ergonomics and bicycle design • Why bikes were originally built from metal tubes • Modern materials and the development of new designs • Options in frames, wheels and tires, transmissions, brakes, control levers, pedals, saddles, stems, and handlebars

WITH A GOOD BIKE, DESIGN, MATERIALS, AND construction are well balanced and suit the intended purpose and cost of the machine. An ultralight, aerodynamic time trial bike made for the Tour de France and built with advanced composite materials, and a crude cargo bike made for hauling bananas to market in Nicaragua and built with crude mild steel, can both be good machines. In the Tour de France, the stakes are high and scores of consultants, designers, scientists, and technicians from several companies may work together on creating a bike especially for the event. High cost is axiomatic. In Nicaragua, the average yearly income is less than many people in America earn in a week, and the typical bike building resource is one person equipped with a hacksaw and a simple gas welder. Low, low cost is essential. For the Tour contender, exotic design, space age materials, and high tech construction; for the banana carrier, a simple design, easily worked mild steel, and rudimentary joinery.

A good bike is honest. It does the job it sets out to do, makes efficient use of materials, and stands up. In Nicaragua, most of the rural bike builders have a pretty fair idea of what they are doing. They have to. The bikes they build to earn their bacon must work well and be reliable, or else the builder goes hungry. Similarly, high tech racing bikes must deliver performance; excuses do not win races.

Whatever the pedigree, whatever the job, good bikes are well found and well executed. There is a ton of technical information in this chapter to help you understand what's what with bikes and which are best for you. If you are cool on tech talk, then please feel free to skim the chapter and come back to it later. It is helpful to understand engineering and construction details, but in the end, all bikes come to the same real time moment: you ride them. A bicycle is a vehicle for you, and while with a new bike it is important to give the machine a fair trial and strive to learn how to get the best out of it, you do the work and the riding, and you either get results, or you don't. Ride, and the difference between an honest bike made to do the best it can, and one that is built badly, or to serve a marketing idea rather than a real purpose, will usually become apparent. A good bike is one you like because it works for you.

THE ELEMENTS OF A BICYCLE

A bike consists of the:
- frame;
- suspension (optional);
- wheels (hubs, spokes, rims, tires);
- transmission (pedals, chainset, gear changers, chain, freewheel);
- brakes;
- handlebars, stem and saddle.

The frame carries the brand name – Trek, Giant, Fisher, Cannondale, etc. – and the components are known as the *specification*. Some bicycle manufacturers make their own frames, others buy them from outside builders, and many do both. Frames vary in quality from crude to ultra-fine, and are produced by firms that range from lone builders through to huge factories. Components are supplied by specialist companies, in various designs and quality grades. Some firms produce specific components such as rims or brakes; others produce *group sets* containing the components of a complete specification. Group sets are identified by a name or model number, as in Campagnolo Chorus or Shimano 105, and are ranked by design and quality, or cost. Sources of components are diverse, but volume sales to bike manufacturers are dominated by the Japanese firm Shimano.

Equipping frames with components from various sources is a method of manufacture somewhat unique to lightweight bikes; the majority of the over 110 million bikes produced worldwide each year are simple machines made in factories that are as self-contained as possible. Until recently, however, a hand made frame was a necessary pre-requisite for a quality bike, and since this market

sector was relatively small, specialization was inevitable. One person or outfit made frames, others made the bits. Now, quality frames are mass-produced, yet the growth in size of the market for good bikes means that specialization in components is still cost effective. Enough bicycle manufacturers need, say, lightweight rims, to give capable rim manufacturers the sales volume to realize greater cost efficiencies than a single bicycle maker might achieve.

Bikes are often judged by the components rather than by the frame, which up to a point can be legitimate. Specialization and the need to have real products to sell has led components manufacturers to make substantial, sometimes even extraordinary, technical advances. Yet for the sake of marketing, they often also introduce spurious gimmicks. For a bicycle manufacturer, retooling to accommodate annual model changes in components can cost millions. As you can imagine, market control is a real issue, and to avoid being a dog wagged by the tail, many bicycle companies make a policy of sourcing components from several different firms. A range of mountain bikes might be based on, say, four different kinds of frames, each

Coventry Rotary Tricycle

with three different group sets, for a total of 12 models.

Makers of bicycles range in size from individual builders producing just a few machines a year, to multi-national corporations producing hundreds of thousands and even millions of bikes annually. Small builders, shops, and firms tend to concentrate on a few models in one or two categories; middle size firms tend to specialize in a few categories, such as racing, touring or mountain bikes, and large manufacturers with extensive distribution networks tend to offer models in every category and price range.

Models from different manufacturers tend to cluster at "price points" – the average retail price for, say, an entry level mountain bike with front suspension – and since large manufacturers buy components and sometimes frames in bulk, comparable models from different makers are often identical, or nearly so.

As a rule of thumb, small builders and manufacturers offer design precision, optimum selection of components, and care in building. Basically, they are specialists, able to give tweaks and touches that can make a bike a bit better or more special – fine hand finishing on a frame, ideal gear ratios for touring in a particular country, a singular color, or just the cachet of an honored name.

Large manufacturers offer value for money through volume production. They can better afford the high capital cost of special equipment needed for working with more exotic materials, and so sometimes are able to offer features and bikes not obtainable elsewhere.

FRAME

Note: this discussion is limited to frames for bikes with an upright riding position. Frames for recumbent cycles have very different design parameters and possibilities, and are covered in Chapter 5, Zzzwwaaaammo! Similarly, many full suspension bikes toss conventional frame design out the window; these are covered in the next section.

The frame is the heart and soul of a bicycle. It translates pedal effort into forward motion, guides the wheels in the direction you select, and helps absorb road shock. How well the frame does these various jobs is determined by the materials from which it is built, the design, and the method of construction. There is no way to work around or upgrade a cheap frame. Components such as wheels are easily changed, but the frame endures and should be the first focus of your attention when considering a bike.

Weight in a bike is pretty well everything, and the most fundamental factor in this department is the frame. The better the frame, the lighter the weight for the same or even greater strength. Related to this are two qualities. The first is resiliency, twang, or flex, which gives better bikes springiness and vitality. This is inherent in the materials from which the bike is made, and is exactly the dynamic difference between heavy, unyielding cast iron and light, flexible tempered steel. The second quality is stiffness, which is related to materials and geometry as well as weight. In a nutshell, a frame with too little stiffness will bend and twist too much, and a frame that is too stiff will not have enough give for comfort. Do not confuse strength and stiffness: a frame made of heavy, weak tubing can be stiff, and a frame made of light, very stiff tubing can be weak. Essentially, frame design consists of trying to strike the best balance between strength, stiffness, and weight.

Steel was once the material of choice for frames, and there were two distinct types: plain heavy for machine-made low price bikes, and refined alloy lightweight for expensive bikes hand built by artisans. The fine steels were strong but required sensitive handling techniques beyond the capabilities of machine assembly. With the bike boom of the 1970s came the development of lightweight alloy steels compatible with mass production techniques. Almost simultaneously, there was a similar evolution in the technology for working with aluminum, which is now the dominant material for topnotch production bikes. Very advanced bikes are made using carbon fiber, aramid, titanium, and other exotic metals and composites.

Steel Tubes

Steel was the original material for bikes because it is cheap, easy to work with, and durable. It is isotropic, with equal strength in all directions. The design problem with an upright bicycle is to create a structure strong enough to support the rider at the three points of posterior, hands and feet, at the minimum expense in weight. With isotropic materials, a hollow tube is the form with maximum stiffness between two points. Hence the classic diamond frame design formed by the triangle of the three main tubes, and the secondary triangle formed by the chain and seat stays with the seat tube as common base.

• Types of Steels

There are many grades and kinds of steel bicycle tubes. Mild steel tubing is rolled from steel strip and electric seam welded. It feels like gas pipe, heavy and inert, and is used for third world utility bikes and sucker bikes (mail order el cheapos and bikes flogged in supermarkets and discount stores). Far better is low carbon, or high tensile (hi-ten) steel, which can be either seam welded or cold drawn. Western bike manufacturers use hi-ten for utility bikes and budget sports bikes.

The next grade up in quality are chrome-molybdenum low alloy steels, or "cro-mo," technically known as 4130. Cro-mo is used extensively for mass-produced midrange performance bikes. There are two types of cro-mo tubing: straight or plain gauge, and butted. Plain gauge tubing is uniform in wall thickness, or external and internal diameters. Butted tubing is uniform in external diameter, but on the inside is thinner in the middle section and thicker at the end(s), for greater strength at the joins. On average, butted tubing instead of plain gauge tubing reduces frame weight by 1 pound.

There are two types of butted tubing: seamed and seamless. Seamed butted tubing is made by rolling a flat strip of steel and welding the edges

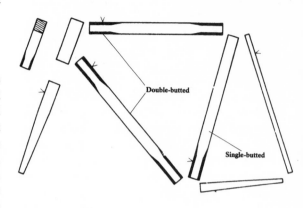

Plain and butted tubing

together. In quality it is about one notch below seamless butted tubing, but at much less cost. It is also more tolerant of machine assembly.

After cro-mo comes an array of exotic alloy steels formulated to have high tensile or draw strength, which permits thinner tubing and reduced weight. Also reduced is stiffness. Frame tubes of this grade have to be handled and worked with care and skill, and are used almost exclusively by small frame builders. Frame tubes are supplied in sets, and design and construction is specific to the intended use, as in Reynolds 531 Special Tourist for touring bikes. There are sets for road racing, time trials, touring, tandems, and so on, and while the distinctions between the different types are real, they are not gospel; for example, in the case of a small rider with a low body weight, a touring frame made with competition tubing may produce better results than a frame made with stiffer touring tubing. Advanced frame builders also mix different types of tubes, to save weight or add stiffness where required.

Frame Stickers

Frames made of any material worth mentioning will have a maker's transfer or sticker, usually on the seat tube just below the saddle. The sticker

Frame stickers

should be specific in the information it provides. Thus, a sticker that says "Reynolds 531ST butted main tubes, forks and stays" means that the entire frame is 531ST double butted. If it says "Reynolds 531ST butted frame tubes" then the seat, down, and top tubes are Reynolds 531ST, and the forks and stays are some other material. In such a case, there may be separate stickers on the forks and stays, with more information.

Some manufacturers of mass-produced bikes have their own name frame material labels, such as "Flash Super-X Cro-Mo" and "Flash Ultra Hi-Ten." In some cases these proprietary brands are legitimate, for there are manufacturers who make or use tubes with special formulations or in premium grades. In other cases, own brand materials labels are just a marketing incantation pasted onto tubing or complete framesets brought in from another manufacturer. If the brand name of the bike is unknown and the frame sticker says "cro-mo" and nothing else, be sure to compare the frame or bike with others of known pedigree and quality.

Framesets made of a mixture of different materials are quite common, and you'll often see a frame sticker or catalog description such as "cro-mo main tubes and hi-ten forks and stays." I prefer a frameset consistent in quality through-

out – the forks are particularly important to performance – but so long as differences are a single grade apart, things will probably work out. Most bike manufacturers are pretty savvy about how to mix and match tubes, but guard against extreme combinations, such as double butted main tubes with hi-ten forks and stays.

Aluminum

Aluminum is now the material of choice for top-grade frames. It's very light, inexpensive, and reasonably easy to work with on a production line. It has a low tensile strength and only a quarter of steel's resistance to bending – and just a third of the weight. These characteristics mean that aluminum frames need to be designed in different ways than steel frames, and thereby hangs a tale.

The traditional sizes for the outside diameter of steel road bike frame tubes are 1.125-inch for the down and seat, and 1-inch for the top (cycle tubing has not yet gone metric). European builders used these sizes when they first began to build with aluminum, and as a result the frames were very flexible and would whip from side to side when pushed hard. This produced an uncomfortable sensation of loss of control for the rider. It was also imagined that whip reduced speed by dissipating energy that would otherwise go into forward motion; if this were true, very stiff frames would consistently win races, and they do not. But irrespective of real or imagined shortcomings, the new aluminum frames were extremely lightweight, and many professional racers began using them (suitably painted over in team colors) on sections with long climbs.

In America, pioneering builders in aluminum such as Gary Klein and then Cannondale decided to enlarge the diameter of the tubing. This increases stiffness, with little penalty in weight, because aluminum is so light. The results were spectacular: where a traditional frame in ultralight steel weighed around 4 pounds, the new aluminum frames with large diameter tubing were 3 pounds or less. More to the point, they were exceedingly rigid, such that some makers secured patents based on the degree of stiffness they could achieve with aluminum.

Strong racers, and more sedate general riders wishing to go touring with heavy loads, were both delighted. At last, they had bikes that did not bend and flex when hammered hard or loaded with heavy panniers. Perhaps best of all, once Cannondale and others began mass-producing aluminum frames, you could run down to the store, hand over mere money, and ride away on a bike as good if not better than the finest European machines.

When Americans tried to enter their new found designs in European races, however, the governing body of international cycle sport, the Union Cycliste International (UCI), panicked at the idea that traditional bikes might be vanquished by technological upstarts, and banned bikes with "oversize" frame tubes. This bit of senile dementia helped speed the shift of the quality bike industry from Europe to America and Asia.

Cycling has always been as much about technological innovation as athletic performance. Our physical capabilities are limited by genetic potential and quality of training. If strength and stamina alone mattered, we could all check into the body shop, get rated and indexed, wear a number, and that would be that. No need to "race." The whole point of competition and the fun of winning is finding and using an edge, whether it comes from being clever or experienced, reaching deeper inside for extra ooommph, or tricking up your bike in some way.

The new generation of cyclists were into performance and fun, and did not care about sticking to "traditional" frames and tubing sizes. Quite the opposite: hot rodding is an American tradition, and folks in the New World quickly made their own way in bike design and manufacture. The concurrent development and spectacular growth of the mountain bike, which, whether built of steel or aluminum utilizes "outsize" tubing, fully established America and Asia as the centers of technological innovation and mass-production of quality bikes. Today, Asian firms can supply

decent enough TIG-welded (tungsten inert gas) aluminum frames at a unit cost less than the price of this book. This is extremely cheap compared to the cost of the quality frames of yesteryear.

That aluminum is relatively inexpensive is good, because it does have one drawback: fatigue. Aluminum wears out and weakens with each movement. Before the computer age, when building do's and don'ts for aluminum were being learned through trial and error, there were incidents of frames or forks snapping apart and sometimes badly injuring their luckless riders. Designers know the material better now, and moreover, we live in a litigious age in which no manufacturer would dare produce a bike with even a slight tendency for structural failure. Aluminum frames are conscientiously overbuilt for strength, and safety is no more of an issue than with any other material.

Some people say that an aluminum frame that has been vigorously used or thrashed will progressively go dead, in the same way that it is possible to blow out a pair of skis in a single hard race. However, aluminum frames are actually massively overbuilt – one reason why they can have an uncompromising feel – and for deadness I suspect a cause other than fatigue. Steel frames also get blown out by hard racers, and yet fatigue is not really a problem with steel. It has been discovered that if these dead frames are reset (put back into true alignment), they can spring back to life!

A problem with aluminum, carbon fiber, and titanium as materials is that frames cannot be reset. One reason steel frames are still popular is that they are easy to fix. Still, the inexpensiveness of aluminum is dimming an image of the frame as the enduring heart of a bike, rolling on through the miles and generations with refreshed components as required. Depending on how hard you ride and how well you look after your bike, an aluminum frame bike will last a certain number of years, and that's it – the bike goes into secondary service, or on to some other career. It's not worth replacing the components, because you can buy a new bike at less cost. In any case, the way cycling technology is advancing, after a few years it is time to enjoy a new bike.

• Grades of Aluminum

Aluminum for bike frames is alloyed with traces of other elements, just like alloy steel, and is grouped in series from 1000 to 8000, according to the main element used. The numbers have no meaning or comparative rank and are only for identification purposes. The most common grade for mass-production bikes is 6061, which contains magnesium and silicon, and is strong, can be cold formed, has good corrosion resistance, and welds well. To prevent cracking of the joints, however, the entire frame must be heat treated in a specialized process, whereupon it becomes T6 aluminum. A stronger, more expensive grade in the 6000-series is 6013 (Cu92) with a high percentage of copper.

Another popular grade for mass production is 7005 or 7020, which is stronger than 6061, but welds, even if heat treated, are subject to stress corrosion, flexing will eventually cause a joint to crack. Frames in 7005 or 7020 need to be generously butted in order to provide enough grip for a safe weld. A similar stipulation applies to 5082, which is popular with French manufacturers. It's strong, resistant to corrosion, and welds well, but cannot be heat treated.

Aluminum frames can also be glued together, which avoids the entire problem of loss of temper through the heat of welding. For gluing, 2014, a common aviation grade, is often used, and so is 7075, currently the strongest grade available.

In development are still stronger and lighter grades in the 8000-series. These should be available soon.

Frame Construction

To discuss the advantages and disadvantages of more exotic metals and then composites, we must first to go into construction and design.

Construction, how a frame is held together, is a major element in quality, and varies in method for different materials. Mild steel frames are usually just stuck together and welded by machine at high temperatures, leaving a smooth join. Quality steels with more carbon content become brittle if overheated, and frames of this material are joined by methods using lower temperatures than welding.

• Lugs and Brazing

The tubes are brazed together using brass (machine or hand) or silver alloy (hand only) as a filler. As an aid to accurate assembly, lugs are used to position the tubes. The important join is between the tubes themselves, and strictly speaking, the lug work does not have to be neat and tidy for a strong join. However, clean lug work is a sign of care and thoroughness that bodes well for the rest of the bike. Moreover, lugs do provide some stress distribution at the joint. On a better quality frame, the lugs should taper down where the tube enters the lug, so that lug and tube more readily flex as one; a lug with a sharp, well-defined shoulder may concentrate stress at one point on the tube. The lug should not extend out over the thin area of the tube. For example, extra long spearpoint lugs have been known to spear tubes.

Fine lug work on an early F. W. Evans bike

• Welding

In metal inert gas (MIG) welding, the filler is material similar to the frame, and when heated, frame and filler become one. The process works well with heavier steels and is particularly suitable for mass production. Thinner tubing requires tungsten inert gas (TIG) welding, which still fuses the tubes together, but a filler is typically used as well. TIG-welding is the common method for volume production of frames in cro-mo and aluminum. However, there are some notable differences in how the two materials are handled.

With cro-mo, the fillet – the bit around the joint – is relatively small; with aluminum it is much larger. The fillet may be left "as is," stippled like decorative frosting on a birthday cake, or ground and filed to a smooth finish; either will hold. Equipment required for TIG-welding steel is relatively simple and inexpensive, but gear for TIG-welding aluminum is quite sophisticated, expensive, and requires skill to use.

• Fillet Brazing

Fillet brazing is done with an oxyacetylene torch and bronze; traditionally, a very large fillet is built up that is then ground and polished smooth. It's a technique for craft built bikes, although it is also handy when a frame (tandems, recumbents, special design bikes) cannot use pre-cut lugs.

Frame Design

The design or geometry of a bicycle frame with an upright riding position varies according to its intended purpose and the type and weight of rider. The two fundamental types of bikes are road and off-road, and within each category there is a similar basic choice: going quickly and responsively, or more slowly and evenly. Generally, performance bikes have quick pedal response and handling, while bikes made for general riding are more stable.

The first crude indication of a bike's character is the wheelbase, the distance between the wheel axles. On road bikes this ranges from 38.5 inches for racing models to around 42 inches for touring models. On mountain bikes the range is from around 41 inches to 45 inches. Wheelbase is an additive function of the relative angles at which the frame tubes are joined, and their length. Tightly built, short wheelbase frames are often described as "stiff," and long wheelbase frames as "soft." These terms give the misleading impression that tight frames have a harsh ride compared to relaxed frames. In fact, wheelbase makes only a slight difference to ride comfort; more important are the type of wheels and tires. Frame design variations are for performance characteristics, degree of stability, and room for mounting panniers.

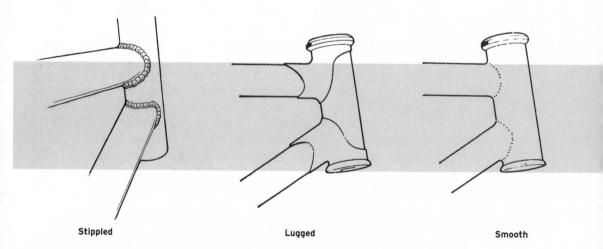

Stippled   Lugged   Smooth

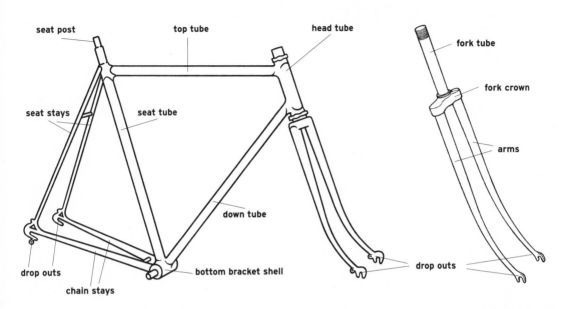

The kick or pedal responsiveness of a bike is largely determined by the tightness of the rear triangle formed by the seat tube, seat stays, and chain stays, or more simply, by the length of the chain stays. On a road racing bike this could be as little as 15.75 inches, leaving no room between seat tube and tire for a mudguard. On sport touring bikes the interval is 16.25 to 17 inches, and on touring bikes it is 16.5 to 17.75 inches. Mountain bikes run hot at 17.5 inches and less, and more sedately at around 18.5 inches. Short chain stays make for quick acceleration and climbing, and nimble handling; long chain stays reduce snappishness but increase stability and room for carrying things.

The speed with which a bike handles, and the degree of directional stability, is largely determined by the tightness of the front end. This is a function of the head tube angle relative to horizontal, or level ground, and the fork rake, which is the distance between the wheel axle and the line of the head tube. The tighter the head tube angle, the faster the bike reacts to steering input. Bikes with fork rakes of 2 inches or more tend to be stable, especially at low speeds; fork rakes under 2 inches give nimble handling and better stability at high speeds.

The bottom bracket height relates to the center of gravity and stability of a bike, and how easy it is to touch the ground with a foot when seated in the saddle. Utility and touring bikes have a low bottom bracket height to aid stability when loaded, and to make frequent stops easier. Racing bikes move the bottom bracket higher for pedal clearance when cornering, and mountain bike bottom brackets are still higher, for clearance over rough ground. One of the things that can characterize a city bike is a low bottom bracket to make stopping and starting easier. However, this means that the pedals are more apt to ground when cornering – an unpleasant, scary experience that can make you nervous about laying the bike over. Although a high bottom bracket can require that you leave the saddle when stopping and starting, adequate pedal clearance is a great aid to confident bike handling.

The design and character of a bike is often described as a function of the angles to horizontal formed by the head and seat tubes. While it is

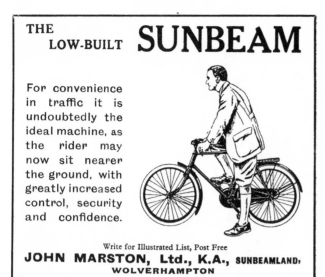
broadly true that a classic "soft" touring bike might be 72° parallel, and a more responsive "stiff" racing bike might be 74° parallel, frame angles depend on the length of the frame tubes and not the other way round. For example, women generally have less reach than men, and short women in particular have limited reach. A correctly proportioned frame will have a top tube of a length that requires steepening the seat tube angle to 75° or even 76°. Despite having a supposedly "stiff" geometry, such a bike will be comfortable to ride.

The stiffness of a frame in a vertical (up and down) plane has little if anything to do with the seat tube angle. Even a very whippy frame with a lot of torsional (twist) and lateral (side to side) movement, will have very little vertical compliance. It's a structural thing, seen everywhere in large four-sided farm gates with a single diagonal cross brace. The gate may rock and sway in the breeze, but so long as the cross brace is adequate, the up and down position won't change. On a bike, in a vertical plane, the forks move but the rest of the frame pretty much stays put. Vertical compliance of a frame is a function of height and length, or wheelbase. A longer or shorter wheelbase does make a difference, but only a very small one.

As a practical matter, if you like to sit tall in the saddle, then a more relaxed seat tube angle down to as low as 68° will work out better; if you like to hunch over for maximum aerodynamic advantage and go so far as to rest your forearms on profile handlebars, then the seat tube angle can pump up to 78° and even higher. The thing to appreciate is that in terms of comfort, this progression is a function of saddle position in relationship to the bottom bracket, not of the frame angles. Essentially, the more weight you support with the arms, the more your legs can dangle in a vertical plane; conversely, the more weight you place on your saddle, the more your hips need to be back from a vertical line through the bottom bracket. Whichever, the important point is that position on a bike is a function of saddle and handlebar position. This provides a jump-off for the question: why the diamond frame?

• New Tricks with Sticks

The diamond pattern frame with a level top tube evolved over 100 years ago and is a perfect design for road bikes and the kinds of alloy steels used through the 1970s. There are other design variations that have advantages, however, and modern materials have characteristics which mean they can and should be handled differently.

I first saw a road bike with a dropped top tube – sloping down from the head tube to the seat tube

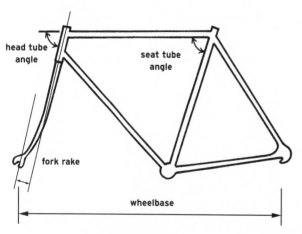

head tube angle

seat tube angle

fork rake

wheelbase

– when I met the American technical guru Fred DeLong, sometime in the 1970s. Fred explained that the inclined top tube on his bike was an old idea, which made the frame stronger, and of course provided extra clearance around the privates, a feature readily appreciated by anyone who has had the misfortune of being slammed in the crotch by a top tube. With the advent of the mountain bike and dynamic off-road riding, a dropped top tube became the norm, not just as insurance against grievous harm, but because a more compact frame is stronger, lighter, and easier to handle. These ideas have moved on to road racing bikes, with the additional benefit of improving aerodynamics. The TCR series introduced by Giant utilizes a dropped top tube/compact frame, something that would not be possible but for that with modern materials, seat posts can be longer (snapped seat posts were not uncommon in days of yore). That the compact frame is effective is evident from the number of other manufacturers who have taken up this trend. I've been riding a TCR, and I can confirm it really is both very lightweight and stiff.

A profound economic advantage of a dropped top tube is that to fit different riders it is no longer necessary to make frames in a range of perhaps ten or more different sizes. Small, medium, and large will cover the lot. Precision fit for individual riders is achieved through different size seat posts

A dropped or sloping top tube is standard for mountain bikes, and increasingly common for road racing bikes.

and stems. In a mass-production bike, this is a huge economy, not just for the manufacturer, but also for the stores, which only have to stock three sizes instead of ten or more. All of this has a vital bottom line for you and me: lower retail prices.

In another one of those moves that leave you wondering how some people make it out of bed in the morning, the Union Cycliste Internationale banned frames with sloping top tubes for racing. They also decreed that a bicycle frame can only be made of tubes of a specific size and configuration. However, the design and manufacture of top level performance bicycles is rapidly wheeling down a very different road.

Composite Materials

Steel and aluminum as frame materials work best in tubular form. Both metals are isotropic, equally strong in all directions. However, the new cutting edge in frame materials, composites, are anisotropic – i.e., composed of fibers strong in specific directions – and the builder can decide which way they go. This means a radical change in design approach.

Composites consist of fibers bound by glue or resin, or by a substance such as nylon. The most common type for bikes is carbon fiber, which in pure form is as strong as the finest steel, never fatigues, and yet is only two-thirds the weight of aluminum. Carbon fiber is somewhat brittle, so frames and components made in this material are overbuilt by a generous margin. They are nonetheless still ultralightweight, yet can withstand more abuse than steel. Frames are also produced in aramid, the material for bullet proof shields and armor and better known by the trade name Kevlar™. Aramid is not as strong as carbon fiber, but is much tougher.

A number of manufacturers produce traditional tubular design frames in composite materials. The tubes are glued together via lugs, made either from cast aluminum alloy or molded carbon. Because a material such as carbon fiber is so light and strong, it has considerable advantages even when shaped into tubing. Replicating the form of a

Windcheetah Mark IA, 1985. The shell is single form, as it were, deformed from a sphere. A noted development of the Windcheetah series was the Burrows-designed Lotus Sport bicycle, which Britain's Chris Boardman rode to a new world record in the 4,000-meter pursuit at the 1992 Olympics.

strong, look great, and are fun to live with. The frame has a decided shape and form, and the large surface areas open up almost limitless graphic and decorative possibilities. I've seen monocoques just as beautiful as the finest paintings. What's more, they are easy to enjoy: while a regular bike has a lot of nooks and crannies and can be a bit of chore to keep clean, a few swipes with a rag and a monocoque is shining.

Monocoque designs are limited to racing and very high-end bikes. Yet composite materials and monocoque construction hold enormous potential for producing not just competition machines with precise performance characteristics, but also a range of general use and utility bikes of better quality and design at lower cost. Realizing this potential, however, is nothing like as easy as rolling off a log. Volume production in composites requires a huge investment and, up until now, few if any bike designers have created monocoques that are much more than aerodynamic, fast, and good looking. There's still a lot of expensive, computer aided design research and development to be done, and as well, considerable production engineering to

metal bicycle, however, is not the best way to use composites.

One big asset of composites is the ease with which they can be worked and shaped into various forms. This allows strength, flexibility, and other characteristics to be placed and added precisely where required. The most efficient configuration for composites is monocoque, the entire frame as a single piece, with the means to hold the wheels, cranks, forks, saddle, and everything else in one cohesive unit. Monocoque means that chassis and body, or skin, are one; more than a few of the slick-looking frames currently labelled as monocoques are in fact glued together assemblies of bits and pieces.

Monocoque designs are aerodynamic, light and

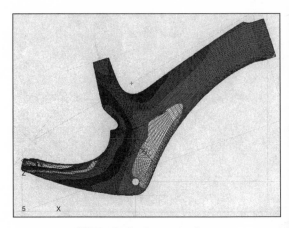

"Weave" of a composite frame.

work out the best manufacturing techniques. Then, too, currently available components are designed for stick bikes; monocoque designs have different needs.

Try to imagine the problem. For more than 100 years, bikes have been made from tubes. The rider's hands, feet, and posterior, and the two wheel axles, are connected by tubes – things you can bend, squeeze, and fiddle with, but that essentially remain lines. Now wipe the canvas clean. You've got the same five points, but connections are now to be made, as it were, with an air brush or spray gun. Fine, you can design something that looks very pretty, and you have some sense of

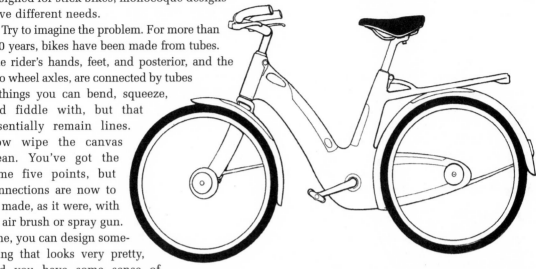

Concept study for a monocoque city bike with cantilever wheels and enclosed chainguard.

how and where to build for strength and flex and so on, but even if you are a leading bike designer, from a technical point of view the final product is likely to lag behind a well-crafted frame in steel or aluminum. The reason is, we know very little about monocoque construction for bicycles, but have a rich fund of experience of building with tubes.

Gerald O'Donovan, chief designer and builder at Carlton/Raleigh for many years, was an artist in steel and reputedly could build a frame with such precision, it would last for only a single race. To protect innocent people from possible harm, Gerald would collect the frame after the event and cut it apart with a bandsaw – a touch of theatre, perhaps, but over a number of different bike building projects I gained enormous respect for the precision with which Gerald could work with steel, and I believe he probably could come right up to the exact edge of what the material could do.

Composite materials are already well-established and monocoque designs, thanks to greater aerodynamic efficiency, are faster than traditional stick design bicycles. As builders learn more about composites, particularly in volume production, monocoque bikes will become increasingly

commonplace. It can't happen too soon. For example, using monocoque construction it is feasible to create a bicycle with everything but the pedals and the wheels completely self-contained and sealed. No external lights, cables, brakes, gears, or chain. All the mechanical bits run in constant lubrication protected from dirt and will last almost forever. Pop off the function specific (speed, off-road, indestructible commuting, wet grip, snow grip, or whatever) interchangeable quick release wheels, give the frame a wipe, and the bike is clean enough to hang in the closet alongside your Sunday best.

Other Materials

• Titanium

Titanium is as strong as steel at half the weight, and free from corrosion and fatigue. Fabricating titanium is difficult, and the cost of tooling (making machines to work it) is high, which makes titanium frames expensive. Still, they are truly beautiful, and regarded by many as the ultimate. Personally, I find the enhanced options offered by composite frames more interesting, but take a look and see for yourself.

• Metal Matrix Composites

Metal matrix composites (MMC) are metals with the addition of small, hard particles. The most prevalent type is aluminum alloy with aluminum oxide or silicon carbide particles. This mixture has improved strength and fatigue resistance, but weld quality goes down, and the material is difficult to machine or work into various forms, such as tubes. Basically, it is more suitable for components than for frames.

• Magnesium

Very, very light, but the stuff is better for parts than frames. Magnesium works best in bulky shapes, and not very well in fine, drawn out shapes. I suppose one could use it to build a boxy looking bicycle, but the chiller for me is that unless precisely and carefully processed and treated, magnesium is highly vulnerable to corrosion.

• Plastic

It should be possible to build nice bicycles with injection molded plastics such as nylon, but major research is needed to understand what bicycle designs will work in plastics. The Itera from Sweden, launched in 1981, was promoted as a revolutionary plastic bicycle and a harbinger of a new era in cycling. However, the machine was so badly done, it set an all-time record for abysmal performance. Not a fair test. The first successful plastic bicycle will probably be a recumbent design, as this configuration is more sympathetic to the use of new materials.

Frame Wrap

The frame is the heart of a bike, and within reason you want the best you can afford. In mass-production, frames for cheap bikes are made with heavy, inert mild steel; for entry level, basic qual-ity bikes, much better hi-ten steel is used; for midrange bikes, cro-mo and other lightweight alloy steels are used; and for top-range bikes, aluminum or composites. Fine alloy steels, aluminum, titanium, and composites such as carbon fiber and aramid are used for hand built frames.

The design of most frames is determined by the function of the bike and how best to use the materials at hand. The classic diamond pattern frame with a horizontal top tube is still used for many road racing bikes, but only because of the dictates of a sport governing body clinging to 1970s technology. With modern materials, a dropped or sloping top tube is practical even for racing bikes and, since it has many advantages, will soon be standard. The future for frames, whether for crafting exotic racing machines or mass-producing inexpensive, plain Jane utility bikes, is in composite materials and one piece monocoque designs.

SUSPENSION

Suspension provides greater speed, control, and comfort. Nothing demonstrates this more clearly than a bike's most important suspension mechanism, the pneumatic tire, which, by flowing over surface irregularities, conserves energy that would otherwise be dissipated in up and down motion, increases traction, and absorbs shocks that would fatigue the rider and rattle loose his or her brains.

No one doubts the benefits of suspension. However, once you set out to equip a bike with suspension mechanisms beyond the air-filled tire, problems arise. One is weight. A suspension device can be very simple and therefore lightweight, but might then have limited effectiveness, which leads to the next liability, mechanical complexity. The problem with suspension is less that of allowing the wheel or some other part of the bike to move up in response to a bump, than of getting it back down in controlled fashion after it has gone up – in other words, have the wheel fluidly follow the contour of a bump rather than bounce up and down. This is accomplished through a process known as damping, which, in simplified terms, is the introduction of progressive resistance to bounce or uncontrolled movement of the shock absorbing mechanism. Damping systems by definition dissipate energy which, unless the bike is freewheeling downhill, comes from the rider. Damping mechanisms can be quite complex and add considerable weight to a bike. Finally, suspension on a bike can lead to an energy draining phenomenon known as "bobbing," where the rider's pedalling effort, rather than moving the bike forward, causes the bike to bounce up and down like a pogo stick.

Suspension *systems* act to absorb shocks to the bike from the terrain. Dual or full suspension means shock absorbing mechanisms for both wheels. A popular option is front suspension only, a hardtail bike. Suspension *devices* act to insulate the rider against shocks from the bike,

and include suspension seat posts and handlebars. How all these alternatives stack up pro and con depends on the design and weight of the suspension system or device, the kind of bike and rider, and the conditions of use.

Road racing bikes do not use suspension, because at the current level of technological development, any performance benefit is nullified by a weight penalty. This could change as suspension systems become lighter and more sophisticated. Off-road is of course where (modern) bicycle suspension began, but much depends on the kind of riding involved. For fast descents, the performance gain from full suspension is sensational, and additional weight is not a problem; the current fashion in downhill off-road racing bikes is for massive, heavy construction. However, in cross country events where there is pedalling up as well as down hills, weight really counts. Races are won on the climbs, because this is where rid-

Been there, done that: Whippet Spring Frame Dwarf Safety Roadster, 1889.

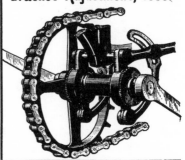

ers spend the most time. At this writing, the majority of cross country racing bikes are hardtails, and bikes with no suspension at all are still very competitive. That said, the pace of technological development is so rapid, dual suspension cross country racing bikes are already turning in some impressive performances, and will doubtless soon be the norm for top-level competition.

For general riding, once speed is no longer paramount, the additional comfort and control provided by suspension is very attractive. Certainly that is how most buyers feel – in midrange mountain bikes, hardtails are outselling equivalent quality classic non-suspension models. Suspension is entirely sensible for much off-road riding, and for many kinds of road riding, too.

Strictly speaking, you do not need suspension on smooth pavement. However, many streets and roads are anything but smooth, and one prime reason for the popularity of mountain bikes is their better handling, safety, and comfort in the face of increasingly harsh urban riding conditions. While a fit, hard charging rider who moves well with a bike is likely to regard suspension as unwelcome additional weight, a bike courier who spends eight hours a day in the saddle may feel that suspension, or at least front suspension, is just great. To go the distance, relief of fatigue can be as important, or even more important, than speed.

From a mechanical standpoint, suspension systems and devices divide into two categories: light, simple, and essentially passive, or heavy, complex, and active. A competition downhill mountain bike is the most extreme example of the latter: full suspension with lots of travel, 7 to 8 inches or more, and highly sophisticated mechanisms that use springs, oil, and air in various combinations and ways. As one levels out to dual suspension cross country and freestyle fun riding models, the amount of travel becomes less, and so does mechanical complexity. Nonetheless, these systems can be structurally involved, with a lot of moving parts and joints subject to rapid wear, and needing frequent servicing.

The next stage in dual suspension is a definite shift: instead of an oil damped coil spring or similar mechanism for shock absorption, there is an elastomer block or rubber ball. These systems are cheap and durable, usually reasonably lightweight, and can be set up to suit the rider's weight and conditions of use. Although this type of design might seem simple – typically, one form or another of a swinging arm hits or pinches the block or ball – it can actually be quite sophisticated. For example, the rubber ball developed by Alex Moulton and used for the rear suspension of his small wheel bikes is an extraordinarily clever device that will outperform many more complex systems. The ball is shaped so that, when compressed, it does a kind of inside out movement that results in both a variable response rate and some damping effect.

Finally, suspension devices such as handlebars and seat posts with springs or elastomer pads are light, simple, and effective within a limited range of conditions. They can't iron out the big bumps and jolts of a fast off-road downhill, but can provide a smoother ride over rough pavement or along a hard dirt path. Rider reactions to suspension devices are apt to be fairly personal. For example, pull up on suspended handlebars, and they move. Not everyone likes this. Similarly, with a suspension seat post, the saddle-to-bottom bracket distance becomes variable. Some people won't mind; others definitely will.

There are many different options for realizing the Holy Grail of suspension, and while with most of them I can make suggestions and offer advice or at least an opinion, when it comes to dual suspension systems, I don't know what's best. Neither does anyone else. The thing is, once you bring in dual suspension, traditional frame design takes a hike. Instead of starting with a frame and then adding suspension, you design a suspension system and build the frame to suit. Many different kinds of systems are already offered, including unified rear triangle inclusive of bottom bracket, unified rear triangle which rotates on the bottom bracket, swing arm high pivot, rear triangle low pivot, linkage in many patterns, parallelogram, and McPherson strut, just to name those that quickly come to mind. Some are highly complex, with lots of parts that can bend or wear out quickly, others are quite simple and long lasting. In addition, a new final answer to suspension, a unified solution to all the different problems of weight, variable chain length and/or saddle to pedal distance, bobbing, response to little bumps versus big bumps, wear rate, and perhaps even cost, appears about every other month.

One option, seen on some decidedly upmarket bikes, is on-the-fly suspension lockout. This feature allows the rider to turn the suspension on or off with a flick of a lever. The bike can be stiff and responsive when climbing or sprinting, and supple and tenacious when howling down a rocky trail. This best-of-both-worlds approach seems to be most popular with riders new to suspension.

A new design worth checking out is the NRS, used by Giant on their XTC range. When this system is set up correctly for the rider's weight, the ride is dead level, with no bobbing, yet it will respond to bumps. It could be an evolutionary benchmark comparable to the first Rock-Shox, and reviews in the cycle press are enthusiastic. I've been out on the bike and like it very much; if you are seriously interested in full suspension, I recommend a look – a suspension bike that does not bob is a machine worth having.

Suspension technology is an evolving area, with a lot of personal preferences involved, and the most important element is – you! How you like a system and how it works for you determines whether it is good or not.

For example, one of the fastest bikes in traffic I've ever used is the Moulton AM-14 with a front fairing (windshield). The Moulton AM-series is an excellent example of a bike completely engineered to take advantage of full suspension. It has small wheels with slim, hard tires (unsprung small wheels are harsh riding, unless cushioned with slow, mushy tires), which provides enough room for the fairing to be three-quarter length and thus quite effective, so the bike has a meaningful turn of speed. Combine this with a slim bike profile, quick handling and low weight, and the result is a machine that can be made to really slide through traffic. Yet if you stand up out of the saddle and try to hammer an AM-14, it will bob. The design is geared toward a riding style that is consistent, efficient, and graceful, rather than sharp and explosive. For some folks, this is just the ticket. (More about the Moulton, a unique design, in Chapter 6, Special Bikes and Trikes.)

Suppose you like fun riding, basically just messing around off-road, ideally in an area with some nice rolling terrain and a few bumps for catching air, plus some sharp pitches for interesting climbs and descents. This sort of go-where-you-like roller coaster riding is exhilarating and perfect for a full size, dual suspension mountain bike. Who cares if the machine is a little heavy? You're out for fun and games, not to win a race. Of course, if you use the same machine for a regular commuting road journey, and you are a vigorous rider, then the weight of dual suspension will be a drag. If you're on a budget, you put up with it, and if you've some spare cash, you start thinking of having more than one bike . . .

For road riders on daily business, suspension can be a welcome comfort, but dual suspension is too much. A hardtail is very nice on those days when you are bushed and can use a bit of a cruise over the rough sections. A proper coil spring fork does the best job, but can need frequent servicing and attention, and adds weight. Almost as good are elastomer suspended handlebars, which don't have a lot of travel, but can take the sting out of rough surfaces such as cobbles. Again, how you might like suspension handlebars will depend on your riding style. If you're athletic and sometimes bunny hop (jump) a sidewalk or pot hole, you won't care for the way suspension bars give when you pull up on them. If you are looking for an easy cruise, then they might be perfect.

Seat posts with a spring or other mechanism so the saddle can move up and down are becoming increasingly popular. Note: a suspension seat post may improve your comfort, it does not help the bike and so does not improve control or tire grip. Also note, when you try to rise a little out of the saddle for a bump or to provide room to whip the bike around underneath you, the saddle does not stay put but instead follows you into the air.

Personally, having spent years riding bikes with hard saddles that were always exactly where they should be, I'm not comfortable with a saddle that follows my nether parts around. For many other people this may be no problem, and that's why I say yes, suspension is worthwhile, but you need to try it yourself to see what you do and don't like. This is particularly the case with rear suspension, which is an open game subject to much change.

Monoblade

A monoblade is a single strut with a cantilever or stub axle to mount the wheel. The method is used to mount both front and rear wheels on HPVs, but on regular bikes, it is limited to the front wheel. The design is stronger, lighter and more convenient than the usual arrangement of twin fork blades.

When you double the diameter of a tube, the weight doubles but the stiffness increases 4.5 times. A monoblade is stronger than a pair of blades of equivalent weight, or lighter in weight for an equivalent strength. As for a cantilever axle, this is how wheels are mounted on airplanes, trains, and cars. Cantilever wheels for bikes made a brief appearance in the late 19th century, and then again in the mid-1980s when Mike Burrows used the idea for some of his time trial bikes, to improve aerodynamics. A single blade has less drag than two. When Mike began designing mountain bikes, the monoblade was again utilized, this time for its weight/strength advantage. There has also been a related concurrent development, the disc brake. Traditional calliper brakes cannot be used with a monoblade – a hub or disk brake can. For various reasons, hub brakes are not suitable for use on mountain bikes, but disc brakes most definitely are. A monoblade is a logical counterpart for a disc brake, which mounts and operates on one side of a wheel, and thus concentrates all of its considerable power in a single location.

As for convenience, with a cantilever axle you can get at the tire without having to remove the wheel from the bike. This would be a liability in road racing, where you need to be able to change

Raven by Cannondale

wheels rather than tires. In mountain bike races, as in real life, there are no support vehicles filled with jack-in-the-box mechanics armed with spare wheels; if a tire goes flat, you've got to mend or replace it yourself, and this is lots easier to do with a cantilever mounted wheel.

So far at least, mountain bike racers have kept clear of the monoblade design. Too radical, I guess. They should look again at airplanes, which have to withstand enormous shock loads. The advantages of the monoblade are decisive, and eventually all competition mountain bikes will be set up this way.

WHEELS

After the frame, the wheels – tires, rims, spokes, and hubs – are the most important components of a bike. The frame is the vitality, the wheels the point of translation into motion. Their effect on performance and comfort is enormous. Once completed, a bike frame is unlikely to go back to the torch or glue pot for changes and modifications. Wheels, however, are easily altered, and offer a

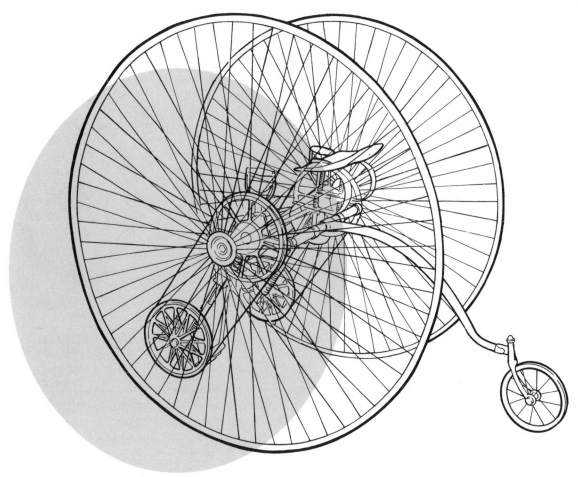

Otto Dicycle by BSA, 1881

range of options regarding performance, durability, and suitability for different conditions.

A traditional metal-spoked bicycle wheel is one of the strongest engineering structures in existence. The spokes are in tension rather than compression – the weight of the bike hangs from the spokes rather than stands on them – and this is why a well-built wheel can support a rolling weight of up to a ton or more. Wheels are made to be as light as possible because weight has a greater effect on a wheel than anywhere else on a bike. To appreciate the truth of the old saying, "an ounce off the wheels is worth a pound off the frame,"

hold a bicycle wheel by the axle ends and move it around in the air, and then do so again while spinning the wheel. The faster the rotation, the greater the "weight," or inertia, and the harder it is to move the wheel into a new plane of rotation. Bicycle wheels are built with spokes and rims to keep weight to the minimum and thereby reduce both the force of gyroscopic inertia, and energy required for acceleration or braking.

Another force that operates on wheels is aerodynamic drag. At speed, ordinary spokes churn the air like an eggbeater and disrupt its flow. This is of little consequence for everyday riding, but is significant when racing. Deep rim spoked, molded one piece, and disc wheel designs all increase the surface area of the wheel to smooth the flow of air and improve aerodynamic efficiency, at some cost in weight.

Wheels operate on a simple spectrum: light wheels are quicker and more fragile; heavier wheels are slower and more durable. The type of bike, rider, and conditions determine the balance of priorities. Wheels for racing on smoothly surfaced roads are lighter and slimmer than wheels for touring with heavy loads on dirt tracks.

A wheel is a package where the components – tire, rim, spokes, and hub – tend to follow suit in weight and quality. Stout tires, wide rims, and thick spokes go with touring and mountain bikes. Light tires, narrow rims, and slender spokes go with road racing bikes. Generally, heavier wheels are better able to cope with bumps, pot holes, and rough surfaces. Much depends on the rider. "Comfortable" for a beginner usually means a wheel stable enough to not skitter at the sight of a pebble. An experienced cyclist, however, is likely to be happier with a lighter, more responsive wheel.

Tires

There are two kinds of wheels: clincher or wire on tires on high pressure rims, usually called HPs, and tubular or sew up tires on sprint rims, usually called sprints. Clincher tires are the familiar type with an open casing, where the two edges of the casing nestle within the lips of a U-shaped rim. The casing edges are reinforced with beads of wire or aramid, so that they retain shape and stay inside the rim when the inner tube is inflated. It's a straightforward design that is easy to manage when changing a tire or extracting the inner tube to fix a puncture.

With tubular tires the casing edges are sewn together, completely encasing the inner tube. A sprint rim has a slightly concave, smooth top with no lips and the tire is held in place with glue or shellac. In case of a flat, a complete tubular tire can be replaced much more quickly than a clincher tire, an advantage when racing. However,

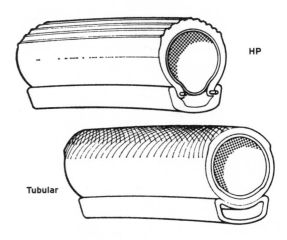

HP and tubular tires.

repairing a tubular is a time-consuming, fiddly business.

Until recently, sprints were decisively lighter than HPs, and hence, despite their hassles, were standard for road racing bikes. Tire technology has advanced enormously, however, and in terms of rolling resistance, clincher tires are now just as fast as tubulars, and only the lightest of sprints have a weight advantage. Most, if not all, racers train on HPs, and many race on them, too. Sprints are still the preferred choice for track events, though.

• Tire and Wheel Sizes

There are two systems for sizing tires, and to keep everybody well on their toes, both are used. Traditional American and British sizes are in inches: 27 x 1.25 means a tire with a diameter of 27 inches and a cross section or width of 1.25 inches. Continental sizes are metric: 700 x 28C means a tire diameter of 700 mm and a width of 28 mm. Neither system is accurate. For example, mountain bike 26-inch tires use smaller rims than road 26-inch tires. A more precise metric system of annotating tire sizes consists of a two figure number, a dash, and a three figure number, as in 32-630. The first figure gives the tire width, the second the diameter of the rim it fits.

The 700C is the same diameter as the sprint rim used for tubular tires, which makes it possible to interchange HP and sprint wheels on the same bike. This is handy for racers who train on HPs, but ride sprints in competition. Note that the 27-inch tire size is not the same as 700C; a 27-inch tire cannot be mounted on a rim for a 700C tire, nor vice versa, and in most cases 700C and 27-inch wheels cannot be interchanged on the same bike. Thankfully, 27-inch wheels are becoming obsolete, although lots of them are still around on older bikes.

TIRE SIZE CHART

Commonly known as	Standard designation
ROAD	
26 x 1.25	32-597
26 x 1.375 (650 x 35A)	35-590
26 x 1.5 (650 x 35B)	35-584
27 x 0.875	23-630
27 x 1	25-630
27 x 1.125	28-630
27 x 1.25	32-630
27 x 1.375	35-630
28 x 1.5 (700 x 35B)	35-635
650 x 35A (26 x 1.375)	35-590
650 x 35B (26 x 1.5)	35-584
700 x 19C	19-622
700 x 20C	20-622
700 x 23C	23-622
700 x 25C	25-622
700 x 28C	28-622
700 x 32C	32-622
700 x 35C	35-622
700 x 38C	38-622
700 x 35B (28 x 1.5)	35-635
MOUNTAIN BIKE	
26 x 1.5	37-559
26 x 1.75	44-559
26 x 2.125	54-559

Mountain bike tires continue to be described in inches, namely 26 x 1.5, 26 x 1.75, and so on. Inch measures are also used for roadster bike tires and, again, note that 26-inch road tires are not the same as 26-inch mountain bike tires. Finally, more than a few hybrid or dual road/dirt bikes use 700C wheels.

Mountain bikes and roadsters generally use 26- or 24-inch wheels, which are stronger because of their smaller diameter and typically more robust construction. Racing and most touring bikes opt for 700C wheels which, with a slightly larger diameter, have less rolling resistance. This is significant in a race or over a long tour. Many hybrid or town bikes also use 700C wheels, which give a bike a touch more speed than 26-inch wheels and, in my opinion, a more elegant appearance. On a town bike, 700C wheels are strong enough if the wheels are of good quality and the bike is ridden well. If strength for aggressive riding is the priority, or if the wheels are not of the first water (say, an entry level bike), then stronger 26-inch wheels are a better bet.

In general, wide tires have a more comfortable ride, better traction on loose surfaces such as gravel and in wet conditions, and are the most durable. Narrow tires have a stiffer ride, less traction, and are more vulnerable to punctures and bruising – but are faster, for both rolling resistance and handling. In the 700C range, typical widths are: 35 mm for hybrids and expedition grade touring bikes; 32 mm for heavy duty touring and mean urban streets; 28 mm for sport tourers and trainers; and 25 and 23 mm for speed riding. Tires at 19 and 20 mm are in the tubular performance class and should only be used by experienced riders.

Tires for mountain bike 26-inch wheels follow similar basic principles except that the width range is from 1 to 3 inches. In general, for off-road riding, one can get by with 1.9- or 2-inch wide tires; however, if the going is muddy, sandy, or very fast down rocky trails, then you want all the tire the bike can wear, at least 2.25-inches. For town riding and the occasional off-road jaunt, 1.5-inch wide tires are fine. And if you want to fly and don't mind fixing flats, the 1-inch jobs are very swift.

• Tire Design

Whether you go for 26-inch or 700C wheels, the range of different kinds of HP tires is quite amazing – everything from rock mushers made for off-road downhill blasting, down to 0.75-inch wide, ultralight treadless road screamers. There are tires for plugging through mud, traction on sandrock, extra grip in the wet, floating on sand, and climbing rock walls. There are tires with dual compound treads to give different performance characteristics when cornering, tires with studs for ice and snow, and tires armored with belts of aramid to help prevent punctures.

How a tire is built affects performance. The tread material can be soft, for better grip, or harder, for greater durability. It can be thin, for minimum rolling resistance, or thick, for greater strength. The casing is made of layers of fabric, with the number of threads per square inch (tpi) ranging from around 35 to 106. A high tpi number indicates a light, supple tire with low rolling resistance and good cornering adhesion, but one that is vulnerable to cuts and bruises. A low tpi number indicates a stout, rigid tire with higher rolling resistance and less adhesion, but that is better able to resist misfortune.

Tread design is a wonderful and most interesting art, but only for wide tires. With narrow road tires, the contact area or "footprint" of the tire is very small, and for grip the most effective tread is none at all. It is the hard road surface that is penetrating the softer surface of the tire, and any voids created by a tread pattern reduce the area for grip. Narrow tires are skittish on slick surfaces (such as rain wet paint stripe lane markers) because the contact area is small and hard.

Off-road, the situation is reversed, the tire is hard and seeks grip in softer dirt, and a tread is necessary for traction. Dirt comes in a splendid variety of textures and colors, from powdery red and yellow dust to black bottomless muck, and hence there are many different kinds of tire tread patterns. Which is best depends on where and how you ride, and while the claims made in advertisements and reviews in magazines can be exciting reading, it is wise to ask around in local bike shops about which models work well in your area.

One point to watch: churning through mud requires tires with beefy knobs, but big knobblies are slow. The current popular solution is a fairly narrow 1.5-inch wide tire with an open tread at the center and knobs at the sides. The tire is fast on harder ground, but when it sinks into soft dirt or mud, the knobs bite in for extra traction. Fine, but be aware that on pavement when the bike is laid over in a corner the knobs can walk sideways at an alarming rate.

No discussion of tires is complete without mentioning one of their most important functions: suspension. The pneumatic tire was a decisive development in the evolution of the bicycle because it increases both speed and comfort. An air filled tire helps smoothen out surface irregularities that would otherwise cause up-and-down energy losses and rider fatigue from vibration. One of your most important performance and comfort tools is a bicycle pump and maintaining the right tire pressures for the riding conditions. I'll talk about this more later.

• Tire Wrap

When sprints were the only high performance tires and ordinary HPs were mostly slow and little different from each other, people made a study of buying tires as cheaply as possible, and used them to grim death, endlessly repairing tubes and casings. Modern HP tires are not devoted to spinning out the pennies; rather, they are a vital, dynamic component of bike performance that you can select for the balance of speed, grip, comfort, durability, and even the looks you fancy – they come in all kinds of colors. Buying new tires is an opportunity for improvement, and although a hot set of tires plus tubes can easily run the cost of a nice dinner for two, the value for money is good. Nowhere else on the bike can you so easily and so greatly alter performance for so little cost.

Spoked Wheels, Traditional

There are three types of metal spokes: galvanized rustless, chrome- or nickel-plated, and stainless steel. Galvanized spokes have a dull finish but are strong. Plated spokes are glittery and pretty but need polishing to prevent rust, and are slightly weaker than galvanized. Stainless steel is generally reckoned the best, but is more demanding of wheel building technique. In design, there is plain gauge, the same diameter throughout, and double-butted, with the stressed areas at the ends of the spoke thicker and the mid-section thinner. Plain gauge spokes are easier to work with, and produce a stiff wheel that can carry on for a while even if a spoke breaks. Double-butted spokes are more elastic and supple, and if correctly tensioned will in theory give an even stronger wheel.

Touring, mountain, and utility bikes are usually fitted with plain 14-gauge spokes. Sporting bikes tend toward 14/15 double-butted spokes, and light racing wheels often pare down to 15/16 and even 15/17 double-butted. It's mostly a question of interest. If you want to get around with the minimum of fuss and attention for the bike, then use plain 14-gauge galvanized. If you enjoy bright, clean wheels and don't mind giving them a little care, like a polish job one night while listening to music or chatting with friends, then use double-butted stainless steel. Wheels are lovely things. They deserve to be pretty. It's fun to watch them sparkle in the early morning sunshine or under street lamps late at night, and is sort of like having company – the bike's way of saying "Whee!"

• Spoke Patterns

To suspend weight, a spoke need only go in a straight line from rim to hub. Known as radial spoking, this pattern is stiff in lateral (side-to-side) and up-and-down directions, but is subject to wind-up from acceleration or braking. To cope with wind-up, spokes are led off the hub at an angle and laced in patterns known as two-, three-, and four-cross, after the number of times the spokes cross each other. The most common pattern is three-cross, which provides the best balance between resistance to wind-up and lateral stiffness. Strength is also a function of the number of spokes used: racing bikes may have as few as 24, while a tandem tourer may have up to 48. The usual ranges are: road and mountain bike 28, 32, 36; touring 36, 40, 48.

Radial spoking is often used for the front wheel on high performance bikes. It is also possible to mix radial and cross patterns on the same wheel. Tradition has it that radially-spoked wheels are stiff, while three- and four-cross wheels are springy and give a softer ride. This appears to be a misapprehension; tests by Mike Burrows show that wheel rims, however laced and whether ancient or new, deflect less than 0.5 mm even under heavy impact.

Rolf wheels are a new design where the spokes are placed side-by-side in pairs. This idea, which

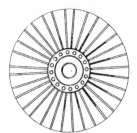

Cross and radial spoking patterns.

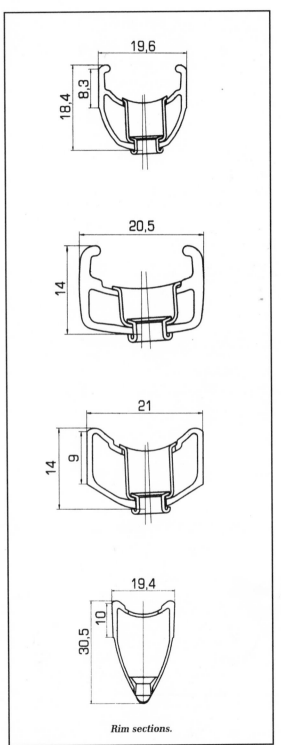

has also been picked up by Shimano, has a definite logic; the rim is held in balanced tension, rather than being pulled in opposite directions in different places. Fewer spokes are used, sprint wheels can have just 14 front, 16 rear. The design is light, yet said to be very strong. I'm sure that as ever, if the wheel is well-built, it will be fine. However, as of this writing it is too soon to know the pros and cons of the design; if you're curious, ask at a high tech bike shop.

There are various new wheel designs that use things such as aramid, continuous lacing patterns, and other innovations. I'm cool towards these, because they are typically very expensive and need special tools and knowledge for servicing. A conventional spoked wheel is still one of the strongest things in all the world, and you can look after it yourself.

• Rims

Rims for traditional spoked wheels are made in steel, aluminum alloy, and composites. Aluminum is standard; composite rims are specialized and very expensive. Don't even look at a bike with steel rims, unless you like running into things. Most bicycle brakes are the calliper type which work by pressing two blocks or shoes against the sides of the rim. In dry conditions this works well with alloy rims, and just barely with steel rims. In wet conditions alloy rims have less braking power, but are still functional. The braking power of steel rims when wet, however, can fade to zero.

Rim sections.

More than once in the rain I've seen terrified riders on bikes with steel wheels careening down a hill and into busy intersections, despite gripping the brake levers with all their might and dragging their feet, too, in desperate efforts to survive.

Although steel rims were once recommended for steamroller strength and durability, modern alloy rims, like tires, are available in a range of weights and strengths, to suit every purpose. Mountain bike rims in particular are made to withstand dreadful hammerings – like 40 mph and more down rocky trails. Steel rims continue to be used only because they are cheap. Even if all you want is a heavy cruiser or utility bike, it will go and stop better and be a far happier machine if fitted with alloy wheels.

For ultimate performance and strength, top line rims are made from specially hardened alloys. Some models are coated with ceramic oxides to improve braking, particularly in wet conditions. Another tactic for better braking is to mill the rim sides, to produce a particularly even, consistent surface. Quality in a rim is important. Although spokes can in theory tension a rim into perfect roundness within a single plane without side-to-side wobble, no wheel builder likes to start with a rim that is out of round or twisted. The job never comes out quite right.

Good quality rims are eyeletted: the holes for the spoke nipples are reinforced with metal eyelets, just like shoes. Rims are formed by joining two ends together, and it is important that the seam be smooth; any roughness or irregularity will play havoc with braking. Generally, box or modular section construction gives the most strength for the least weight. Part of the rim is hollow – in cross section, shallow rectangle, or box. Rims that are sturdier can use a simpler channel section design shaped like a U. Rims for downhill mountain bikes are wide and shallow to help absorb impacts.

A good match between tire and rim widths is important. Most rims that accept 32 mm wide tires will accept a slightly narrower 28 mm tire, but not a 25 mm model. It's more than a yes or no fit. A rim and tire work together and have an opti-

mum performance profile. When a tire is too narrow for a rim it tends to take the shape of a wedge, and impact resistance and grip are greatly reduced. The wheel is more easily damaged by bumps, the ride is hard, and bike handling is skittish and uncertain.

There is less of a problem if the tire is too wide for the rim, but at low pressures the tire can swim about within the rim, so that the bike feels indeterminate and queasy when cornering. When tire and rim are correctly matched, the profile is similar to a button mushroom, with the tire (cap) wider than the rim (stem). Ride is firm and handling is certain; the bike is "willing" to take a corner.

Aero Wheels

There are several design options for reducing the aerodynamic drag of a wheel. All involve trade offs in weight and/or the stability of the bike in windy conditions. When speed is paramount, the weight trade off is clearly worthwhile. However, in gusty conditions an aero wheel on the front can have a traumatic effect on bike stability and handling. Although some people claim that a similar problem can occur with an aero wheel on the rear, in practical experience I've not found this to be so. In fact, it is common to run an aero rear wheel and a regular or deep rim front wheel.

• Deep Rim Spoked

Deep or aero rims are made of aluminum or a composite with a metal sub-rim for braking. Wheels with shallow aero rims of 50 mm depth or less are controllable in most conditions and can be used for road racing and general riding; wheels with aero rims of 60 mm depth or greater are more of a handful and are best limited to time trials and track events.

The HED wheel is a well known deep rim design. Another very interesting model designed by Mike Burrows for Giant Bikes uses plastic spokes shaped like blades. Unlike ovalized metal spokes, which are not thin enough to be fully aerodynamic, the blade spokes are flat as can be.

• Molded

Moulded wheels with 3 to 5 aerodynamic "spokes" can considerably reduce air drag, provided they are correctly designed. Aerodynamics is a complex and tricky subject, and many molded wheels deliver more looks than performance. The yardstick is the Specialized Tri-Spoke, which has a proven race winning pedigree and a price to match. The airfoil sections of the Tri-Spoke are so effective it is claimed that in a slight cross wind they act like a sail and help push the bike along. A bike with a Tri-Spoke wheel on the front can be a real handful in windy conditions or if hit by an unexpected gust from a hedge opening or passing motor vehicle.

• Disc Wheels

Fes of Germany, which produces world class racing bikes, does a good one piece, fully enclosed disc wheel. Otherwise, as with molded wheels, most disc wheels are not really aerodynamic, and are not worth the hassle and extraordinary expense. Moreover, solid disc wheels exist only because of misbegotten UCI regulations; it is far cheaper to use add-on discs over regular wheels. Even cardboard or light plastic cut to shape and carefully taped in place will work perfectly well. Use a full disc on the rear wheel only.

Hubs

Alloy hubs are universal on decent lightweight bikes. They are attached to the bike with conventional axle nuts or via quick release (Q/R) levers. Quick release hubs are standard for racing bikes and handy on pretty much any bike. Some people say Q/R levers make a wheel easy to steal, but whether a bike has Q/R or bolt on hubs, when locking it you must secure the frame and both wheels.

The hub in the illustration is a high flange (H/F) design used for racing and sport riding. The flange is the part with all the holes where the spokes are attached. According to theory, the stiffness of a wheel is proportional to the flange diam-

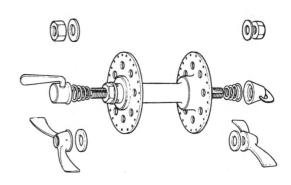

eter squared. Hence, commuting and touring bikes often use low flange (L/F) hubs for a softer, less stiff ride, while performance bikes usually have H/F hubs for greater responsiveness. Opinion is divided as to which type is stronger. A high flange reduces the load on the spokes, but increases the angle at which the spokes join the rim, trading one problem for another. Tandems require high flange hubs to allow room for additional spokes. For solo bikes, flange size is less important than the overall quality of wheel building. (In America, hubs are sometimes called large and small flange, so if you see an American advertisement with the term L/F hub, it may mean a high flange and not a low flange model.)

Cheap hubs can deform at the spoke holes, promoting spoke breakage. Established brands are Campagnolo, Shimano, Mavic, Specialized, Hope, and Formula. Most hubs have cartridge bearings and are sealed to keep out water and dirt.

Ye Total Wheel

Wheel quality depends partly on the quality of the components and design, but the thing that makes a good wheel is – a human being. Automatic wheel building machines can make a good start at building a wheel, but the final, crucial touch is human. One important function of a bike shop is to check and true the wheels before a new bike is given to a customer. A craft, an art, building and truing wheels is something like playing a banjo or guitar. You learn all the strings and the notes, you practise 1-2-3-4, and then one day your fingers have the music.

Good, hand made wheels can cost as much as a basic bike but have superior performance and strength, and will outlast half a dozen sets of cheap wheels. Wheels on sub-basic quality bikes are typically crude and may not last for more than six months of regular commuting or even make it through a heavily laden tour. One important reason why many people upgrade from cheap bikes after a year or so is that they become fed up with dodgy wheels and broken spokes.

A point in favor of the mountain bike 26-inch wheel for general use over the slightly larger 700C is that the smaller size is inherently stronger, which can be helpful if the bike is a budget model – but only for conventional riding. If the intention is to ride very heavily laden, or vigorously off-road, then in terms of wheel quality the minimum requirement is a middle rank bike. To put this in

Tuning up

another perspective, hand built wheels are very popular with keen mountain bikers.

Wheels offer many options. They can transform a bike, and you are not just limited to one pair. It's increasingly common to run two sets of wheels, one for heavier going, the other for sport and fun. You can have a road bike with light, fancy wheels for fast rides and stronger wheels with stouter tires for commuting and loaded touring. A mountain bike can wear full gnarlies for off-road and urban wasteland jaunts, and change to another set of wheels shod with narrower, semi-slick tires for road riding. If you go this route, it makes for an easier life if the wheels are set up at the same time, with identical rims and free-wheels. This way, you don't have to fiddle with readjusting brakes and/or derailleurs when changing wheels.

TRANSMISSION

The transmission converts power at the pedals into work at the rear wheel – motion. There are three main types: single gear, hub multi-gear, and derailleur multi-gear.

Single Gear

A single gear transmission consists of the basics: pedals, cranks and chainwheel, chain, rear sprocket, and freewheel. It's simple, strong, and reliable, and fine for riding flat terrain at a relaxed pace. But for climbing hills and acceleration in stop-and-go traffic, one gear ratio (number of times the rear wheel turns for each complete revolution of the cranks) is limiting. Humans do not generate lots of energy, and what they do muster tends to be optimal at specific pedalling rates. If you use a low gear ratio (fewer turns of the wheel for each complete rotation of the cranks) good for acceleration and climbing hills, you'll run out of breath trying to spin the cranks fast enough for speed on the level. If you use a high gear ratio (more turns of the wheel for each complete rotation of the cranks) good for speed on the flats, climbing will agonize your muscles and eventually bust your knees. The way to flexibility is a hub or derailleur gear system with multiple ratios.

Hub Gears

Hub gears are internal; the mechanism nests safely within the rear hub shell where nothing can get at it. The design is nearly 100 years old, is used on utility bikes all over the world, and is tried and true. The classic basic model has 3 speeds, with adequate range for ordinary utility use over moderate terrain. Models with 4 and 5 speeds have more precisely spaced gear ratios and slightly greater range. The Shimano Nexus, with 7 speeds, is a nice unit, with well spaced ratios in the lower gears.

Hub gears are easy to use, reliable, long lasting, and clean. Most are controlled by an external shift trigger or twist grip that can be operated to select any gear you want at any time, whether the bike is moving or not. (The relatively rare semi-automatic 2-speed hub is pedal operated; when pedalling is paused, the unit shifts up or down.) Hub gears need only a single chain, wider and stronger than the type used for derailleur gears, which can be covered with a chain guard or even fully enclosed to protect it from dirt as well as prevent stains on clothes.

The intervals or jumps between gear ratios on basic 3-speed hubs are large, which makes it difficult to maintain a steady, efficient pedalling rate. This problem eases off considerably with the 7-speed Shimano Nexus, and disappears entirely with the Rohloff 14-speed Speedhub 500, which provides as many ratios as the usable ratios in a 27-gear derailleur setup. There's also a 12-speed Sachs hub, but it weighs a ton.

The Speedhub 500 is a top end unit at an eyeball spinning price, designed for off-road mountain biking, where an internal gear hub has several advantages. It can be shifted at any time, is protected from dirt and assault – there's no exposed derailleur to be damaged or snatched away – the single chain is taut and not subject to suck or unwanted escapes, and the rear wheel is stronger

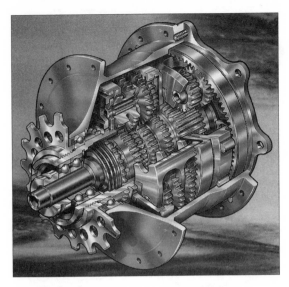

Speedhub 500

because it does not have to be dished to make room for a freewheel.

Sounds good, units such as the Speedhub 500 may become popular for their practical advantages, but there is a rub: the mechanism of a hub gear consumes some of the rider's energy. Most hub gears have a direct drive gear ratio, and use a sun and planet gear mechanism to indirectly achieve gear ratios above and below that of the direct drive. The amount of power lost depends on whether the gear selected is direct or indirect and on the pedalling rate, and ranges from as much as 20 percent in indirect ratios down to 2 percent in direct drive. Losses are more acute in lower gear ratios. Oddly enough, the hub gear I like the most for street use, the Shimano Nexus, has only indirect gears. The ratios are well-spaced, however, and the shifting action is very clean. That the Nexus is enjoyable despite some inefficiency demonstrates the chief asset of hub gears: convenience.

Derailleur Gears

Derailleur gears live in the open air, exposed to wet, dirt, and knocks. They are mechanically

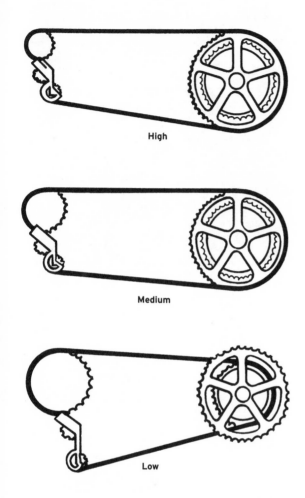

High

Medium

Low

times for each rotation of the cranks – speed. Small on the front to large on the rear makes the wheel go around fewer times for each rotation of the cranks – torque.

There are two broad types of derailleur systems: competition; and general use, touring, and mountain biking. In road racing the need is to keep the human power plant churning away at peak efficiency, and gear ratios are tightly clustered in a narrow range: close ratio gears. In general riding, touring, and mountain biking, the need is to extend the work range as widely as possible. There are many things to do, from sailing along at speed with a boosting tail wind to climbing stiff gradients while laden with camping gear to churning through mud, and so the gears are broadly spaced apart: wide ratio gears.

In general, road racing bikes have two chainrings at the front, and eight to nine sprockets at the back. Bikes for general riding, touring, and mountain biking usually have three chainrings at the front, and from six to nine sprockets at the back. The spread of gear ratios is normally fairly even, but many variations are possible. For example, many road sport touring bikes use three chainrings; two are large and close to each other in size, as on a racing bike, and the third is a small "granny," to provide low gears for hard climbs. More information on the subject of gear ratios in Chapter 10, Fitting and Gearing.

• Derailleurs

A derailleur (or "mech" in bikie parlance) moves the chain from sprocket to sprocket (rear), or chainring to chainring (front). The rear mech also keeps the chain taut by wrapping it through a spring loaded arm. With close ratio gears, less chain is needed to bridge the difference between the largest and smallest chainrings and sprockets, so competition mechs tend to be compact and lightweight, with a short arm for wrapping the chain, and to operate quickly. With wide ratio gears the sprocket and chainring differences are greater and there is more chain to gather in. Touring and mountain bike mechs have longer arms and may be mechanically more elaborate,

rather crude: to change gear ratio, pieces of metal poke at the chain, knocking it from one sprocket or chainring to another. And yet, derailleur gears in good condition can be up to 99 percent efficient in delivering power to the rear wheel, in any ratio. This is why they are the universal choice for performance bikes.

The number and range of gear ratios in a derailleur system depends on the number and size of the chainrings on the crankset (the business with the pedals), and the number and size of the sprockets, or cogs, on the freewheel (the spiky business on the rear wheel). Large on the front to small on the rear makes the wheel go around more

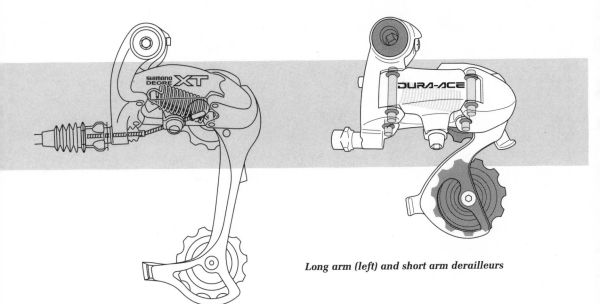

Long arm (left) and short arm derailleurs

and do not shift as quickly as competition derailleurs.

Derailleurs come in basic, good, better, and best quality grades. They've been around for a while now, and the days when an expensive derailleur unit could go out of sync and self-destruct in milliseconds, or worse, sail into the spokes of the rear wheel and transform the back of the bike into a useless mangle, seem to be over. Most modern derailleurs work. The differences relate to weight, range or capacity, mechanical sophistication, speed of shifting, strength and reliability, and finish. The Japanese firm Shimano dominates the components field for production bikes, with a wide range of equipment from economy budget to top-line high performance.

The derailleur was devised in its first seriously successful form in 1933 by Tullio Campagnolo, a name that has stood ever since as the pinnacle of elegance, efficiency, and reliability in cycle components. The Campagnolo Record series derailleurs are reckoned by many as the best ever made, and for generations of road racing cyclists, an "all-Campy" equipped bike was in a class above the rest.

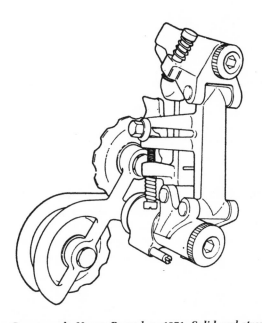

Campagnolo Nuevo Record, c. 1971. Solid and strong, this model was assembled with nuts and bolts rather than one-time rivets, and thus could be tuned for optimum performance. When the bolts and bushings did finally wear loose, only a few replacement parts were needed to restore the mech to as new condition.

RIDING FIXED

Multiple gear ratios provide mechanical flexibility, but it is also important to extend the range of the rider, and a useful aid for this can be riding a "fixed" gear. This is a single sprocket without a freewheel, so that when the back wheel turns, so do the cranks. The only way to stop pedalling is to stop the bike.

Riding fixed is a traditional European method for winter training. At the end of the road racing season the multi-gear bike is put away, and replaced with a fixed gear machine. Sometimes the bike is a track model made for the job, but often it is an old, stripped down road bike that won't be too deeply offended by the grunge and grime of winter. The classic gear ratio is 63 inches, which is low and easy to spin.

The bike is used for everything. With only one gear ratio, the rider is forced to learn how to spin the cranks at blinding speeds. There's no other way to make the bike move, or stay with it on downhills. The rider becomes progressively more supple, fluid, and fast. In the spring, on returning to the multi-gear bike, the rider is a tiger.

In the 1980s Campagnolo were slow off the mark in responding to the rapidly rising new market in mountain bikes, and firms such as Shimano and Sun Tour came to the fore. Now Campagnolo has bounced back with new equipment that many, particularly in the road division, regard as the ultimate for light weight, beauty and luster, and by no means least – performance.

There are, of course, many other components firms, from small workshops producing all titanium parts and custom milled chainrings, to larger companies with established pedigrees in high quality and race winning equipment. One of these to watch is the French firm Mavic, who in addition to producing outstanding wheels are introducing new technologies for derailleur gears (see Shift Control, below).

• Shift Control

The derailleur is under spring tension, and the shift control is the means for moving it from sprocket to sprocket (or chainring to chainring) and then holding it in position. The shift control must function precisely, or else the chain may become misaligned and ride roughly or jump unexpectedly from one gear ratio to another.

The first shift controls were friction levers, mounted on the down tube so that the cable runs were as short and direct as possible. The levers did not have preset stop points for selecting different gear ratios; when shifting, the derailleur was aligned for smooth running by ear and "feel." Some people mastered the technique easily, others never did.

As bikes became popular for general use as well as racing, and mountain bikes appeared, shift levers moved up to the stem, out to the bar ends, and onto the handlebars. Mountain bikes in particular promoted handlebar thumb shifters so that gear changes could be made without relinquishing the grip on the handlebars and brake levers.

Then came a decisive development that Shimano, with their SIS range, was the first to make work successfully on a large scale: indexed gears, where the shift control has preset stops for each gear ratio. Nudge a lever or button and snick! you have the right gear, perfectly aligned. There were teething problems for a couple of years, but indexed systems from Shimano and other manufacturers became the new standard in perfor-

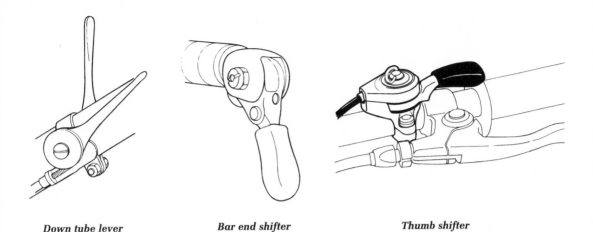

Down tube lever   *Bar end shifter*   *Thumb shifter*

mance. Shift controls have since become even more mechanically sophisticated, with spring-loaded thumb and trigger levers capable of initiating crisp, flawless shifts, and ergonomic in design, so that their use is intuitive.

All this gee whiz performance sometimes comes at a price: where the old friction type lever had few parts and was held in place with a single bolt, some modern indexed shift control units have more than 100 parts, and are not user serviceable. If one packs it in while you are on a ride, there's no easy fix, and a complete replacement unit (which with some designs may also include the brake lever and mount) can cost a mint.

Many therefore welcomed the introduction a

while ago of the Grip-Shift, a handlebar twist grip indexed system with only a few moving parts, all of them simple. Brilliant. The Grip-Shift is easy to use and maintain (be sure to use the right lubricant – see Chapter 21, Bike Care). Its one weakness is that it does not like mud. Too much grit, and the mechanism will stick and jam – not a catastrophe in general riding, but fatal in competition. It takes a fair old dip in the sludge to produce this effect, however, and clever folks find ways to protect the works with silicone impregnated rubber sleeves and boots.

As to which is best, grip or lever, that's a matter of personal preference. Although I consider simplicity a virtue, I have to admit that Shimano's Rapidfire shifters are marvelously easy and quick.

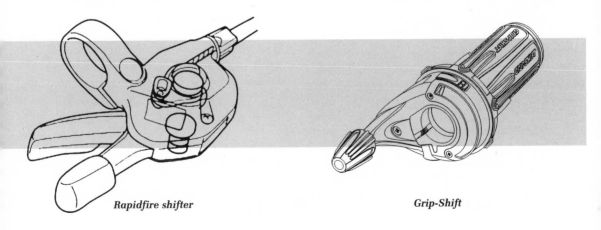

Rapidfire shifter   *Grip-Shift*

Road racers have also benefited from progress: Shimano completely reset the standard in shift controls for drop handlebar road bikes with a new design dual brake and shift control lever. These all-in-one units, which are of course also now produced by Campagnolo and others, greatly enhance bike control and safety, and are all one talks about when setting up serious road bikes.

Until recently, the design of derailleur controls has hinged entirely on various ways and means of using wire cables to accurately move and position the derailleur. I have long thought that a better method would be to power the derailleur with an electric motor, and thereby end the whole business of fiddling with cables. There have been attempts to do this, but the one that has got it together is the electronic Mektronic from Mavic. This gear shifting system is completely wireless; there are no cables, not even the electric wire I had envisioned. Push a shift button (there can be several, in various convenient locations) and a signal is transmitted to the electronic derailleur, which then executes the shift. A particularly clever feature of the Mektronic is that the shift is made not with an electric motor, which would use a lot of juice, but with a power take-off from the chain (technically, from an eccentric cam attached to the jockey roller).

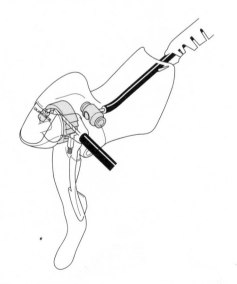

Shimano brake/gear lever

The Mektronic operates slowly and needs more development, but I reckon that electronic gear shifting is the next step. Some people will recoil at the idea of a "batteries included" sign on a bicycle, but from a mechanical standpoint, electronic gear shifting is simpler than complex shift lever controls and cable wires and housings. An electronic derailleur is bolt on and go, and aside from the cage arm, it lives inside its own little housing, safe from the wet and dirt that make life hard for ordinary derailleurs. The greatest benefit, though, might be convenience: touch a button and you get a shift. Part of the ethos of a bike is that you move with it as one, and while I enjoy the skill satisfaction in executing a well-timed double alpine shift with old fashioned friction levers, a push button electronic shifter is dead easy to use. For competition, and fun riding, that's a vital difference.

• Combined Systems

It is possible to mix hub and derailleur gear systems on the same bike, and come up with a blinding number of gears. Usually, this is pointless. However, one device worth mentioning is the Mountain Drive, a two-speed bottom bracket planetary gear system. Basically, it is a hi-lo transfer system, available in two configurations. One is a complete change of range, double (or half), which is most useful for heavily laden utility vehicles climbing gradients. The other is an overlap change which, with derailleur, provides more progressive steps rather than an outright hi-lo change. The second type is used with machines that need speed, such as HPVs.

I've not tried a Mountain Drive. However, it has been fitted to many good machines. A trade-off in efficiency for stump pulling power or speed might be worthwhile. The testimonials look good, and if you're interested, further information is available from:

Mountain Drive, Florian Schlumpf, Ing.HTL, Dorfstr 10, CH-7324 Vilters, Switzerland. Tel: 081 723 80 09. Fax: 081 723 83 64. E-mail: schlumpf_ing@bluewin.ch. Web: www.schlumpf.ch.

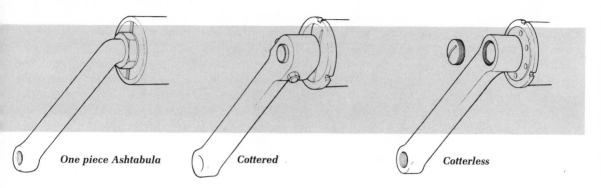

One piece Ashtabula   Cottered   Cotterless

Crucksets

Cranks and chainwheels are made of aluminum alloy or steel. More exotic metals are sometimes used for fancy and ultralightweight bikes. Designs vary in the method used to attach the cranks to the bottom bracket axle. The Ashtabula is a one piece crank, chainwheel, and bottom bracket in steel, used for cruisers and kid's bikes.

Cottered cranks are fastened to the bottom bracket axle with a wedge-shaped cotter pin, and are usual on cheap roadster bikes. Aluminum alloy cotterless cranks use a recessed bolt to fix the cranks to the bottom bracket axle, and the design is used from everything from basic bikes to superbikes.

Cotterless cranksets vary considerably in type and quality. Low-end are one-piece cranksets with a fixed chainring, found on basic grade roadsters and el cheapo specials. When the chainring wears out, the whole unit has to be replaced.

Cotterless cranksets with detachable chainrings divide into two types, long arm doubles and short arm triples. Road racing bikes need high, closely-spaced gear ratios, and to save weight typically use only two chainrings fairly close to each other in size. For maximum strength, long arms are used to mount the chainrings. General, touring, and mountain bikes need a wider spread of gear ratios, and usually have three chainrings, fairly evenly apart in size and mounted on short arms.

Detachable chainrings can be replaced when worn, and make it possible to set up or change gear ratios for specific riding conditions. A heavily laden tourist headed for steeply pitched terrain, for example, might fit two very small, closely spaced chainrings, and one medium size chainring. This will concentrate most of the ratios in a low range for climbing.

In the past, detachable chainrings were a necessity because manufacturers made so many dumb mistakes when specifying bikes. Often, heavy bikes for general riding and touring were fitted with long arm competition cranksets and race gearing. Because of the long arms, it was impossible to fit smaller chainrings and thereby achieve the lower gear ratios these bikes so desperately needed. Watch this point if you are ever picking up a 15- to 20-year-old bike with a view to upgrading it.

Competition   Touring

I'm pleased to say that manufacturers now seem to understand the subject of gearing quite well, and essentially, most bikes have a good or even excellent pattern of gear ratios. We can thank mountain bikes for this: off-road machines simply must have a good selection of gear ratios, and once the idea of using gearing appropriate for the function of the bike was established, it spread across the board. Nonetheless, you should always check that the gear ratios on a prospective bike are suitable for your purposes – be sure to read Chapter 10, Fitting and Gearing – and if the brand of the components is unknown, that replacement spares are available.

A periodic new idea is that of oval chainrings, which vary the gear ratio during each revolution of the cranks, in accordance with the strong and weak parts of the rider's power stroke. The seemingly logical way to set this up is so that the ratio increases on the downstroke and decreases when moving through top dead center. Several years ago, though, Shimano enjoyed a good deal of success with an ovaloid crankset known as the Biopace, which was rather curiously set up so that the gear ratio reduced on the downstroke. The thinking here was that the increase in pedal speed produced more power and momentum for moving through the dead or weak position at the top of the stroke. A further thought was that this timing

made it easier for the leg muscles to synchronize the transition from downward to upward movement. In this last idea, the Shimano technicians just might have rumbled something, at least for novice cyclists.

Round chainrings work because they give one a break, and optimize speed and torque. Muscles need an interval in which to relax, so that blood can flow, distributing oxygen, and carrying away waste products. In fact, champion cyclists are hallmarked not so much by strength (although it obviously is important) as by their efficiency at refreshing their muscles. Their greater respiratory and cardiovascular capacities mean they can sustain a faster pace and keep it up for longer.

The Shimano Biopace is an example of a lie that was true. People said it was comfortable, and novice cyclists struggling to come to terms with pedalling probably found it so. However, experienced cyclists do not pedal, they spin the cranks, at speeds ranging from, say, 70 rpm to past 100 rpm. It's a definite skill (see Chapter 11, Riding Basics, for more information), one that for sure is the route to optimum power, and it is difficult to learn let alone achieve if pedalling resistance is constantly changing.

The Biopace and other oval rings still have loyal fans. No harm done, in fact, oval rings can have their advantages, principally low speed torque for climbing, and comfort for people who pedal slowly.

Chains

Chains used to be cheap and simple. Now they come in a variety of colors and designs, are made with better quality steels, and are stronger, lighter, and faster. There are two main types: standard width for standard freewheels and narrow width for compact freewheels. Narrow width will work on a standard freewheel, but not vice versa. There's also a special narrow chain for 9-speed freewheels.

Chains are often designed to be used as part of a complete transmission system from a single manufacturer. Mixing different brands of chains

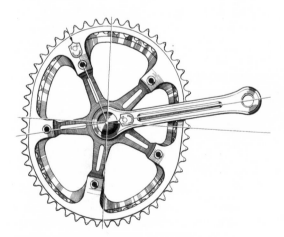

Oval chainring

and freewheels sometimes results in ragged performance, particularly with indexed systems. Shimano hyperdrive transmissions require a hyperdrive chain. However, I've often switched transmission bits around to improve performance, and have a fondness for high quality chains. There are some really nice ones available now, strong as a tank, and if you look after them they will last for long time.

• Belt Drive

Derailleur systems cannot use belt drives, nor can any bike with a standard rear frame triangle. You'll find belt drives now and again on folding bikes, the one application that makes sense, because they are clean. Otherwise, a belt drive does not have the mechanical efficiency of a chain.

Freewheels

The freewheel is attached to the rear hub and holds the sprockets, or cogs. These may be between 5 and 10 in number. As a rule of thumb, basic quality general bikes have 6 or 7 cogs, touring and mountain bikes have 7 or 8, and road racing bikes 8 or 9. A 9-speed freewheel requires more wheel dish – insetting the hub by using shorter spokes on the freewheel side of the hub – which weakens the wheel. A 9-speed freewheel on a mountain bike may be flash, but 7 or 8 is safer.

With a triple chainring, an 8-cog freewheel will theoretically produce 24 different ratios or speeds, and a 9-cog freewheel 27. However, derailleur systems always have some unusable ratios, because to keep the chain reasonably aligned between the chainrings and sprockets, it cannot be run in extreme crossover positions (such as from the small front ring to the small rear cog). A further number of ratios are lost through duplication; for example, big ring to a middle size cog may produce the same ratio as middle ring to a smaller cog. Thus, a 27-speed setup may produce only 14 usable ratios. There are more options to work with, however, to ensure that those 14 gear ratios are patterned so that the intervals or

jumps between them are even, and shifts are fast and precise.

Old fashioned and cheap freewheels thread into the hub. Pedalling winds the freewheel on tight, and it is rarely easy to get it back off. A cassette type freewheel slides onto a spline and is much easier to install or remove. Some freewheels have the sprockets fastened with rivets, which lowers cost, but means you cannot change the gear ratios. This can be an acute limitation.

Freewheels are highly stressed, and reliability is paramount. Fixing a broken freewheel is an odious pastime, even in a shop, and usually impossible in the field, because special tools are required.

Pedals

Pedals are like shoes: intimate and varied in function, fit, and comfort. The pedals on many production bikes are so-so and will need replacing within a year. If they are good quality, they still may not be the right type for you. When buying a new bike, sort out the type of pedals you want. Most shops are cooperative about making substitutions, and while a big upgrade may involve a price adjustment, the cost will probably be less than buying new pedals later on.

Beginners tend to want an open pedal, so they can easily put a foot on the ground when necessary. In fact, for most kinds of riding it is safer and more effective to have your foot secured to the pedal. If your foot slips or is knocked off the pedal the result can be extreme loss of control. In any case, for maximum power and efficiency, you need to spin the cranks around rather than merely push on the downstroke. For this reason, securing the foot to the pedal is universal practice for road sport riding, and commonplace even on bikes used in stop-and-go traffic. In the case of mountain bikes, the type of pedal depends on the kind of riding involved.

Essentially, there are two kinds of pedals: platform and clip-in. As the name suggests, platform pedals support the shoe and may be used open, without attaching the shoe. Rubber platform models are the basic type used on utility bikes. They

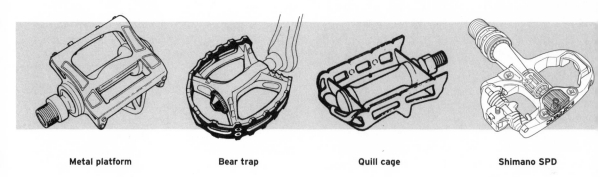

Metal platform   Bear trap   Quill cage   Shimano SPD

provide full support for the foot, can be used either way up, and do not accept toe clips. Cage design platform pedals save weight by eliminating some of the platform area; the sole of the shoe touches only the cage sides. This means that for long rides, cycling shoes with reinforced soles or at least ordinary shoes with stout soles are required. If a soft shoe such as a trainer is used, the cage sides will bite into the foot and cause fatigue and numbness. Parallel cage pedals have the same shape on each side and can be used either way up, and are designed for touring and general riding. Mountain bike parallel cage models tend to be robust, with the cage sides deeply serrated to give shoes a firmer grip. Most cage pedals will accept toe clips and straps.

Quill cage pedals for road sport bikes are designed to be used with toe clips and straps and cleats. They can only be used from one side, the bottom is rounded to save weight and give extra clearance when cornering. A cleat is a small plastic or metal plate attached to the sole of the shoe. It has a thin slot that engages with the rear cage side of the pedal, and when the toe strap is snugged down, the foot is secured to the pedal. Quill pedals are still made and used, I guess because some people are accustomed to them, but have long since been supplanted by clip-in pedals.

Clip-in pedals require a special type of shoe, with a metal or plastic cleat on the sole. When the rider steps on the pedal, the cleat fits and locks into a spring-loaded mechanism. The grip is tena-

cious, but will release when the rider twists his foot. Most if not all of these mechanisms are adjustable, so that the force required for release can be a little or a lot. Somewhat confusingly, clip-in pedals are sometimes called clipless pedals, because there is no toe clip.

With some clip-in designs, the cleat mounts onto the sole of the shoe and protrudes, so walking is awkward and impractical. Externally-mounted cleat designs such as Look are intended for road use. The Shimano SPD system is more flexible; the cleat is recessed within the sole of the shoe and does not protrude, so one can walk without waddling like a duck. SPD type pedals are suitable for both road and off-road use. There are a wide range of SPD type shoes, produced by Shimano and others, from Arctic boots to sandals and everything in between. In terms of comfort and style, most people will be able to find something at least reasonably to their liking. SPD type shoes will also mount cleats for Time A.T.A.C. pedals, another popular brand noted for resistance to fouling by mud.

Clip-in pedals for road bikes are one-sided, to pare away as much weight as possible and also provide maximum clearance for cornering. The pedal's small contact area means that the shoe has to be strong and rigid to provide enough support, which can limit the shoe's usefulness for walking. Pedals with more platform area are becoming increasingly popular, especially for general sport riding and touring. Campagnolo Pro-Fit pedals are particularly good, because the design features a wide platform that improves stability and provides greater support for the foot.

Clip-in pedals for mountain bikes are often double-sided, so that the rider can quickly engage the pedal. In size, they range from quite small, which means they are inconvenient if you do not have the appropriate shoes, to rather large, with a bear trap cage to support the foot. These are handy if you miss engaging the cleat, do not want to be locked to the pedal, or are wearing shoes without cleats. Another variation is a cage pedal with a plain platform on one side, and a clip in mechanism on the other.

Good clip-in pedals are designed with "float"; the foot is not rigidly locked to the pedal, but can twist a few degrees to either side. This is exceedingly important, because legs and knee joints do not move and rotate in perfect flat planes, and damage can result if they are forced to do so.

The business with shoes and pedals needs to be analyzed in terms of your own particular preferences and circumstances, remembering that you might eventually be running two, three, or more bikes. The broadest, most flexible system is SPD. Time also makes pedals for both road and off-road use, and are much liked at high levels of competition. If you are serious about road sport, you should consider Look or Campagnolo pedals, for support and comfort over long distances.

A good set of pedals will challenge your wallet. However, with regular maintenance good pedals last a long time, and in the long run are more economic than cheap pedals, which usually do not last more than a year or two. On the other hand, if you fall and bust a pedal, then the economic advantage shifts to less expensive models. Modestly priced pedals perform perfectly well, especially if you look after them. I've had good luck with MKS pedals.

Pedals are a critically important point of your interface with a bike. It's worth reading over the chapters on the various kinds of riding and the information about shoes in Chapter 9, Accessories, to form a clear idea of your needs before making a selection.

BRAKES

Bicycle brake designs differ in their balance of braking power, weight, mechanical precision, and expense. They are a dynamic part of bike performance, and it is important to know how different kinds of brakes mix and match with different kinds of bikes. You can't possibly enjoy yourself on a bike unless you understand the brakes and know what you can do with them. For example, compact side pull brakes are fine for road racing bikes, because they have all the stopping power that lightweight machines with thin tires can safely handle. Using a similar type of brake on a cheap, fake mountain bike is a ticket to grief, because the design does not have enough rigidity and power to manage the greater forces generated by the heavy bike weight and tenacious wide tires. There are three basic kinds of brakes: hub/drum, disc, and calliper.

Hub/Drum Brakes

Hub (or drum) brakes subdivide into two general categories: pedal-operated and hand-operated. The pedal-operated version is known as a coaster brake, and is found on beach cruisers, some European utility machines, and classic American paperboy bikes. A coaster brake has limited power and capacity. Under conditions requiring a quick stop it tends to lock up the rear wheel, causing the bike to skid rather than slow down. It has poor heat-dissipating qualities and can burn out on a long downhill. Coaster brakes are fine for use in flat countries like the Netherlands. To their credit, coaster brakes are not affected by ordinary wet conditions. If something goes wrong with a coaster brake, remove the wheel and take it to a bike shop for overhaul or replacement. It is complicated to service.

Hub brakes work by pressing two pads or shoes against the inside shell that is part of the wheel hub. Good quality hand-operated hub brakes can be powerful, sensitive, yet smooth in performance, and effective even in wet conditions short of complete immersion. They are fairly straightforward to service. They are better for smaller rather than larger wheels (which have a longer "lever" for exerting force on the brake), and are a common choice for high performance, small wheel HPVs. However, it is worth noting that these hub brakes are typically custom built, or are extensively modified commercial production models. Unfortunately, manufacturing good quality hub brakes involves proper production engineering and thus cost. So far, the hub brakes for cycles produced by manufacturers such as Sturmey-Archer and Sachs have been basic in design and cheap in quality, and performance has been uneven – sometimes dangerously so. The only mainstream model I've used that has decent out-of-the-box performance is the Shimano Nexus, a unit suitable for utility bikes. Otherwise, to obtain the kind of performance hub brakes are capable of delivering, it is necessary to resort to custom builders at custom prices.

For mountain bikes, hub brakes have two drawbacks: weight and a dislike for swims. To get really serious power, you have to go up in size to the point where weight becomes a burden. You might be able to live with this on a downhill

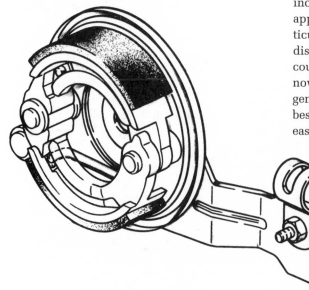

Drum brake, section

mountain bike, where weight is not a big factor. Problem is, if you ford a stream or otherwise find a way to get water into the works, the brake is worthless until it has dried out. Since disc brakes offer even better performance and are not as badly affected by water, they are the current premium choice for mountain bikes.

Where hub brakes shine is on utility bikes. They've got a nice, smooth action, enough power for urban conditions, and work in the wet. As of this writing, the only one worth considering is the Shimano Nexus. I hate to be down in the mouth about the Sturmey-Archer and Sachs models, but they've had years in which to get it right and have not done so. One option is to see what a custom service can do by way of modifying and improving a stock unit.

Disc Brakes

Disc brakes are where life is at. They are the most powerful kind of brake, and more important, operate with unparalleled smoothness and precision for maximum bike control. They have greater depth than other types of brakes, and are less inclined to snatch, so greater braking force can be applied without locking up the wheel. This is particularly useful for mountain bikes, and while disc brakes first came into use for expensive cross country and downhill racing machines, they are now increasingly available on midrange and even general use bikes. Except for weight, they are the best: outstanding in performance, reliability, and ease of servicing.

Disc brakes require a specific type of mounting on the frame and a special hub. It is possible by using conversion kits to retrofit disc brakes to bikes designed for calliper units, but it is better to have a bike designed at the outset for disc brakes. There are two types of disc brakes: cable operated and hydraulic. In general, the hydraulic type is better. See Hydraulic Calliper Brakes, below, for a discussion of how hydraulic systems operate.

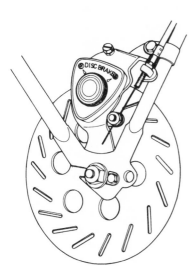

Early disc brake

One caution: disc brakes are great, but quality is important. Some of the mechanical complexities are subtle, and for trouble-free performance straight out of the box you need one of the better brands such as Hope. As disc brakes become increasingly popular, I expect both quality and cost to move within bounds. If you are into mountain biking in a serious way, they are the only route to go. If I were buying a midrange bike, I would rate this feature ahead of suspension.

Calliper Brakes

Calliper brakes are the most common type, and function by pressing a pair of blocks (pads, shoes) against either side of the wheel rim. Calliper brakes offer a good balance between weight, stopping power and cost. They come in a variety of models and, depending on the quality of a particular brake and match with bike type, performance in dry conditions ranges from good to very good to excellent. In wet or muddy conditions, braking capacity can decrease – sometimes considerably. Calliper brakes

are straightforward in terms of engineering and good quality units can be manufactured at reasonable cost. They are relatively simple to service, although adjusting the blocks can sometimes be fiddly. There are three significant design types – side pull, cantilever and V-brake – plus a couple of others I'll mention so you know what they are.

• Side pull Brakes

Side pull brakes pivot two calliper arms on a single bolt and are made in two versions: inexpensive for cheap bikes, and decent to jewel-like for use on road sport bikes. Cheap side pull brakes have long, widely-spaced arms to reach around mudguards and thick tires. They are stamped out of steel and chromed to prevent rust. The spindly design and crude manufacture result in a sloppy

mechanism with poor performance. Perversely, cheap side pulls are common on bikes that have a real need for decent brakes: heavy utility machines, fake mountain bikes, small wheel bikes with steel rims, and worst of all, bikes for kids.

As they have for decades, cheap side pulls work well enough on a nice day in unexceptional circumstances. Sprinkle some water on the rims, though, or ask for performance when it matters – Mom or Pop with a full load of groceries trying to stop for a dog, or junior trying very, very hard not to sail under the wheels of a big truck – and cheap side pull brakes won't cut the ice.

Cycling is not about being scared out of your wits or dying for sake of money. That manufacturers have supplied inferior brakes for years, when better are available, is morally if not legally criminal.

Do not buy any kind of a bike with cheap side pull brakes. They are too dodgy. Even if all you want is a very simple utility bike or cargo machine, be sure to spend the money or otherwise take the trouble to ensure it has decent brakes – either good hub brakes, V-brakes or cantilevers (see below), or a combination of both. Mark Twain once wrote: "Get a bike. You will not regret it if you live." Heed!

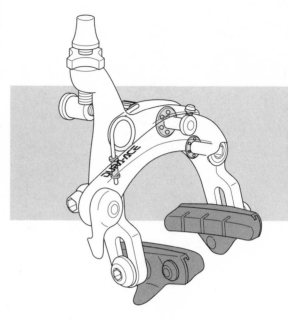

Quality side pull

Quality side pull brakes for road sport bikes are a dimension apart from the long arm type. They are cast in alloy and milled to precise tolerances. Better models are cold forged for greater strength and rigidity. The mechanism itself is tidy and compact, with short arms, because with close frame clearances and slim tires the rim is close to the frame. Feel through the brake lever is positive; this type of brake is designed more for sensitive control at racing speeds than for raw stopping power, although it has that, too. Top brands are Campagnolo and Shimano, both have a range of double action pivot design models.

• Center pull Brake

A center pull uses a backplate to mount two pivot bolts. There are two brake arms, one on each pivot, linked by a yoke cable attached in turn to the brake cable. The design has a greater mechanical advantage than the side pull design, and was once common on touring and general use bikes, and top flight models were sometimes used for road racing bikes. It has been entirely

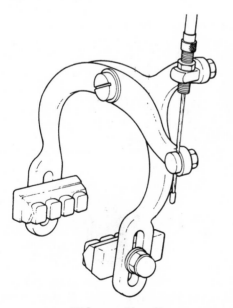

Wide arm side pull

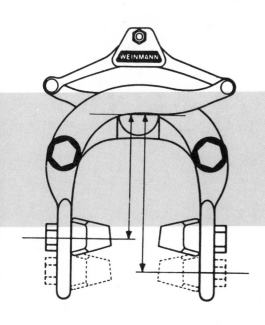

Center pull

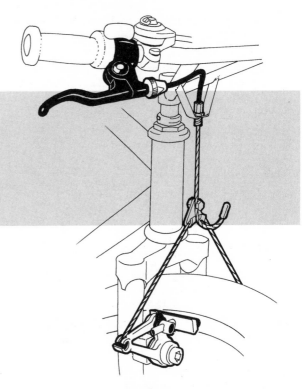

Cantilever

replaced by the lighter and more powerful cantilever design.

• Cantilever Brakes

Cantilever brakes pivot on two bosses (mounting points) brazed onto the fork blades and seat stays. Separate calliper arms on either side of the wheel are joined by a yoke cable (or straddle wire), which is pulled by the brake lever cable. Cantilever brakes work fairly well, and are adequate for a town or utility bike, and light off-road riding. They are also often seen on touring bikes. Where more performance is a definite requirement, as with mountain bikes, cantilever brakes have been replaced by the more powerful and effective V-brake.

• V-Brake

V-brakes use independent pivot bolts and arms but, as with a side pull, the cable housing is attached to one yoke, and the cable wire to the other. The long arms of the V-brake provide a greater mechanical advantage and more power.

That no cable hanger is required means that a V-brake can be used with wheel suspension.

V-brakes are powerful, and it is important to use them with brake levers made for V-brakes. If used with levers made for cantilever brakes, they are likely to snatch and grab. Because of their power, pad and rim wear can be rapid, especially in muddy, gritty conditions.

The V-brake is the benchmark standard for top performance in cable-actuated mechanical calliper brakes. They can be a little tricky to adjust, but then, so can cantilevers. For safety's sake, I think a V-brake is about the minimum one ought to have. Be aware: brakes with enough power to handle a descent on steeply pitched terrain in wet, muddy weather means that on a road in dry conditions, if you slap down the brake levers too hard, the rest of your journey will be airborne and short. With serious brakes,

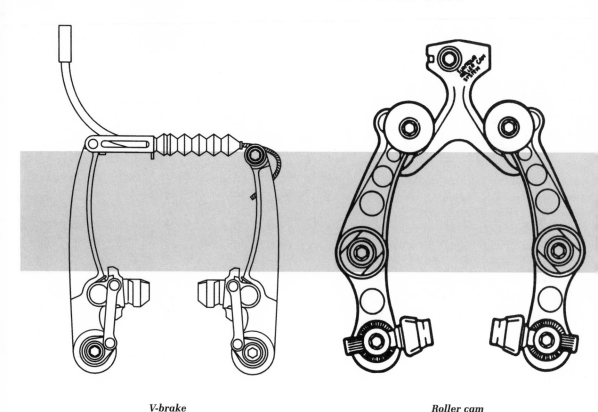

V-brake   *Roller cam*

it is important to learn and practice your braking techniques until they are second nature (see Chapter 11, Riding Basics).

• Roller cam and U-brake Designs

Two calliper designs no longer in production, but that you might find on older bikes, are the roller cam and U-brake. Both use mounting bosses located in different positions than the bosses for cantilever or V-brakes, so upgrades are out.

The roller cam uses two separate arms and pivot bolts, but instead of the arms being pulled together, a wedge shaped metal plate or similar device pushes them apart. The design has a high mechanical advantage and performance is good, but it is intricate and apt to foul in muddy conditions.

The U-brake, a.k.a. the old fashioned road center pull, operates in a similar manner to roller cam

brakes, but via a straddle wire. It is not as powerful as the roller cam, and can mush out on steep descents. Although the roller cam has its fans (I've got one), I have never heard anyone swear fealty for a U-brake.

• Hydraulic Calliper Brakes

A hydraulic control system uses fluid under pressure to operate a remote mechanism, and is both more powerful and precise than a cable wire system. Hydraulic brakes have been standard on motor vehicles for decades, and bicycle versions function in exactly the same way.

The brake lever drives a piston that compresses fluid in a master cylinder connected by a flexible tube to a slave cylinder inside the brake mechanism. There's a second slave cylinder on the other side of the mechanism, linked to the first with a tube. In operation, fluid from the master cylinder flows into the slave cylinders and drives a piston in each, pushing the brake blocks against either side of the rim.

Hydraulic calliper brakes mount on the same bosses as V-brakes and cantilevers, but do not have pivot bolts. The brake shoe emerges straight from the brake mechanism to press against the rim. The compact design of the mechanism increases the amount of power it can exert, and there is enough so that one might be able to damage a weak rim. This raw strength is somewhat offset by increased sensitivity and precision of control. A big plus is that hydraulic brakes are pretty well self-contained and protected against dirt and wet; keeping the hydraulic fluid in means keeping other things out. You can wash the brakes with a hose without fear of carrying away vital lubricants. Another plus is that servicing is minimal. Aside from an occasional tweak of an adjusting screw for the brake lever travel, there's no tricky adjusting of blocks. Topping up the brake fluid and bleeding air out of the system is simple, and replacing brake shoes is literally a snap.

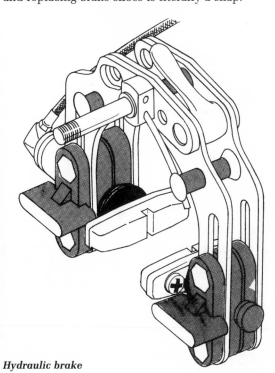

Hydraulic brake

Hydraulic calliper brakes are first class, expensive, and generally limited to fairly fancy high range bikes, though some manufacturers are now offering them on commuting machines. Hydraulic brakes can be retrofitted to many bikes, but again, you are talking real money, and also retiring or selling on all of the old system. Still, when I modified a mountain bike for my daughter to ride to and from school, I fitted hydraulic brakes, because I wanted her to have the best.

Brake Levers

There are two basic brake lever designs: flat handlebar and drop handlebar. Levers for long reach side pull brakes are simply a means to make the brakes work. Almost all flat handlebar levers for other types of brakes are more sophisticated. They are shaped for comfort under steady use, and so that a couple of fingers can rest at the ready on the lever without relinquishing a firm grip on the handlebar. Most have an adjustable reach, so that the lever can be positioned where it is best for your hand size.

Brake levers for V-brakes often have a means to adjust the speed with which the lever moves the cable, and thus the amount of lever pressure required for a given amount of braking force. This can be a useful feature for novices.

Brake levers for drop handlebars all have the same general shape, but subtle variations from manufacturer to manufacturer can be important. This is because a lot of riding is done with hands on the hoods, and the fingers resting on the levers. Make sure that the levers fit your grip, as some makes are only suitable for large hands. There really is nothing to beat the combined brake and shift lever controls available from Shimano and Campagnolo.

Brake Blocks

You want blocks made of synthetic material, not rubber or leather. Brake blocks harden with use and you can generally with good effect replace them before they have completely worn away.

Original equipment is fine, and there are also models from specialist manufacturers. I've found the Kool Stop range to be reasonably priced and very effective. One option for increasing brake performance is to fit abrasive compound blocks. These work especially well in wet conditions, but both blocks and rims wear away more quickly. An effective compromise for all but extreme conditions is a dual compound block, with the leading portion abrasive compound and the main portion standard compound.

Brake Wrap

Cycle brake technology has seen enormous advances in recent years, and this is one area where you should have high standards and expectations. Do not fool around with long reach side pull brakes on bikes that will see regular use. This type of brake is antique, and bikes so equipped ought to be used only on special occasions in good weather. Yes, there are lots of bikes with long reach side pull brakes, but it is time to draw the line on this one. Four wheel rather than two wheel brakes have been mandatory for cars for years. Long reach side pull bicycle brakes are the equivalent of two wheel car brakes – not good enough.

Hub brakes are primarily useful for utility bikes, though in tweaked versions they can be good for small wheel speed machines. They are also sometimes used on tandems. Disc brakes are the kind to have if you want the latest and best. Calliper brakes are the most common type, and represent a good balance between performance, weight, and cost. For road sport bikes the norm is classic: a well made, compact side pull. Other road bikes can get by with cantilever brakes, but the V-brake is better – which in some circumstances could be very important. For serious off-road riding, the V-brake is the least you want. Finally, hydraulic calliper brake systems offer tremendous power, sensitivity of control, and minimal maintenance.

Brakes are much more than just a means to stop. They are a dynamic element of bike perfor-

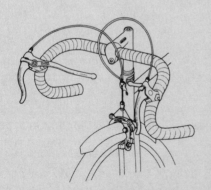

SUICIDE LEVERS

Years back, one disaster inflicted on unsuspecting cyclists by marketing flacks was the "safety" or dual brake lever. This was a long extension from the brake lever that ran underneath the straight section of drop handlebars, originally developed for touring bikes so that an upright riding position with maximum aerodynamic resistance could be used when braking on long descents. The term safety suggests that a second lever might help avoid an accident, and for the record, the truth is precisely the opposite.

Dual levers have to travel a long distance before the brakes engage, and if the system is not adjusted to tight tolerances, it is possible that using the "safety" lever will not produce any braking effect at all. Even when adjusted properly, dual levers need 20 to 30 percent more distance for a stop than standard levers. This is not safety! We called them suicide levers. If you encounter them on an old bike, remove and discard them.

mance; how well they work is important to your riding technique, style, and pace. Good brakes help you to be one with the bike. And to think when I was a kid most of the neighborhood bikes had sneaker brakes – a foot jammed against the back tire.

HANDLEBARS, STEM, AND SADDLE

I wish bike manufacturers would supply their machines without handlebars, stem, saddle, or pedals, and leave selecting these items to the bike buyer and shop. These components are the points where rider and machine interface, and it is important that they are right for each individual. People are like blades of grass: similar, but never exactly alike. A small variation in stem length, for example, can be the difference between a bike that gives you an aching back after a few miles or one that you can ride forever. For more information on setting up a bike so that it is right for you, see the chapter Fitting and Gears.

Handlebars and Stem

Handlebars and stems are usually made of alloy. Some downhill mountain bikes use steel handlebars, not for economy but for bombproof strength. Another option that is both lightweight and very strong (but multi-$) is carbon.

• Road Sport

Downswept bars are the classic type for road racing bikes, and are held in place with the stem, the height and length of which determines the position of the bars. It is especially important to get the length of the stem exactly right, and one way to do this is to fit a sizing stem, use it for long enough to determine your ideal position, and then fit the appropriate stem. Some shops have sizing stems for exactly this purpose. Another route is to buy the adjustable stem designed by Mike Burrows and made by Giant. This clever bit of equipment will give you ongoing flexibility in handlebar positions.

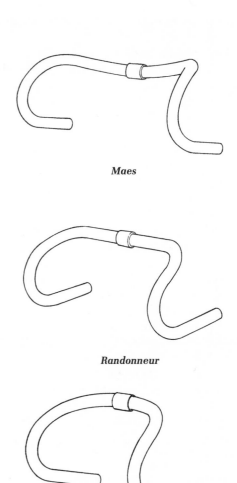

Maes

Randonneur

Pista

Downswept bars are available in several patterns. The most common is the Maes, a square, shallow drop pattern suitable for racing, touring, and general use. Randonneur bars are for touring; the tops are upswept to give more riding positions, and the hooks are shaped to place the brakes nearer to hand. The Pista is a pure racing pattern, round and deep, with little purchase for riding upright. Cinelli bars and stems are classic designs, well tried and popular, and lovely to look at. When a good builder showing off a spiffy bike points to the bars and says "Cinelli," that's all that needs to be said.

The multi-position is a flat handlebar developed for touring. The shape is utterly distinctive, with the bars formed into two hoops, like two question marks joined by their ends. The multi-position looks a little odd, but gives a variety of riding positions.

Profile bars have the ends pointing forward and up, rather like horns. They were originally developed for time trial and track events, but are now quite common on road sport bikes. They provide good support for the rider, a strong grip point for the hands, and ready access to brake and gear controls. Paired with an adjustable stem, profile bars give many options, from low and fierce for racing, to high and relaxed for touring.

Elbow rest bars enable a rider to stretch out and extend the arms forward and together, like a swimmer diving into water. The bar ends are close together, and the forearms rest on padded supports. Elbow rest bars improve aerodynamic efficiency and/or comfort and are fine for time trial and triathlon events, but can reduce bike control

and are not suitable for mass start road racing or riding in traffic.

Elbow rest bars are available as clip-on additions for normal bars, and as complete units. Some models include the stem as well.

• Utility

Flat bars as fitted to roadsters and utility bikes follow the shape of a squared-off bucket handle, with the ends pointed toward the rear of the bike. They are fine for an upright riding position, and work best when paired with an adjustable stem. A few degrees of rise or upsweep increases the number of possible positions.

• Mountain Bike

There are two kinds of stems for mountain bikes: quill, the traditional design inserted within a threaded fork tube, and Ahead, a design that fits over the end of a threadless fork tube and holds it in place. The Ahead type is lighter, stronger, more reliable, much easier to adjust and, because it is popular, has the most variety in sizes and colors. It's standard on hard core mountain bikes. However, height adjustment is limited, in fact zero if there are no spacers in the system. An adapter can be used to give 2 to 3 inches of travel, but this adds weight.

Quill stems can be moved up and down within the fork tube, enable a more upright riding position, and are common on entry level mountain bikes and on town bikes. Quill stems are available in various lengths, and in adjustable models.

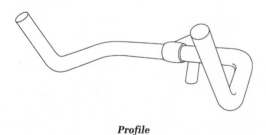

Profile

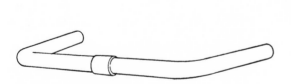

Bucket handle

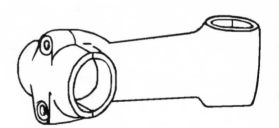

Ahead stem

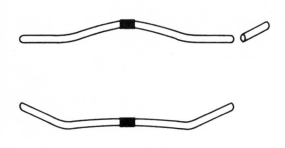

Mountain bike

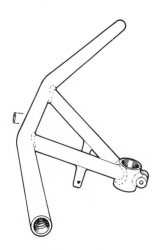

Bullmoose

With an adapter, an Ahead stem can used with a threaded fork intended for a quill stem. You can't go the other way round, though. If you buy a serious mountain bike, it will almost certainly have an Ahead stem, so take particular care that it holds the handlebars in the right position for you.

Most mountain bike handlebars are simple: straight but for a backward sweep (or "layback") of around 5°. However, for strength, the materials and construction may be sophisticated, with special heat-treated or cold-drawn alloys and double and triple butting. The number of riding positions can be increased by fitting bar ends, for a shape like that of profile bars. Bar ends come in many

different shapes, and are definitely something you need to try for yourself.

Downhill and slalom mountain bikes favor riser bars, which, in addition to a sweep of perhaps 5° to 10°, have a shallow rise of around 25 to 50 mm. For extra strength, some models have a cross brace. Riser bars are also good for cross country and general riding, because they can be twisted for subtle variations in configuration.

A type of handlebar you'll find only on classic mountain bikes is a one piece design called the Bullmoose. It's bombproof, comfortable, and provides a convenient platform for carrying a map case, jacket, or sack of potatoes. The cross brace on a riser bar accomplishes much the same thing.

Saddle

There are two basic types of saddle. The mattress design is wide and comfy and can include coil springs or other shock absorbing mechanism. It's made for use with an upright riding position that puts most of the rider's weight on the saddle. The racing design is long and narrow and made for use with riding positions where the rider crouches and some body weight is supported by the arms. The range of "racing" saddles is broad and varies from minimalist models that are little more than a rail, to plush, padded models akin to mattress saddles.

Saddles are personal, and fit and comfort are very individual. What is bliss for one person can be torture for another. Bike manufacturers do their best to supply appropriate saddles – lean and hard on competition machines, wider and softer on general use bikes – but when buying a bike this is one area to explore as thoroughly as possible, in case you want to substitute a different model.

All leather saddles are the classic type and can be very comfortable after 500 miles of riding. The leather gradually molds to your particular shape, and there is a mechanism for maintaining tension as it softens. Some people try to shorten the break in interval with neatsfoot oil baths, baking in hot

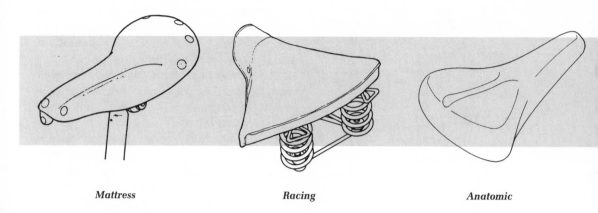

Mattress   **Racing**   **Anatomic**

ovens, and beatings with rolling pins, but manufacturers sternly advise that such measures will shorten the life of the saddle.

Water definitely will damage a leather saddle, a point to consider if you expect to do wet, muddy off-road riding, and/or to keep the bike clean with a hose. Otherwise, you can carry a saddle cover, plastic bag, or shower cap to use in case of rain.

If you get on with a leather saddle, you may never find better, but it takes time and the development of a hard behind. Brooks Pro is the classic, but Ideale also have nice models.

Plastic saddles are cheap, and feel like it. For any distance work they bite and chafe, and in hot weather you swim in your own sweat. Ugh. They are light, though, which is good for short distance races.

Most saddles consist of a plastic shell or base, some foam or polymer padding, and a cover, which can be plastic, leather, or a more exotic material such as aramid (Kevlar™), for scuff resistance. Some have an anatomic design, with the base shaped to allow extra room for more padding where the pelvic bones make contact.

One option to check out are saddles with a hole or depression to relieve pressure on the genital area. It's not just a fashion trend. In the old days, female riders used to carve up their saddles to make them more comfortable. This design feature has been introduced for mens' saddles as well, because long hours in a hard, full saddle can cause penile numbness. (If you even suspect this is happening to you, lower the nose of the saddle one or two degrees.)

Women please note: females have wider pelvic bones than men, and require a saddle designed for their physique. If you are buying a bike, you might well be offered a model proportioned for males, which is fine so long as the bike fits you, but be sure to change the saddle.

Everybody: when you buy a bike, make sure you like the saddle, and exchange it for another if you don't. There are many different models, ranging in price from the equivalent of a few beers, to a case of champagne. Other than suggesting that novices start with a fairly wide and soft model, it is impossible to make specific recommendations, because comfort is so personal.

Two of my friends set off from London, England to India on their bikes, and within two days were each swearing a blue streak at their saddles – one a leather Brooks Pro, the other a Sella Italia foam filled anatomic. Discomfort mounted and when raging pain brought the duo to a halt a few days later, as a last resort they switched saddles. Suddenly all was bliss, and they completed the rest of the 6,000-mile journey without complaint. The only way to know which saddles are suitable is to try them for yourself. When you find a saddle you like, keep it!

BIG WRAP

There are many different types of bicycles, some are general use, others are highly specialized. They are made by hand in workshops by artistans, and mass-produced in factories by global companies. Hand builders usually make function specific, quality bikes; large manufacturers typically produce comprehensive ranges of models in different price grades. However, the days when hand building was the only route to quality are long gone; modern materials and technologies mean that mass-produced bikes can be of the finest quality, and remarkable value for money.

A good bicycle is one where design and materials work in harmony to fulfill the intended function of the machine. The chief parameters of bicycle quality are weight, vitality, and mechanical sophistication. In the upward pro-gression from steel roadster bikes, there is an increasing use of alloy steels, aluminum, and then finally, titanium and composites such as carbon fiber and aramid. The weight sheds fast: decent entry level bikes are under 30 pounds, midrange bikes hover around 25 pounds, and top range bikes are not much over 20 pounds, and are sometimes less.

Sport bikes were always pretty good. The big improvement is that where once utility bikes were uniformly heavy and dull, now they, too, are becoming increasingly lightweight, vital, and mechanically sophisticated. The bikes we ride to work, to collect groceries, and to just get around, are fun as well as practical. This is one of the great advances, and is largely due to the mountain bike, which has stimulated unparalleled progress in cycle technology and, above all, made the case that riding any kind of a bike should be fun.

PAST AND PRESENT.

Zzzwwaaaammo!

Recumbents and human-powered vehicles (HVPs) • Aerodynamics • Search for a better bicycle • Origin of HPVs • Speed record challenges and street machines • Health, safety, and performance advantages • Selected machines and resources

TWO DECADES AGO, RECUMBENT CYCLE manufacturers the world over could be counted on the fingers of one hand. Today there are hundreds of builders and new designs, and sales are pitching up like a jet plane on take-off. Recumbent cycles are featured on large stands at cycle shows, and some individual shops are selling over 500 units a year. Many of the big manufacturers of traditional bikes have introduced recumbent models, or have them on the drawing boards.

Recumbents have arrived, but they are not cycles in the ordinary sense of the word, and they do not run in the usual commercial channels for conventional bikes. Classic road racing bikes draw their ethos from the Tour de France, mountain bikes from the legendary Repack downhill race, but recumbents are at once about easy rider relaxation and safety – elderly folks with full touring paraphernalia cruising long distances in armchair comfort – and cutting edge technological sophistication and performance – HPVs streaking along public roads at over 70 mph.

HPV Contest Entry, 1969

Recumbent cycles are a land vehicle subset of a movement devoted to exploring and expanding the capabilities of human-powered vehicles of all kinds, including land cycles, boats, submarines, and aircraft, and the development of a range of machines and devices from ice cream makers to agricultural pumps. The human power movement mixes sport and fun with the excitement of technological innovation and developing the machines and tools that can help bring about a better, more socially and envir.onmentally benign world. The quest involves some of the best brains and nicest people on the planet, has a clear and useful purpose, humor and charm, bags of personality, and best of all, is completely accessible by you and me. The shared vision, the feeling of being a part of building the future, is tempered by the determination – aptly expressed by the British Human Power Club motto – "to have a laugh while doing it." Human-powered machines, and recumbents in particular, are clean and green, but above all, they are plain old-fashioned sheer fun.

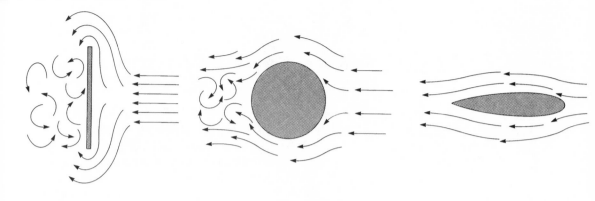

Air flow patterns

How did all of this come about? What exactly is a recumbent or HPV? Might one of these machines be good for you? For the last question, the simple answer is yes, it could be. Recumbents have some real advantages. To understand these machines, and where they might fit into your life, we need first to delve into some physics and the history of the future.

AERODYNAMICS

Air is thick stuff. When an object moves, the surrounding air must separate and flow over the object, and then reform in its wake. At low speeds this movement is not particularly evident. For a cyclist on an upright safety bike moving at 12 mph, the resistance from internal mechanical friction (bearings, tires, etc.) is about the same as that for aerodynamic drag. Increase speed to 20 mph, however, and bike and rider now displace some 1,000 pounds of air a minute. Increase again to 30 mph, and pushing through the soup now consumes up to 90 percent of the rider's total energy.

What makes aerodynamic drag so strong? Essentially, air is sticky, and has its own ways of moving. The sticky bit is friction drag, the movement of air molecules over each other, which occurs because air does not flow directly over an object, but rather over a boundary layer of air next to the object. Friction drag is a function of the kind of surface or skin of the object, and its overall shape. Beyond the boundary layer, how air moves around an object is a function of shape, and in enormously simplified terms, if you push air out of the way with a flat, thin object such as a pie plate, then it is slow to rejoin on the back side of the plate. This loss of air or partial vacuum in the wake of a moving object is a retarding force known as pressure drag. Shape can be used to ease the return of the air: add a dunce's cap to our pie plate to make a cone shape, and life becomes easier. Instead of tumbling helter-skelter over the lip of the plate in a series of turbulent vortices that generate drag, the flow of air smooths out and moves down the cone to break at a later point with less turbulence and drag. In aerodynamics, exit shape is more important than entry shape. For an effective reunion of separated air, an aerodynamic taper must be at least 4 to 1, that is, a length four times entry shape width. On this score, most of the world's so-called aerodynamic bicycle tubing has at best a 2 to 1 ratio, and hence little if any aerodynamic advantage.

The idea of improving performance by reducing aerodynamic drag dates from at least 1896, when a man named Challand built a recumbent bicycle in Belgium. In the period 1912 to 1933, starting with Etienne Bunau-Varilla in France,

Oscar Egg

conventional upright bicycles fitted with egg shaped fairings set numerous speed records.

But the proofs of performance that influenced history came between 1933 and 1938, when a relatively unknown Frenchman, Francois Faure, riding a recumbent bicycle called a Velocar, built by Charles Mochet, shattered speed records for the mile and kilometer. In response, in 1934, the world governing body of cycle sport, the Union Cycliste Internationale (UCI), banned recumbent bicycles and aerodynamic devices from racing.

As the 20th century progressed, cars, trains, aircraft, and even roller skates all went through tremendous technological evolution and development. Not bikes. The lack of competitive incentive for new cycle designs, and the rise of the motor vehicle into a dominant role in transport, canonized the safety bicycle. There were lone builders and riders of recumbent cycles in America, Britain, and France, but the evolution of cycles remained limited to detail improvements until two widely separated and probably initially independent events occurred.

In 1967, David Gordon Wilson, coauthor with Frank Whitt of the highly respected book *Bicycling Science* (MIT Press), launched the first modern design contest for human-powered vehicles through the magazine *Engineering* in Britain. The brief was to improve on the safety, comfort, and usefulness of the bicycle, and reduce the effort consumed in overcoming aerodynamic drag. The contest was judged in 1969, received widespread publicity, and led directly to the development of modern recumbent bicycles (see What Is a Good HPV? below).

As has often been the case, another crucial strand of development originated apparently

Velocar

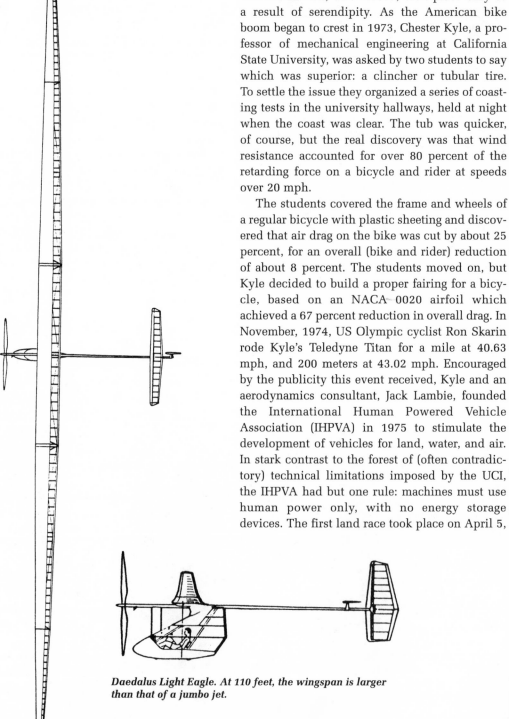

without knowledge of what had gone before or was concurrent, and indeed, took place only as a result of serendipity. As the American bike boom began to crest in 1973, Chester Kyle, a professor of mechanical engineering at California State University, was asked by two students to say which was superior: a clincher or tubular tire. To settle the issue they organized a series of coasting tests in the university hallways, held at night when the coast was clear. The tub was quicker, of course, but the real discovery was that wind resistance accounted for over 80 percent of the retarding force on a bicycle and rider at speeds over 20 mph.

The students covered the frame and wheels of a regular bicycle with plastic sheeting and discovered that air drag on the bike was cut by about 25 percent, for an overall (bike and rider) reduction of about 8 percent. The students moved on, but Kyle decided to build a proper fairing for a bicycle, based on an NACA 0020 airfoil which achieved a 67 percent reduction in overall drag. In November, 1974, US Olympic cyclist Ron Skarin rode Kyle's Teledyne Titan for a mile at 40.63 mph, and 200 meters at 43.02 mph. Encouraged by the publicity this event received, Kyle and an aerodynamics consultant, Jack Lambie, founded the International Human Powered Vehicle Association (IHPVA) in 1975 to stimulate the development of vehicles for land, water, and air. In stark contrast to the forest of (often contradictory) technical limitations imposed by the UCI, the IHPVA had but one rule: machines must use human power only, with no energy storage devices. The first land race took place on April 5,

Daedalus Light Eagle. At 110 feet, the wingspan is larger than that of a jumbo jet.

1975, with a speed of 44.87 mph for the winner, a streamlined tandem bicycle. There were only 14 weird and whacky machines at that initial event; most of them crashed more often than not, but the human power movement never looked back. Freed from the constraints of the UCI, machines built and competing under IHPVA auspices proceeded to rewrite the record books and quite literally go where none have gone before.

The old dream of human-powered flight is a reality many times over, with the most sensational accomplishment being the crossing of the English Channel in 1979 by Bryan Allen, pedalling Gossamer Albatross to win the £100,000 (then about $170,000) Kremer Prize. A more difficult but less acclaimed event was a 72-mile flight from Crete to mainland Greece, by the MIT backed Daedalus in 1988. Current human-powered aircraft (HPA) are now pushing the envelope for in-flight maneuverability and speed.

On water, a human-powered boat (HPB), Flying Fish, was the first successful human powered hydrofoil, and the world 200 meter speed record at an impressive 21.28 mph (18.50 knots) is held by the Decavitator from MIT. But naturally enough, land vehicles are by far the most widespread activity, and speed and distance records have been broken one after the other ever since the inception of the IHPVA. Pedalling all on their lonesome, individuals have exceeded 70 mph in a sprint, and covered more than 50 miles within an hour. A free rein for innovation has resulted in some truly diverse creations, but recumbent designs are the mainstream. Collectively, they're known as human-powered vehicles, or HPVs for short.

A safety bike is technically an HPV, but in practice the term is used to cover any machine that is not a standard upright design. This differentiation means there is a natural tendency to compare HPVs with safety bikes, which is not always appropriate. The safety design is refined and, as far as it goes, near perfect; HPVs are a completely new class of vehicles with different characteristics, in designs that are varied and very much in evolution.

QUEST FOR SPEED

The four central elements governing the speed of an object through air are frontal area, smoothness, shape, and power. A recumbent bicycle has about 20 percent less frontal area than a conventional upright bicycle. This is mostly due to reduced frontal area and a more streamlined shape. Things begin to move when the flow of air is smoothed with a fairing (body shell or cover). Compared to an upright bike, a fully faired recumbent has up to 80 percent less aerodynamic drag, or 70 percent less energy consumption. It takes 200 Watts (W), about 0.26 horsepower (hp), to maintain 20 mph on an upright

Concept water velocipede, 1895.

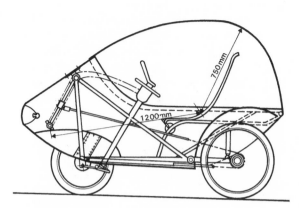

HPV Contest Entry, 1969: J. Stradowski, Poland.

bike, and only 64 W (0.085 hp) for the same speed in a fully faired recumbent.

From this point onward the physics of speed becomes a good bit more complicated. With truly fast HPVs, shape is a major consideration in aerodynamic efficiency. It's one thing to arrow through a set of traps (timing gates for a specific distance) on a race track in still air, and quite another to cope with variable wind conditions and the turbulence created by other vehicles on a public road. Rider position and power delivery is another factor. Set the rider fully supine for maximum aerodynamic efficiency and he or she will have a good view of the sky but not where they are going. It will also be more difficult for them to screw on maximum power for short periods.

These elements interact and balance in complex ways, and to suit different purposes and the needs of different kinds of people, there are many different HPV designs. The line up for a race meet, particularly a practical vehicle competition, is likely to include bikes, trikes, front steerers, rear steerers, hinged machines, machines that incline from side-to-side, and what else. But the bottom line is clear: HPVs are the most efficient vehicles in the world. Per distance per weight carried they consume less energy than anything else going. They are indeed fast. No UCI legal bike is ever going to come anywhere near to 70 mph on level ground, or covering 50 miles in an hour. But the

impressive maximum speeds HPVs can reach is not as important as their efficiency. What this means in practical terms is that HPVs can cruise at higher speeds, for less effort – which is the part that matters for us ordinary folk.

A cyclist fit enough to be classified as an athlete will usually be able to average around 18 to 19 mph on a racing safety bike. Riding 25 miles within an hour on such a bike is an accomplishment that takes real effort and merits genuine pride. In a good HPV an ordinary person in reasonable health can average 20 mph. If she or he trains and becomes fit enough to output 0.25 hp for an hour, which many people can do, average speeds will start climbing toward 30 mph. In other words, in an HPV most people can achieve riding 25 miles within an hour, and on a regular bike most people cannot.

The fundamental requirement for greater efficiency and speed is a fairing that smooths and eases the movement of air. In my view an HPV is more specific than just non-UCI. It is a vehicle with a fairing – full or partial – that significantly improves aerodynamic efficiency. A recumbent is an open, unfaired machine. Most HPVs are based on recumbent designs, but not necessarily so. Alex Moulton's upright AM bicycle, for example, has exceeded 50 mph fitted with a full fairing.

On the subject of terminology, in 1998 the IHPVA changed its structure and name, in a shuffle doubtless confusing to anyone who was not at the table for the deal. The IHPVA and the human power movement inspired the development of HPV clubs and associations all over the world, many of which became subchapters of the IHPVA. This eventually became unworkable, because the IHPVA was primarily an American and Canadian organization, and so in 1998 the original IHPVA was reformed as the Human-Powered Vehicle Association (HPVA), with members in the United States and Canada, and at the same time a new IHPVA was formed, a committee comprised of representatives from national human power clubs and associations from other countries. The alphabet is the same, but the identity is different. The job of the

IHPVA is to set the rules and requirements for international competitions, and to keep the record books. National organizations run their own competitions, and are free to vary from international rules if they wish. This is a good arrangement, because while there is (more or less) common ground for international competitions and records, the various national groups have their own priorities. In Europe especially, the human power movement is extremely strong, annual European HPV Championships have been held for many years, and the development of practical street vehicles is well advanced. This is a direct reflection of the fact that average journey distances in Europe are about half those in the States, which makes everyday use of HPVs for transport a realistic proposition.

The human power movement is now truly international, and we should never forget that the genesis was with a few early academics who perceived the need for evolution and development in cycle technology, and to meet it, quite brilliantly founded an organization under which such development could take place, provided incentives by sweet talking industrialists and other sponsors to put up large cash prizes for just-out-of-reach accomplishments (such as cracking 65 mph on pedal power alone), and embroiled the resources of their various universities in human-power projects. Once this initiative was formed, a seed as it were in good soil, the rest of it, like Topsy, just growed.

WHAT IS A GOOD HPV?

The evolutionary history of modern HPVs has two strands: competition and street. The first consistently successful HPV in both speed trials and road races was the Vector from California, a low slung recumbent tricycle mounting a smooth, tear drop shaped body shell. It looked futuristic and fast – and was. In 1980 it set a world speed record at Ontario Speedway that stood unbroken for many years. The Vector was also an able contender on road racing circuits. Demonstration runs on public roads produced point-to-point average speeds that had many people speculating on when they, too, could buzz the highway patrol on their way to work. But although the Vector was offered for sale to the general public, it was not a practical street machine. It was expensive, rider comfort was poor, both vision and visibility were severely limited, and there was no provision for lights and signals. It was a racing machine, built to break records and explore new ground in knowledge.

Enter street. Recumbent bicycles were an early line of development for street usable machines that could be produced inexpensively. The configuration is more or less a tandem rearranged to seat one person, the stresses are much the same as with an ordinary bicycle, and building does not involve untoward problems for anyone familiar with bikes. Designing and building a good recumbent trike, however, is a demanding business,

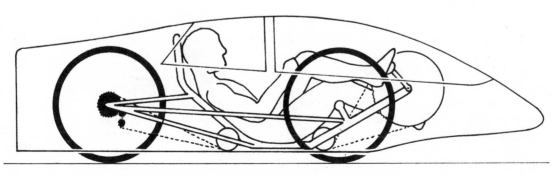

Vector

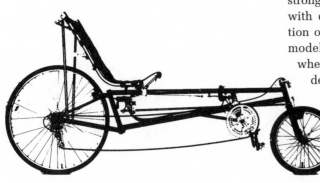

Avatar 2000

because a trike is subject to high lateral forces and must be strong, and the nuances that give good handling are more slight and critical than with a recumbent bicycle.

At the 1980 New York bicycle show I encountered an LWB recumbent bicycle designed by David Gordon Wilson, the Avatar 2000. The idea was new to me, but looked worth a try, and I ordered a machine for delivery later that year. Before it arrived, I had the good luck to encounter Wilson at Velo-City, an HPV congress in Bremen, Germany, and see him riding the new machine and hear about its benefits. The congress, too, was an eye opener for me, and I began to learn about HPVs and something of the history of the development of the Avatar.

When Wilson organized a design contest for human-powered vehicles through the British magazine *Engineering* from 1967 to 1969, he was interested in developing a safer bicycle than the upright design, which can still "come a cropper" just as nastily as an old high wheel bike. Inspired by the contest, one H. Frederick Willkie II contacted Wilson in 1970 and asked for designs he might build. Working from sketches supplied by Wilson, Willkie constructed two SWB prototypes, Green Planet Special I (1972) and II (1973). Wilson purchased the latter, and modified it into a new machine named the Wilson-Willkie (WW), which showed promise but was hard on the front

tire, and could still pitch the rider forward under strong braking. Wilson then formed an association with commercial manufacturers, and the evolution of the SWB Avatar 1000 into the LWB 2000 model essentially involved moving the front wheel forward to lighten the load on it, and decrease rolling resistance. Further benefits were that the brakes could be used full force, with no tendency for the bike to cartwheel, and tracking accuracy, or steering, was much improved.

There were other assets, as I discovered once I had my own Avatar 2000 out of the box and rolling through London streets and along English countryside lanes. One was that 0012, as she was called after her serial number, could be heeled way, way over in a corner without any need to stop pedalling. This gave a precise degree of control, and I became convinced that the Avatar would be able to outcorner the Vector on a tight course.

Following a tryout of the bare machine at the 1981 Aspro Clear Speed Trials in Brighton and on the Goodwood GP circuit, Derek Henden designed and built a fairing, the drivetrain was modified with crossover gearing, and with Aussie solicitor and pedicab driver Tim Gartside as engine, we were off to the races. In the 1982 Aspro in Brighton, the machine, christened Bluebell, surprised us all by turning in a very competitive straight line sprint performance. The next day, in a circuit race at Brands Hatch, after a slow start, Tim and Bluebell showed their speed by overtaking the Vector going past the stands. The incandescent paroxysm of excitement and wild cheering of our motley crew was short lived; on the next turn Bluebell lifted into the air, lost traction, and sailed off the course to end up smashed to smithereens.

Talk about serendipity. Bluebell's strength was also an Achilles' heel. Derek had approached designing a fairing by asking what is the optimum way to fit a shape around a rider, not what is the optimum shape and how can we squeeze a rider into it? The Vector and other maximum speed designs sought to get away from the air by crouch-

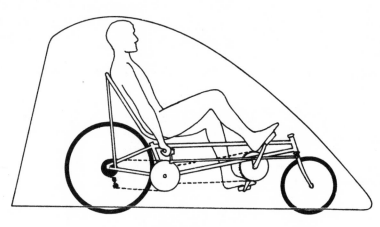

Bluebell I

ing close to the ground and presenting the smallest possible frontal area. There were already some existing upright designs based on recumbent bicycles, but they still had flat bottoms that sought close contact with the ground to minimize air flow. Derek chose to work with aerodynamic forces rather than hide from them, and designed a complete fairing shape around the rider that would actively smooth and ease the flow of air. The result was a three dimensional flow shell with a pointed nose and a long, high tapering tail, a huge affair that looked very much like a shark's fin. A true airfoil, it was fast and slippery and stable when upright, but given to lift – the same kind as for aircraft – if caught by a cross wind when heeled over in corner. We had set out to build a road racer, and done well but to our surprise, had also created a streamliner, a machine that might well be able to best the Vector for speed as well as handling.

The next upcoming event was the 1982 IHPVA Championships in California, but the shoestring financed Nosey Ferret Racing Team was in debt and could not afford to compete. Derek and his wife Linda went off for other business in California, and a few days later Tim and I looked at each other and, with hardly a word, realized we just had to go for it. We braced the bank for an increase in the loan, and I smashed my china piggy bank to give Tim breakfast money. At the

airport, in an epic performance of pleas and appeals to patriotism (by an "Over Here" American and an Aussie from down under?) before an audience of a dozen bemused airline officials and cargo handlers, we persuaded them to meet our audacious request: carriage of Bluebell and a huge fairing and what else, for free, as Tim's personal baggage. There wasn't enough money for me to go, too.

Tim was reunited with Derek and Linda at the Championships in California, and when Bluebell, huge and ungainly compared to the other sleek, low slung entries, rolled up to the start line for the

sprints, the announcer running the PA system actually laughed. But it was a fine, fine day. Bluebell left the line, built up momentum, and the announcer's jibes turned into excited exclamations of profane amazement as Tim shot through the traps at 51.9 mph, blowing off the Vector, and setting a new world record bicycle speed for 1982-83 in the process. Things were never the same in HPV design after that.

The Vector team retired from competition. They sold one machine to a German competitor, who used a modified version as the staple design for an HPV racing team over the next several years. This team set several IHPVA speed records for various distances (but not the benchmark 200 meter sprint), in private and at no small expense, in La Paz, Bolivia, at 12,000 feet (where thinner air gives a 5 to 10 mph gain over sea level). Yet just as Bluebell beat the original Vector in head-to-head competition, over the next decade whenever Bluebell machines met the Vector clones at IHPVA or national events, in both sprints and road races and whether the racing was fair or foul, the Bluebells consistently bested them. In fact, Vector bashing was a Bluebell tradition, something our riders were expected to be able to do as a matter of course, because we had stronger competitors to beat.

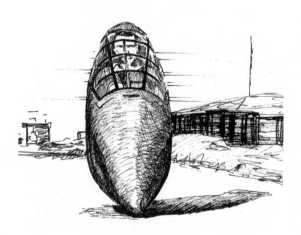

Bluebell II at Eastway

Others had been working with bicycle recumbent designs for some time, and in 1984 at the Brickyard, Indianapolis, Tim Brummer's Lightning X-2 floated by at 57.39 mph. (A new version of Bluebell with Doug Adamson riding had 65 mph on the back straight in practice, and our high hopes, but in each official sprint run the chain derailed – that's racing.) In an important precedent, the Lightning X-2 had a hinged front lid for self-entry, and trap doors for the feet to permit self-starting and stopping. Next, the $18,000 DuPont prize for the first HPV to break 65 mph fell to Gardner Martin's Easy Racer Gold Rush, ridden by Fast Freddy Markham. The current world speed record now stands at 72.74 mph, set by Sam Whittingham in the Varna Mephisto.

Bluebell also had competition at home in Britain in the form of a slim, fast monocoque HPV, the Bean, created by the father and son team John and Miles Kingsbury (also producers of the SWB recumbent Kingcycle). In 1990, Pat Kinch rode the machine to a new hour record of 46.96 mph. The current record is 50.4 mph, set by Lars Teutenberg riding the Whitehawk, designed by Andy Gronen. A new Bean from John Kingsbury looks promising for an even higher speed.

With a top-notch machine, the right conditions and a fast course, and a world class rider, we can expect to see a 80 mph sprint one of these days; but setting land speed records is now a specialized activity that can involve considerable expense. Although much design is still by eyeball and intuition, machines have to be carefully built and finely finished. For record attempts, the track has to be perfect in terms of surface and gradient, the weather has to cooperate, and riders need to be world class athletes in peak shape. Getting all this together costs a bomb in and of itself, and in addition, all the characters involved have to eat and think about earning a living. It's rare for an HPV race team to last through more than one or two record attempts or projects, though of course manufacturers such as Easy Racer and Lightning in America, M5 in Holland, and Windcheetah in Britain are proving long lived. As recumbents and HPVs become more popular, manufacturers and publicity seeking firms hopefully will provide the sponsorship and support for serious record attempts.

The European HPV scene was always primarily about the development of street vehicles for everyday use, and this has been an increasing focus for the IHPVA as well, through practical vehicle competitions, circuit racing, and point-to-point races on open roads held in compliance with traffic laws.

Speed record HPVs mostly have ultrasmooth body shells made from exotic materials such as aramid and carbon fiber. But a significant advantage of the recumbent bicycle is that the shape takes easily to a fabric fairing. The usual method is to have solid nose and tail cones, and stretch fabric between them, something like a sock. Such machines do not have the top speed of flat out streamliners, but are still very quick, and more important, are very light and can accelerate and climb briskly. They are also a lot more affordable, not just in initial cost, but also in general handling.

The other popular recumbent option for street use is the tricycle. This is a more difficult design to build well, and challenging to fit with an effective fairing. Nonetheless, tricycles are stable, and easier to push to the limit of performance without going over the top. In long distance races and in variable conditions this can be an important advantage.

The pattern that has emerged from events in Europe and America is that fully faired bicycle recumbents have the edge for speed, but only if conditions are good. If the weather becomes dirty, or there are bad cross winds, the faired tricycles have a much higher survival rate. In any case, there may not be much in the difference. Pete Penseyres rode the Lightning X-2 from Seattle to Portland in 7 hours and 30 minutes, covering 192 miles at an average speed of 25.6 mph. The winner of the 1986 Seattle

to Vancouver race was Chico Expresso, a tricycle that covered 166 miles in 7 hours 5 minutes at an average speed of 23.4 mph.

In 1989, the Easy Racer Gold Rush Replica and a Lightning F-40 battled it out in a 3,000-mile race across America. Each team had four riders, used in relays. The Gold Rush, although street modified was still a streamliner with a very cramped riding position, and reportedly no rider could stay in it for more than an hour. The F-40 was completely a street machine, a fiberglass nose cone with a windscreen, and a cloth fairing stretched over a light aluminium frame. The rider's head was out in the open, not perfectly aerodynamic, but a whole lot better for comfort and navigation. The Gold Rush team held the lead almost all the way but then lost the route, and the F-40 won, with a time of 5 days and 1 hour, at an average speed of 24.5 mph.

An even clearer portent that same year was seen in the Tour de Sol, a seven day stage race through the Swiss Alps, using the old, high roads through the passes and not the modern bypass tunnels. It's normally a race for solar-powered vehicles, but that year HPVs were invited to participate. We had two entries: the latest Bluebell, shortened to a CWB configuration in an effort to reduce the area of the fairing and make the

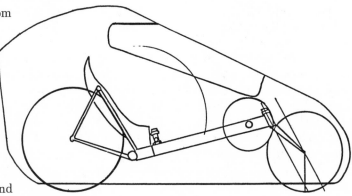

Bluebell III

machine more stable in cross winds, and an earlier extra LWB shark fin version named Eric which had seen many races, and still might do well.

The lead Bluebell had mechanical difficulties and rider Glen Thompson eventually blew up on one of the gruelling climbs, completely overcooked by heat and lack of ventilation. In Eric, amateur rider Danny Tungate did well to place third, despite sending the staid Swiss race officials into a tizzy by clocking 70 mph on one stretch. (There was a 50 mph limit for the solar-power vehicles, but fortunately, no one had actually thought to specify this provision for bikes.) Decisively in the lead was Bram Moens, riding a lightweight carbon fiber M5 SWB recumbent bicycle with a simple fairing. The M5 wasn't as fast as Eric on level ground, but it could climb with wonderful speed.

As ever, for practical road performance weight was decisive, and so was rider comfort. The various attempts by HPV racing teams to make their fully enclosed bicycle streamliners street usable were successful only to a point. As highly aerodynamic machines, they are vulnerable to chance winds. One reason for the success of the Bluebell HPVs was that they frequently crashed, so we became very good at building new fairings and trying out new ideas. That's fine for evolution, but not for riding the street.

Another limiting factor for streamliners is that the human engine is air cooled. On a regular bike there is plenty of fresh air, but inside a streamliner, even if you have air scoops and openings, there is not enough ventilation. (At one stage we considered using a variation of a Moon suit, a garment that would water cool the rider.) The importance of this cannot be overemphasized. I remember the finish of a keenly contested HPV road race on a hot summer day. As machines stopped, they toppled over, riders half in and half out, some slack sprawled in heat prostration and dehydration, others uncontrollably kicking and convulsing with painful cramps from constricted riding positions. It was like being in a war zone. This was only an hour long race. Believe me, the comfort issue in distance riding is important not just

Pegasus - A four-rider vehicle

to performance, but also to well being.

Start with a streamliner's vulnerability and weight, throw in real world stop-and-go riding and climbs, hot sunshine to raise interior temperature to gasping and fry the rider's brains, or rain to turn the windshield opaque with condensation, and the advantage for distance riding goes to a machine with a simple sock fairing and the rider's head in the open air – or a trike.

When streamliners were first abuilding, Mike Burrows of Norwich, England designed and built a recumbent tricycle, the Windcheetah SL, as a practical street vehicle for training riders of record attempt machines. The Speedy, as the machine is popularly known, turned out to be both practical and fast, with exceptional agility and cornering ability. It was one of those marvellous creations that, by genius or design or both, was exactly right: easy to use, yet totally exhilarating. A complete novice could climb in, go for a short spin, and come back with a beaming grin.

Burrows produced a kit from which a Speedy could (with considerable engineering skill) be assembled, thus allowing the breed to propagate, and over the years these machines have garnered many road racing victories, and first and second placings in practical vehicle competitions. They are not as fast as the trim SWB recumbent bikes, but on the other hand, a fully faired Speedy is a realistic proposition for everyday use, whereas a fully faired recumbent bicycle is not. When Mike entered a practical vehicle competition in Canada, he rode from his home in Norwich to the airport, and then from the Canadian airport to the event. You can't get much more practical than that. And in any case, faired trikes can be very quick; the current End-to-End record (Land's End to John O'Groats, about 900 miles) of 41 hours and 4 minutes) was set by Andy Wilkinson riding a Windcheetah. As for speed, when Wilkinson broke Olympic cyclist Chris Boardman's record for the 37.75-mile TT circuit on the Isle of Man by over five minutes (1-18-38), he was clocked on one downhill stretch at 75 mph.

Settling into the faired Speedy for the ride home. On a regular 7-mile commute through the heart of London, 25 minutes was a good time, and 22 minutes was possible.

Bicycle recumbents are inexpensive, easy to build, fast, and versatile. Many manufacturers offer a range of models with increasingly sporting performance. Easier-to-use street and touring versions feature lower bottom brackets and smaller wheels; sporting versions use larger and even equal size wheels, to minimize rolling resistance and align the rider's body for minimum frontal area.

Tricycle recumbents are more complex to design and build, and are typically more expensive. They are stable, and perhaps best suited to street and touring use. However, their stability means they can more easily and safely be pressed to the limit. A recumbent bicycle still feels in many respects like an "ordinary" safety; a low down trike has a quick agility which, to be fully appreciated, has to be experienced.

sores or chafing. The chest cavity is open and free to breathe. On LWB models the ride is like a tandem bicycle – steady and comfortable. On SWB models and on trikes, bumps can be felt with sharp awareness, but there is no harsh shock rammed up the spine. Many recumbent designs now feature rear suspension to alleviate this problem and produce a silky ride. LWB, SWB, or trike, there's no pain in the neck, back, arms, or hands. Riding a recumbent is literally relaxing in a comfortable chair.

WHAT'S IT LIKE?

Broadly, compared to safety bikes, recumbent cycles have superior comfort, braking, handling, and speed. Fully faired HPVs are like cars.

Comfort

The recumbent position is very relaxed and kind to the body. There's no problem with saddle

Weather

On a bare recumbent you've got the same exposure to weather as on a regular bike. You need to dress appropriately and carry extra rain clothing. Riding in a cold rain is rarely much fun. However, adding a partial fairing and/or windshield, which many people do, provides a noticeable improvement: the rain no longer pelts your body, and while you still get wet, it's not the thorough soak-

ing you can expect if caught unprepared while on an upright bike.

In a faired HPV, the weather is immaterial. In my Speedy, I normally wear shorts and a shirt. If the temperature falls to freezing, I add another light shirt. If it gets really cold, say below 25°F, I wear a light jacket and full length trousers. On warm days, I open up the convertible top. It can be set in stages: half open or completely open. If it rains, I zip up the top, slip a shower cap on my helmet for a mini umbrella and tuck a towel around my neck to stop water running in, and enjoy the spray. I've taken many trips this way through steady downpours, and whiskers aside, usually arrive as dry as if I had been indoors. I've got a hard shell roof that can provide nearly 100 percent protection, but it's confining and claustrophobic and my body heat produces constant condensation on the windshield. It's more comfortable to keep the head exposed.

I'm not crazy about using a full fairing in hot weather, and in fact run two machines, one bare and open, the other faired. The open machine is for whizzing about, and good weather, and the faired one is for fast, long trips, and those dank November and January days when it's nice to have something between you and the elements.

Stability and Crashes

LWB bikes tend to be light at the front wheel and wag back and forth in crosswinds. There's no real problem, just more movement. The lighter loading also makes the front wheel more willing to climb over ruts and ride up on snow. SWB bikes are better balanced and less prone to movement, but once the front wheel loses traction, it's harder to recover. However, if something goes wrong it is easy to put down both feet. The classic example is what happens if a stick goes through the front wheel. A safety bike will cartwheel and send the rider to the ground head first; besides painful scraping and cuts, a characteristic type of injury from this type of fall is a broken collar bone. A SWB bike might rear up and pitch the rider forward to land on their feet – riders sometimes even do this on purpose as a flashy way of arriving someplace – but is unlikely to cartwheel. An LWB bike will simply stop.

If a recumbent bike goes down in a corner, the rider is already close to the ground and slides rather than falls to the road surface. The landing is on hip and shoulder, the seat takes most of the impact, and damage, if any, is usually limited to road rash (strawberry burns).

Trikes are stable, and this is very handy in heavy traffic. It's also great when you want to go; close to the ground on three wheels that can be drifted through a corner, I'm not worried about hitting a pothole and being smashed to the ground on my face, or skidding on an oil patch and going down to collect road rash or broken bones. Trikes can be rolled, but by and large, only if you really foul up. It depends on the particular machine;

some models are designed for stability and are almost impossible to tip over. Overcook a corner, and the vehicle understeers (front wheels point inside the arc of your actual path) and scrubs off speed. On performance trikes such as the Speedy, it is definitely possible to lift a wheel, and on fast corners the rider must counterbalance by leaning to the inside. So long as this is done, matters usually stay in hand and if necessary speed can be scrubbed by understeering.

I'm one of those people who prays for snow. Sliding through a corner in a plume of snow crystals isn't just fun, it's ecstasy. On most trikes the back wheel is fairly lightly loaded. Get your timing right on a slippery surface or loose gravel and you can break it loose with power, and slide through a corner in a full three point drift. It's not the fastest way to corner, but it sure is lots of fun.

In a collision crash a bare recumbent is a better bet by far than a safety bike, and an HPV is simply another dimension. I've seen lots and lots of crashes in competition and at record attempts, and only rarely has the rider suffered more than a dusting and minor grazing. I still remember watching a bare Speedy crash in a round-the-houses race on London streets. It was an early model inclined, in a corner, to suddenly tilt up onto two wheels and arrow off in a straight line. In this incident, the luckless rider careened across the road, bounced off a parked car, mounted a 6-inch high curb, hit a parked mountain bike and tossed it into the air, and finished by smashing into a fence of iron railings.

Damage to rider: a cut on the shin needing one stitch. Damage to machine: none. Both were off to see the sights of the town within the hour.

An HPV with a body shell is remarkably safe. At San Diego, California, Tim Gartside in Bluebell hit a steel pole head-on at nearly 50 mph. The machine did a midair flip and disintegrated; the fairing was made out of material essentially similar to McDonald's hamburger boxes. Bluebell came to rest with the forks and head tube torn out by the roots and the fairing shredded to bits. Tim walked away with a few grazes. It's a safe bet that on a safety bike he would have been critically injured or dead. Nor was the incident a fluke. Richard Crane did exactly the same thing in a later edition of Bluebell, when he hit a stout wooden post head on at 45 mph while going for the hour record. The impact was severe enough to lance strands of carbon fiber deep within the wooden post, but like Tim, Dick walked away with only a few grazes.

I always liked the tale of how Easy Racer got the DuPont prize. On a start up run, Gold Rush went down at 62 mph, spinning and scraping away down the road. In most cases this would have been the end, but the fairing was made of bullet proof aramid, so there was no damage. The fall may have even been to the good, because an irked Fast Freddy Markham climbed right back into Gold Rush and charged through the 65 mph barrier.

Swimming a Speedy

Visibility and Riding in Traffic

The most common objection to recumbents and HPVs is that they are unsafe in traffic because they are too low to be seen. This simply isn't so. Recumbents and HPVs attract a lot of attention. My faired Speedy, for example, is far more noticeable than any car, however fancy or expensive. For pulling crowds it can cut a $200,000 Ferrari dead. It's got real spirit. More to the point, in traffic, other road users notice and make room for the Speedy far more readily than for a safety bike. It's not just that the Speedy is unusual. To other road users, it is a proper vehicle that looks and behaves like a car, and they give it more respect than a bike. I often use the faired Speedy in traffic because it is the best and safest machine for the job.

A bare recumbent more or less has the same restrictions as an ordinary bike. You don't want to go snaking through stopped traffic, asking to be caught by an opening car door. You're careful to keep some stopping distance when trailing behind another vehicle. On LWB machines you've got to nose out carefully at intersections, particularly if thoughtless motorists have parked their cars close to the junction and further obscured the view.

In a full HPV that takes time to exit, you learn to stay clear of traps. You never want to be on the inside of a corner between a wall or railing and a big truck or bus. You watch carefully for any idiot motorist in front who might reverse suddenly. The fastest reversers seem to be the ones who take the least trouble to check if anything might be in the way. Vulnerability to this type of hazard is a genuine disadvantage of an HPV in traffic, and just one incident of this type is more than frightening enough to make you permanently wary of the problem.

Recumbents and HPVs like to ride the high side (a place you'll read about in Chapter 12, Traffic: Fast Is Safe), out in the open, and clear of the poor motorists and their laggard cars. Rather like motorcycles, they can filter along on the outside, passing when the way is clear.

Once in a while there's a public transport strike in London, and a massive influx of cars. I like to go out in the Speedy and blow by hundreds of cars at once. Funny thing is, the motorists cheer.

Most motorists are charmed by recumbents and HPVs. They think the idea is great. A few cluck mournfully and suggest that you are incredibly foolish. A very few are aggressive. The main factor seems to be status. The cars that feel compelled to blow off an HPV at a traffic light or behave nastily are usually cheap models with go faster stripes, or look-at-my-money performance cars. Once in a while they get a rude surprise on the next corner.

Many people riding HPVs have had experience at racing and mixing it up at close quarters. When a car bullies and tries to shunt them aside, they sometimes push right back. It is perhaps not the sensible thing to do, but a machine like my faired Speedy is a lot better for a paintflake-to-paintflake argument with a car than a safety bike.

Take note that a bit of fun and sport is one thing, but the hyper-aggressive traffic conditions prevailing in some American cities is quite another. The US is a big place with a great deal of variety; some areas are cycle friendly, others most definitely are not. Where traffic is a war zone with constant combat between armored cars, and the terrain is sprinkled with bomb crater potholes and jagged steel plates, you need an agile machine capable of fast escapes – first choice is a mountain bike. You'll have to take your own reading on the conditions in your area, and if they are not good, then a recumbent or HPV, like a fine road racing bike, may be a sport machine you use only for fun rides in the countryside.

Performance

• Agility

I can't decide which is more fun down a twisting country road; a recumbent bike or trike. Like a regular bike, a recumbent banks over. The difference is, you can keep on pedalling, and this gives a completely different dimension of control. On a

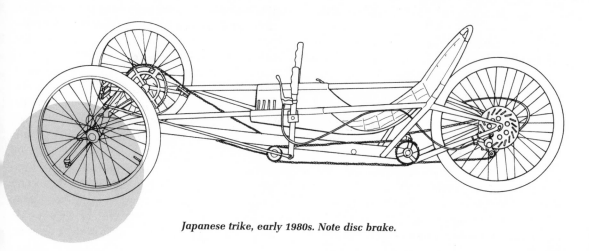

Japanese trike, early 1980s. Note disc brake.

regular bike, you line up for a corner and ride it out for better or worse. You can't pedal, because you're likely to ground and go flying. On a recumbent bike you can pedal all the way through the corner. If you need more lean, you back off the power. If you've got room to spare, or need to pick up the machine a bit, you screw on the juice.

A trike is stable, and extremely agile. Other things being equal, not in the least the skill of the rider, recumbent bikes are probably faster than trikes through corners. This said, more than once I've watched a pack of bikes and trikes go into a corner and seen a bike go down while the trikes survived.

Summarily, you have to work hard to overcook a recumbent bike in a corner, but they can go down. A trike with a low center of gravity is incredibly agile and a great survivor – but beware of negative camber corners!

• Braking

A recumbent will outstop a safety bike by a wide margin. You can just put out the anchors for all they are worth. If they are real stoppers, like the modified moped drum brakes on my faired Speedy, or the incredible Hope disc brakes now available, you can stop on a dime. It does not do to rely on your brakes to get you out of trouble. Nevertheless, the immense stopping power of

recumbents and HPVs is a great boost to confidence and morale.

• Speed

"How fast can you go?" is a question I get at every other traffic light. The answer is: "Depends on the rider."

Recumbents are faster than regular bikes. They've been whipping them since the 1930s, and that's why they are banned from UCI sanctioned events. Overall, a recumbent is about 10 percent faster than a safety bike. But the real advantage is not in maximum speed, which can only be sustained for a few seconds, but rather the speed attained for a given effort. Crudely, 20 mph on a recumbent takes 25 percent less power than 20 mph on a safety bike. That's a whopping improvement, but note that this differential is only relevant at higher speeds, where aerodynamic drag is more significant. In regular traffic, at speeds between 12 and 15 mph, there is no practical difference between a recumbent and safety bike.

HPVs are like recumbents, only much more so. Much depends on the machine in question. At 20 mph, a streamliner like Bluebell is just loafing. I doubt if it needs more than 20 percent of the power necessary to drive a safety at the same speed; 50 Watts (W), or about 0.06 horsepower (hp) should do it. For a machine like my faired

Speedy, I'd guess around 100 W or 0.12 hp. But it is probably more relevant to answer the question in real life terms.

If I am just going somewhere in the faired Speedy, it will be at 18 to 19 mph. Any good rider on a road sport bike can pull alongside, and many do. If I make a more solid effort, the speed notches up to around 21 mph, a rate that I can keep up for a while. The good rider is now working fairly hard. What happens next depends on the distance and people involved. Good riders can give me an argument, particularly if hills are involved. Really good riders can leave me behind if they want, because I can't keep up over 22 mph for a long time. But although my steady power output level is modest, the efficiency of an HPV is high, and at about 100 to 125 W, I am working only half as hard as the sport bike rider, who is pushing out around 200 W. I wait for a stretch of level ground or slight downgrade, press harder, and it's usually so long.

I try to avoid sprints, at least in traffic. When I'm fit, I can see 30 mph on level ground, and 35 to 45 mph on downgrades. I've been clocked at 55 mph on a steep descent.

The thing to appreciate is that as HPV riders go, I'm on the slow side. An interesting comparison is that on a regular urban commuting journey, I would average 15 to 16 mph, sometimes 17 mph, on a lightweight mountain bike with road tires. In the Speedy, if I was up on the cam, and lucky with the traffic, I could do the same trip at an average speed of 20 mph.

• Power

In a recumbent riding position the back is braced, and it is possible to generate much greater thrust and power than with a safety bike. If you want to screw it on for a moment, you can go like you wouldn't believe. However, the high thrust is strictly momentary. In a recumbent your body weight does not help press down the pedals; turning the cranks is completely up to your legs, and for this reason, the cadence (crank revolutions per minute) range for effective power is narrower than with a safety bike. To be a good

and happy recumbent rider, you must be able to spin, and need to use the gears precisely. On the other side, an HPV can be a great oldster's machine. What you do is ram in thrust and whiz up to speed, then jump the gears to a big ratio that you just slowly trundle, taking a rest from the burst that got you going.

Some respected cycle authorities claim that the upright riding position is best for power. Work done in Britain by the Kingsburys and others seems to indicate that the body is a fuel cell, and the rate at which it drains is more a determinant of performance than of how the work is done. Or: if you're used to doing things one way, you might not be as good doing them another way. We've always recognized that for top level performance, recumbent riders have to be extensively conditioned and trained. Different muscles are used, as are different skills.

I personally think that the recumbent position is healthier. On a regular bike, you can stay aboard and keep on going even when, if you stopped, you would not be able to stand up, much less walk. On a recumbent you can only go so far as your legs will take you. Once they turn to rubber, like it or not, riding for the day is done.

Hills and climbing are supposed to be the weak point for recumbents and HPVs. Ha. Depends on the hill, the conditions, the machine, and the rider's technique. There isn't a lot of difference between a recumbent and a safety of equal weight. With the recumbent you must spin.

HPVs typically pay a weight penalty for aerodynamic efficiency. Climbing grades over 6 percent, a UCI safety bike at, say, 21 to 22 pounds will outclimb an HPV at, say, 32 pounds. (It would also outclimb a standard bike at 32 pounds.) However, once the grade is less than 6 percent, the HPV with greater aerodynamic efficiency is faster.

If it's a steady 1,000-meter climb, then weight is all important. If it's rolling terrain, then even a heavy HPV will be fast. At speeds beyond 12 mph aerodynamics have a telling effect. If a hill is short, giving the pedals some stick will conserve momentum.

HOW MUCH IS A HUMAN POWER?

Power is measured in odd ways. Most of us understand it in terms of horsepower (hp), an fps unit of power based on the foot (12-inch kind), pound, and second as units of length, mass, and time. Thus, one horsepower equals 550 foot-pounds per second. However, most scientists and technicians use SI units, for which the derived power unit is the Watt (W), equivalent to 1 joule per second. A joule, heh, is the work done when the force of 1 newton is displaced through a distance of 1 meter. It takes 746 W to equal 1 hp.

One time at the York Cycle Rally, Bluebell rider Tim Gartside had a go on a bicycle ergometer run by the British National Team. He held a cracking pace for 5 or 10 minutes or whatever, and then did his thing, standing up out of the saddle and sprinting, registering a peak of 1.9 hp before the rig started to come apart. This kind of power output, even for a few seconds, is very, very rare.

A common benchmark is the performance of world champion Eddy Merckx, who produced 455 W for 1 hour on an ergometer. A healthy, well-conditioned cyclist might be able to keep up this rate for perhaps a minute. A trained, healthy person can put out about 700 W for a few econds, and about 180 W for 1 hour. Over a longer period of a few hours, an average cyclist produces 50 to 75 W or about 0.1 hp.

Parking

An SWB bike is a tidy affair and has much the same space requirements as a regular upright bike. A nose cone and/or a boot tail can mean a tighter squeeze in a hallway, but does not add too substantially to the overall bulk. An LWB bike is pretty much like a tandem upright; slim enough, but needing room fore and aft. Most LWB bikes are fairly easy to pick up and handle.

A bare recumbent trike is a fairly substantial piece of kit, and can be awkward to handle. Most are designed to fit through a standard doorway. However, in real life, as you go through that doorway, having to turn around a corner or jig past the boiler or whatever, handling a recumbent trike can require deft maneuvering and a certain amount of strength.

A trike with a full fairing is like, well, a small car cut down the middle. It no go through the door. I can get mine into the house, but only through a large window. I long ago decided that any big faired machine in regular use would have to live outside, just like my neighbors' cars and motorcycles. I don't like exposure to possible vandalism, but the parking spot is beside a window right next to the house, and reasonably safe. When the machine is in use, it's left out on the street, usually up on the sidewalk in front of the house. I can park anywhere I want though, at no cost and no risk of a parking ticket.

Getting the faired Speedy out from under cover, unlocked and set up (or putting it to bed) is a bit of a production compared to simply picking up a bike, and does not happen unless the journey is going to be of some length. The LWB and SWB machines, including the full faired Kingcycle, handle very easily up and down the front steps and in and out of the inner hallway.

AN HPV FOR YOU?

I'm sold many times over on recumbents and HPVs. However, while a bare recumbent is in a sense simply a lowdown version of a bike (or trike), a faired HPV is a personal vehicle, with utility, performance, and safety standards that no upright bicycle can emulate. If you are one of the majority who take little journeys here and there at distances of 10 miles or less, often by yourself, then an HPV is an answer that takes a lot of beating. It's simple, comfortable, quick, safe, easy to park, weatherproof, requires only organic fuels, and provides healthy, life giving exercise. It's not push button, you've got to pedal, but at speeds above 12 mph it's easier than an upright bike, where most of the energy is consumed by aerodynamic drag. And if you like sport and a turn of speed, then HPVs are really worth considering: fast, much easier to take to the limit, and safer than an upright bike.

HPVs transform the concept of a personal vehicle. With a car, one buys personality; with an HPV, you express personality. After all, you're the engine! Are you fit and feisty? The HPV for you may be a lightweight, high performance model in which you move with grace and speed. Or per-

haps you are a grandad or granny, healthy enough, but with no interest in dashing about. You'd like a machine that is first and foremost comfortable – you never did like bicycle saddles – that will get you around the neighborhood, has room for little Johnny or Kathy, and can even trundle your clay pots to the kiln for firing, or whatever. There's an HPV for you, too.

Recumbents and HPVs set out to improve on the performance of safety bikes, and in this respect can whip them flat, but the most important gains are greater comfort and increased safety, and a broader range of applications and more flexibility in meeting the needs of different riders. At the same time, for sheer fun, a sporting/performance recumbent or HPV is a sonic blast without equal. With a car, motorcycle, or other powered vehicle, the central issue in performance is how light and feathery a touch you have for control. Famously, car racing drivers have the reflexes and skill to drive at "nine-tenths," a hairline inside the edge of traction and control.

In a recumbent or HPV you are the engine as well as the driver. This gives complete engagement and awareness. What's on the line and happening is you, not your control of another force, and this is why I laugh when car drivers pull

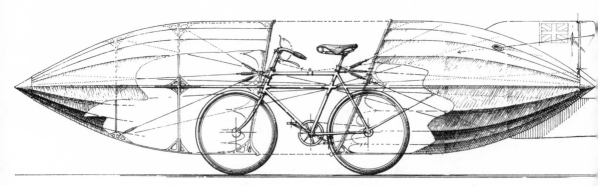

Fantascycle by David Eccles

alongside and rev their engines. They're not even in the same class. Want to race? Really race, with everything you've got? Get in an HPV.

Should you consider a lowdown machine? Yes, definitely. It's not an either/or choice. I run both ordinary bikes and trikes, and recumbents and HPVs. You might start with a bike, then add a recumbent or HPV – it all depends on what works for you.

FINDING OUT MORE

At the end of the chapter I discuss a few specific recumbents and HPVs, but this is mostly to cover classic bookmarks and give some idea of the kinds of machines around. Laid back riding is a fast developing scene and for current information you'll need to do your own research. This is good, because the personal nature of these machines means you should not buy one without trying several to see which you like best. Most of the shops specializing in recumbents and HPVs are set up for test rides, and many have access to private tracks or car free areas.

Periodicals

The magazine to be sure to get is *Recumbent Cyclist News*, a US bimonthly that's hoisted the recumbent colors with enthusiasm since 1990. With a solid personal touch from editor/publisher Robert Bryant, issues are filled with scuttlebutt, news, test reports, technical and touring articles, reader dialogues, and plenty of ads, classified sales, and wants. Many back issues are worth obtaining, for example, a special edition devoted to homebuilt recumbents. Each March or thereabouts they have a buyer's guide issue.

Recumbent Cyclist News, PO Box 2048,
Port Townsend, WA 98368, USA.
Tel: 360 344 4079.
E-mail: bob@recumbentcyclistnews.com.
Web: www.recumbentcyclistnews.com.

The annual publication *Encycleopedia* is an international guide to alternatives in cycling hat covers folders, recumbents, HPV's city bikes, family bikes, cargo carriers, mobility, trailers, accessories and more. Although manufacturers pay to be included in the guide, appearance is by invitation only, and text is originated by the publishers, Velomedia. They don't bother with duff products, only things of interest, and the result is a unique, fascinating showcase of new, unusual, and very beautiful things in cycling. Each issue also has a corresponding video film showing all the various products in action, so you can see how folders fold, how a recumbent looks, and so on. If you like bikes of any kind, you'll enjoy this publication. Produced in Britain by Velomedia and available from the US distributor:

Overlook Press, 2568 Route 212,
Woodstock, NY 12498, USA.
Tel: 485 679 6838 and 800 473 1312.
E-mail: overlook@newstep.net.
Web: www. overlookpress.com.

A British magazine devoted to laid-back riding is *Recumbent UK*, which is intelligent and well written, with a good mix of news, technical articles, stories of interest (what riding the end-to-end Speedy is like), and cycle and product tests. The tests are quite good, and often compare machines in groups. This is useful, because recumbents and HPVs vary in character, and "best" is relative to the match between the natures of the rider and particular machine. There's a shop and manufacturer guide, HPV and recumbent ads galore, and a sales and wants classified for used machines.

Recumbent UK, The Laurels, Church Hill,
Olveston, Bristol BS12 3BZ England.
Tel: +44 01454 613497.
E-mail: richard.w.taylor@btinternet.com.
Web: www.recumbentuk.hpv.co.uk.

Books

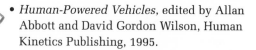

- *Human-Powered Vehicles*, edited by Allan Abbott and David Gordon Wilson, Human Kinetics Publishing, 1995.

The human power movement in action! This A4, 280 page, well-organized compendium of articles by leading scientists, designers, and builders is a thorough exposition on the dynamics of human power, and the history, technology, and future of land, water and air vehicles. Plenty of useful illustrations, photographs (mono), and charts. This is an information book that stimulates the parts others cannot reach. A must have for anyone interested in human-powered vehicles.

- *Bicycling Science*, by Frank Rowland Whitt and David Gordon Wilson, MIT Press, 2nd edition 1982.

First published in 1974, this is the classic work on the ergonomics and mechanics of cycling. Comprehensive, fundamental, and essential.

- *Bicycle Design*, by Mike Burrows, Open Road, 2000.

Mike Burrows, founding chair of the British Human Power Club, designer of record-breaking HPVs and bikes and now head designer for Giant Bicycles, is famous for being clear and to the point. The focus is on what you need to know to go fast; covers the lot, from ergonomics to aerodynamics and the mechanics of cycles. Entertaining, informative, and must have.

- *Richards' Ultimate Bicycle Book*, by Richard Ballantine and Richard Grant, Dorling Kindersley, 1992.

Now available in paperback. Major section on recumbents and HPVs. A little dated, but very high quality pictures.

Electronics

An annual HPV CD with lots of pictures, and information on events, organizations, products and shops, is produced by:

Oliver Zechlin, Rudolf-Breitscheid Str. 10, D-90547 Stein, Germany. E-mail: hpv-cd@zechlin.com. Web: www.zechlin.com.

A good start point on the Web is the site of the International Human-Powered Vehicle Association: www.ihpva.org. The site includes plenty of links to clubs, projects, and manufacturers throughout the world. Another site with many links is: www.recumbents.com.

Associations

One good way to learn about recumbents and HPVs is to connect with the Human-Powered Vehicle Association of North America. The HPVA has chapters in various states, which organize regional races, tours, and other events. These are often a great way to meet HPV enthusiasts, ask questions, and possibly try out machines. Once a year there is a national championship, with several days of speed trials, road races, tours, seminars and workshops, and many other events. The exact program will depend on the resources of the host organization, but these events are usually fascinating, with a rich selection of interesting machines and people.

The HPVA produce excellent publications. This includes the biannual *HPVA News* and three to four issues per year of the journal *Human Power*, edited by David Gordon Wilson with associate editors from Europe and Asia, filled with hard core technical news and articles. The latter publication is also available by direct subscription. The HPVA also have a mail order store with books, symposium proceedings, other papers, and videos available. For HPVA membership contact:

Jean Seay, PO Box 1307, San Luis Obispo, CA 93406-1307 USA.
Tel: 805 545 9003. Fax: 805 545 9005.
E-mail: Jean Seay exec-vp@ihpva.org.
Web: www.ihpva.org.

Dennis Turner, 7 West Bank, Abbot's Park, Chester CH1 4BD England.
Tel: +44 01244 376665.
E-mail: recumbent_dennis@compuserve.com.
Web: www.bhpc.org.uk.

In North America and Canada, human-power clubs and associations are an evolving scene. Various groups, some affiliated with the HPVA, are emerging to organize races, speed challenges, and other events. There are also many small clubs specific to an area, or to a project, perhaps at a university or college. Best bet for tracking these down is to check with the publication, *Recumbent Cyclist News* (address above).

You might also want to look on the other side of the Atlantic. The European HPV scene is both fascinating and of course somewhat different. There are regional events in most countries, and an annual European HPV Championship held on a rotating basis in various different countries, which attracts competitors from everywhere. There are more machines than you can count, and always a tremendous amount to see and learn. Most championships also include seminars and workshops, with some of the top researchers from around the world. If you are interested in HPVs and/or bikes and go to one of these events, I think you are pretty sure to have a wonderful time.

The HPV movement is particularly strong in the Netherlands and Germany, and also of course in Britain, home of the British Human Power Club (BHPC). The BHPC have a pithy quarterly newsletter with news, articles, race reports, ads, and a sales and wants section. Would-be home builders can acquire the hugely useful *So You Want To Build An HPV?* which spells out some of the do's and don'ts of design and construction.

Information and membership details:

LEARNING TO RIDE

Do your initial rides in a quiet area free of motor vehicle traffic.

A trike is fairly straightforward. Sit in it, ask/figure out how the controls work, and set off. Stay calm. It's too easy to become intoxicated and whiz about with increasing abandon. We usually have to rein in first time trike riders after a while, because the excitement and fun has them pushing a little hard. A point to watch, particularly with a trike, is fastening your feet to the pedals. It's fine to take a short spin with open pedals, but the majority of recumbent and HPV riders use clip-in pedals. Holding one's legs up in the air

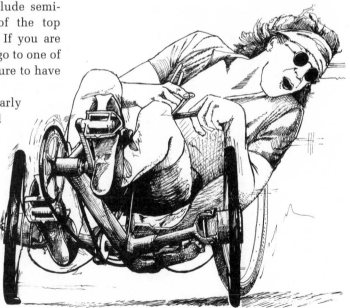

Andy Pegg riding an early model Speedy. When cornering hard with a trike, it is essential to lean to the inside – note stress to tires.

on open pedals can be tiring, and if a foot should slip off a pedal as a result of a bump or other mishap, strike the ground, and then go under the machine . . . ugh.

Cornering technique with a trike will depend on the particular machine. Some models are rock-stable and will simply scrub speed if you enter a corner too fast – up to a point. More sporty trikes usually need body English; lean your upper body inside the turn, hooking your elbow on the seat if necessary.

For your first ride on a recumbent bike, a CLWB or LWB model with a semi-reclining position will be easier and more fun than an SWB with a high bottom bracket. Find a bit of ground with a slight downslope, and use your feet to scooter yourself along until you get the hang of the balance and steering. Be sure to sit back in the seat. When you can glide for some distance, raise your feet to the pedals and keep on going. Remember to put your feet back down when you stop – honest, some people forget.

For starting from rest, it's important to be in a gear small enough to push without strain, yet big enough to get you going. Balance the bike with one leg, raise the other to the pedal, and position the crank at about 10 o'clock. Start a firm stroke on the cranks and, as you get going, bring up your other foot to the pedal and smoothly put it to work. It's simple enough, but it has to be right; if a take-off aborts you usually need to come to a complete stop before you can try again. This can be frustrating in traffic. Naturally, uphill starts can be rather tricky. Avoid these when you can.

Seems obvious, but . . . don't go out in heavy traffic in a recumbent or HPV until you feel relaxed and confident with the machine. A session or two in an empty parking lot, and a few early morning rides while most cars are still asleep should do it.

THE MACHINES

Recumbent bikes are available in all grades, from simple runabouts at about the cost of a basic or midrange ordinary bike, to titanium or carbon frame machines equivalent in cost to a small car with an internal combustion, chemical fuel engine. A decent performance or touring model will cost about as much as a top quality safety. Trikes are more complex, and run to more money. Full HPVs with fairings, suspension, disc brakes, proper lights, and so on are personal vehicles, and initially expensive because they are lightweight and efficient enough for use with low power, organic fuel, biological engines. This makes the long term running cost sensationally less than for chemical fuel engines. Cheap insurance, no registration or licensing fees, and no parking tickets!. Even the capital cost represents good value for money; time trial bikes as used in the Tour de France cost more, and are not nearly as fast.

If you don't have much money, it is more than possible to cobble together a recumbent for yourself. I've seen plenty of viable machines made by converting old BMX bikes, Choppers, tandems, and folding bikes. I've also seen disasters. If you go the DIY route, save yourself trouble and get hold of the booklet *So You Want To Build An HPV?* produced by the British Human Power Club (see above). Many manufacturers sell plans for home builders, and this route can be educational and satisfying, as long as you genuinely enjoy this sort of thing and lots of it. None of the kits or plans offer a cheap, easy way to get a recumbent or HPV.

This selection of machines is not comprehensive, and is just a start. On the Web, lists of manufacturers are maintained by:

RCN: www.recumbentcyclistnews.com
IHPVA: www.ihpva.org
BHPC: www.bhpc.org.uk

I've listed a number of machines from abroad, giving the manufacturer's address, because they will have the most up-to-date information on US dealerships. For some scant but perhaps helpful information on sizing and setting up recumbent cycles, see Chapter 10, Fitting and Gearing.

Bike-E

Wide range of CLWB bikes, including an off-road model. Very easy to ride, an excellent first machine.

Bike-E, 5125 SW Hout Street,
Corvallis, OR 97333, USA
Tel 541 753 9747 and 800 231 3136
E-mail: bikee@bikee.com
Web: www.bikee.com

Dragonflyer

Touring and commuting trike with mid-weight suspension, folding rear wheels and stays.

Earth Cycles, 1500 Jackson St. NE,
Minneapolis, MN 55413, USA
Tel: 612 729 4035
E-mail: e-cycles@spacestar.net
Web: www.spacestar.net/users/e-cycles/

Easy Racer

LWB and CLWB bicycles in racing and touring models. Upright handlebars. Optional Zzipper fairings and body socks. An IHPVA '75 original and longest in the business. The Easy Racer Gold Rush Replica, now also available in titanium as the TiRush, is reckoned by many to be one of the fastest and best LWB machines around.

Easy Racers, PO Box 255-W, 200 Airport Blvd.,
Freedom, CA 95019-2614, USA
Tel: 831 722-9797
Fax: 831 768-9623
E-mail: info@easyracers.com
Web: www.easyracers.com

Greenspeed

Australian trikes in touring, sport, and tandem models. Well-known for quality construction and stable handling. Independent brakes, which makes it possible to execute some fancy cornering techniques.

Greenspeed, 69 Mountain Gate Drive,
Ferntree Gully, VIC 3156, Australia
Tel: +61 3 9758 5541
Fax: +61 3 9752 4115
E-mail: info@greenspeed.com.au
Web: www.greenspeed.com.au

Lightning

SWB racing and touring models. The Lightning P-38, a very fast and able road machine, is available in a range of different frame materials. The R-84 model in carbon fiber has a listed weight of 19 pounds. Zzipper fairings, body socks and streamlined panniers available. Lightning do the full faired F-40, one of the faster road HPVs available.

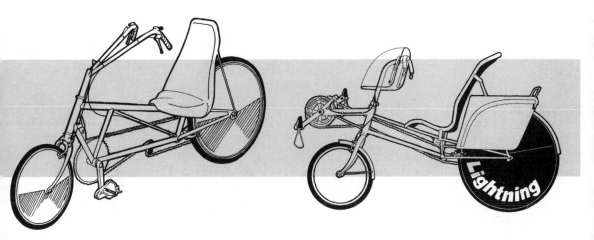

Gold Rush

Also list an M5 Low Rider codesigned with Bram Moens of Holland, a pure racing machine well low down even by recumbent standards.

Lightning Cycle Dynamics, Inc.,
312 Ninth St., Lompoc, CA 93436, USA
Tel: 805-736-0700
Fax: 805-737-3265
E-mail: info@lightningbikes.com
Web: www.lightningbikes.com

Kingcycle

British SWB bicycle now out of production, but some 450 were made, so used ones are available. Faired version worth seeking out, because fairing is one of most efficient around. Nose and tail cones, sock middle. Very fast. Large boot will carry a creditable amount of shopping.

M5

M5 are an established brand well-known for lightness and speed. They do several mouth-watering SWB machines, ranging from easy ride, small front wheel models, through to lightweight racing machines. The Street Legal model, a fast tourer with rear suspension, is reasonably priced. Their Low Rider model holds many records.

M5 Ligfietsen, Nieuwe Kleverskerkseweg
23, 4338 PP Middelburg, The Netherlands
Tel: +31 118 628 759
Fax: +31 118 642 719
E-mail: info@m5-ligfietsen.com
Web: wwwm5-ligfietsen.com

Moulton AM-14S

Moulton AM-14S

Upright safety bicycle, but full suspension and small wheels allow fitting a three-quarter length Zzipper fairing. Very versatile, quick, and comfortable. One of the great machines, for more information see the Moulton entry in Chapter 6.

RANS

Established manufacturer of recumbent bikes with a range of LWB and SWB models, including some interesting tandems. Popular and reliable, one of the safer makes for buying secondhand.

Rans Inc., 4600 Hwy 183 Alt.,
Hays, KS 67601, USA
Tel: 785 625 6346
Fax: 785 625 2795
E-mail: info@rans.com
Web: www.rans.com

M5

Street Machine GT

Street Machine GT

SWB bike by HP Velotechnik of Germany, with under seat steering, dual suspension, and an extensive range of options including hydraulic calliper or disc brakes, carrier racks, lighting systems, and front and rear fairings, the latter with an enormous boot. Three different seat sizes. Produced since 1993, refined and well-made, with very smooth handling. Designed for daily use and touring, not racing, but performs well. A full spec version will run to some change, but of the SWB bikes I've tried, this is one of the best. HP Velotechnik has a web site at www.HPVelotechnik.com, and information is also available from their British distributor:

Bikefix, 48 Lamb's Conduit Street,
London WC1N 3LJ England
Tel: +44 020 7405 1218
Web: www.bikefix.co.uk

Trek R200

Interesting SWB bicycle from a mainstream manufacturer with above seat handlebars, rear suspension. Uses a crossover drive to produce 44 gears. Small wheels. Easy to ride.

Trek USA, 801 W. Madison St.,
Waterloo, WI 53594 USA
Web: www.trekbikes.com

Trice

Stable tricycle with secure handling. Touring/commuting version with large boot. Other models are a SWB bike, an in-line tandem, and a low rider bike, the Festina.

Inspired Cycle Engineering,
Unit 9B Spencer Carter Works,
Tregoniggie Industrial Estate,
Bickland Water Road, Falmouth,
Cornwall TR11 45N England
Tel/Fax: +44 (0)1326 378848
E-mail: tricehpv@globalnet.co.uk
Web: www.cycling.uk.com/bikeshop/trice.htm

Windcheetah SL

The Speedy! Recumbent tricycle. Very agile and quick, winner of many practical vehicle con-

Windcheetah Mark IIIA

tests and road races. By my lights, the best all round street HPV in the world – fast and thrilling, yet safe, easy to handle, and comfortable, too. Partial fairing and boot available, also a full fairing (suitable only for racing). Frame in aluminium or carbon fiber. Many options, including hi-lo dual range bottom bracket gear, electronic gear shifters, disc brakes, hi-power lights.

Advanced Vehicle Design, L&M Business Park,
Norman Road, Broadheath, Altrincham,
Cheshire WA14 4ES England
Tel: +44 (0)161 928 5575
Fax: +44 (0)161 928 5585
E-mail: bob@windcheetah.co.uk
Web: www.windcheetah.co.uk

COMING ATTRACTIONS

I like to think about new HPV designs for increased speed or performance, and one frustrating problem area is the crankset. Providing enough room for the feet to whirl around creates a high nose section that obstructs the forward vision of the rider. This difficulty has been considerably eased by the new Kingsbury K-Drive, a crankset where the pedals move in an oval path, but the gear ratio remains constant. (In contrast to an oval chainring, where the gear ratio is variable.)

The K-Drive permits using a lower nose section with better penetration for speed and efficiency, and wider field of vision for the rider. This is especially important for street vehicles, and my guess is that we will soon see a new generation of user friendly HPVs based on the K-Drive, or variations thereof.

I hope that we will also see strong development in the area of inflatable and suspended fairings. I've always been charmed by the way dolphins can alter their shape to improve hydrodynamics. In land vehicles, a similar ability to change shape could be very helpful in realizing maximum aerodynamic efficiency at various speeds, and in changing conditions. An inflatable fairing might be capable of flexibility in shape, and would also be lightweight yet strong.

Another thing needed for aerodynamic efficiency is a fairing with suspension, which, according to Mike Burrows, is necessary for a consistent, smooth laminar flow with an efficient break-off point. A vehicle that is strongly aerodynamic needs to be able to move with the wind. If the fairing is rigid and/or rattled by road shock, then the laminar flow will be disrupted.

I can see a recumbent machine with an inflatable fairing that has different stages. For in-town use, where speed is not the main issue, the fairing is quite compact, and serves primarily as protection for the rider – a kind of air bag in the event of a fall. On the open road, engage the air pump connected to the bottom bracket, and the fairing

expands to a more aerodynamic shape, for greater speed. It's all very simple, but also extremely sophisticated, because both vehicle chassis and fairing have independent suspension controlled by smart fluids and electronics, capable of reacting within fractions of a second. Guided by the rider, the machine is as much a creature of the air as the land, and constantly adapts to changing conditions as it quite literally flies along.

Indeed, a small band of hardy and daring folk even go so far as to fit inflatable, pop out, delta shape wings to their vehicles. They climb high hills and mountains, come screaming down roads or even open slopes, pop open the wing, and launch themselves into the air for long gliding flights – 25 miles is the record, but 100 miles is sure to happen soon. There is a rumor that one inventor has fitted a folding pusher propeller to an ultralightweight bike glider and made a flight of 200 miles, but has not reported it because she is too busy flying around having fun.

Think I'm kidding? All the things I've mentioned – delta wing flying trikes, inflatable structures and fairings, aerodynamic controls, smart fluids and electronics – exist. All that's needed is for someone to put them together.

Perhaps you?

Special Bikes and Trikes

Small wheel bikes • The Moulton Series • Folding bikes • Tandems, in-line and side-by-side • Tricycles: the racing "barrow," adult trikes, and shopping/utility trikes • Mobility cycles • Reproduction and replica cycles • Children's bikes from starter trikes to BMX and freestyle machines

SMALL WHEEL BICYCLES

ALL OTHER THINGS BEING EQUAL, SMALL WHEELS have greater rolling resistance than large wheels. However, small wheels have less mass, and accelerate and handle more easily. They are stronger, and have less aerodynamic resistance. They take up less space and thereby open up new possibilities in cycle designs. All good so far, but as you will see, making efficient use of small wheels requires comprehensive design engineering; in terms of quality and performance, bikes with small 16- to 20-inch wheels range from crude and abysmal to refined and excellent.

Shopper Bikes

The classic shopper bike has a step-through frame, 20-inch wheels, a large bag on the rear, and a quick release wire shopping basket on the front. On paper, the idea looks neat and sensible: a one-size-fits-all utility bike that can haul groceries or serve as a general runabout. The reality is that most models are heavy and slow, unstable, and sometimes impossible to stop. They are cheaply made, with gas pipe frames, steel wheels, and crude, long arm calliper brakes. The wide, soft

tires used to cushion the stiff ride of the small wheels make for hard pedalling. The typical shopper bike from a mainstream manufacturer is a case study in bad engineering and execution of a decent design idea.

It need not be so. Moulton bikes (discussed below) are among the world's finest. I've also tried out some excellent lightweight small wheel city/shopper prototype designs, with features

Shopper

such as alloy wheels and hub brakes. These bikes are just great when you need an easy get-around machine, as when photographing bike races, or when you need to go to some place while wearing good clothes. A small wheel bike can carry things more easily, and is more compact and manageable than a standard 26-inch wheel roadster. We do not have decent small wheel shopper bikes because mainstream manufacturers have assumed that customers for these bikes are downmarket, and have engineered quality down to a ridiculous level – in gas pipe models a weight of 40 pounds and even more is not uncommon.

Fortunately, two forces for good are at work. The market for quality bikes is continuing to grow and expand, and utility cycling is becoming increasingly upmarket. Once there is the prospect of viable sales volume in several national markets, one of the giant global manufacturers will risk the large capital investment in modern materials and manufacturing technologies necessary to produce a good, lightweight, small wheel utility bike at affordable prices. Until then, if you want a general runabout suitable for many family members, seek out a lightweight, small frame mountain bike and fit it with a long seat post and quick release clamp, and adjustable stem. If you need to haul things, get a trailer, which is easier to manage and far more commodious than a wire basket, or a cargo bike (see Chapter 14, Cargo Cycles and Trailers). Or rob a bank and spring for a Moulton.

Moulton Bicycles

In 1962, Alex Moulton revolutionized bicycle design with the introduction of a small wheel bicycle equipped with full independent suspension for both front and rear wheels. This eliminated the need for soft, slow tires; instead, the wheels were light and stiff, and shod with narrow, hard, high pressure tires. The bikes were comfortable, yet very fast, and their credibility as speed machines was decisively established when rider John Woodburn used a Moulton to set a new Road Racing Association Cardiff to London record.

Alex Moulton wanted his new design manu-

Moulton deluxe, Series II

factured by Raleigh who, in a move foreshadowing their reaction to the mountain bike two decades later, declined the option. Alex went into business for himself, and soon became Britain's second largest manufacturer, with production at 1,000 units a week, export sales to 30 countries, and sublicense production in the United States, Australia, and Norway. There were many different models in addition to the Speed, including an outback Safari, a commuter/shopper, and a folder. Particularly in Britain, Moulton bicycles were whizzing out of the shops, leaving rival cycle makers standing flat.

A beleaguered Raleigh launched its own version of a Moulton, the RSW 16, one of the worst bikes ever made, and a clear demonstration that the historic firm, then under different ownership and management, had truly lost its marbles. Nonetheless, the competition from Raleigh and a host of other manufacturers who leapt aboard the small wheel bandwagon pinched Moulton Bicycles; in 1967, the firm was sold to Raleigh, with Alex Moulton as consultant. To make a long story short, despite an eventual production of more than 250,000 Moultons, Raleigh engineers, if there were any, fouled up, introducing soft tire variations and competing models of such poor quality and performance as to bring the entire idea of small wheel bicycles into disrepute.

Alex Moulton reclaimed manufacture of his design, and in 1983 moved strongly upmarket with the introduction of the AM-series with 17-inch wheels, a marvelously sophisticated design with a space age geometric frame and advanced suspension. These are finely-made bikes, justly celebrated and enjoyed for their comprehensive engineering excellence. Later, Moulton introduced the less expensive APB-series with larger 20-inch wheels now available through Pashley Cycles. The range also includes an off-road "Land Rover" model, which has capable and comfortable if not startling performance in the dirt. Latest is the New Series Moulton, with 20-inch wheels, silver brazed space frame, and revised suspension with anti-dive geometry and fluid damping. One model, known as the "Bentley," features a belt drive.

Many people will tell you that the Moulton is the finest bicycle in the world. They have a good case. Among the advantages that accrue from combining suspension and small wheels is flexibility. For example, small wheels make room for wide, platform carrier racks so that bulky, heavy loads can be carried without loss of stability. A Moulton is a practical machine for shopping, or for laden touring. Alternatively, the small front wheel leaves enough room to mount a three-quarter length fairing (windshield), which means greatly improved aerodynamics and a new dimension in speed. Other things being equal, only a full bore HPV can catch a faired Moulton, and the sleekest road racing bike in the world hasn't a hope.

If you try sprinting a Moulton with a burst of pedalling energy, the suspension will bob up and down like a pogo stick. Although the suspension can be tuned for a hard or heavy rider, a Moulton is not designed to be hammered. The idea is to have a bike that is efficient and fast, yet comfortable and elegant. Over a distance, the reduction in fatigue awarded by the suspension is worth more to performance than the ability to snap off in a sprint.

Only a single hex key is needed to disassemble a Moulton into two halves. There's a carry bag for the bike, and while the package cannot be classified as slim and neat, it is quite manageable enough for travelling.

Bentley Moulton

Moulton bikes are a unique design, the only truly new and successful one since John Kemp Starley's 1885 Rover Safety. The current models are machines of such class and distinction as to be instant classics. And depending on the model, they can be expensive. The cost is fair enough for what you get, and for many people, Moulton bikes are it: brilliantly engineered, beautifully-made, and wonderfully versatile machines, a continuing source of pleasure, satisfaction, and pride. Other people agree completely that Moulton bikes are great, but have other things they'd rather spend their money on. It is a question of temperament and interest, not right and wrong. If you enjoy innovative engineering and superb building, and can write four digit checks without flinching, then be sure to look over the Moulton ranges.

For further information you might want to contact the Moulton Bicycle Club. The club does a newsletter, and also sells an excellent book, *The Moulton Bicycle*, by Tony Hadland, which covers the Moulton story from 1957 to 1981.

The Moulton Bicycle Club, c/o Malcolm and Jenny Lyon; 2 The Mill, Mill Green, Turvey, Bedfordshire MK43 8ET, England.

Web sites include Alex Moulton Bicycles, www.alexmoulton.co.uk, the US dealer Hed Cycling Products, www.hedcycling.com, and Tony Hadland, www.hadland.net.

Folding Bikes

In folding bikes you can have a machine that folds easily into a compact, light, easily handled package, but which does not ride so well and has limited range, or a machine that folds into a larger and less manageable package, but that rides well and can cover distances. The key to success with a folder is that the folding ability directly serves a useful or essential purpose. Otherwise you are better off with a full-size bike.

There are many sound incentives for folding bikes. It can be difficult or outright impossible to get a full-size bicycle aboard a train, and when you do manage the trick, you often have to pay an extra charge. However, a disassembled or folded bicycle inside a bag or box can go along, no problem, and no fee. For people who commute to work by train and want to use a bike at both ends of the journey, and for tourists who want to use trains to reach nice cycling areas, a folding bike is an effective answer.

Folding bikes are flexible. If there is an unexpected downpour of rain, you can fold the bike up, hail a cab, and be on your way, snug and dry. There's no need to carry a monsoon kit. A folder also pretty much eliminates security problems and having to carry heavy locks, because you can take it into your place of work and stash it under a desk, check it into a restaurant cloakroom, sling it under a grocery shopping trolley, and so on. A folder is handy if you have limited storage space, or want a bike aboard a yacht, aircraft or land vehicle.

To work well, a folder must reduce to a compact package that is light and easy to carry. El cheapo versions are effectively no more than a gas pipe, small wheel bike sawn through the middle and then rejoined with a massive hinge. These things are disasters as bikes, and do not so much fold as collapse into a large, flapping mangle of sharp protrusions and filthy greasy bits. This, and a weight of 40 pounds, make them completely impractical to carry.

Happily, good quality modern folders are in another class. The benchmark in compact folders is the Brompton, a well-made, tried and true machine that folds in 15 seconds or less into a neat package with a volume of 3 cubic feet that locks together, so it is easy to carry. The Brompton has small 16-inch wheels but is equipped with rear suspension, and rides and handles remarkably well. Weight from just under 25 pounds. Optional luggage and racks are very effective, and a Brompton is a good load carrier. A Brompton is not a distance machine, but it is probably the best compact folder available.

For distance riding and also rather more money, the Birdy is a high tech folder with full suspension and a weight of 22.5 pounds. It folds into a fairly small package of around 6 cubic feet, which is manageable but not as neat as the Brompton. Available in several different models, the Birdy is a refined machine that needs to be used with skill; rough, hard-charging riders could experience mechanical problems.

One of the best high performance folders around is the Bike Friday, with 20-inch wheels. It folds within 15 seconds to a package about twice as large as Brompton, and can also be disassembled in about 30 minutes to fit into a hard shell case when travelling by air. Weight from 25 pounds, several different models available. Another quality machine that has been receiving accolades for good performance and folding ability is the Bernds, with 20-inch wheels, rear suspension, and front and rear pannier racks.

Dahon are a well-established manufacturer of folding bikes, and also supply other manufacturers, so you'll find Dahons running under other colors. They have a range of bikes, from small wheelers to a full-size police pursuit model. Most of the reasonably compact models are fairly slow and heavy.

Brompton

A full-size bike with 26-inch wheels that folds is the Montague, now marketed by BMW. I've never ridden one, but the design has been around for a while and reviews in the press and testimonials on the Internet are very enthusiastic.

If you like fiddly things, you might want to look into the Swift from Animal Bikes. This is a 22 pounds, 24-inch wheel bike with unified triangle rear suspension, that folds in three stages. Stage one is a straightforward quick fold with the wheels still on so the bike will fit into the boot of a car. Stage two, wheels removed, the bike will fit into a small suitcase, and stage three, wheels off and carried separately, the bike will fit into an aircraft hand luggage case.

A good and cheerful source of up-to-date information on folding bikes is:

A to B Magazine, 19 West Park,
Castle Cary, Somerset BA7 7DB England.
Tel: +44 01963 351649.
E-mail: post@a2bmagazine.demon.co.uk.
Web: www.a2bmagazine.demon.co.uk.

TRAVEL BIKES

A travel bike is designed to reduce to a manageable package within a reasonable amount of time, say 10 to 15 minutes, for use on long distance journeys, typically holidays involving air travel.

The low cost option is to place a full-size bike sans carrier racks or mudguards in a standard soft shell bike bag. Remove the wheels, lift out the stem, detach the rear mech, remove the pedals, and nest these items within the frame, fit spacer blocks on the drop outs, lower the saddle, swaddle the lot in miles of bubble wrap, and bundle it all inside the bike bag. You need to be mechanically familiar with the bike but the job can be done quickly once you know the procedure. All would then be fine – but for baggage handlers.

One day while waiting to board at an airport somewhere in California, I glanced out the window just in time to see a baggage handler whirl full-circle like a discus thrower and send my bike bag flying over 20 feet through the air to land with a violent crash in the back of a truck. After that, I went out and purchased a hard shell case, with little wheels to make it easy to trundle. However, I do not use it often, because it is just too big. Getting it to and from an airport can be a major production. The pros manage, but they have to; for ordinary travel, an oversize hard shell case can be a real millstone.

Bike travellers now have an easier solution. A brilliant gadget, the S & S bicycle torque coupling system makes it possible to break down a full-size bicycle to fit, with wheels, into a suitcase measuring 26 x 26 x 10 inches, well within airline requirements. The coupling, a threaded lug used to join frame tubes, is beautifully engineered and made. On a standard road bike, a set of couplings adds about 8 ounces of weight, less than that of a water bottle. By all reports, the couplings actually increase rather than decrease the stiffness of the frame, and have no adverse effect on ride quality. A bike with S & S couplings can be disassembled and nested into a baggage handler proof case in less than ten minutes.

For some people, the S & S couplings are a dream come true, and many fine bikes have been fitted with them, either as a retrofit conversion, or as original equipment. Firms such as Merlin and Santana build bikes with S & S couplings, and the list of frame builders includes some of the best in the world.

As the folks at S & S point out, it is better to build a new bike with the couplings, because a retrofit involves repainting the frame tubes. To date, S & S couplings are available only for steel or titanium frames, and must be fitted by a frame builder or cycle manufacturer. S & S will advise on authorized outlets. For information contact:

Steve Smilanick, S and S Machine,
9334 Viking Place, Roseville, CA 95747, USA.
Tel: 916 771 0235. Fax: 916 771 0397.
E-mail: steve@sandsmachine.com.
Web www.sandsmachine.com/index.html.

Cost depends on the particular kind of bike and whether the fitting is original or retro, and should be recovered out of saved airline charges in ten or so trips. More worthwhile, perhaps, is the peace of mind knowing that your bike is well protected.

TANDEMS

Tandem cycling is a special world. In terms of sport, tandems are fast, because bike weight per rider is less, and wind resistance is cut in half. A tandem will outrun a solo bike on a downhill run, and over gently undulating terrain the greater mass helps to iron out small hills and maintain

momentum. Tandems are supposed to be slow on climbs, but in fact, if the riders are strong and coordinated, and the frame is strong (see box notes), a tandem can ascend with speed. The long wheelbase gives excellent stability and a smooth ride.

On the social side, togetherness is a definite plus of tandem cycling; it's easy to talk, and there is something very pleasant about the shared physical effort. A tandem is good for riders who tend to separate and spread out when riding solo bikes; the weaker rider can relax on the easy parts of a ride, and put in the muscle when necessary. There's a large and interesting collection of skills to learn before the pilot (front) and stoker (rear) can work together smoothly, and do heed that this process has been the making of some people, and the undoing of others.

A tandem can be a good way to share road riding with small fry not yet of an age for riding on their own, and also a neat way of doing the school run. A tandem is big, though, and can be awkward to handle in traffic. It can be virtually impossible on trains and buses. You'll need ample storage space, too. Many of these problems can be solved through the use of S & S couplings (see Travel Bikes, above).

Only a quality lightweight (35 to 45 pounds) derailleur gear tandem is worth owning. Heavyweight

Invincible Tandem

Swallows tandem

models as sometimes seen in rental fleets are just too much work. With the weight of two riders, first-class brakes are essential. A lightweight racing tandem for use by experienced riders might get by with calliper V-brakes. Otherwise, drum or disc brakes are what you want. Wheels must be strong and should be made using tandem hubs with thick 11 or 15 mm axles, 40 or even 48 spokes in 13 or 14 gauge, and stout rims.

Upright riding position tandem models are road racing or touring with 700C wheels, and mountain bike touring or off-road with 26-inch wheels. Tandems are made in various grades of quality, with a range of options, including suspension. There are also recumbent tandems, which are interesting and useful and my own preference. A nice one made in England is the Trice X-2. For information contact:

Inspired Cycle Engineering,
Unit 9B Spencer Carter Works,
Tregoniggie Industrial Estate, Bickland Water Road, Falmouth, Cornwall TR11 45N England.
Tel/Fax: +44 01326 378848.
E-mail: neil.selwood@btinternet.com.
Web: www.ice.hpv.co.uk

Tandem Resources

A tandem represents a considerable investment, there's a lot of choice, and it is essential to do some research, test riding, and thinking – all with your co-rider – before you buy. Two books you can peruse are *The Tandem Book*, by Angel

Rodriguez and Carla Black (Info Net Publishing), and *The Tandem Scoop*, by John Schubert (Burley Design Cooperative). You need to find a shop specializing in tandems, with a good selection, which hires out machines or will let you take extended test rides. They should provide instruction via a spin or two with an experienced rider. Information and advice can be obtained from:

The Tandem Club of America, 306 Union St., Morganton, NC 28655-3729, USA.
Web: www.mindspring.com/~strauss/tca.html.
Newsletter.

Tandems Ltd, 2220 Vanessa Drive,
Birmingham, Alabama 35242-4430, USA.
Tel: 205 991 5519. Fax: 205 991 7766.
E-mail: tandems@mindspring.com.
Web: www.tandemsltd.com.
Catalog for tandems, parts, information.

The Tandem Club, Box TC,
Cyclists' Touring Club, 69 Meadrow,
Godalming, Surrey GU7 3HS England.
Web: www.tandem-club.org.uk.

The US *Tandem Magazine* (www.tandemmag.com) is full of useful articles, tests, and general information. A web site with links to clubs, manufacturers, and much more is: www.shell.rmi.net/~wherrera/tandem-bike.html

Side-by-Side Bicycle

A tandem in a class of its own is the companion, or sociable bicycle, with the saddles set side-by-side rather than in line. It looks weird but works well and is easy to ride. Anyone who can ride an ordinary bike can just get aboard and go.

A side-by-side is not suitable for long journeys because the large frontal area creates poor aerodynamics. However, on local excursions and tours where speed and distance are not important, it is a complete stone gas. You can talk, hold hands, and even kiss. See also side-by-side recumbent tricycle, below.

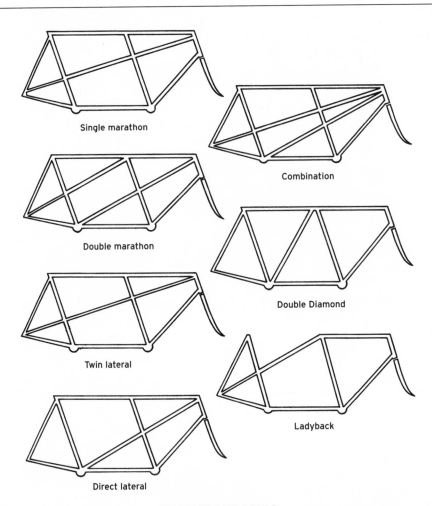

TANDEM FRAMES

Tandem frames are designed to reduce lateral (side-to-side) flex while still retaining a reasonably comfortable ride. Two popular compromises are the marathon and twin lateral designs. Both use long diagonal tubes running from the head tube all the way back to the rear drop outs. These provide bracing against the flex caused by powerful pedalling and sharp changes of course. With the marathon, a single tube splits at the seat tube to run on either side of the rear wheel; with the twin lateral, two thin tubes are used for the entire length.

The double marathon has two diagonal bracing tubes for a very still and strong geometry. The direct lateral, which is popular with American builders, uses a single diagonal tube from the head tube to the rear bottom bracket, and beefy chain stays. The stiffest and also heaviest design is the combination, which uses both marathon and direct lateral tubes.

Double diamond frames are common, because they are easy to build, but tend to flex at the bottom bracket. The ladyback design is too flexible for serious riding.

TRICYCLES

There are trikes and there are trikes! Low rider trikes, popular in retirement areas, usually have 20-inch wheels to keep the weight down low and are stable as long as they are not pushed hard. A large rear basket for carrying groceries, gold bars, or extra ammunition is a popular accessory. These machines offer much-prized mobility to people otherwise restricted owing to infirmity, poor balance or coordination, brittle bones, or other problems. One type of tricycle has a fixed gear, so that the pedals and wheels move together, and people with limited motion in their legs have sometimes found that the exercise provided by this arrangement improves leg mobility.

In my opinion a better option for those who do not wish to risk involuntary contact with terra firma is a recumbent tricycle. These are comfortable, and wide track general use and touring versions are difficult if not impossible to tip over. Braking is better, too. See Chapter 5, Zzzwwaaaammo! for more information.

At the other end of the spectrum from the senior trike is a machine known in Britain as a "barrow" — a lightweight, upright tricycle with 26-inch or 700C wheels. In no way is this an old age toy. Many experienced cyclists have come a cropper first time out on this trike. It must be steered around a corner, a sensation completely at odds with the handling of a bicycle, and rider weight must be counterbal-

Higgins Ultra-light, c. 1950. The rear axle includes a differential, so that power goes to both rear wheels.

anced to the inside on even a moderate bend. It's easy to lift a wheel, and downhill bends must be approached with particular caution.

Part of the appeal of racing trikes is that they are eccentric and challenging. Many adherents are crack bicyclists out for still more thrills. But trikes also have practical advantages: they are good for carrying things, can stop and park without difficulty, and stay upright under slippery conditions. We ran a big tandem trike as the family cycle for some years, and the different combinations of adults, kids, and babies we were able to get aboard the thing were dazzling.

For something unusual, a Victorian type tricycle with the stoker position at the front is made by:

Taylor Cycles, 375 Birchfield Road, Webheath, Redditch, Worcestershire B97 4NE, England. Tel/Fax: +44 01527 545262.

Another variation that is a good load carrier and a lot of fun is a side-by-side sociable recumbent trike, the Gem, made by:

Crystal Engineering, Unit 9B Spencer Carter Works, Tregoniggie Industrial Estate, Falmouth, Cornwall TR11 4SN England. Tel: +44 0777-355-3773. Fax: +44 01326 317789. E-mail: peterross@crystalengineering.fsbusiness.co.uk. Web: www.cycling.uk.com/bikeshop/ross.htm.

Low rider upright tricycle

Viscount Bury, K.C.M.G. on a Humber Roadster

Devotees of barrows should get in touch with:

The Tricycle Association, 24 Manston Lane, Crossgates, Leeds, West Yorkshire LS15 8HZ, England. Tel: +44 01532 605290.

• Tricycle Builders and Shops

Roman Road, Rogers, and Longstaff do kits for converting solo and tandem bicycles into trikes. These work, but mechanical proficiency is required to carry out the conversion, and the work is best done by a shop that has done it before.

Ken Rogers, 71 Berkeley Avenue, Cranford, Hounslow, Middlesex TW4 6LF, England. Tel: +44 020 8897 9109.

Bob Jackson Cycles,
Unit 1, 9 Union Mills,
1 Dewsbury Road, Leeds, West Yorkshire LS11 5DD England. Tel: +44 0113 234 1144. Fax: +44 0113 234 1000.

Longstaff Cycles,
Newcastle-under-Lyme, Staffs, England. Tel: +44 01782 561966. Fax: +44 01782 566044

Roman Road Cycles, Ddôl-Las, Ffarmers SA19 8JP Wales. Tel/Fax: +44 01558 650336. E-mail: romanroad@Ddol-Las.telinco.co.uk.

ODDITIES

Sailing Tricycle

RANS manufactured a sailing tricycle. These have a sail (about 30 square feet) just like on a boat, and will see 50 mph – be sure you have enough room! It's not listed in their current catalog, but perhaps there are still a few to be found.

RANS, 4600 Highway 183 Alternate, Hays, Kansas 67601 USA. Tel: 785 625 6346. Fax: 785 625-2795. E-mail: rans@media-net.net. Web: www.rans.com

Ride On Water

The Shuttle-Bike Kit will convert your bicycle into a watercraft. The bike is held on a frame between two pontoons, and pedalling powers a prop drive that can be steered with the handlebars. The kit is claimed to weigh 11 kg, and to fit into a small back pack. Contact:

SBK Engineering, Via dei Pioppi 22/7, 27029 Vigevano (PV), Italy. Tel: +390381 20140. E-mail: sbkkit@tin.it. Web: www.shuttlebike.com.

Pedal-powered watercraft have come a long ways from the typical holiday area machines, and can be both fun and practical. For more information on these, contact the HPVA:

Jean Seay, PO Box 1307, San Luis Obispo, CA 93406-1307 USA. Tel: 805 545 9003. Fax: 805 545 9005. E-mail: Jean Seay exec-vp@ihpva.org. Web: www.ihpva.org.

MOBILITY

A wide range of cycles and machines are available for disabled people, who number in the millions. "Wide range" means just that: there are many different kinds of disabilities, and hence designs include everything from detachable wheelchair tandems to ultralight hand-powered racing recumbent trikes. The annual publication of Velomedia, *Encycleopedia*, invariably has an intriguing selection of mobility machines. Obtainable from:

Overlook Press, 2568 Route 212,
Woodstock, NY 12498, USA.
Tel: 485 679 6838 and 800 473 1312.
E-mail: overlook@newstep.net.
Web: www. overlookpress.com.

Basically, if you are a special-needs person and can get out the door, with or without help, then one way or another you can go for a ride. Most (good) machines are produced by small firms, and can run to a bit of money. If you are interested in handcycles, be sure to get in touch with Ivacare, they make some truly lovely racing recumbent handcycles, standard upright models, and a child's model. They've have been around for a while and have agents worldwide.

Invacare Top End, 4501 63rd Circle North,
Pinellas Park, Florida 33781, USA.
Tel: 727 522 8677. Fax: 727 522 1007.
E-mail: Infor@invacare.com.
Web: www.invacare.com.

REPRODUCTION ANTIQUES

Modern versions of antique cycles are either reproductions (faithful copies) or replicas (rideable modern equivalents). Two firms producing a variety of bikes and trikes based on 19th century designs, plus one or two classic American paperboy bikes, are:

Classic Cycle Vertriebs GmbH, Talstrasse 38, 61476 Kronberg, Germany. Tel: +49 06173 78121. Fax: +49 06173 78122. E-mail: classic-cycle@t-online.de. Web: www.classic-cycle-de.

Rideable Bicycle Replicas Inc., 2329 Eagle Avenue, Alameda, CA 94501, USA.
Tel: 510 769 0980. Fax: 510 521 7145.
E-mail: mbarron@barrongroup.com.
Web: www.hiwheel.com.

Rideable Bicycle Replicas have been around for awhile. Years ago, one of their machines completed a 1,000-mile tour down the length of England without a single mechanical problem.

If you are interested in a high wheeler or a Star, I recommend obtaining *Collecting and Restoring Antique Bicycles*, by G. Donald Adams (Tab Books), with directions for riding. It is just as easy to "come a cropper" with a modern high wheel bike as with a veteran model.

Reissues of classic mid-20th century American paperboy bikes — balloon tires, cowhorn handlebars, and mock motorcycle styling with gasoline tanks, shock absorbers, horns, and acres of chrome — are increasingly popular, but are often either cheaply made, or expensive enough to blow your socks off. If the style of these machines appeals to you, I think it would be more fun to find an original and fix it up (see Chapter 19, Veteran and Classic). Veteran (pre-1910) cycles often command high prices, but classic machines of the 20th century, while sometimes pricy, can still be found for reasonable sums. This is part of the fun. An original machine will appreciate in value, while a replica will not.

The Dursley Pedersen

In *The Evolution of the Bicycle 1867–1939*, Tom Norton describes the Dursley Pedersen as "perhaps the most comfortable and novel cycle ever designed." Launched at the 1897 Stanley Show in London, the bike had two unique features: a hammock saddle woven from 45 yards of silk cord, and a frame made entirely from very

Dursley Pedersen

slim lightweight tubing, in a sophisticated design based on principles used in bridge construction. Comfortable, elegant, and extremely light (a folding model produced for the British Army around 1900 weighed a scant 15 pounds), the distinctive Dursley Pedersen was the first of the deluxe type of cycles to become popular with middle and upper classes.

The original Dursley Pedersen was produced until 1914. The design has since been revived a number of times, and replicas are available from:

Swallows, The Old Bakery, Market Street,
Llanrhaeadr ym Mochnant, Oswestry,
Shropshire, SY10 0JN England.
Tel: +44 01691 780050. Fax: +44 01691 780110.
E-mail: info@swallow-tandems.co.uk.
Web: swallow-tandems.co.uk

CHILDREN'S BICYCLES

For a child, a bike is motion and growth incarnate, a key to freedom and a tool for learning new skills. However, children's bikes are often regarded as toys to be bought as cheaply as possible, and the market is littered with models bright with color but crude in construction and mechanics. A common downmarket feature is to use plastic sleeves for bearings, which is like using glue as a lubricant. Even when new, plastic sleeve bearings have

high resistance, once worn, they can be impossible for tiny legs and muscles to move. El cheapo kids' bikes are bad value, because after the initial flutter of excitement children rightly leave the stupid things to rot.

A decent child's bike costs a reasonable piece of change, because it is just as complex to make as a full-size bike. But the return value in terms of work and play is incredible. I've watched many young children (under age 4) play with bikes for one or two hours at a stretch, every day, for months on end. They just keep on whizzing and whizzing. If you're looking for something to get the kids out of your hair, bikes are one of the best things going.

A good bike gives genuine play value, and it lasts. You can pass it down in the family, or sell it and recover a substantial portion of the purchase price. If you are on a tight budget or have a swarm of offspring to mount, then buy used. Basic quality is more important than newness, and anyhow, working with dad or mom and sprucing up an old bike is, for most children, more interesting and useful than spending money at the store.

The First Machine

Most children are ready for a bicycle at about age four or five, depending on individual development, coordination, and interest. A child may enjoy a bike at age two or even sooner, but not necessarily as a means of transport. The initial use

Pashley Pickle

LEARNING TO RIDE - DISCOVERY METHOD

The best way for anyone, young or old, to learn how to ride a bike is to discover the trick for themselves, in exactly the same way the bicycle was discovered. Go to a quiet open area, such as a park, and change the bike into a hobby horse: remove the pedals (15 mm wrench, left side pedal unscrews clockwise), and lower the saddle so that the rider can touch the ground with their feet when mounted. Show the rider how the bike steers. Let them push with their feet, as with a scooter. Show them how to use the brake. After they can start and stop, put them on a bit of ground with a gentle downgrade. Each individual scoot will progressively become longer and longer. When they can travel for a good stretch without touching the ground, replace the pedals and watch them go.

   This method is infallible. Do not use training wheels, or attempt to assist by holding the bike yourself. The discovery method usually works within 20 minutes, often less, but if your protegé wants to take longer, don't push; the whole point is that they do it themselves.

may be as a house or as a study in mechanical engineering. Let the child move at his or her own pace and he or she will eventually figure out what the thing can do. Keep a careful eye on matters. A toddler can easily catch a finger in moving bits.

As a starter machine for a very young child, a proper tricycle is far more safe and stable than a bicycle with training wheels. The Pashley Pickle is an excellent, sure-to-please chain drive tricycle that is a ridiculous amount of fun. Ours is much loved, and is now on hold for the next generation.

A child's first bicycle should have:

- Pneumatic tires. Solid tires are hard to pedal, provide a harsh ride, and give bad braking.
- Ball bearings for the headset, bottom, bracket, and wheels. Plastic sleeve bearings give bad handling and steering, poor efficiency, and wear out quickly.
- A large seat range adjustment so the bike can grow with the child.

- Brakes that work. It's surprising how many do not. The type is a matter of what suits the individual child. I prefer calliper rim brakes, because they are easy to service, but the hands of many young children are too small to operate the brake levers. If this is the case, go for a pedal-operated coaster brake.

You might to have to search for a while in order to find all these features in a bike suitable for small fry age four to seven. Availability improves considerably with bikes for children age eight and older, indeed, whole new worlds open up.

Most major manufacturers of quality bikes such as Fisher, Trek, Giant, and others, produce one or two good small wheel junior mountain bikes. These are great basic first bikes, tough and durable, yet with enough performance for real riding. From here, the sky is the limit – there are models with full suspension, multi-gears, V-brakes, and just about anything else you might find on an adult bike. A good value trick is found on FlexX models from Giant; an adjustable stem and a pivoting seat tube, so that the riding position can grow with a child from age 8 to 13.

BMX started out as dirt track racing, and then blossomed into incredible forms such as freestyle, with levels of bike handling and riding skill that have to be seen to be believed. BMX is play taken to a very high degree of work and dedication, and is utterly real time. Mechanically, BMX bikes are superior to most adult bikes. They have to be. Junk iron can't cut a bunny hop or place in a race.

All you have to do is pick up a good BMX bike to appreciate why any kid would want it. It's light. It'll go. And it's unbelievably tough. It is made to leap into the air, zoom off things, crash – and come back for more. Does your nearest and dearest have a chance of being hurt doing this kind of thing? You bet. But not mortally, in fact not even seriously, if he or she uses the right gear – a helmet, full-length pants, elbow pads, and gloves. And the payoff is participation in a sport that looks flash, but requires commitment and hard work, and the development of good sense and courage.

Allied sports of great appeal to youngsters are downhill racing, freestyle riding, and slalom competitions. There are special kinds of bikes for all of these, and they don't come cheap. Downhill is an especially testosterone-charged sport, and any sensible parent is likely to ask: hey, is this safe? Does this make any sense?

I say yes. I've never believed in the business of aping adult activities by putting kids on junior road bikes and dragging them on 50-mile tours. Kids like riding, sometimes for long distances, but roads are not the place for it until they are age 13. Until then, most haven't got the attention span to cope with the dangers. Too many get wiped out; per mile cycled, the highest accident rate by far is for under-16s.

The kind of downhill racing that occurs today sometimes scares the heck out of me, and I have a better-than-passing familiarity with this sort of thing. There are mind-boggling spills and crashes in freestyle and slalom, too. But on the plus side, these sports involve learning real skills, and how to extend your limits without overstepping them. These are

valuable lessons for living. So if these sports are what a kid genuinely wants to do, I'd rather make sure they have good equipment and get started right.

Pick out a good kid's bike the same way you would an adult bike: quality materials, alloy components, and sound building. Go to an event or two, see what bikes are in action, and ask people what they think. A good sport bike can cost; junior mountain bikes are pretty reasonable, but crack freestyle or BMX machines can run a mint. You and yours may be in for some real talk about money and finance, and this is a good thing. Working together to figure out what your collective resources are, and how they might be managed, is important for learning how things happen, and for togetherness. Good bikes should neither grow on trees nor be out of reach.

Hey, if you are a keen cyclist and your kid prefers table tennis, don't be disappointed. Get better at table tennis.

Some Advice on Selecting a Bike

Choosing the right bicycle(s) for you • Adaptability of bikes • Reasons for specialization • Quality and price • Bikes for women • Custom bikes

BEFORE SELECTING A BIKE, PAUSE AND CONSIDER if you might want to eventually have several machines. Budget, storage space, or other factors might limit you to one bike, or your desire may be specific: a folder, perhaps, or a bike for sport activities to be pursued only at certain places, as with skiing or scuba diving. However, cycling is the best means for getting around ever invented, and highly useful in a wide range of activities. Once you take up with bikes, you'll find that they work their way into many spheres of your life. Run a machine for commuting to work and soon enough you'll be taking spins for fun, and conversely, if you take up cycle sport you'll soon find that a bike is very handy general transport. If you think cycling will be an increasing part of your overall lifestyle, you might want to plan ahead, and work on building a stable of function-specific bikes. Ultimately, this pays off in increased convenience and fun.

On the other side, there is a good case for having just one bike. Strong road sport bikes and light mountain bikes are both fairly versatile, and can be set up so that with a change of wheels and accessories, the machine can be transformed from a commuter into a road tourer or off-road explorer. Snap on a trailer and you've got a cargo carrier. All-in-one bikes can be mechanically clever and

thus satisfying in themselves, and there is a special companionship in sharing many jobs and adventures with one machine. It is fun, indeed important, to use a bike enough so that you really get together with it.

Still, one of the joys of bikes is that it is possible to enjoy a flash new machine once in awhile, without suicidal expenditure. Treat! And one of the best treats ever is riding a bike designed expressly for a particular purpose. Interested in what it feels like to glide on a quiet road through rolling countryside? You can do it after a fashion with a roadster, and even fairly well with a pared down mountain bike or commuter rig, but there is nothing to beat riding a light, lean, road sport bike, because then, legs and heart willing, you fairly fly. The machine weighs hardly anything. You lean against the land and then with wings on your feet you actually move with it. A dance. It's a feeling and a joy like no other.

If you've got, say, a commuter bike, and a hankering for some fast open road riding, then to give the experience a real try it is worth obtaining a proper road bike. If the song of the road doesn't sound, you can sell (or trade) the bike on to someone else, and you won't have spent that much.

There are also practical reasons for having a stable of bikes. One is convenience. There's no

messing about changing a bike around for a particular task. Shopping? No fumbling with panniers or a futile search for the trailer hitch which has found a clever new hiding place. You just trundle out the shopper/cargo bike and go. What's more, the job of managing the shopping is done properly, quickly, and safely. A load that is a breeze for a cargo carrier can be a real handful for a regular bike. Late start for work? There's no where are the locks? Lights? Rain clothes? The commuter bike is there, full street outfit always aboard, lights charged, ready to go.

Having a spare bike or two to loan out is handy when you want to catch a film with a friend, go to a bar, spend a day in the country – or turn someone else on to bikes.

Finally, having more than one bike will likely make your life happier. Bikes are helping to make a better world, and the more bikes and the easier it is to use them, the faster and sooner things will keep on changing for the better. I don't want to get too sentimental, but bikes are a giving thing. They feel good.

Right. When selecting a particular bike, pick a type and model suitable for your immediate needs and budget, but push both areas a little so that your bike has some open potential. Suppose, for example, that fitness is a priority, and that you would like to get in some vigorous exercise over a regular 5-mile commute to and from work, and on occasional day rides. A commuting bike would be fine for the commute, but once you were seasoned you would find edge of capacity riding out of character for the bike. A solid, fast road bike would better encourage "going for it." On the other hand, if the roads for your 5-mile commute are in bad condition or are crowded with frustrated, aggressive motorists, and there are alternatives – dirt trails, old railroad lines, parkland – a sporty mountain bike might be the best answer. You'll still have all the room for improving fitness you can take.

Avoid underbuying. The confusing array of fancy machines in a bike shop can lead you to retreat into an "aw, shucks" hillbilly mode and to perhaps opt for a bike good enough for local use, but that gives only a taste of what is possible when going for more. A year or two later you are back at the shop, laying down the money for a better machine.

Cycling is a real time activity, and this can lead some people to feel that the moral right to ride a quality bike should be won with athletic performance, not purchased with mere money. Do not let this point of view push you away from a quality bike to a "good enough" alternative. Cycling is poor no more. Go for better, it's more fun, and cheaper in the long run. There is nothing, nothing, nothing wrong with spending money on a bike.

Equally, don't go over the top. It's not so much that you might overspend, but rather that you need some experience before you can get the most out of a fine bike. An ultralightweight road racing bike has to be handled with skills acquired only through practice. Similarly, a very high tech mountain bike will be mechanically demanding, and might need servicing almost every time it is used. If you are new to looking after bikes then a more straightforward (but still lightweight) machine will be more enjoyable. Remember, too, that a really fine, expensive bike is not something you can leave lying around loose, or locked up on the street.

Evaluate your own needs carefully, and then go for a bike that has some fun in reserve. Some bit, some thing, some aspect, that tickles your fancy and scratches a dream. This is an important trick

for success with a bike. At root, fun is the reason for cycling, and fun is personal. If you're really taken with the idea of stepping off a train, doing a clever bit of sophistry on a collection of bits removed from a bag, and then elegantly riding away on a bicycle, then try a folder (but read about them first, in Chapter 6, Special Bikes and Trikes). If you fancy the idea of wowing neighborhood kids by giving them rides in a pedicab, then go for it. Pick what works for you.

One cautionary note: anti-establishment machines are fun. It's relaxing to drift down the road on an Old Faithful held together with rust – sort of like joining hands with the stream. But that kind of thing is for lazy days when you are on your own time. If you are looking at a bike as a pragmatic tool, then you want a good one that works cleanly and well. More, you want a bike that is just that little bit better and more satisfying – a machine that you can move and grow with.

The Exact Machine

The problem with recommending specific bikes is that brand names, bike models, and prices can change rapidly. Like people, bicycle manufacturers have good times and bad. A well-established company may merge with another, and until the two groups harmonize, quality may suffer. Equally, a once great company that has been on the skids for years may come under new management and produce a sparkling range of bikes.

Elements that can make a brand of bicycle good or bad include the quality and efficiency of the manufacturer's management, financial structure, production engineering, distribution, marketing, shower facilities, and kind of coffee they serve. All this before we've even come to the essential bit: engineering and design.

Thirty years ago, many people in the bike industry never rode bikes. Now, most of them do. That difference is absolutely crucial, because in many bike firms the people have real hands-on knowledge about bikes, and a genuine feeling for cycling. Making bikes is not like manufacturing TV sets without a care for what programs will appear on the screen. Bikes are cultural and emotional, they are about living, they are meant to be used, and today's better firms, large or small, consist of people who really care about making the best bikes they can produce. There's much more to the story, but summarily, if you buy a reputable brand, you should be on reasonably safe ground.

With good firms competing to deliver more for less, and with continuous technological advances and changes, the bicycle market is dynamic and seasonal. If you are out to get the most for your money, first work out a solid idea of the design, quality level, and features you want, and then look around and see what's going. Talk to people. Read catalogs. Trawl cyberspace. Cruise bike shops. Most will have particular lines of bikes to sell, but that in itself can be a recommendation. Good shops sell good bikes. Yes, they will want to persuade you to take what they have, but like food in a restaurant, what's on for the day may be the best thing. In any case, you are looking for a good shop as much as you are looking for the right bike (for pointers on bike shops, see Chapter 8, Buying a Bike).

Eventually you will focus on one or two bikes and shops. What you fancy most may cost more than you can afford. Look for value, see what can be done, but avoid buying on price alone. If the gap is large, think about lowering your sights: better a good quality, basic bike than a poor midrange bike. Perhaps you can find a break on a model clear out, or a demonstrator. If your budget really won't stretch, and your heart is set on performance, then consider a used machine.

Never let price chasing lead you to a discount store. These places do not sell worthwhile bikes. In Chapter 8, Buying A Bike, I explain the vital role of a bike shop in ensuring that a bike works. This especially applies to inexpensive, basic bikes. Even if all you want is a heavy steel runabout, buy it from a bike shop. Basic machines from reputable manufacturers cost more than chain store el cheapo specials, but they work. In fact, it's amazing how much usability and reliability can be packed into a basic bike – by manufacturers and shops who know what they are doing.

If you are not of a mind to go comparison shopping, pick out a good bike shop (see Chapter 8) selling the kind of bikes you like, go there with cash in hand, discuss your needs and be fitted up with a machine within or nearly within your budget, and ride it away that very day.

Techie, Feelie High Class Bikes

A few small firms manufacture limited quantities of bicycles built to standards of excellence in engineering and quality that are nothing short of remarkable. These bikes are so classy and lovely, they are often enjoyed more as creations in themselves than for what they can do. However, they can also be astounding to ride, and some people will have no rest in life until they have acquired a truly exclusive high performance model from makers such as Klein or Merlin. For the pleasure they can bring, these bikes are a worthwhile investment, despite their high expense.

Cautionary note: car manufacturers have taken to producing bicycles. Automotive engineers are capable and well-equipped, and some of these bikes are interesting. However, the presence of a prestige car brand on a bicycle is not an assurance of quality.

Custom Bikes

A custom-built bike with a unique, made-to-measure frame, finished and decorated exactly as you wish, and with your own choice of equipment, is thoroughly personal and can be very satisfying. Be advised that complete, off the shelf bikes will meet the needs of most people in terms of fit, and are far better value. What you pay for is custom.

There are a few old-time master framebuilders around and their work is in great demand, but there are also many young, new framebuilders who do excellent work at competitive rates. Many are to be found in smaller communities and rural areas, where overheads are low.

A custom bike is conversation and interaction. The builder will talk with you, analyze your needs, discuss options, and hopefully let you see the frame being built. It is wonderful fun, and really interesting, but remember that time is money and be prepared to pay a fair price for a custom service. There is no comparison with what is on offer down at the store.

Regarding the design and details of a custom machine, make all the suggestions you want, but never ask a frame-builder to do something he or she does not want to do. The responsibility for success rests with the builder, and it is best to stay within the bounds of their experience and range.

A custom bike, a machine that is yours alone, is one of life's great pleasures. In view of the cost, it should wait until you have had a bike or two and have a sound idea of what you want.

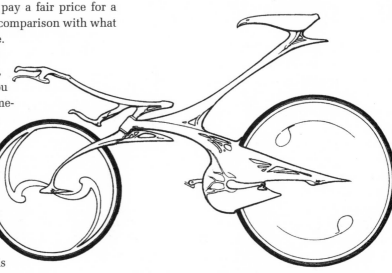

Gandalf Special

Women

You are unlikely to wear a skirt while mountain biking or in a road race! Some women may assume that they would like to have a bike with a traditional ladies' open frame. However, this design is structurally weaker and less responsive than a frame with a level or sloping top tube. In any case, sloping top tubes which are now the norm, give plenty of room. The case for an open frame is not one of gender, but convenience; it can be useful in the case of a roadster or cargo bike, when ease of mounting and dismounting does matter, and performance is secondary.

The gender difference that counts in frame design is: women have longer legs and shorter torsos than men. If you are female and over 5 ft. 7 in., then in most cases by using a smaller frame and shorter stem you will be able to get a good fit. If you are under 5 ft. 7 in. – and I believe around 75 percent of women are – then it is better if the frame is proportioned correctly for your physique. Briefly, this means a shorter top tube, and steeper seat tube. If you are quite short, consider a bike with a 24-inch front wheel. This allows the bike to be proportioned correctly without fouling up the handling qualities, and to have a head tube of reasonable size.

A well-known builder specializing in bikes and components

Why?Bike

for women is:

Georgena Terry,
140 Despatch Drive,
East Rochester, NY 14445, USA.

Trek, Giant, and Cannondale have bikes designed for women, and in time so will most of the other manufacturers. It's the coming thing: surprise! women are different.

Bike weight has a greater effect on power-to-weight ratio for light people than for heavy people. In general, women should place lightness at the head of the list of priorities when obtaining a bike. Wheels, which are important in perfor- mance, can usually be slimmer and lighter. Make sure that components such as the stem, handlebars, and cranks are the right size for you. (See Chapter 10, Fitting and Gearing). If you go for a bike with suspension, make sure it is set up correctly for your body weight.

The Women's Mountain Biking and Tea Society (WOMBATS), is a fun off-road cycling network for women, and a good tonic for anyone:

WOMBATS, Box 757, Fairfax, CA 94978 USA.
Tel: 415 459 0980.
Web: www.wombats.org

Buying a Bike

Why bike shops • Picking out a shop • Test rides, the buy, and taking delivery of a new machine • Breaking in a bike and the post sale mechanical check • Used bikes • Options for where and how to park/store your bike • Bike security • Bicycle storage • Locks • Insurance • Hanging

BIKE SHOPS

The best place to buy a bike is a bike shop. You can make an initial savings by buying from a discount store, but are virtually guaranteed a string of headaches and problems that will in the end cost you more. First, the bikes stocked by discount outlets are usually inferior, because reputable manufacturers shun such places. Second, even if by a fluke you should happen to find a good bike at a low price in a discount store, it will still be no bargain.

Manufacturers build bikes up to a point; final assembly, adjustment, and tuning is carried out by the shop mechanic who sets the bike up for the customer. Discount stores sell price, not bikes, and do not employ trained bicycle mechanics or have workshops equipped with proper tools; they sell their bikes still in the box and unassembled, or at best, have them put together by some innocent armed with pliers and a hammer. When post-sale problems arise, discount stores have no means to do repairs, much less understand the problem. The options are a refund – good luck – or a replacement, which will probably take weeks or months.

In bike shops, capable and qualified mechanics know how to assemble new bikes quickly and cor-rectly, how to test and check that everything works, and iron out any defects. This last is important. Even the finest of machines can have problems. I was out recently on a new test bike, a top-of-the-line model, and discovered that someone at the factory had cross-threaded and stripped the mounting bolts for the front disc brake. This

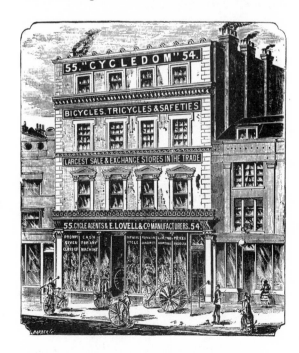

kind of problem, which could have serious ramifications, is more than a discount store could understand, let alone handle, but is a dead easy fix for a bike shop, which has both the knowledge and the right tools for the job.

Buy from a bike shop, and it is 100 percent their responsibility to produce a working bicycle. You'll want to check their work, but chances are they will do the job right. You get a free post-sale safety check, when a mechanic goes over the bike and ensures that components are in correct adjustment and that everything is snug and tight. You get a guarantee on parts and labor good for a year or more, and if some problem arises, the shop will be available right away to fix it, and will have any necessary parts in stock. If you buy a bike with a manufacturer's warrantee, let's say on the frame for 10 years, and something does go wrong, obtaining satisfaction from the maker is a whole lot easier if you have a bike shop on your side.

How about buying a bike at a discount outlet, then taking it around to the shop for servicing? In the old days, shop owners would turn livid and run such people straight out the door. They're smarter now. Of course service is available – at fair rates. Democracy! Let's see: a bike with, say, a sticking headset, wheels out of true, a dragging brake shoe, and a few other problems. Surely nothing serious, just little annoying things to touch up . . . hmmm, the head tube has to be refaced with a special tool, the wheels are the devil's work to put right, the "few other problems" are time consuming – and the bill for this work exceeds the savings that were made by purchasing the bike elsewhere. The extra you pay in a bike shop buys a lot and is money well spent.

What about mail order and web site outlets? Many offer tempting price breaks, especially for folks on a budget. Mail order can also be convenient, particularly if you live far from a decent bike shop. Well, it depends on what you are buying, and what sort of resources you have. A component such as a pedal is straightforward and is easy to install, but to set up a complete bike or install a complex suspension system you need to be, or have access to, a bike mechanic with a full selection of tools. Mail order is typically most successful with groups of riders who already have a fair idea of what they are doing and what equipment works for them, and have pooled their resources and tools to save money. If you are in with such a group or club and like this route, then fine, go for it. If you are more or less on your own and not very familiar with bikes, you are better off dealing with a shop.

A good bike shop offers informed counsel and advice. They will steer you right on your choice of bike, and over time, provide advice about accessories, equipment, riding techniques, events, and all sorts of matters. You'll have your bike serviced from time to time. All this stuff is important, you need straight information and good work, and you want an on-going relationship with a bike shop that you like and trust. Such a relationship is enjoyable, educational, and in the end will save you money.

PICKING OUT A SHOP

Buy from a shop that sells, uses, and knows about the kind of bikes you like. If you live in the sticks and are after an upmarket machine, this may mean travel afield, as the bulk of sales for such bikes are through perhaps a few hundred top shops. If you want a specialized machine such as a tandem or a recumbent, then the number of good shops will be even fewer. In such an instance you should get in touch with the appropriate clubs and organizations to obtain information on recommended shops. You might have to travel, but this can be fun. Some specialty shops and manufacturers are focusing on service by offering try-out sessions where you are fitted properly, given instruction, and can try out various machines. Accommodation at reasonable rates is usually included. This is a brilliant way to buy a bike. Another very good way of trying out high-class bikes are cycle road shows with demonstrator bikes that tour the country, stopping in various areas for a few days. Sometimes these are tied to local shops.

If you live in a metropolitan region or if you want a midrange bike, then a greater number of shops will qualify. Most of the big, well established shops can handle many different kinds of bikes.

It is important for a shop to know about the kind of bikes you want, but don't automatically head for the bright lights. The more local the shop, the better, because convenience means a lot. Most repair problems with new bikes are minor and can be sorted out within minutes. Bike shops typically give first priority to customers who bought their bike from the shop. If a local shop does not stock your heart's desire, see if they can order it for you. If what they've got is different, take a good look. All other things being equal – as they often are with mass-produced bikes – the convenience of a local shop could be a good reason to switch brands.

Check the Yellow Pages and ads in cycling magazines for the locations of shops near you. Ask friends and whoever else you can find which shops they like; word of mouth is the best recommendation. Bike shops live on customers, and good shops first, foremost and always, look after their customers. There's no satisfying everyone, you can always expect to hear a few chuffs and moans, but usually, when talking about a shop, people should report that they were pleased with

the service or happy with the bike they purchased, and yes, think you should go there.

Visit the shops and sort them out. Bike shops vary a good bit in character. Some are dedicated strictly to mountain bikes, others to changing the world with interesting but plain looking utility machines. Some are small and cramped, others are big and modern and have lots of bikes on display. It's nice if the shop is big and inviting, but don't be too quick to judge by appearances. Bikes take up room, rent on a good retail location can be astronomical, so even in good shops space may be at a premium.

Attitude matters most. There should be clear evidence that the staff of the shop ride bikes and one way or another are involved in cycling. Whether this is lycra-clad road racing, aramid-armored off-road downhilling, or natural cotton cycle activism, is only a matter of taste; what counts is the involvement. I repeat, a bike is not a TV set. It may be made of metal and rubber and various other supposedly nonsentient things, but it is a biological machine. Cycling is an activity, and a shop where the bikes all look alike and the staff treat you with glassy-eyed indifference or synthetic politeness, is one to avoid. You're looking for evidence of character: a photo or two on the wall showing someone at an event, a notice

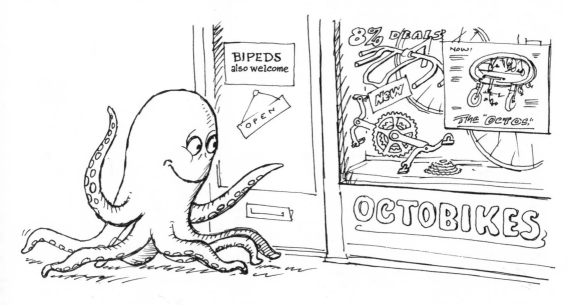

board with some clippings, say about road racing or HPVs or classic bikes, leaflets about campaigning for cycle facilities, that sort of thing. If you know how to read bikes, see if you can spot what the staff are riding (easy if you hang around at closing time); this can be educational, and sometimes very impressive.

When you go into a shop, someone should speak to you within a few minutes of your arrival, if only to say (when the shop is busy) that they will be with you as soon as possible. When a sales person attends to you, and you say you are interested in a bike, they should straightaway proceed to obtain information about the kind of machine you are interested in, your riding experience, and price range. Make some allowances here. US and Canadian bike shops are among the best in the world, but there are still some good shops with staff that would flunk sales school by a mile.

If you say something like, "Well, I'm interested in a commuting bike, or a nice mountain bike with suspension," and are taken over to a machine and told "this is the only thing to have," then it does not matter what the bike is; politely thank the sales person for their time, and get clear of the joint. Whether the sales person does it directly, or through indirect chatter about this and that, they must first form an idea of *your* wants, experience, and price range – help them with this process if necessary – and then suggest looking at two or three bikes. If the machines are up your alley, look them over and ask any detail questions that come to mind, and in the process check out the following:

- What sort of servicing does the shop offer? What is the guarantee? A free post-sale service should be standard.
- Will you be able to take test rides? If you cannot take test rides, go elsewhere. Test rides are an essential part of the evaluation and buying process.

A good shop may be ready with a demonstrator and offer a test ride then and there. If you like everything that has happened so far, you may want to take a spin or two and perhaps slide right along into the next stage, The Buy. There's no need to cover every shop in town, particularly not if you already know from your own research that the shop you are dealing with is a good outfit.

A likely possibility is that the bikes you'd like to try will have to be set up, in which case you are likely to be offered a later date for test rides. Play fair and agree only if you think the shop is a genuine prospect for The Buy. Ask if there are any leaflets or catalog information on the bikes that you can take away and study. This will help you to do your homework. For example, you like the look and price of a bike but for the fact that it has V-brakes fitted with modulators (a kind of anti-panic safety device) that you don't like. However, a switch to another make of V-brake will be neither difficult nor expensive, so the bike is a contender.

THE BUY

Once you've boiled your options down to two or three bikes and one or two shops, you're ready for the main event: The Buy. To ensure the best attention of the shop, avoid doing this on Saturday, Friday evening, or Monday morning, which are times when they are apt to be busy. Wear suitable clothes and shoes and have a bit of tissue or rag handy in your back pocket.

Before whizzing off on a test ride (or any strange bike) check that handlebars and saddle are tight, brakes are firm, and wheels run free and true. Ensure that tire pressures are correct and within the range marked on the tire. Simple stuff, but I can't tell you how many times a poorly adjusted component on a strange bike has taken even a very experienced rider by surprise. Make sure that the handlebars, brakes, and saddle are tight! As for tire pressure, this is important for both the objective and subjective feel of a bike, and is one of the things that simply needs to be right.

Vary the pace of your test ride: try out low and high speed handling, riding over rough surfaces, cornering, and braking, but don't press the bike too hard, or expect too much. Any new bike feels strange for awhile. If you are actually uncomfortable, and the feeling persists, ask the advice of the shop. Sometimes an adjustment of saddle height or stem length will cure the difficulty. If not, try another bike.

You are not looking to find the very, very best bike, only which one you like the most. There are definite differences between bikes, but bike testing is highly subjective and even so-called experts are regularly fooled by the power of suggestion. Tell a tester, "Check out the smooth ride on this new Wonderfiber frame," and most times they will come back saying, "Yeah, great, incredibly smooth!" Send another tester off without saying anything about the Wonderfiber frame, and likely they won't notice a jot of difference. It's not that these people are stupid or incompetent, only exactly what I said: bike testing is highly subjective.

Beware of not liking something that might be good for you. Henry Ford used to fit soft, plush seats in his cars. They were terrible for long term comfort, but felt great in the showroom. So, for example, if up until now you have been aboard roadsters and mountain bikes and try out a high performance road bike, you may find the crisp handling a bit scary. Or perhaps it is your first encounter with a straight, unmodulated V-brake that clearly has the power to send you right over the bars if you use it carelessly.

There is nothing wrong whatsoever with a bike having performance potential that you can and will learn to use. That's exactly what you are looking for. It is just fine if you need to ride a bike with a little tenderness and respect for what it can do.

When you've found the bike you like the most, the one that you think with a smile of riding home, buy it. The whole game is not to stuff you aboard a bike, but to match a bike to you. Your tastes might change later, but in the here and now, the thing that will work best is the bike you like the most.

Discuss any substitutions you need on your new bike; a shorter stem, a better saddle, or different pedals, to name a few common swaps. Although you are trading one item for another, the shop is entitled to charge (gently) for labor, and any difference in value of components, which might be significant if you are upgrading from,

The New Bike

say, basic cage pedals to top quality clip-in pedals. Then there are accessories such as lights, helmet, carrier racks, a lock, and what-else, depending on your needs. Also possibly marking the bike and/or registering it (see Security, below). Sort it all out and get the money down to the bottom line.

If you are buying a lot of gear all at once, you are entitled to ask for a price break, but be aware that, although bikes are glittery and shiny and some components cost an absolute bomb, running a bike shop is not like having a private mint. In fact, margins in the retail bike trade are tight, and the majority of bike shops stay afloat only by dint of hard work and a love of the life. You should already know from previous cross-checking if the price for your bike is fair value, and if it is, my sentiment is that you should take it.

How you pay for a bike is your business. As always, for best price nothing beats cash. If you need credit, so far as I know, banks do not finance bikes the way they do cars, but there's always a first time. Some bike shops offer credit at favorable rates. Ordinary credit cards are of course rather expensive, but your circumstances might be such that the savings of a bike offsets the cost of credit. Like I said, your business.

Whew! The deed is done. The shop may ask you to return for the bike later that day if there is time, the next day if not, and is entitled to a deposit. Ensure that the sales receipt has the frame number of the bike, and your name and address.

TAKING DELIVERY

Anticipate that any new bike will have something wrong with it. Dealing with a good bike shop minimizes this possibility, but does not eliminate it. When I picked up a new dream machine from one of New York City's finest shops I was too bedazzled to give it anything but a cursory inspection. As I accelerated away from the shop the rear hub and freewheel exploded in a blizzard of metal flakes and chips. The problems you might encounter are not apt to be so spectacular, but even minor glitches such as slightly loose handlebars can have dramatic consequences, if they give way at a wrong moment such as under stress of hard braking. Plan on giving your new bike a 100 percent inspection. You make a new bike yours, and safe, by taking charge of it. Personally.

Collect the bike at least two hours before shop closing, so you have time to sort out fine points and make adjustments. Bring along the tools you need. Look the bike over carefully, checking that the bits are tight and tidy, and of course that the brakes and gears work.

For the rest of it, there is no need to subject the shop to the sight of a review of their work, or to obstruct their premises. Take the bike out for a spin, and check the following:

• Frame and forks for straight alignment. In an area clear of traffic, ride holding the handlebars as lightly as possible, hands off if you have the skill. The bike should go straight, in control, without pulling to one side. Stop, stand behind or in front of the bike and see that the wheels are in line (it helps to have a friend along for this one). Next, hold the bike by the saddle only, and wheel it around. If the frame or forks are out of alignment, it will tend to veer to one side. If this happens, make sure that the cause is not the layout of the brake and/or gear cables, or a rough spot in the headset bearings.

Check that the front wheel is centered under the fork crown, and equidistant from each fork blade. If it is not, remove the wheel, turn it around, and put it back in. If it now cocks to the other side, the wheel is off. If it assumes the same position as before, the fork may be misaligned.

A crude check for frame alignment can be done with a long piece of string. Remove rear wheel. Tie end of string to one dropout, lead it forward and around the head tube, then back to the opposite dropout. Make sure the string comes out of each dropout in the same way. Tie string drum tight. On either side of the bike, the distance between the string and the seat tube should be the same. If the difference is more than 1 mm, there may be a problem.

A bicycle that will not track accurately is tiring and unsafe to ride, and a bike which fails these tests should go back to the shop. Keep in mind that this kind of thing can be subjective, you can easily talk yourself into believing a bike pulls one way or the other, and tests such as with pieces of string are crude. Be diplomatic and polite when speaking to the folks in the shop. They will have the proper equipment for checking the alignment of both frame and forks, and will need to see for themselves. If the cause is, say, a slightly bent fork, and it is steel, a fix may be simple. Forks in aluminium, titanium, and carbon fiber, and suspension forks, cannot be realigned and should be replaced. If a frame needs resetting, that is a job for a professional, and again, it's on only for steel frames.

• Wheels should spin easily. When the bike is held clear of the ground the weight of the valve stem should push the wheel around until the valve positions at six o'clock. Note, however, that several factors can cause the valve to settle into another position: tubes and tires are not always uniform in consistency; the wheel may be festooned with safety reflectors and, if it is a rear wheel, the freewheel might present some resistance to turning.

• Wheels should be centered in fork arms and rear chain stays. If a wheel can be moved from side to side and there is a clicking sound, the hub bearings are out of adjustment. Check that the rim is true by holding a pencil next to it and spinning the wheel. Brace the pencil on a fork arm or chain stay. Side-to-side movement of the rim should not exceed one-eighth of an inch.

• Pluck the spokes. All should be evenly tight and give the same sound. Note that on the rear wheel, the freewheel side spokes will have a different tone.

• Brake blocks should hit the rims squarely and not drag when released.

• Gears should work smoothly, with no slippage or unhappy noises.

• Pedals and chainwheel should spin easily but without side-to-side play.

• Check that all nuts and bolts are secure. Every one of them. You might need to wait until you are home and have access to more tools before you can do them all.

You might imagine that so comprehensive an inspection is excessive. After all, it's a new bike, and should work. All I can say is, I have bought many bikes, for myself, for family, and for friends, and there was something wrong with every one of them. I rejected a few outright. You stand to possibly save yourself a lot of grief if you invest some time at the outset on a careful inspection. More positively, carrying out a thorough series of checks puts you straight to grips with your bike as a machine, and learning how it works.

On the other side, don't get carried away. If the bike is a basic model, it cannot sing with quality, nor can the shop be expected to spend all day fiddling with it. What you have a right to expect of any bike, whatever it costs, is that it is safe and roadworthy.

After a few days and/or riding 50 miles or so, again check that all nuts and bolts are secure. Every last one. New bikes "bed in," there is microscopic wear where parts meet or are joined together, and it is common, for example, for the brake bolts to work loose. Crank bolts will need tightening. The mechs will probably need adjusting, and the cables will almost certainly need to be tightened. Read through the appropriate sections in the Maintenance part of this book for details. I put bike inspection and maintenance as something for you to do because the sooner and more you learn about your bike, the better. However, if you do not know a wrench from a screwdriver, do not be intimidated. The important post-sale service by the shop fully covers tightening the bike up, and adjusting it to run smoothly. If all goes well, as it should, you will have plenty of time in which to make mechanical friends with your bike.

USED BIKES

Used bikes are a great way to save money. There are plenty of them around, in all shapes and sizes, conditions, and ages. Crudely, you can expect to pay about 75 percent of street retail for a bike in excellent, near new condition, and 50 to 60 percent of street retail for bikes that are two to three years old and in average condition. "Street"

means the true selling price in shops, not the manufacturer's suggested retail price.

Sources for used bikes depend on where you live, what you are looking for, and your own initiative. Some shops sell used bikes, but turnover is quick and you usually need some luck to catch the machine you want. Cycling magazines often have classified ads; look in the magazines that are about your kind of cycling, and again, move quickly if you want to score. If you are interested in specialized machines, such as a folder or a tandem, or a sharp old classic, then join an appropriate association or club, because their newsletters and journals often have for sale ads. A rich source of bikes of all kinds is cyberspace.

If your aspirations are modest and money is tight, look around locally. There are millions of forgotten bikes in garages, attics, and sheds. They often have a minor fault such as a broken cable, and are no problem to make roadworthy. We're not talking neglected Colnagos or other great prizes here, only working-grade bikes such as Ben's Fuji 12-speed, left in the garage when Ben emigrated to New Zealand. His mom is now happy to be rid of the thing for a few bucks. Ask around your neighborhood, put up BIKE WANTED notices in laundromats and on

bulletin boards, and you might turn up a bike for a song.

Local newspapers usually have classified ads with a few bikes for sale, but be wary of "trader" ads that repeat each week. Sometimes a sale of household effects includes a bicycle. Auctions are sometimes good. A good bet in the spring are local bulletin boards at universities and colleges. Put up some cards yourself, or take out an ad in the student newspaper. Naturally, the more prosaic a bike you seek, the sooner you are likely to find it. But if you just keep putting out the word wherever you go, something will eventually turn up.

Whatever you are looking for, when following up leads where the initial information is minimal – "Nice adult bike" and "Mountain bike" – eliminate machines which are not the right size or the type you want. You must have the right size, and you should buy what you need, because it is expensive and often impractical to, say, convert a racing bike into a touring machine. On the other side, if you are looking for a commuting bike, it is no great expense to fit an old mountain bike with mudguards and lights.

When you go to see a bike, try to find out its history. It's best if you can talk to the owner. Was she or he interested in the bike and in taking care of it? If it is a relatively new machine, where was it purchased? Is there a service history? Does the bike appear looked after, or as if it has been left out in the rain?

Does the owner ask questions of you? Do they care that the bike is suitable for your needs? Better to pay more for a well-loved bike than less for one with a dubious or unknown past. This can cut another way, too. I once purchased a really lovely curley stays Hetchins from a man in the north of England, at a price both he and I knew was very reasonable. What he cared about was that I had travelled 200 miles to see the bike, and really wanted it. We had a nice time together, chatting and looking over his stable of bikes, he had a couple of handsome Jack Taylor machines, and I went home with a long-coveted Hetchins, in a beautiful ruby red. Buying used can be a lot of fun.

Equally, you could wind up with a lemon. If

you don't know about bikes, bring along a knowledgeable friend. In inspecting a bike, cover all the points listed for a new machine. Pay particular attention to the frame. Wrinkled paint on the forks or where the top and down tubes meet the head tube can indicate that the bike was crashed. So can a coat of nice new paint. I know of cases where badly-repaired, crash-damaged bikes have fallen apart, killing their unfortunate new owners. What you want to see are a certain number of inevitable nicks and scrapes, but no major dents, rust spots, or welds.

Count into the cost of a used bike a complete overhaul and lubrication, and replacement of cables. Note condition of tires, brake blocks, chain, and be guided accordingly on price. Read the sections on Maintenance and Repair to learn how to assess components for wear and useful life.

In the matter of price, you will find at times that people have an inflated idea of what a bike is worth. A common sequence is, "Cost $XXX, selling for only $YYY". Well, $XXX might be what they paid for it, but the average retail price of the bike when new might be another story. Rummage through back issues of cycling magazines, ask friends, etc., but develop your own information and make your own calculations as to what a bike is worth. Do not feel bad about sticking within the limit of what you can afford or want to spend. If a bike is a great bargain, but outside your range, someone else will have the treat – or perhaps the vendor will lower the price.

If you are looking at an expensive machine and/or one with full suspension or other sophisticated components, it could be worth arranging for an examination by a competent bike shop, at your expense. A confident vendor will probably agree to a sale price "subject to survey." If the seller pushes that a bike is a bargain, anyone with a lick of sense would whip out the money, then pass. You want a decent price, sure, but the foremost thing is to get a good bike.

One temptation that might come your way is a stolen bike. There are lots of them for sale. Many street markets are venues for stolen machines, and in some areas you can order the type of bike you want. Prices are incredible, 25 percent of list and often less, for bikes that are all but new. With such flourishing activity, it hardly seems a crime to get a bike this way. It is. Buying a stolen bike is stealing, of a particularly low, cowardly, and contemptible kind.

BICYCLE CONNECTION

In my hometown of Woodstock, New York, we've got this great guy, Mike. A preacher with a small church up on Overlook Mountain, Mike is a bike nut. He runs a kind of repair service known as the Old Spokes Home, and is constantly connecting people and bikes – everything from reconditioned clunker, single-speed "Woodstock Specials" to full-bore road racing machines. It's not just – as you might guess – that I personally like Mike and appreciate his enthusiasms. He puts bikes together very capably, with a nice feeling for integrity, at good value. If there is someone like Mike in your area, then this could be an excellent route for acquiring a bike. You'll probably need to be patient until you find what you want.

RECYCLE BIKES

If you are broke, dig up a bike for free. Try the recycling center, scout out rubbish dumps. People sometimes throw away complete working bikes, but more often, you will find incomplete and damaged machines. Pick the best bits off three or four such wrecks and build a bike. It's a lot of work, and you will have to improvise tools and exercise ingenuity, but it can certainly be done.

KEEPING YOUR BIKE

This is a serious problem, and it can have a major effect on the kinds of bikes you ride and where and how you use them. In the US, millions – yes, millions – of bikes are stolen every year, and not just on the street; most thefts are from homes, garages, and apartment storage areas. Once a bike is gone, it's unlikely to come back. Local registration programs are spotty; some towns have them, others do not. There are two nationwide registry programs (see below), but not all police know about them. Most of the bikes the police find are sold at auction.

You want to prevent a theft from occurring in the first place, and it is important to realize that this will be a daily agenda. You might think a lock is the answer. No. There are strong locks, but none are proof against attack. Lightweight chain and cable locks are worthless; many can be cut apart faster than they can be opened with a key. High security locks vary. Some are pathetic and a rotten way to swindle people of their money, others are strong enough to leave most thieves gasping for breath – but not always. It is less a matter of the strength of the lock – any of them can eventually be broken – than the talent and resources of the particular thief. Many locks that can ably resist crude physical attacks can be opened quickly and quietly with a professional lock pick, a tool that is unfortunately readily available. Finally, and very sadly, the kind of lock you use may not make an iota of difference, because many thieves will simply cut the frame to steal the components and accessories.

One reason bike theft is such a problem is that thieves operate with relative impunity. When an attempt at theft takes place, even if there are plenty of people around, unless they have been previously enlisted it is unlikely that any of them will interfere.

I once arranged a bike theft for a magazine article. We locked a bike to a fence railing on a busy street, positioned a photographer in a nearby building, and sent in our own professional thief. The deed was accomplished in seconds. A voluminous raincoat concealed the actual snipping of the cable lock, which the thief tidily tucked away in a pocket before riding off on the bike. Nearby people did not notice a thing. We could not believe how easy it was. We repeated the experiment six times, making the theft progressively more and more obvious. On the final go, the thief marched up to the bike, hauled out the snips and cut the cable in full view of nearby pedestrians, and still got away with the bike. One person watched, but did nothing.

If you use a bike solely for recreation and sport, the issue of theft may not be a great problem. If you use a bike for transport, then out on the street, there is no lock that you can absolutely count on to resist attack, and few places where the public will act to prevent a theft. The only way to know for a fact that your bike will not be stolen on the street is to not leave it there in the first place.

A good bike should be kept indoors. This is usually simple enough at home. At work, it is increasingly common for employers to provide secure cycle parking and changing rooms with showers, because employees who cycle to work are more punctual, take fewer sick days, and are more productive! Providing cycling facilities is a lot less expensive than providing car parking. Businesses that want to be in the vanguard are going this route not just because they like being green, but because it pays.

Workplace parking for bikes is what some business types call a win-win situation, and where you work, whether you are the president or the janitor, you can score Brownie points and gain considerable personal convenience by initiating parking for bikes. There's usually some nook or cranny that will serve: a little used storage room, space down in the basement or utility room, and so on. If not, look afield; a nearby garage or other facility might be suitable. For the cost of a single car space, 20 or more bikes can be parked. If your workplace is too small, look around: there might be a nearby business with enough employees to make creating cycle parking facilities worthwhile.

Paid bicycle parking is a growing option. These establishments provide secure bike parking, showers, and changing rooms, lockers for your riding gear, and even repair and maintenance facilities. Some have their own shops, so you can book your bike for service while you are at work. To see if there is one near you, check with bike shops and your local campaign group.

Locking on the Street

Sometimes you will just have to lock up on the street. The essential point to grasp is that there is no absolute defense. Your strategy is to make a theft difficult enough so that a potential thief will move on and try elsewhere.

Most thieves only know how to break one kind of lock, and carry one specific tool for this purpose. One core trick for improving your odds is to use two or three different types of locks: a hefty U-lock, say, backed by an equally strong chain or armored cable, and a lighter but still strong shackle, or a long length of cable. The problem here is weight, and some people get around this by leaving a collection of locks at their regular journey destination, and carrying only one lock on the bike, for emergency use or for when locking up for short periods of time.

• Guarantees

Some locks are sold with guarantees that promise to pay you the value of your bike up to a stated amount should the bike be stolen as a result of the failure of the lock to prevent the theft. Such guarantees are largely useless. The problem is that most theft claims made under lock guarantees are fraudulent, and to protect themselves, lock manufacturers and distributors have in place a formidable array of formal requirements and conditions. For a guarantee to be effective, you must within a specified time period register your bike with the manufacturer, showing a bill of sale or valuation from a bike shop (no payment if a different bike is stolen). You'll have to say if you have any other insurance, and any misreporting on this or any other information can invalidate the guarantee. In the event of a theft, you have to file a police report within a specified period and produce copies of same. In many cases, you've got to demonstrate that you used the lock properly, and in many if not all, you have to produce the broken lock – and I can't count the number of times I've heard of both bike and lock vanishing. Finally, and by no means least, the guarantee payment is less whatever cover you may have from insurance elsewhere. Since home insurance often covers a bike – more paperwork and trouble – the payout from a lock guarantee when it finally comes is peanuts. I understand well enough why lock makers and distributors are stiff about guarantee requirements. But the upshot is that guarantees are no substitute for proper insurance (see below), and more to the point, are no assurance that a lock is going to work. As a marketing ploy, which is all they ever were, guarantees are dead.

• Good Locks

What's a good lock? I do not have nice things to say here. For starters, you can eliminate locks with round keys. These were great – until lock and security firms made sophisticated round key picking tools freely available to anyone with a few dollars in their pocket. If you are shocked, don't be; think of how easy it is to obtain master keys for cars, which are rather more expensive than bikes. At any rate, locks with straight keys, while not unpickable, at least are more difficult to pick than round key mechanisms. However, it needs to be a straight key which pushes the lock pins sideways, not up and down as with common household keys.

According to the police, the majority of bike thefts are not carried out by organized international crime cartels and trained thieves armed

Lock frame and wheels . . .

with sophisticated lock picks or powerful gasoline-powered orbital disc cutters. Most thefts are committed by opportunists equipped with basic implements such as poles, axes, pry bars, and pliers. The squelch on this seemingly good news is that this lot, too, can melt through all but the stoutest of locks in seconds. Yes, most of the high tech locks touted as the ultimate in security and sold for enough money to fund a big party or a workable used bicycle, can be blown apart by any Neanderthal with enough brains to use a hammer or iron bar.

Only a few locks are able to put up stiff resistance to a sustained physical attack: the heaviest, top of the line shackle U-locks, and ultraheavy hardened chains secured with a mini U-lock. The massive Kryptonite New York U-lock is a top seller and is extremely strong, but the current model has a round key, and for me at least, this is a big downer. I don't buy the idea that bike thieves are all cretins, because I know of many instances when very fine bikes have been stolen in circumstances that were selective to say the least, with no apparent resistance from the lock. Other Kryptonite models have not done well in tests.

I've been using Abus Granit U-locks from Germany, which feature a pick resistant straight key. The locks have the usual quality features such as hardened exterior, center crossbar lock mechanism, and double locking (both ends of the shackle, or U-shaped portion), and a mounting bracket for carrying a lock on a bike that works. Abus also has a neat little mini U-lock called the Swing, made for the front wheel on a scooter and only big enough to do a bike frame tube, but small and light enough to carry for emergency use or as a back up for a primary lock. Abus locks are not backed by a pay-for-your-bike guarantee, but are endorsed by a spate of European testing organizations.

Abus also do a Granit model which is a steel cable armored by hardened steel cups. This is a heavy piece of equipment, but at around 2 kg still lighter than the ultimate business in security: thick, hardened steel chain joined with a mini U-lock made for motorcycles. These weigh around 3 kg and are what I use as a primary lock when securing on the street. I like their flexibility,

because this makes the locks more adaptable, and also easier to carry – get the twist right, and you can double-loop a chain into a fairly compact bundle. The Kryptonite New York model chain is a tower of strength, but again, the lock mechanism is a round key. The Squire ML2L chain has a straight key lock.

In giving you a few particulars on brands, I want to emphasize that high security locks can and do vary enormously in performance. I once was toasted in a national newspaper, because in a cycle magazine test report I had dismissed a new model of lock with the statement that it had been destroyed in one second. The newspaper article indicated that my report was possibly biased because of my commercial association as a distributor of high security locks in Europe, an activity which in fact had discontinued long before. I guess the lock manufacturer, and the lazy journalist who cast aspirations on my credibility without contacting me for my side of the story or to check facts, just could not believe that one of their locks had been flinderized in a second.

You had better believe it. I've busted more locks than I can count, and know of lots of instances where particular types of locks had specific vulnerabilities. On the other hand, if I were given a random selection of locks to test, I'd get through some very quickly, while others would have me reaching for tools that are too time-consuming for practical use on the street. Hand the same bunch of locks to someone else, and you'll get a different result. There's no consistency, partly because technical experts and bike testers do not have the single-minded intensity of a thief, and partly because knowledge about lock breaking techniques is diffuse.

• Using Locks

No lock is invulnerable, but a decent lock, properly used, will put up enough of a fight to perhaps win the match. Your entire strategy for dealing with thieves in terms of locks is not to aim, as it were, for a knockout defense, but to last for enough distance to wear out an attack. Here is how to use locks on the street:

• Always lock your bike. A snatch takes but a moment. Thefts where the owner left their bike for "just a few seconds" are legion. If you do not have your hands on your bike, it should be locked up. If you are on a sport ride by yourself, you probably should carry a lock, as any number of things could arise to separate you from the bike. If you buddy up, then you can stand guard for each other when ducking to the toilet or getting a cappuccino. The same logic applies to commuting runs, even when you have a battery of locks permanently stationed at your destination.

• Lock your bike to seriously immobile objects such as heavy railings, lamp posts or parking signs. Make sure your bike cannot be lifted free of a pole. Trees are generally no good, because they can be cut. Ditto wire mesh fences.

• Use at least two and preferably three high security locks of different types. Lock the frame and both wheels. Ideally, use one lock to do the frame and rear wheel, another lock for the frame and front wheel, each lock to a different stationary object. The third lock should be used as suits the type: a mini U-lock can be yet another defence for the frame, a long cable lock can be twined through all the various bits such as saddle, wheels, etc. Forget alarms. Also forget disabling the bike by loosening the axle quick-release levers; a thief can just carry the bike away.

• Fit locks tightly, leaving as little room as possible for inserting tools, pry bars or jacks. With U-locks, try to avoid exposing the cross-bar (the bit with the lock mechanism) to a lever or car jack attack; place it where there are soft, tangled bits of your bike (ulp!) and not next to a pole or railing which could lend support to a pry bar or jack. To reduce bulk, some folks use a small U-lock around the rear wheel inside of the stays, and a pole. A wheel and tire are diffi-cult to cut, and the resilence of the tire helps defeat prying or shock attacks.

• Be selective about where you lock up. Obviously, avoid dark alleys and out-of-the-way locations where thieves can work undisturbed, but do not let the fact that a location is well-lit or well-travelled beguile you into thinking it is safe. Certain neighborhoods and locations are a bad bet at any time. In my north London neck of the woods, parking a bike at the local sports center is equivalent to throwing it off a cliff. Bone up on your territory.

• Try to enlist help. Although many thefts have occurred in broad daylight in view of hundreds of onlookers, more than once I've had a bike saved by an alert citizen who was willing to interfere. The cashier at the movies, the newstand vendor, the greengrocer, the waitress and chef at the cafe, are all potential allies. Speak to them, ask them to keep an eye out for your bike however they can, and then if they notice something funny happening, they are more likely to do something about it, if only to give a shout – which might be enough. If they don't know it is your bike, then seeing someone fiddling with it, how are they to know it is a theft? This is where you start to get into lifestyle – buy your stuff from small stores on the

"The only practical War Cycle."

streets where you lock up, slide some change to a bum, make friends around, say hello to folks – and you might improve the odds in your favor. Yes, there are those who will watch a bike theft with no more than idle curiosity, but there are also plenty of people will lend a hand if they know to do so.

And of course, you're one of those, yes?

At Home

Home and safe? Not quite. As stated, many bike thefts are from homes, garages, sheds, apartment storage areas, and yards. You've got to lock up at home, too, and how you do it will depend on your circumstances. As on the street, it's not much use just locking the bike to itself, because a thief can carry it away and then open the lock at his or her leisure. You need to fasten the bike to a railing or other substantial fixture, or install a bracket. The latter type of equipment ranges from relatively inexpensive simple wall brackets held in place with expanding bolts, for use with your street lock, to complete locking systems such as the top-rated, gulp-priced Serious 500. Brackets might slow a thief down, a system such as the Serious 500 would probably stop them cold.

Try to place the bike out of sight. Keeping a bike handy (but locked!) by the front door or in front of the house is fine when you are going in and out, but the permanent parking spot should be out of view of the street, and ideally, casual callers as well. Here, we are getting into the broader area of parking and storage, which is a little difficult, because I don't know your particular circumstances. But whether space is tight or free to burn, these are the priorities that should be balanced:

• Access. Ideally, you want to be able to come and go with your bike with ease. If every departure and arrival is a major production, you won't use your bike as much. If an entrance hall or something similar is part of your abode, this can be good location. If the ceiling has enough height, you might be able to hang the bike on a wall. There are many brackets available, some offer

ingenious, space-saving ways of holding a bike, any of them can be fastened in place with big screws or bolts which you can make theft resistant. You lock the bike to the bracket – an arrangement which is anything but invulnerable, but still a hassle for a thief.

• Storing a bike outside under a cover is no good. Aside from the fact that the bike is more vulnerable to theft, there's rot and rust from condensation. If you want your bike to last, keep it indoors.

• Bike-specific area. It's no good banging a bike into a closet used for linens or swell clothes, because things are sure to get dirty. In any case, you need an area for helmets, pumps, tools, and other bike-related gear. Look your place over and consider the possibilities. Is there a boiler/utility room for the house? Could a space be converted? Is there space above? With high ceilings, you can often rig some kind of pulley system to send a bike aloft; if you go this route, make sure that all fittings are double secure.

A garage or shed is great in terms of convenience, but these locations are usually more vulnerable, so you need to beef up the general level of security and strength of locking systems. Many garage doors are made of paper thin aluminum which can be cut with a dull knife. Garden sheds are often made of wood boards which can be ripped off with any old thing. You'll have to study up on possibilities for reinforcement and adding more locks, and if you are not handy at such things, get someone to do it for you. An expense, but consider yourself lucky – having a nice, secure shed or garage means you can go to town on the number of bikes, easily manage big tandems and HPVs, and probably have a neat workshop, too.

If you have your own house, or can get enough people in a building to cooperate, one possibility is to create a bikeport, outside in the case of a small home, inside in the case of a larger bulding. An advantage here is that from the get-go, construction can be security conscious, with the bikeport made in concrete, brick, or cinder block, and fitted with barred windows and a bombproof door. Be sure to provide ventilation and consider having a small fan and/or heater unit to minimize damp and condensation.

Another tactic for urbanites is to rent a garage and share it with other bike owners. I get nervous at the thought of 20 to 30 bikes in one place, but this sort of arrangement is standard practice in cities such as Amsterdam, where space is really tight. For a garage owner, it's a good deal: the take from 20 cyclists is double the top charge for a car. It's dead easy to provide racks for 20 or more bikes, and security is not bad – the garage is locked, and bikes are locked to the racks.

You'll probably have to use some ingenuity to sort out an efficient and secure bike parking scheme for yourself. It's worth the effort. You want the bike where it is handy without falling over it, and it should be safe.

After the Fact

You've got four bike theft contingency options: documentation, marking, registration, and insurance.

• Documentation. Keep a record of your bike's particulars, including the serial number, which is usually stamped on the bottom bracket. Take pictures of the bike. These will be invaluable if the bike is stolen and you want to post "Wanted" notices.

• Marking. Make up small cards which say "This bike was stolen from" with your contact details. Have the cards laminated in plastic and insert them into the head tube, seat tube, and anyplace else they might be found. Have your name, address, and telephone number stamped onto the bottom bracket. Cards, and also electronic transponders, can be found and discarded. Obliterating a name and address stamp leaves a scar which says "hot bike" to any bike shop or conscientious individual.

• At least two organizations run national registration programs. For a fee, you register the bike, and are given a tag sticker to place on the bike. The tags are difficult to tamper with or remove, and if the police recover the bike, help your chances for getting it back. The tags also appear to have a deterrent effect.

National Bike Registry, 2855 Telegraph Ave., Suite 304, Berkeley, CA 94705 USA.
Tel: 800 848-BIKE (2453) and 510 665 0280.
Fax: 510 665 0285.
E-mail: staff@nationalbikeregistry.com.
Web: www.nationalbikeregistry.com.

Bike Star, 3030 North 3rd St., Suite 200, Phoenix, AZ 85012 USA.
Tel: 602 241 8547.
Fax: 602 241-8571.
E-mail: info@bikestar.org.
Web: www.bikestar.org.

• Insurance. I have mixed feelings about insurance for bikes. For what it costs to cover just the daily use machines in my family – never mind Sunday specials and test bikes – I can buy a new bike every year. Insurance costs anywhere from five to twenty percent of a bike's worth, depending on where you live and the value of the machine. Yet it has to be said that if you cannot afford to replace your bike, you should insure it. Even an unsuccessful or partial (of components) theft may do terminal damage to your bike.

Another dimension of insurance is third party cover. Should you be held liable in an accident, this could be invaluable. If you are worth a fair piece of change, cover this flank.

The cheapest way to obtain insurance is as an extension of a household contents policy. You'll probably have to take out an all-risks or special bike extension, and read the small print with care. Most such policies have a low limit.

Racing and touring associations and organizations, and many campaign groups, offer insurance policies for members. Terms vary, and can include loss, damage, and theft, and new for old inclusive of accessories. Check around, and be sure to ask at your bike shop, because they are ones who get the replacement business, and might know which insurance firms deal with claims promptly and fairly.

§!X@!*§•!

What we should do is hang bike thieves – slowly, starting fairly early in the morning, only on national holidays. That way, we could all be there, and we would have plenty of time for setting fire to their toes and torturing them in unspeakable, fiendish ways.

I hate bike thieves, and so does anyone who has ever lost a bike. But the fantasy of applying draconian measures to them is a non-starter. I will defend a bike from an active theft, but after the fact, extracting revenge in the guise of punishment is neither humane nor practical.

The justice system does not rate bike theft. Bike thieves do not go to jail. Folks, you can go out and steal a car, commit grand larceny and 40 other crimes, and if you play your cards right, only get a

slap on the wrist. Where are we going to get hard time for a bike thief? In any case, unless a thief is caught in the act of stealing, there is no way to prove that he or she is guilty. Someone in possession of a stolen bike only need say "bought it off someone on the street" and they go free.

What about the police? Mixed results. Depends on the city, and country, too. I received a lot of interest and help when I circularized a whole bunch of police stations with "Wanted" notices in pursuit of a stolen machine. Officers called and wrote to me to say that they and their families would keep an eye out for the bike. I do not think the police like bike thieves very much, either.

Unquestionably, there are police officers who have made and continue to make real efforts toward preventing bike thefts and restoring recovered bikes to their owners. I'm glad, but the fact remains, few stolen bikes are recovered, and most of them are sold at auction. On a broad scale, the police do not have the resources for this kind of problem.

What if you catch someone trying to steal your bike? Chase them off. If a thief is belligerent, you are entitled to defend your property and person.

What about if you see someone riding your recently stolen bike? This is a difficult situation. I know of many instances where people have gone to the police saying "Hey, I just saw a guy on my stolen bike," only to be told: "Get lost." A few individual police officers might make like the cavalry, but in most cases they will not. What you are left with is personal intervention, and you need to think very carefully about this one. Confront the rider and demand your bike back, and you are likely to be told to **** off. If you attack to get the bike, you can be in a world of trouble. Bike theft is minor, violent assault is not. Incredibly, you could be sued!

What about a citizen's arrest? You know, a bit of fancy hung fugu, a march down to the police station, and triumphant "Got the villian here!" Guess what, vigilante attack or quasi-legal citizen's arrest makes no difference, because anyone riding a stolen bike is innocent. How do you prove they stole it? This is one reason why police often refuse to become involved. They know it's a non-starter.

If you catch someone in the act of stealing your bike, you're not obliged to be kind. However, if you encounter someone riding a bike you think or even know for a fact is yours, attacking that person is out of line. What if you made a mistake about the bike? What if you harmed someone who, say, had barrowed the bike from someone else, who in turn, did not know it was stolen?

Or how about wider consequences? I once loaned a first edition Stumpjumper bike to a friend, he turned his back for a moment while outside his building, and the bike was stolen. I had the serial number and other details, and the theft was reported to the police. A day or two later another friend who lived in the same house called to say "Hey, I saw your bike, followed the guy to his house!"

I shot over to my friends' apartment, and asked: "Right, what are you gonna do? Go over and get it? Call the police?"

My friends looked at me sadly. "Richard, they know where we live. It's a whole houseful of young men. If we go over there, or call the police on them, they'll come over and burn down the entire building. We're not going to do a thing."

With a sense of profound shock, I realized that my friends were absolutely right. It was not a question of courage – my friends were brave and strong. It was a matter of commonsense. The neighborhood was a tough one and firebombings were common. My bike, however much sentiment and value I attached to it, was not worth the lives of my friends (who later made up the loss in other ways).

Bikes are stolen all the time, no matter what precautions are taken, and the thieves steal because one way or another, they can get away with it. It is not a matter of poverty, social inequality, diminished opportunities, or bad mother's milk. Elsewhere in the world, other even less fortunate people do not steal. Mercy and consideration are exactly the qualities thieves lack, and there is no simple answer to this problem. In the end, theft is something that is around, like rain. If you run bikes over a lifetime, you are likely to lose at least one or two to thieves.

ALTERNATIVES

I noted down the cost of a stout home security system, three strong locks, and insurance, and the total came to enough to buy a decent bike, with suspension. Crazy, eh? If you have to lock up on the street, you might want to consider one of the following alternatives.

• Junkers

A serviceable, used roadster or old clunker can be purchased for less than the cost of a high security lock. It should preferably be rusty and beat-up, and as unattractive as possible. This is the default option in countries like the Netherlands, where the street machines are heavyweight roadsters, and fine bikes live indoors and only go out for Sunday rides.

• Disguise

Suppose you want to ride for good distances and really need a performance bike? One possibility is to have a bike shop custom build you a bike that is lightweight and mechanically sound, but rigged to look like a wreck. This means getting an old but lightweight frame, stripping off the transfers and splotching it with old paint and touches of rust, selecting components that are outdated but still functional, and burying the lot under a coating of oily grime. Tear the saddle cover. True artists decorate the bike with fake bird droppings. From a shop, a machine like this can be fairly pricy – there's a fair bit of work involved – but think of it as a custom bike with a difference. No, I'm not joking. I've got a bike exactly like this, and I like it a lot.

TESTIMONIAL.

To Messrs. Hillman, Herbert & Cooper, Ltd.

Ghostland, December, 1889.

Dear Sirs,—I left the old world through an accident, the result of a fall from a so-called safety bicycle by one of the too numerous jerry makers, who, being without the means to build cycles with limbs of steel, resort to the fatal practice of casting in large pieces.

My present object in writing to you is to express my unbounded gratitude for the "Premier" cycle you made for me. It carries my weight well, and although the roads are full of clinkers and other rough products of combustion, the grade of steel of which it is composed is so fine, and its temper so excellent, that the 5,000,000 miles I have traversed upon it have not impaired it to any appreciable extent.

In contrast to this I have seen machines brought here by ill-advised Ghosts, which I will simply describe as *not* "*Premiers,*" made of such common soft material that they have melted like butter in the sun.

You will be somewhat astonished at the number of miles I have ridden in this land, but the fact is that one has to take a deal of exercise to keep one's form as a Ghost, and I prefer to take all mine on a "Premier." Besides, a Ghost has to be in many places at one time, and that means fast travelling.

I congratulate you on that wonderful ride on a "Catford Premier" safety by Holbein!!! **324 miles at one go!!!** If ever that man comes to these parts, where the physical conditions are so different to those you are familiar with, and gets down to the weight of a healthy Ghost, he will do about 1,000 miles a day.

I have learnt with great satisfaction that you have made more cycles than any other maker during the past season; that your factories are the largest, and your machinery the finest in the world. I should wonder how your rivals find purchasers were it not for the fact that I know all cyclists are not able to get your wonderful machines, the supply, great as it is, being limited.

I enclose my photo, taken by an old gentleman in these parts who has only just commenced the photographic art. The likeness is not a very good one; you may therefore not recognise the features of,

Yours very truly,

JOHN NOTELEKS.

• Folding Bike

Folding bikes with 20-inch wheels have enough performance for moderate journeys, and are a definite option for eliminating many security problems. Few 20-inch wheel folders easily reduce to a really compact package, however, and this can be awkward at times. Folding bikes with small 16-inch wheels can be very compact, and therefore manageable in almost any situation, but typically are only good for short journeys. See the chapter Special Bikes and Trikes for more information.

DIRECT ATTACK

Successfully protecting your bike when you are not around is only one aspect of bike security. Depending on your age and sex, and the value of your bike, you are also subject to direct assault while riding. Usually this crime occurs in parks and other isolated places, and to a lesser extent, in slum neighborhoods. In form, it can range from seemingly friendly and casual interest on the part of strangers who "would like to try your bike out," to someone leaping out from behind a parked car, knocking you flat with a club, and riding away on your bike. This has even happened to entire packs of racers.

Once assaulted, there is little you can – or should – do unless you are an action freak or have experience in physical combat. No bike is worth a cracked skull or a knife in the gut. You would not have been jumped in the first place if your opponent(s) did not have an advantage.

On the other hand, it is sickening and degrading to be ripped off. If you're up against three guys armed with knives and clubs, pack it in. You don't want to be only a fading memory. Think of those who love you. However, if you are simply up against an aggressor who is forcing you into the role of victim, then stand your ground and fight. Better, attack. On principle. It's OK to lose the bike, the crown jewels, a million pounds. You are worth more. What's not OK is to lose your own self respect by quitting when you might have had a fighting chance.

Spirit matters. I've seen little old grannies back down nasty drunks. Most bullies are motivated and stimulated by cowardice. Deep inside, they are scared themselves, and bullying is a way of denying this. If they sense rabbit in someone else, they go for them. If they sense fighting spirit, they may back off. There are lots of circumstances where you can and should fight, win or lose.

Where you draw the line is up to you. Fighting takes experience. Bullies may be cowards, but many of them are seasoned, and can be quick and vicious. Know what you are doing; foolish bravery can get you killed. In any case, do not let a violent encounter take you by surprise. Think about and prepare for it now.

For example, one kind of attack consists of a group of people fanning out across a street with the obvious intention of stopping you. Forget negotiation, you might as well just hand the bike over. If there is room, hang a fast U-turn and get gone. If you are already trapped, shake off any victim mentality/impulse to hit the brakes, and instead yell like a maniac, pour on the power, and head straight for one of the people blocking you. Don't fake. Try to hit them. Keep an iron grip on the bars. In the end, most anyone will make a scrambling effort to get out of the way. You can do this kind of thing only if you are prepared. Otherwise, you will just roll to a stop in dumb surprise, and one of the crowd will relieve you of your bike.

Understand basics. On the street, when someone wants to make contact with a stranger, the right thing is to give a hail or wave or other indication of interest in such a way as to give freedom of choice in response. It's called open hands/no weapons. If a few people suddenly cross the street and intersect your intended path, or otherwise cut down your options, this is a very aggressive act and you've genuine cause for alarm. Vanish. It's not just the bike. One friend of mine who ignored the portent of a gang of four men moving into his path was knocked off his bike by a simple touch on the handlebar, and then for fun, was propped up against a fence and methodically beaten to a pulp. He was kicked in the head more than 30 times and is happy – and lucky – to still be alive.

If you can avoid confrontations in the first place, so much the better. Do your exploring of new places by daylight, and stick to routes you know at night. Stay out of isolated areas in parks at any time, and out of parks altogether at night. If you travel though rough areas move along at a smart pace, and at night stay on well-lit, well-travelled streets. Above all else, be alert. Look for likely ambushes and people who seem unduly interested in you. Do not assume that all other cyclists are your allies.

I have put the information about bike security problems and some of the fun situations and people you can meet while cycling in this chapter because you need to make a realistic evaluation of the pros and cons of owning a bike. If you work in a bad neighborhood and your employer won't let a bike on the premises, my advice would be to get another job, but perhaps that isn't possible. If you are a woman in an urban area, you are a more likely target for direct assault. If . . . if . . . I think that the advantages of owning and using a bike way outweigh the disadvantages, but riding a bike does expose you to the world in new ways, and it would be unfair not to tell you about some of the problems you could encounter.

Accessories

9

Anti-puncture products • Carrier racks, panniers, and bags • Catalogs • Child seats • Clothing • Computers • Helmets • Lights • Pumps •Wheel discs • and more

WHEN BICYCLES WERE JUST FOR KIDS, CYCLE accessories were tinny and cheap. Worthless equipment is still sold in supermarkets and other price driven outlets, but the renaissance in cycling and in quality bikes has stimulated the development of a wide range of well-made, truly functional accessories. There's some really good stuff around, which is great, because the right selection of extra equipment can make a crucial difference in cycling efficiency,

CATALOGUES SENT FREE UPON APPLICATION.

comfort, and pleasure. Think about and choose your accessories with care. Keep in mind cycling's first law: weight is everything. Ensure that each item works well and will stand up to use, and expect to pay for it. The outlay for a full commuting or touring outfit can easily equal the cost of a bike. If you are on a tight budget, do not be lured by "good enough" cheap equipment, as it will only cause irritation. Improvise instead, and acquire better when you can afford to do so.

Air Pollution Masks

Air filter masks serve primarily to block large particles and grit. Some models utilize straining materials such as charcoal, which probably at least cut down one's intake of nasty chemicals and substances. My impression, however, is that the worst air pollutants march right on through. In any case, I've found that masks inhibit breathing and cause glasses to mist over. In the end, I think it's a personal thing; some people are comfortable with masks, others are not. It's a case of try and see. See Chapter 12, Traffic: Fast is Safe, for more information on the subject of air pollution.

Anti-puncture Products

Punctures are the bane of the cyclist, and not a year passes without the introduction of a new product claiming to eliminate the problem. Here's a brief run-down on the main types.

• Liquid Sealants

These can be used with Schraeder and two-piece Presta valves. Up to about 4 oz of liquid sealant is inserted through the valve into the inner tube. If you have one-piece Presta valves, the tube can be cut, the sealant inserted, and the tube patched. Also available are inner tubes already filled with sealant. The liquid is able to seal punctures and small cuts, but not large slashes, as from glass. If the tire suffers a major blowout the sealant can create a thorough mess. It can also put paid to a tire valve. After six months to a year the solvent evaporates, reducing the effectiveness of the sealant.

Sealants can be effective for specific situations, such as thorn-littered roads or trans-Sahara expeditions, over limited periods of time. If you do a high number of miles on littered urban streets and are plagued by punctures, and are prepared to replace the inner tube/sealant combination every six months or so, then using sealant may help. Otherwise, these products are more trouble than they are worth.

• Tapes

These are thin ribbons of plastic or aramid inserted inside the tire between the casing and the inner tube. Extraordinarily tough and pliable, they are effective at warding off punctures from ordinary broken glass, nails, and thorns, but not items such as needle sharp carpet tacks. However, the tape itself can cause punctures. This seems to happen when the tape changes position away from the central bead of the tire, or if the wrong size is used, or if the tape is of poor quality with sharp edges.

Using tape in a light, narrow section tire noticeably degrades performance. One might as well use a heavier, more durable tire in the first place. For beefing up heavy duty commuting tires, tape can be a help, but the tires need to be deflated once a month and the position of the tape checked. In comparison with sealants, which can be messy, tapes are clean and do not complicate mending a puncture.

• Belted Tires

Tires with a belt of aramid or wire mesh embedded in the casing are effective at reducing the number of punctures, and do not have the problems of loose tapes. They are expensive – too bad if a catastrophe strikes early – and increase weight and rolling resistance, but they do work.

• Heavy-duty and Thorn-proof Tubes

Thick inner tubes with tiny bores, and tubes made of special substances that resist penetration, are effective at reducing the number of punctures. Thick tubes are heavy, however, and really cut down performance. Special substance tubes such as latex are a gamble; fine so long as they work, but expensive when they don't – which can be sooner rather than later.

• Flint-catchers or Nail-pullers

Small half-loops of wire that ride just above the tire and brush off shards of glass, pebbles, and other nasty things. Most effective with tubular and smooth tires. Near impossible to fit if you use fenders.

• Solid Inner Tubes

No! Fitting a solid inner tube and tire onto a rim is typically the kind of event you will remember, with pain, for the rest of your days. Riding is even worse. Solid tubes are heavy and magnify the gyroscopic qualities of a wheel, making it fatally difficult to change direction when riding. Definitely a case of once tried, never again.

• Solid Tires

Double no! One hundred percent puncture proof and 100 percent useless as a tire. High, high rolling resistance and a boneshaker ride that will destroy a bike, if the rider lasts that long.

• Summary

The pneumatic tire was invented and developed because it gives decreased rolling resistance and greater control and comfort. It works because there is air inside. Why mess around with the basic concept? If you want to go faster, use a lighter, more supple tire; if you want more protection, use a heavier, more robust tire. On my mountain bike, I often use big gnarlies when riding in the city during the dark months. They're a touch slow, but tough as old boots.

I replace tires before they become too worn or beat up, keep them inflated hard, try to stay out of trouble by veering around broken glass and other unfriendly debris, and carry a spare tube and a puncture repair kit as a matter of course. Also a pump. I'd rather rely on myself than a product that might or might not work. Most punctures can be mended in minutes. If there is bad weather or a real hurry, I use the spare and mend the puncture later at home, when warm and cosy.

Bells and Horns

Your own squawk box is a wonderful noise maker – quick, reliable, and wonderfully expressive. You can issue a friendly whistle or call, or shout loud enough to lift an errant motorist out of their seat or freeze a pedestrian in their tracks.

The traditional cyclist's bell has some charm and little else. Excited kids, stumbling old folks, and people like me who are part deaf cannot hear these little bells. In any case, tinkle-ding is too weak to be audible in the rough, brawling conditions which often prevail in urban traffic.

The other extreme is represented by freon and air-powered horns, which have more than enough volume to give dumb pedestrians brown pants. The problem here is that the main motivation for their use is revenge and retribution rather than safety. I speak from gleeful experience. Golden Flash, my first 10-speed, mounted a gift from my father, a long, great monster brass Bombay taxi driver's horn. It had a deep, vibrant, penetrating bellow which sounded like the air horns on the biggest truck in the world. It completely paralyzed

wandering pedestrians, and wiped motorists back into kindergarten.

On a bike, you're vulnerable, and when pedestrians go into your path without a care for your safety, it is natural to be startled and then angry. They would not be so reckless if you were a big bus or truck. Of course you want to blast them. I won't say no, either. Right up the . . . but people, if the situation is tight, your hands belong on the handlebars and brakes, not fiddling with horn buttons. If the danger of collision is acute, you definitely will not have the time nor presence of mind to go for a button. The thing you've got right on tap, pretested, and programmed for automatic independent action, is your ability to yell. Horns and bells are useless extra weight.

A median path of sorts is a whistle, which is sharp and loud and will catch the attention of many pedestrians, but again, not all of them. Problem is, although you hang a whistle on a string around your neck, you've got to ride holding it between your teeth if you want instant blaster effect. It's the sort of thing that irked cyclists do for a while, and then drop.

Cables

In the course of regular maintenance on your bike the brake and gear cable wires and housings will have to be replaced. These are technologically sophisticated items and can be fairly expensive. An excellent upgrade which will give both better performance and greater long term economy are Nokon Trac-Pearls, a new cabling system from Germany. The outer casing is formed from a combination of short aluminium rods and beads that you custom fit to your bike. This results in an articulated casing which is more flexible than the standard type, yet is also less prone to compress. Cable runs can be shorter and neater, and performance is smoother and more powerful. The casing is durable, which is economical because only cable wires have to be replaced. Various colors. I haven't been able to track down a US source yet, but try your local cycle gems shop, or try over the pond from:

Sonic Cycles, 48 Lambs Conduit Street, London WC1N 3LJ ENGLAND. Tel/Fax: +44 020 7405 1099.

Car Racks

There are two kinds of racks for carrying bikes on cars: rear mount and top mount. Rear mount versions are less expensive and usually designed for quick attachment to the vehicle. One type holds two to three bikes in a stack, which means that preventing the bikes from scratching each other requires extra padding, and getting this all right and tight can make loading up a production. I prefer the straight on (bike pointing in same direction as car) type of rack which keeps the bikes apart and individually accessible, such as the Cradle by Rhode Gear.

Top mount versions cost more, attach easily enough but are usually intended to be a semi-permanent mounting, and will hold up to six bikes. The machines are away from the road grit that tends to accumulate at the rear of a vehicle, but beware low overhangs. The Thule and LP models are stout and well made.

Avoid using car racks if you can. Their high aerodynamic drag increases fuel consumption — less of a problem in America than elsewhere in

the world, but still, why waste money? More to the point, bikes held out in the open for prolonged periods in bad weather at highway speeds take a beating, and can have water hammered into various vital nooks and crannies. Covers and protective accessories are available, but using them is a nuisance.

With the wheels off, a bike becomes a surprisingly compact package. Two people and two bikes can fit into most small cars, and middle size cars and up should be able to manage three of each. If you have a large party of people and a mess of bikes, consider using a small, covered trailer. This way you get plenty of space for extra baggage, wheels, and things. Also, when you get where you are going, the trailer provides a kind of mechanical base camp for the bikes.

Carrier Racks, Panniers, and Bags

• Bags and Packs

On all rides you need to carry a few essentials: a spare inner tube, puncture repair kit with tire levers, a pump or tire inflation device, and a multitool. The handiest way to carry bike bits is in a seat or wedge pack underneath the saddle. These packs come in a range of sizes and designs, from compact models with just enough room for the essentials, to large expedition rigs that can handle hefty quantities of gear. There's every size in between, and many models are expandable; undo a zip and they double in size. This is useful for holding a light jacket or vest.

Wedge packs usually have two types of mounting: either a Velcro strap and buckle combination, or a snap on/off cleat system. The former is better for tight, no sway mounting, the latter is more convenient for frequent on/off use, or if you have several different bikes. Whether you opt for small or large, simple or fancy, useful features are built-in reflective strips, and a mounting point for an LED rear light. (Otherwise, if the light is mounted on the seat post, the bag may obscure it.) Altura, Trek, Blackburn, and Topeak are all good brands, but see what is going – the shops are full of nice looking models at reasonable prices.

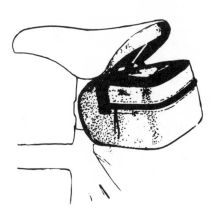

At least two kinds of riders are not keen on wedge packs: all out mountain bikers, and people who frequently lock up on the street. An increasingly popular option, particularly for mountain biking, is a waist pack or bum bag. Like wedge packs, these range from simple models to elaborate designs with multiple compartments and water bottle holders. Bum bags are good, because the weight is down on the hips where it does not foul up balance or bike handling too much, and bits and pieces are easy to hand. Also, when you park and leave the bike, your stuff automatically comes with you.

For around town use, the classic cyclists' cloth slingbag is really one of the most convenient things going. It travels with you on and off the bike and will manage books, papers, and a container or two of milk or juice. There are also large courier versions that can tote bulky loads.

For something with enough room to hold a helmet, some gear, and odd shopping, I prefer a knapsack or light back pack. Again, these are available in very simple versions that are fine for knocking around town, to sophisticated models designed specifically for cycling. Some of these are very technical, with anatomical harnesses, suspension to keep the pack off your body, special provision for various bike bits, hydration systems, extra loops, and all sorts of clever bits. They work very well. Around town, and on what you might call the casual trail, I use a simple day pack

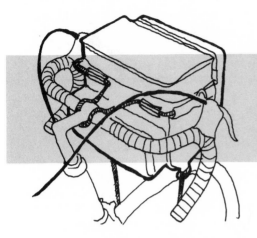

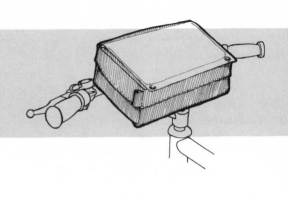

picked up for a song at a sale years ago. When the going counts, say an off-road ride in winter, I reach for a technical back pack that allows comfortable movement, but will stay with me even in a fall. Good brands are Karrimore, Trek and Altura.

Conventional wisdom used to be that the bike, not the rider, should carry the load. However, for mountain biking, using a back pack keeps the bike limber and versatile; in town, it keeps your stuff with you when you're off the bike. On long road rides and with heavy loads, it definitely is better to let the bike or a trailer (see Chapter 14, Cargo Cycles and Trailers) do the carrying. Starting at the front, if you've got a straight roadster bike, then a traditional old-fashioned wicker basket (wire in a modern version) is surprisingly useful. You can just chuck things in and go. As long as the load is not too heavy, steering will still be OK. Avoid the type which uses a support rack resting on the head tube; when the handlebars are turned, the rack scratches the head tube.

On a road bike with drop handlebars, some people elect for a handlebar bag, usually with a wire support. These hang well out in front, which has a rotten effect on steering. Bags made for flat bars, positioned over and behind the bars, are great; there's ready access for maps and bits, and no effect on steering.

• Panniers

Panniers mounted on carrier racks are the next sequence, and here the possibilities are quite dazzling: large bags, small bags, itsy-bitsy bags, bags that shrink or grow as required, bags that convert to back packs, and more. For around town use and for specialized applications such as photography, or carrying vital supplies of cool beer, you might find a padded trunk or rear pack bag useful. These sit on top of a rear carrier and usually have some kind of expansion feature.

Road warriors who need to trundle papers, computers, and what else back and forth from the office should have a look at a briefcase pannier. Some of these are very technical indeed. I quite like the Altura Workstation, which looks like your typical computer/multi-compartment bag, but which will mount to a pannier. A clever feature is an offset mounting, so that the bag will not foul a rider's heels. There's also a proper rain cover.

A type of pannier that can be a useful all-round carrier is made for holding bags of groceries. It has mesh sides and folds up out of the way when not in use. These panniers will also digest sports equipment, tools, or whatever.

• Carrier Racks

Carrier racks are required for mounting panniers, and are very useful on a working bike. Really robust models can support a passenger. Two-up on a bike is common in countries such as the Netherlands, where bikes are part of the transport structure.

For around town use, a lightweight alloy carrier rack with a spring clip will manage briefcases, parcels, and moderate loads. At the other extreme, a big, heavy steel rack such as seen on old-fashioned roadsters will handle pretty much anything you can fit on it. Most people prefer a good quality alloy rack for both lightness and strength. Look for four point fixing (drop outs and seat stays), which is better than three point (drop outs and brake bridge). Some models are characterized as "fast," meaning they are lightweight and weaker. Pointless. The carrier is for loads and might as well suffer the few extra ounces needed to do the job properly. I like Blackburn racks because they are strong and durable; I've one that has seen several bikes.

For touring and/or lots of baggage, use carrier racks front and rear to even out the load. It's important not to go too big on the rear panniers, because excess weight can unhinge the bike. At the front, for road touring, use a low rider design carrier rack that holds the panniers alongside the axle. This gives an enormous improvement for handling. If the mission is off-road, a traditional design front rack with a loading platform on top may be better, as low slung panniers tend to catch on branches and rocks. If you have a lot to carry, give serious consideration to using a trailer (see Chapter 14, Cargo Cycles and Trailers).

Prices for all this stuff vary; some are reasonable, others will make you blink or gulp. Once you know for sure what you need, it's usually a very worthwhile investment. If you are short of the ready, improvise. Bash together a rack from discarded lawn chairs and other aluminium bits, and stick on an orange crate. Some people have gone around the world with no more.

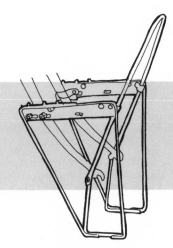

Low rider carrier rack

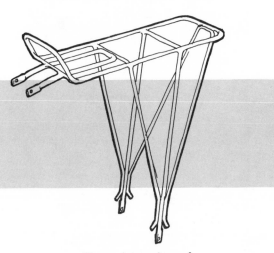

Four point carrier rack

Catalogs

Catalogs are fun for browsing and seeing what's around. Many are also full of useful tips and information. Keep in mind that catalogs pitch for sales and read their product descriptions with a pinch of salt. Bike shops usually have a larger selection of goods to choose from, and can give straight answers to questions such as "Which is best?" and "Which will do the job without breaking the bank?" There's also nothing like actually getting your hands on an item and trying it out. Play fair; if you deal with a shop and get good information from them, then give them the business. Yes, the price for an item might a few dollars more, but you save time and do not waste money on unsuitable gear.

Of course, buying mail order can be mighty convenient. If you know what you want, then with a single telephone call, the stuff is delivered right to your door in just a couple of days. And it is fun to look through catalogs, or cruise the net.

Another factor is price. Plenty of cycling equipment is really expensive. Many shops have web sites and sell all over the world. Last time I looked, there were over 150 listed. Some are very competitive on price, and offer savings that many people cannot afford to ignore. Fine – so long as you know what you are doing. If you hit a snag with, say, a fancy crankset, or a new set of brakes, and resort to a local

shop to sort it out, you may wind up spending more than if you had gone to the shop in the first place.

I've included a few international firms for interest and products not obtainable elsewhere. As a matter of note, US prices for European products are on average 25 percent less than in Europe, and as for the prices of US stuff in Europe – don't ask.

Bikes & Bits, F. W. Evans, PO Box 118, Leatherhead, Surrey, KT22 7YS England.
Tel: +44 01372 227979.
Fax: +44 01372 227978.
Web: www.evanscycles.com

Full of useful tips and straight on product information. If you go to Britain, Evans have a chain of shops where you can check out gear.

Bike Nashbar, 4111 Simon Road, Youngstown, OH 44512 USA.
Tel 800 627 4227.
E-mail: mail@bikenashbar.com.
Web: www.bikenashbar.com.

Plenty of goodies, and some amazing sales.

Encycleopedia, The Overlook Press, 2568 Route 212, Woodstock, NY 12498 USA.
Tel: 485 679 6838 and 800 473 1312.
E-mail: overlook@netstep.net.
Web: www.overlookpress.com.

European and not mail order, but does cover unusual and interesting products.

Performance Bicycle Shop, PO Box 2741, Chapel, Hill, NC 27514, USA.
Tel: 800 727 2453.
Web: www.performancebike.com.

Long in the business, good value proprietary products.

Colorado Cyclist, 3970 E. Bijou St., Colorado Springs, CO 80909-9946 USA.
Tel: 800 688 8600. Fax: 719 591 4041.
Web: www.coloradocyclist.com.

General cycling equipment.

The Third Hand, 12225 Highway 66, Ashland, OR 97520 USA. Tel: 541 488 4800. Fax: 541 482 0082. Web: www.thethirdhand.com.

Specialty in tools. A favorite.

Velo, 1830 N. 55th St., Boulder, CO 80301-2700 USA. Tel: 800 234 8356. Web: www.velogear.com.

Books, posters, clothes, gifts.

Child Seats and Trailers

Carrying a child on a bike is fun, and it is worth doing the job properly. A basic moulded plastic, rear mounted seat can manage a child weighing up to 40 pounds, and should include a wrap-around spoke guard to prevent feet from tangling in the spokes. These seats will also neatly hold a box of groceries. Ideally, the mounting hardware should be self contained and not depend on an existing carrier rack. Models are available that attach and detach within seconds. Use a mountain bike, or a road bike with a stiff frame. A so-called ladies' step through or open frame (without a top tube or crossbar) is not a good choice, because the extra weight of a child at the rear can induce frame whip and unstable handling.

One way around the handling problem caused by a heavy load at the rear is a seat that attaches directly to the crossbar and places the child between the adult's arms. I've a neat wicker model from China that just slips over the crossbar when needed.

Basic seats are exposed to the weather and do not provide sufficient support for the head if the child falls asleep. A nice example of a more refined design is the Babybike from Holland. This is a three-in-one baby seat, bike seat, and car seat. On a bike, the seat snaps into a rack with shock absorbing springs. There's a tent cover for complete protection against the weather, and a three point harness plus a belt. Information from:

Babybike Nederland bv, Postbus 372,
1400 AJ, Bussom, Netherlands.
Tel/Fax: +31 35 695 1908.
E-mail: babybike@tip.nl.

Nearer to home, the Rhode Gear Limo child seat doubles as a child chair when off the bike.

Another route for carrying children that works very well is a trailer. There are models that can quickly adapt from child trailer to stroller, and many can handle two children, or one child plus a good load of baggage. Some people worry about placing kids in a "vulnerable" trailer, but I think that overall, it is safer.

Although a rear mounted child seat can supposedly manage up to 40 pounds, once the weight goes over 20 pounds, bike handling starts to be comprised. Most trailers can handle up to 100 pounds. Also, in order to provide weather protection, most trailers have what amounts to a cage construction, which gives a child greater security than an open seat. A child trailer also doubles as a very effective load carrier for shopping, transporting a mountain of fishing gear to the pond, or as a ruse to facilitate bank robbery getaways. Finally, unhitch the trailer and you've got a regular bike, without a massive thing on the back. I've tried 'em all and for both long term use and fun, with children under age four trailers are the best route to go. There are lots of nice trailers coming onto the market, and good place for information on current models is the publication *Encycleopedia*, available from:

The Overlook Press, 2568 Route 212, Woodstock, NY 12498, USA.
Tel: 485 679 6838 and 800 473 1312.
E-mail: overlook@netstep.net.
Web: www.overlookpress.com.

If you want information on a range of trailers of all kinds, try:

Two Plus Two, Cliffe Fair Place, Cliffe High Street, Lewes, Sussex BN7 2RD England.
Tel/Fax: +44 01273 480479.
E-mail: twoplustwo@pavilion.co.uk.
Web: www.twoplustwo.uk.com.

Once a child is about age four, he or she can ride the back of a tandem and join the fun via a junior pedalling attachment. Tandems, especially good ones, can be expensive, but pay off as a long term investment. Children aged eight and up can ride on the road in the company of adults, but it's a nervous business because the adults must be 110 percent on the ball. As a rule of thumb, children need to be age 13 before they have a sufficient attention span to be safe when cycling on roads. A tandem as family transport can have a long life, and in any case, when no longer needed, can be sold on to another family. See the tandems entry in Chapter 6, for more information.

An interesting variation of the tandem is a half-bike or trailer that attaches to a regular bike. As with a tandem, the child can pedal and join in the fun, but take rests when needed.

Clothing

Cycle clothing is made for comfort and function and makes riding a lot more enjoyable. Take a simple thing like touring shorts. A good pair will have a lined crotch for comfort, and pockets with flaps and buttons so things don't get lost. Chill weather? There are jackets and trousers which are faced with nylon at the front to break the wind, but with regular fabric at the back for ventilation and ease of movement.

After shoes (see separate entry), good shorts and trousers are a priority. You can cycle in regular clothes, but they often have seams in the wrong places. The opposite way round works though; clothing comfortable for cycling can be used for other activities as well.

Current fashion is for roadies to have smooth, sleek clothes, and for mountain bikers to have loose, baggy clothes. However, smooth, close fitting clothes move easily and reduce the prospect of chafing. This is why

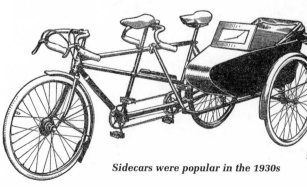

Sidecars were popular in the 1930s

some baggy clothes are made with snug fitting liners – function within, style without.

Tops are a matter of personal preference. There are all sorts of wonder fabrics around, designed to wick perspiration away from your skin, and which dry quickly. Try one and see, lots of people like them. Others prefer natural fabrics such as cotton.

Next is a good jacket for adverse weather. Roadies and fast movers have a wide choice of garments designed not for 100 percent protection, but rather to brunt wind and rain while still providing ventilation through features such as mesh side panels. These clothes are very lightweight and usually reasonable in price.

General riders and people out in bad weather will want a heavier jacket that can provide serious protection. On a fishing boat you can go for plastic and rubber garments. On a bike you generate heat and perspiration, even on a cold day, and the only route to go for waterproofs are breathable fabrics which allow your perspiration vapor to escape but do not let water in. The best fabric I've found over the years is the original: Gore-tex®. At least in my experience, others work, but not as well, or for as long.

The classic cycling all weather jacket is cut trim, and long at the back. It's fine in the summer, but in winter can be tight if you want additional layers of clothes underneath for warmth. My basic

outer layer garment for cycling, and almost all other activities, is a ski/mountaineering lightweight parka, decidedly oversize and extra long, with a built in hood. In summer, it's light and roomy enough to be reasonably well ventilated and cool. In bad weather, there's plenty of room for inner garments; I can even wear it over a suit jacket. The hood fits tidily over a helmet. Yet the parka is still light enough to roll into a compact bundle and be carried on the handlebars or in a bum bag.

I get a lot of use out of a parka, from rain forests to winter alpine peaks, and rate it my single most important garment, but I'm still staggered by what a good one can cost. I should not be so skinflint, because with care a good jacket will last for many years. One trick is to check for seasonal sales; ski shops, for example, often clear their stock in early Spring at half price. You might get lucky at a garage sale. Another method is to just make do. I can't count the number of times I've used a garbage bag as a waterproof (just tear holes for your head and arms). For additional wind protection, slip flat newspapers inside whatever you're wearing. For additional warmth, stuff crumpled newspapers, bubble wrap, or anything else that will help maintain an insulating layer of air between your body and an outer garment.

See also entries for gloves, helmets, rain gear, shoes.

Computers

Cycle computers provide useful information and like watches, range from inexpensive models with basic functions to more sophisticated models that can interface with PCs. Typical functions are: clock, elapsed time, current, maximum, and average speeds, and trip and total distances. A nice option is cordless. Routing wires to sensors neatly and keeping them out of harm's way can certainly be done, but life is easier if you don't have to fiddle with wires at all. On the other hand, hard wired models are possibly more reliable.

Better cycle computers can track your cadence, or pedalling rate. This is particularly useful for training and for learning how to maximize performance. Better still are models that include a heart rate monitor. This feature is especially useful for fitness conditioning. The top-line models have more functions than I can count, and can download data into a PC. I've had consistently good results with Cateye computers.

There are cycle computers that will tell you what gear you are in, your altitude, where you are in the universe, and your stars for the day. Hey, there's a limit. The best cycle computer is still your own thinker.

Cycle Bags and Cases

Large soft cloth bags and hard shell fiberglass cases designed to hold a bike with the wheels off can outfox the anti-bike contingent when travelling by air, rail, or bus. Most will not accept a bike with fenders or carrier racks.

Cloth bags are inexpensive, lightweight, and versatile. You can cram them full of clothes and other gear. At journey's end, once the bike is out, the bag can be folded up and carried on the back of the bike, or for a time, over your shoulder. Stripping down a bike and swaddling it in protective layers of bubble wrap, clothes, and cardboard can take a bit of time, but with practice goes well enough. The most major limitation is with airline baggage handlers. Lost and damaged baggage is the leading consumer complaint

against airlines. An in-depth psychological study conducted by the nefarious firm Clabbercut & Slade ("We got it made") has established that a high percentage of baggage handlers conform to the Weisbader-Snasburton Enema Profile for failed authoritarian personalities. As lowly baggage handlers, they are consumed with especial rage against the people who have given them baggage to handle, and in the darkened catacombs of the baggage halls vent their anger on guess what. What's more, they particularly dislike anything different or out of line, that might indicate a bit of fun, such as a bike bag.

I don't want to be too hard on the airlines, I've had a lot of brilliant luck with them, but the fact remains that if you want to transport a full-size bike, then a hard shell fiberglass case is the only means with a fighting chance of success. These cases are expensive, fairly heavy, and big. They have little trundle wheels to make handling easier. They are big enough to be a real headache in a taxi or small vehicle. Unlike a cloth bag, they don't fold up; at journey's end you'll have to figure out what to do with it. In short, a fiberglass case is a pro's solution, one that works but at cost in convenience.

Still, on a big cycling vacation, you might want to take your own bike. If flying is involved and a fiberglass case is not the answer, you can obtain an old cardboard box from a bike shop, and reinforce it with internal layers of plywood and anything else that might resist attack and abuse.

Consider a lateral move: renting bikes. At one time this meant having to put up with gas pipe wrecks bent into amazing new configurations, but the rental market is now much, much better, and you can book quality machines at many destinations. It can also be a neat way to try out n ew machines.

Finally, if you travel a lot by air and want your own bike, then consider having a purpose-made travel bike with S & S couplings. With these, it is possible to reduce a bike to carry on luggage (see travel bikes in Chapter 6).

Fairings and Windshields

Air has plenty of substance for a cyclist. At 30 mph, 90 percent of the rider's effort is just to overcome air resistance. Smooth the flow of air, and the rider's lot becomes easier. A higher top speed is possible, of course, but the really useful advantage of improving aerodynamic efficiency is that fast cruising speeds require less effort.

The Zzipper fairing is a clear, bubble shaped windscreen which improves aerodynamic efficiency by up to 30 percent, for an increase of about 10 percent in speed. The gain is more pronounced at high speeds, and works out to a gear 10 inches higher than would otherwise be the case. On long downhill runs the increase in velocity is very evident and exciting, and air pressure on the screen makes handling somewhat steadier. Cross winds are another story, and the turbulence from a large truck overtaking at speed will put a Zzipper equipped bike out of track by about 12 inches instead of the more usual 6 inches. On very gusty days it is better to leave it off the bike.

The Zzipper fairing is useful for fending off rain and snow, and helping to keep the rider warm in cold weather. In terms of cutting down effort, it is most useful for touring and open road riding,

and not of great moment in stop-and-go town riding. The fairing mounts and dismounts within seconds, so it is very much the sort of thing you can use when you want to do so. Information from:

Zzipper, POB 14, Davenport CA 95017 USA.
Tel: 831 425 8650. Fax: 831 425 1167.
E-mail: ZZipdesign@aol.com.
Web: www.bikeroute.com.

Glasses

For urban riding a pair of glasses will spare grit in the eyes, and at speed in the country eliminate burning of the eyes by the wind, or direct hits by bugs. Plain glasses are available for those who do not want to compromise their view of the world. Sunglasses are of course a fashion item but I've never regarded them as really necessary, except in extreme conditions such as desert travel or when snow and ice are mixed with strong sunshine. Look for glasses that ride clear of the face, to help minimize condensation problems. You may also want to use an anti-fog product.

Gloves

I think of gloves as essential, and rarely ride without them. In the short term, hands can stand a lot of wear and tear. In the long term, gloves help prevent stiff fingers and hands. The main reasons though, are comfort and protection.

Cycling gloves are fingerless, with ventilated mesh backs and padded leather palms. The padding helps prevent numb hands from pinched ulnar nerves when riding with a portion of your weight on your hands. Some people (like me) have shallow placed ulnar nerves, which are extra vulnerable, and gloves padded with gel substances are particularly effective at insulating against vibration and shock. For winter riding there are full-finger gloves made with Gore-tex® or other materials that are wind- and waterproof, but that allow your hands to breathe. Mittens that allow your fingers to keep each other company are warmest for very cold weather.

The protection aspect is simple – a fall. I tilted an HPV one day while not wearing gloves and made the mistake of putting my hand down on gritty pavement at speed. Now I always wear gloves.

Handlebar Grips, Pads and Tapes

There are all kinds of foam grips and sleeves available to give more or firmer padding on the bars. Grips for straight bars come in various designs and textures and claims for increased performance. Make sure they work when wet. With drop bars, tapes are part of the decoration scheme, and many riders like cork tapes for comfort. For more padding, tapes with micro-cells are available, and for ultimate comfort, neoprene foam sleeve Grab Ons. These last are popular for distance riding, and go for the real McCoy, because the imitations are inferior. In a pinch, stop by a builders' store and check out what they have for insulating pipes.

Heart Rate Monitor

Like cycle computers, heart rate monitors range from basic, inexpensive models to sophisticated, expensive units that can be downloaded into a PC. A number of top models combine heart monitor and cycle computer functions.

Heart rate monitors are very useful for fitness training, and when used in combination with a cadence sensor and/or a cycle computer, for honing your cycling skills. Experienced riders using this equipment for the first time usually make very interesting discoveries about how hard they are actually working (or not), and how this bears on riding technique and speed.

In a way, heart rate monitors with information about the engine can be more useful than cycle computers with information about the bike. This applies particularly to older riders, who need hard exercise, but within limits.

If you can afford one of the top models and like this sort of thing then by all means have a play. Much more interesting than silly toys that add

and subtract numbers or tell you the time in Bolivia when you're in Tokyo. I do advise, however, that when you are huffing and puffing with effort, dealing with a complex computer/monitor with a multitude of functions and buttons can be distracting and even impossible. I suggest starting out with a fairly straightforward model, and then if you like this sort of thing, go further. A simple, basic combined heart rate monitor and cycle computer at a reasonable price is the Cateye HB 100. A good value heart rate monitor as used by Tour de France winners and with plenty of bells and whistles is the Cardiosport Heartsafe TZ, with the more upmarket Autozone offering additional features. A well known brand is Polar, with models from simple and basic, through to technological marvels such as the cordless Polar XTrainer Plus, which with additional sensors can give cadence and altitude. Any of these units can also tell time.

Helmet

What is it, a hundred thousand, perhaps a million years of evolution that has gone into making your head? You're born wee little, unable to look after yourself without help for a number of years, just so you can have a big head with a large brain and the means to participate in a society which, among other things, is structured for people to use their brains in cooperative endeavors that improve their lot and keep the show going. That our particular civilization has seen false starts, blind alleys, widespread destruction, and plenty of brains that we could have done better without, is neither here nor there. Good or bad, better or worse, your brains are you.

One snag. A human is a tough customer – ask any other critter on the planet. Yet if you drop a human head a distance of just two feet onto a hard surface, the skull can fracture.

You wear a helmet when you ride a bike so that if you should fall and smack your head, you have some protection against damaging your skull and/or your brains. That's it. If you ride off a 200-foot cliff or get pulled underneath the wheels of a large truck, a helmet won't help one bit. A helmet is strictly for the low-key kind of trouble you can get into with a bike which mainly, is falling off. Broken bones mend, cuts and scrapes heal, but leaked or scrambled brains like Humpty-Dumpty's may never go back together again. Barring fluke accidents, a helmet substantially increases the level of protection for your skull. It means that to be taken out forever, you've got to be properly smashed and pancaked, not just given a tap in the right spot.

There is a fierce amount of misunderstanding on the subject of helmets for cyclists. Various misguided do-gooders want to make helmets compulsory for cyclists. This mistake has already been made in, of all places, Australia. The result has been a marked decrease in the number of people who cycle. Now if riding bikes is dangerous, and fewer people ride, they should be better off, yes? Nope, in Australia, the net result has been a loss of life through diminished longevity and an increase in health problems. Staying home safe in bed is poor risk management because it is bad for your health. Get people out on bikes and while some do get snuffed, the rest live longer and healthier lives. According to the British Medical Association, the health benefits of reducing coronary heart disease, obesity, and hypertension by cycling, outweigh the risks of accident by around 20 to 1. Making cycle helmets compulsory will produce precisely the opposite effect of saving lives – i.e., people will live worse (at greater cost to health services) and die sooner. If a whiff of this kind of thing comes around your neighborhood, shoot it down.

A more fundamental problem is that making helmets compulsory for cyclists is grabbing the wrong end of the stick. It's like saying prevent rape by fitting people with chastity belts. Cyclists fall off their bikes, and on this score I'm all for wearing a helmet. But the true great danger to cyclists is just one thing – cars and the design of roads.

It is sometimes said that if all cyclists wore helmets, many hundreds or even thousands of lives a year might be saved. The idea is flawed, but let's ride it out – if all the people in cars and buses

were made to wear helmets, perhaps 30,000 lives a year could be saved. Wouldn't that be much better? Let's aim higher and cut the speed of all motor vehicles at all times and in all places to 25 mph. That one might save 50,000 lives and spare several hundred thousand maimed and injured. Ridiculous, eh? Not practical, eh? Right, I guess it is a lot easier to jump up and down on a few cyclists and say the roads are dangerous and therefore they should wear helmets.

I am a practical person, and I take a lot of precautions against being hurt by motorists. Yet in my heart I have always agreed with the venerated and famously crusty cycle historian Derek Roberts, who says simply that it is not up to cyclists to stay out of the way of cars, it is up to motorists to avoid us. The answer to the question "But surely it is a good idea for all cyclists to wear helmets?" is no.

Cyclists in the Netherlands, a country where bike riding is univeral, do not much bother with helmets. When a motorist/cyclist collision occurs, they throw the motorist in jail. Automatic. They don't necessarily hang the person, but jail is mandatory. This has had a big cooling effect on motorist/cyclist collisions. In the Netherlands, the cyclist/car accident fatality rate is just 10 percent of the UK and US rates – 0.8 against 8 per 100 million kilometers.

One reason the Netherlands, and to a lesser extent, countries such as Germany and Denmark, can place the onus of responsibility on motorists to avoid cyclists is that they have transport infrastructures designed to cope with bicycles. Yes, but as I've personally seen first hand, there are still plenty of conflict points between bikes and cars – and it is the cars that take the trouble to stay out of the way. There is a fundamental, utter difference in attitude.

In America, there has been progress in treating cyclists respectfully, but we've a long, long way to go.

So far as helmets are concerned, the ironic thing for me is that when I started cycling, only a few racers wore head protection, albeit a scant network of padded leather strips great for fresh air but of little use when piling into a tree. I sat down and thought the whole matter through and came back up swinging hard in favor of wearing hard shell helmets. It doesn't matter if you look like a nerd and kids laugh when you pull up to the grocery store, I said. Wear a helmet whenever you cycle. It's inconvenient. So is not being able to think or talk because your head has been pounded into jelly. Make a personal decision, I said, and swim against the crowd.

Now, you are expected to wear a helmet. There's a real bias. If a motorist creams you and it is 100 percent their fault, and you are not wearing a helmet, you may very well wind up the loser in any legal contest. The world, or at least a part of it, has decided that sensible, law abiding, upright, good cyclists wear helmets. The thinking is something like, roads are dangerous, ride a bike without a helmet and your deliberate vulnerability is a further burden on all responsible people trying so hard to drive their cars without hurting anyone.

Ah, what bilge . . . but no matter. I still stand by what I have always said: wear a helmet whenever you cycle. Folks, I been around, I done seen what happened. The one I always remember was

a nice girl in Amsterdam, she was just sitting on her bike, stock still, not doing a thing, fell off her bike and hit her head. She is still in a coma in a hospital bed.

My son went out on a hot mountain bike, crossed up somehow, and piled into a bunch of logs. He was knocked unconscious, scraped and gored pretty good, and lucky not to break a collarbone. It's a safe bet the damage would have been worse if he had not had a nice new Bell helmet firmly planted on his head. There are a million stories like this. They all say the same thing: wear a helmet just in case.

It's simple. Your head is the most vulnerable part of your body, and as you might expect, the leading cause of cyclist deaths is brain injury. Wearing a helmet greatly reduces the risk of brain injury. This applies whatever kind of cyclist you are: general, off-road, or road racer.

The silly thing about "should I or shouldn't I?" is that a helmet is actually a useful thing. On hot, sunny days it provides shade. When the rains fall, it helps keep the wet off your head, and if covered with a shower cap, becomes a neat mini umbrella. Most models feature a visor, also useful against sun and rain; by tilting your head down slightly, the sunlight or raindrops are kept out of your eyes, improving both comfort and vision.

Early helmets, a.k.a. "brain buckets," were not well-ventilated and on hot days could overheat a rider. The problem is, cycling is warm work, some 25 percent or more of your body heat radiates from your head, and it's an air cooled unit. Reduce the flow of air and you become

Brain bucket

awash in sweat and eventually cook out. I know about all this stuff especially because I cycle very warm and even in winter use a light, well-ventilated helmet.

The first requirement of a helmet is that it is comfortable, or else it may not be used at all. Happily, modern helmets are designed for good ventilation, and models are available that maximize the flow of air. You should already know if you tend to run hot on open throttle, and be guided accordingly. When in doubt, go for a cooler design; you can always add a cover for additional warmth.

The second requirement of a helmet is that it fits. If it slops around on your head, it won't provide protection when you need it. Many helmets are designed so that you can use Velcro-backed pads to adjust the fit. Another common feature is a retention system which hugs the back of the head.

A helmet should sit squarely on your noggin, somewhat above your eyebrows and not tilted back, or to either side. The V-straps on each side should be adjusted to converge just below the earlobe and the chin strap should be snug. You should not be able to pull the helmet off from the front or back.

Good helmets are expensive. I'm a fan of quality when needed, but frankly do not understand why one helmet can cost three or four times more than another, or as much as a cheap bicycle. A good value helmet is the Bell Forza 2. For top performance, I like the Giro Exodus (mountain) and Boreas (road) models. Bell, Giro and Specialized are all good brands.

A cycling helmet is a piece of sporting equipment, and as such, increases the enjoyment of cycling. The idea that wearing a helmet is somehow odious is an assumption made by people who do not use helmets, and just is not so. After a time, wearing a helmet becomes a habit, a natural item of clothing. As far as the terminator part of the business goes, I hope you make it through life without a scratch, but it is unrealistic to ride a bike and expect that you will never crash. If you ride a bike and want to increase your chances of staying with the fit and living, then wear a helmet.

Kickstand

A kickstand is a useful item on a utility bike. You can park in front of a shop without leaning the bike against the window and giving the shop owner fits. On a sport bike a kickstand is dead weight. A cure for the tendency of a bike to fall over when leaned against a pole is to fit a parking brake. Carve a clothes peg or so that it can be wedged into the brake lever. Or use a bit of elastic or rubber band to hold down the brake lever. With calliper brakes, another method is to slip a bit of cardboard between the brake pad and rim.

Lights

Lights are for seeing, and for being seen. For the most part the two functions are separate. To see where you are going, you need a concentrated beam of light; to be seen by other road users, front or rear, you need diffuse lights which are visible from various angles of incidence or view. In addition, be-seen lights should by their nature help other road users and especially motorists to understand that you are a cyclist. As it happens, it is a good idea to have two independent lighting systems, so one can be for the cause of seeing, and other for being seen.

Lucas candle lamp

For seeing where you are going, it is simple enough to establish the type of lights and level of power required for your particular riding circumstances. Well-lit urban streets are a breeze; dark off-road trails usually require plenty of juice. Being seen is a whole different game. It is a matter of catching the attention of others, and it is easy to underestimate how difficult this is to do. Many cyclists think they can be seen when in fact they cannot. It's a natural mistake. They're out there, panting and pedalling away and moving all over the place, and surely obviously visible. The real case is very much otherwise.

The noted cycling author Fred DeLong took the trouble to replicate a series of car/bike collisions. He used the actual vehicles, equipment, and clothing involved in the original collisions, or duplicates in identical condition, at the same locations and times of day. In nearly every instance, and despite the use of regulation cycle lights in some cases, the problem was that the motorists could not see the cyclists, *even knowing they were there.* Other experiments with cyclists and motorists confirm that cyclists believe they are visible long before motorists actually see them.

The essential problem is that motorists drive too fast for safe control within the distance they can see, and the speed of their ability to understand what is happening. At night, on a dark road with little interference from other light sources, the main beams on a car have pretty good range. Still, a car travelling at 70 mph is moving at over 100 feet per second. In theory, a driver with his or her eyes glued to the road will be able to spot a cyclist in sufficient time to slow down or stop, which at 70 mph takes 315 feet. You can see where this is headed. If the motorist takes a second or two to glance at the instruments or adjust the radio, look at a passenger, or even simply have a good yawn, they can be on top of a cyclist before they know it. On dipped beams, the effective range of car headlights can be 75 feet. A car moving at 30 mph will need all of this distance for a stop.

A clear road is one thing. In the real world, motorists have to cope with sorting out a confusing welter of lights of sharply varying intensities. There are other cars with headlights bright enough to reduce an oncoming motorist's vision to a fragment of road space, traffic signals, street lights, lights from buildings, instrument lights, and reflections in rear view mirrors and on the windshield, which itself may be spotted with bugs or smeared with dirt. Bombarded with information inputs and typically partially out of control in terms of reaction time and maneuvering space, motorists concentrate their perceptive abilities on looking out for primary hazards – things big and powerful enough to impinge on a 5,000-pound vehicle. This concentration raises the level of their stimulus threshold, the point at which they take notice of things.

There is a big difference between seeing something in a mechanical sense and knowing what it is. Motorists operate by perceptual sets, a mental construction of what lies ahead. If you like, they draw a picture and drive into it. To preserve the integrity of that construction, especially if (knowingly or unknowingly) the motorist is pushing the margin of control, the stimulus threshold raises and holds back new data until such time as it conclusively alters the picture for current events. A motorist knows right away that a pair of oncoming

Lucas Silver King oil lamp

headlights means another vehicle, and because the distance between headlights is relatively consistent, also has an idea of how far away the vehicle is, and how fast it is moving. A single weak light, however, is just one of many inputs and could be anything, at any distance from the windshield to the horizon line. The motorist might see the light in the physical sense that a stimulus is delivered to the brain, but until the old grey matter has enough information to know what the light is, or identify it as requiring attention, the message is likely to be ignored.

• LED Lights

One of the best tools for telling motorists that you are a cyclist is a blinking LED light. Blinking or moving lights are four times more conspicuous than steady lights. For a motorist, a blinking light means heads up, be alert, possible big picture change involving significant velocity or temporal space difference – i.e., the presence of a slow moving vehicle, or a physical obstacle. In addition, LED lights have a distinctive rapid blinking pattern which many motorists (not all!) immediately recognize as characteristic of a cyclist or pedestrian. This does not automatically make you safe, but at least now you are in the picture.

LED lights are wonderful. They are very visible, reliable, lightweight, and cheap to run. A bright rear LED blinking light is the VistaLite VL700 Eclipse. In common with most other models of rear LED lights, it is dual mode and can be set for blinking or to give a steady light. Another bright and durable model is the VistaLite 300. Cateye LED lights are all pretty good. Most models are retro-reflective, so that even if the batteries have expired, the unit still acts as a reflector. See what's going, as manufacturers constantly bring out new models. If you want a light claimed to be visible a mile away, try a VistaLite VS3001R Rear Strobe. It's brighter and more effective with an amber lens. If you want to get really serious, a source for very high intensity strobe lights are dive shops and boat chandlers.

Some people claim that strobe lights are too strong and may startle motorists. Yes! The people

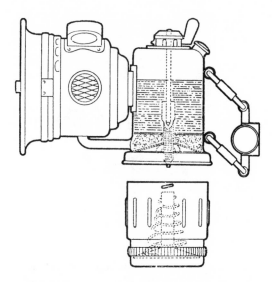

"A modern type of acetylene lamp. The calcium carbide is placed in the lower chamber, and when the water is turned on the gas passes through the perforations at the top, through the felt and along the pipe to the burner."

who think cyclists can get by with dim lights should be taken out on a dark night, and put on a fast, narrow road aboard bikes equipped with old, flickering lights and fading batteries. The survivors would thereafter behave.

You have a right to preserve your life. Get a blinking LED light, or a high intensity strobe if you want to go all out, and use it. Mount your rear blinking light at motorist eye level, up high and unobstructed. Off the back of a saddle wedge pack is good, and on the seat post is fine, so long as nothing obscures the light. Careful of coats with long tails. If you have a carrier rack, it's usually best to mount it off the back of that, or else loads on the rack may obscure the light. Another trick is to wear the LED light yourself. They clip easily to the back of a reflective belt or vest. Make sure the clip is secure. As a supplement, I like the models that mount to the back of a helmet. They are small, but quite visible and effective. Another useful supplement are gloves with LED lights. See the entry Turn Signals for more information.

Microphote oil lamp

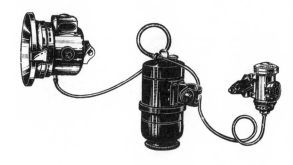

Lucas Calcia King carbide set

Although in some places blinking LED lights are legal for bikes, in others you are supposed to have a steady rear light. Check out the situation in your area, because if you are involved in a collision with another road user, not having legal lights can be very expensive if a claim for damages is involved – insurance companies are ruthless about taking advantage of technicalities. Blinking lights are more effective, but to cover all bets you probably should also have a steady light.With generator lights (see below) it is possible to have a steady rear light as part of the system. However, this involves wiring which is vulnerable to snags and breaks, and many people use a generator for the front light only, and mount a battery light on the rear. For long battery life, steady LED lights are unbeatable. A good LED rear light is the Cateye TL-AU100. Mount your primary rear light as high as possible, on the center line of the bike so that it is visible from both sides. Do not attach it to a chain stay, as it will be invisible from one side, and could possibly foul the wheel. Mount your reflector, however, as low as possible, so that it is more likely to be caught by low beam car headlights.

• Front Lights

You should have an almost white (they're often a kind of greenish yellow) blinking LED light at the front. These are fairly new and it's not yet established just how effective they are. The thinking is that motorists will identify the rapid blinking as a cyclist. Since you should have a backup light anyhow, the idea seems worth a try.

For a primary front light or lights, there are a range of possibilities. The two basic types of lighting systems are battery and generator.

• Generator Lights

Generators take power off the wheel, and while old-fashioned models have a fair amount of drag, modern ones are much more efficient – the best need less than 5 W, which means an efficiency of around 70 percent. This is very good. Power is adequate for road riding, but not for fast or tricky off-road riding. Wires must be run between the generator and the lights, and these can snag and break. The system is permanently attached to the bike, which can be a problem when locking up on the street, because bikes with extra goodies attract thieves and vandalism.

Basic generator lights go out when you stop the bike. This does not matter if you also have an LED light. Better generator lights often include a storage battery, to keep the lights on for awhile – anywhere from 5 to 45 minutes. This can be handy for map reading and roadside repairs. At high speeds generators produce a lot of juice,

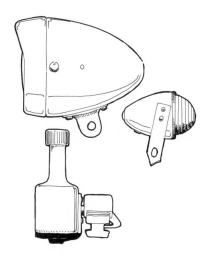

Bottle generator system

the time, even if the light is not in use, and while drag is much less than for a bottle unit, it is still noticeable. If it is a high class unit such as the Schmidt Original, however, the residual drag is equivalent to climbing 1 foot per mile – not something you'll notice.

The big asset of generator lights is that they are always there and cost nothing to run. They are great for utility and local use bikes. For this sort of thing, my advice is to go with a basic, inexpensive bottle type, unless the bike has a hub generator as original equipment. For touring or extended use, quality units such as the Dynosys LightSpin or Schmidt Original are the route to go. Initial expense is high, but running cost is far more economic than battery lights.

As said, many people use a generator for the front light only, to avoid running wires to the rear. This makes sense for a sport bike, but on utility bikes I'm happy enough to have a complete front and rear system.

Generator lights are not especially popular in America. I don't even see them in the usual catalogs. However, they are favored by working cyclists, so a shop that supplies and services courier and delivery bikes should be able to help. Some tips: most bottle generators are single wire systems, that earth or ground through the bicycle itself. The generator mount includes a sharp pointed screw designed to grind into the bicycle frame for earth contact. Ecch. This causes rust and is not reliable. Better to use two wires, and make a proper ground contact via a bolt. Use robust wire, and be meticulous about routing and fastening wires. You can form coils for extra slack by winding the wire around a nail or pencil. A handy way of insulating and protecting connections is with silicone bath sealant.

which can blow out bulbs. This is cured by fitting a zener diode (voltage regulator), which is standard on better units.

There are two types of generators: bottle, which run by pressing against the tire side wall, and hub, where the generator is built into the hub unit. Bottle generators cost less, and are engaged only when in use, but have the highest drag. The AXA-HR is cheap and reliable, and has a built-in voltage regulator, which is good if you want to run brighter halogen bulbs. My fancy has been caught by a new bottle model, the Dynosys LightSpin Lite, which has ball-bearings and a new magnetic design that reduces drag to a very low level. Spin the roller, and instead of dragging to a stop it keeps whirring away, rather like a spinning top. It has a storage battery, too. If you cannot find one in the US, try:

The Cyclists' Touring Club, Cotterell House, 69 Meadrow, Godalming, Surrey GU7 3HS England.
Tel: +44 01483 417217. Fax: +44 01483 426994.
E-mail: cycling@ctc.org.uk.
Web: www.ctc.org.uk.

In general, hub generators are best in terms of reliability, efficiency, and power, but are "on" all

• Battery Lights

These are available in a wide range of sizes and power capacities, from little micro-jobs that only just show the way ahead, to dual headlight 32 W units that could probably illuminate the Grand Canyon. Cateye even have a 84 W headlight, the Stadium, quite powerful enough to completely

The Cateye HL-500 Micro Halogen is a powerful 2.4 W light which runs for three hours on four AA batteries. A nice thing about this light is that the casing is transparent, so the light is visible from all angles. If you want more run time, lights with C-cell batteries will last for about six to eight hours, but at 1.25 W are not as bright. Lights with D-cells last longer, but because of their weight, are prone to fly off the bike and self-destruct. They are also notorious for poor reliability, failed switches and contacts, and rattles. A better method is to house D-cells in an independent unit, and use them to power a light such as the Cateye HL-500 Micro Halogen 2.4 W. This gives a strong, reliable light, and about 12 hours run time. Cateye sell a power supply case for this purpose which fits into a water bottle cage.

If you ride regularly at night, then you don't want to be spending bagfuls of money on batteries, or for that matter, be spreading used batteries around an already polluted landscape. The obvious route to go is rechargeable. Fine, but be aware of their limitations. One is that when a rechargeable battery expires, it does so all at once, without warning. There's no "get you home" fading orange glow. You have to track your journey times and recharge on schedule. Best if you have an established routine. Some of the better lights with dual low and high beam outputs have a low battery warning indicator, so you can shift to low beam for a longer run time.

Many rechargeable units can be damaged by overcharging. "Smart" units with automatic control do not come on stream until you are spending a goodly sum of money, for advanced high power systems. This is very naughty of manufacturers. Put a light on charge and forget, and poof! an expensive battery can be damaged or even shot. Often, a replacement battery is unobtainable; you have to buy the whole shebang, light, charger, and battery, all over again. Bah.

Finally, in my experience, rechargeable batteries often work well only when fresh off the charger. If you charge up a light and then try to use it a few days later, it may be dead as a doornail, or piffle out unexpectedly.

blow the night apart, along with your wallet. It runs for three hours, too.

Battery lights have two big assets: flexibility, and as much power as you are willing to carry. They can be whipped on and off the bike in a flash. This is good for sport bikes and street machines, and useful if you need to read a map or mend a puncture. The power bit is variable, and trades off with weight. The lights themselves are compact. It's the batteries. You can get a bright squirt out of a small battery, but not for long. So as a simple rule of thumb, the more power, the more battery, and the more weight.

If you are a sunshine rider and only need lights on odd occasions for short distances, then a straightforward lightweight battery light will do.

All in all, with rechargeable lights, it is worth going first class: plenty of power, dual mode, and smart recharge.

The VistaLite 600XR Road Toad with a 1.8 W output is a town light, with a wide angle lens and diffuse beam designed to catch the eyes of motorists rather than show the way ahead. I don't give it a big hand, it does not hold a charge well, but it's cheap and legal.

VistaLite VL400 series lights are designed to throw a beam for seeing, and range in output from 2 W to 10 W, running from one and one-half to three hours depending on the size of batteries used. Cateye have several models, including a 2.4 W with AA Nicad batteries, and at 6 W with a 6-volt lead-acid battery carried in a separate pack. Both of these types will run for about three hours.

For lighting with real authority, 6- and 12-volt systems are available, with headlights at 10 W, 12 W, 15 W, 20 W, and more. These systems are definitive, the problem is that run time is measured in minutes rather than hours. Because the lights themselves are relatively compact and light-weight, many people set up a dual mode system, with a 10 W or 12 W as the main use light, and a 15 W or 20 W for special occasions. Used this way, most systems will provide over two hours run time.

A flexible high power system is the 6-volt VistaLite 500 series, because components are interchangeable with the 400 series. This means that in addition to 10 W (beam) and 15 W (flood) lights, a 2 W light can be used for long run times. There's also a kit for mounting a light on a helmet. This option is really great for off-road riding.

High power lights at 10 W and up are serious-ly expensive. They are for people who want, or need, performance without compromise. Well, we complained for decades about the fact that lights for cyclists were all cheap and near useless. Now we do have some very good lights available, and I'm afraid we have to pay for them.

• Home-brew systems

There are several options for DIYers and the economy-minded. One is to put together a system using moped or motorcycle lights and a battery and charger. Performance is not bad and cost can be lowered by scavenging parts from junkers, but batteries of this type are not designed for deep dis-charge cycles and weight tends to be a problem. It is perhaps better for work bikes and pedicabs.

One system I've used a lot consists of generator halogen lamps powered by a 6-volt lantern bat-tery, the kind used for large hand flashlights, and widely available. This gives a fairly good light, and the battery will fit neatly into a water bottle cage. I've never actually counted running time, but the battery will usually last a month or longer, and this is powering both a front and rear light, and a brake light. One nice thing about this setup is that you can also have a bottle generator aboard the bike, at not much cost in weight. Should the battery expire, or you find a 20-mile downhill stretch, you can use the generator.

• Lights Wind-out

Being seen is critical; a cyclist's risk of fatal collision with a motorist is four times greater at night. People who ride in the dark without lights and identification aids are playing Russian roulette. A little bit of visibility is not good enough. Be bright! See also the reflectors entry in this chapter for more important information on this subject.

Being able to see where you are going is impor-tant outside of towns, away from street lights. For road riding, generator lights can handle most situ-ations and are economic to run, but may drag unless they are an expensive, quality unit. Battery lights will provide as much performance as you want, at a price in weight and cost.

Fenders

Fenders increase air resistance as well as weight and are not used on road racing bikes. On training bikes, or bikes often used in bad weather, fenders will prevent wet and dirt from spraying into your face at the front, and all over your back and posterior at the rear. They also help keep grit out of the works.

The classic image of a mountain bike is sans fenders, but in fact, some form of protection is very useful for off-road riding. I like mudguards, as they are called in Britain, and many is the time I've sailed unblemished through muddy bogs that left unprotected riders looking as if they had been dipped at a chocolate factory. For this kind of use, clearance must be as high as possible, to prevent mud from building up and possibly jamming a wheel. A popular option, minimalist and less apt to foul, is to use a Crud Catcher, a short guard that clips on the down tube, and a short clip-on guard for the rear. I personally like a full length fender at the front, and a bobtail at the rear, with a flap. Only three hex bolts hold each fender, so they can be mounted or removed quickly.

Plastic fenders are light but eventually warp, if they don't crack first. Better by far are chromo-plastic models, which will stand years of abuse. SKS are good.

Odometer

You might spot one of these on a classic. It's a tiny mechanical gizmo mounted on the fork blade and uses a toothed wheel ticked over by the spokes to count the miles.

Pumps

Lots of options here. First, I heartily recommend investing in a proper floor or track pump, as this will make the important task of keeping your tires correctly inflated a breeze. It really only takes a few strokes to hit 100 psi in a narrow 700C tire, and half again more to push 50 psi into a 2-inch wide 26-inch mountain bike tire. Another plus is that your riding pump or inflation device will only be for contingency use, and can be light and portable. Basic quality floor pumps are quite inexpensive. Because I get so much use out of a floor pump, I much prefer the better models, for both efficiency and durability. They can be maintained with replacement parts, and will last for decades. Zefal is my favourite, but Blackburn and SKS are also excellent.

For many years cyclists routinely carried long frame pumps, suspended between brazed-on pegs or frame tubes. These pumps still work very well and I have fond regard for the top quality and strong Zefal HPX. For less money, the SKS Supersport will do a perfectly good job.

Frame pumps tend to get in the way when you are carrying a bike – especially mountain bikes – and are too long to fit easily into a case or bag when locking up on the street. One solution is a shorty or mini-pump, compact enough to fit into a case or bag. These come in an assortment of models and sizes. Some are designed to be carried on a bracket next to the water bottle cage, others are compact enough to fit inside a large seat wedge pack. Naturally enough, the bigger ones pump more easily, and the Blackburn Mammoth Twin-Head and Dual Stage models are both excellent. At half the size, the Blackburn Shorty Mammoth still delivers good performance and will fit inside a large wedge pack. Do realize, though, that where a floor pump may inflate a tire to max pressure in 20 to 30 strokes, a mini-pump is likely to need 100 or more.

For high portability and no sweat whatsoever, many people rely on CO_2 inflators. They are pretty much all you will see at a race. As with hand pumps, these come in a variety of models with various features designed to enhance the degree of control over inflation capacity and pressure. Innovations is the leading brand. CO_2 inflators are marvellously light and of course convenient, but once you've exhausted your supply of cartridges,

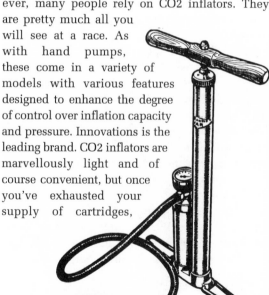

you're done. A compromise solution to this problem is the Innovations Second Wind combination CO2 inflator and hand pump. This can use either threaded cartridges, or the more widely available threadless kind. The hand pump is small and needs plenty of action, but will work as a back-up.

In gadget catalogs you'll find offers for electric air pumps that claim to be able to fill anything, including bicycle tires. In my experience none of these work very well, if at all. Best, fastest, and easiest is a proper floor pump.

A separate tire pressure gauge is useful for precision. Although most hand pumps include a pressure gauge and/or an inflation setting, the readings may or may not be accurate. With modern tires, 5 to 10 psi one way or the other can make an important difference.

You might at some point want to inflate a tire using a gasoline station air line. Don't. Although cycle tire pressures are high, the volume of air is small, and in only seconds the tire can overinflate and blow to smithereens, with an almighty bang. If you must use an air line, doso in very short bursts.

Rain Gear

How much protection you need or want depends on your circumstances and personal preferences. Weathering a shower on a short training ride or journey to work is one thing, riding all day in a downpour is quite another. Another factor is temperature: on a hot day it can be refreshing to ride through a cooling drizzle; in cold weather, however, wind chill on a wet cyclist can produce hypothermia. Don't underrate this risk. My closest brushes with becoming frozen stiff have not been on sub-zero winter expeditions, but on cool nights in the mountains when caught out by rain while wearing only shorts and T-shirt, with a 15 to 20 mile downhill run home. It's amazing how truly, desperately cold you can become. This problem is not uncommon for tourists who have spent most of a hot, sweaty day climbing to the top of a pass, and then encountered rain while descending the other side. If a mix of wind chill and rain ever becomes a prob-

lem and you cannot scavenge additional protection from a wastebin or other resource, use a small gear and pedal rapidly to keep circulation going in your legs (or pedal backwards), keep clenching and unclenching your hands, and if it gets really bad, stop and jog around for a bit until you warm up.

Minimum rain protection, more to ward off chill than to stay strictly dry, is a light nylon jacket which can fit tidily under the saddle and thus always be available. A budget alternative is a plastic rubbish bag with holes for your head and arms. Ordinary plastic shopping bags can be tied on your head and feet.

A classic cycling cape is an anachronism. It drapes over the shoulders, back and handlebars, allowing air to circulate up from underneath, and as well, road spray from your tires, splashes from other vehicles, and an occasional duck. A cape also makes life very interesting in windy conditions.

With modern clothing, waterproof but breathable fabrics are the answer to avoiding wet from within as well as without. Cycling jackets are function specific, and while usually cut trim, have long sleeves with adjustable cuffs and a long back. A hood is a great asset, and I like the kind

The
HYDROMAC
(R·g)
UNIVERSAL
SMOCK
for LADIES
(as Illustrated).

that are attached to the jacket and either roll up or live in a little pouch. Detachable hoods are always elsewhere when you need them. Make sure the hood is compact enough so that your vision is not impaired when you turn your head, but large enough to cover a helmet. A hood and helmet combination (or helmet cover) is very effective, because the helmet keeps the hood from touching your skin and becoming all clammy. If the helmet has a visor, you can tilt your head so that the rain stays out of your eyes. Helmet covers are available, although I'm happy enough with a lightweight shower cap.

As related in the entry for clothing, above, I like to base my cycling and outdoor outfit on an oversize mountaineering parka. This allows flexibility in adding layers of clothing for warmth. The best fabric I've found is Gore-tex®, but garments in this material are expensive. If your need for a rain jacket is as a contingency measure rather than a main use garment, then a cheaper breathable fabric may be adequate.

For full protection, you need trousers, cut with room for knee movement, and large enough to fit over other clothes. I prefer the kind that have a full bib front and shoulder straps. Note that in

Brooks leggings, c. 1936

warm weather you can wear waterproof trousers with just undies underneath.

Little touches: a pair of lined rubber gloves, as sold in hardware stores and garden centers. Don't forget to cover your saddle, if it is leather. Saddle covers are available, but a plastic shower cap or carrier bag works perfectly well.

Rearview Mirror

A rearview mirror can warn of impending danger, and aid faster, safer riding in traffic. Little mirrors which mount to the helmet or attach to eyeglasses have a small field of vision and don't do a proper job. Far superior are mirrors which mount to the handlebars or brake levers.

Reflectors

In darkness, good lights are your main means for signalling your presence to motorists, but do not always quickly identify you as a cyclist. It is difficult to judge distance to a single light, and in any case, lights can fail. Reflectors provide a good back-up, and can help identify you as a cyclist.

Rear, front, wheel spoke and pedal reflectors are a legal requirement. A big red rear reflector is definitely useful. Mount it as low as possible, so that car headlights on low beam catch it easily. An alternative or supplement is a reflectorized rear mudguard flap. White front reflectors are useless. They are only required because many cyclists do not use lights. Also useless are wheel spoke reflectors, which are only visible when a cyclist is already broadside to a motorist. They imbalance a wheel, and when setting up a bike I throw them away. Similarly, tires with reflective sidewalls are eye-catching, but only when a cyclist is actually crossing a motorist's path.

Pedal reflectors are great. Their low position is picked up by car headlights, and they have a distinctive pattern of movement. Active, moving reflectors are four times more noticeable than static reflectors. For this reason, reflective strips on the backs of shoes are also very effective.

Basic reflectors only reflect light to a source when in one position. Retro-reflective materials reflect light back to a source regardless of the angle of incidence. Millions of microscopic prisms do the trick. They must be sealed under plastic or other clear covering for effectiveness when wet. An excellent product when made of retro-reflective material is the Sam Brown belt, a lightweight combined belt and shoulder slash that can be used with whatever you are wearing. Also good are lightweight reflective vests. If you use ankle clips or bands, make them the reflective type.

When I set up a bike for regular night riding, I make liberal use of retro-reflective dots, stickers, and tape. These can be applied to panniers, helmet, crankarms, pedals, and bike frame. Every little bit helps.

Shoes

This topic is also discussed under pedals in Chapter 4, because the kind of shoes you use depends on the type of pedal you have. All I'll say here again is that for comfort, efficiency, and safety, I absolutely prefer clip-in pedals. These require shoes set up for the appropriate type of cleats. However, if you also want to ride wearing ordinary shoes, there are plenty of clip-in pedals with wide cages for full support.

One case of sorts for old-fashioned toe clips and straps is that these pedals can be used with regular shoes. If you have particular style requirements in footwear and are riding short distances, this might be the route to go. Otherwise, for comfortable cycling, it is definitely better to use cycling shoes with additional support and strength in the soles. There's quite a range of styles available, in three main categories: racing, training/general, and off-road.

Racing shoes are quite stiff and firm. They often have double closure, an inside lace-up, and an outer with straps and buckles. You can walk in them, but not for any great distance. Training/general shoes are perhaps the largest and most useful category. Closure is usually single, and the shoes are soft enough to wear for general activities. Finally, off-road shoes usually feature textured soles, for more grip in dirt, and may be cut higher on the ankle, for more support and to help keep out small stones.

Spoke Guard

A thin plate mounted on the rear wheel that prevents the rear derailleur from catching in the spokes. With a properly adjusted derailleur this should never happen, but should the derailleur malfunction or break (as has happened to me), then down you go, and likely with the bike as a write-off.

Trailers

Trailers are absolutely super for hauling around groceries, laundry, children, and all manner of things. There's a wide range of trailers available, to suit everything from off-road single track touring to heavy duty transport. Most models attach and detach from the bike in seconds and can free you from any need for carrier racks and panniers, which is nice if you have a performance machine.

For information on specific models of trailers, see Chapter 14, Cargo Cycles and Trailers.

Turn Signals

Electric turn signals mounted on a bicycle are not separated widely enough to give a clear indication of direction. Some people wear a strip of retro-reflective material around the wrist or on the back of a glove. However, when a cyclist makes a hand signal at night, the outhrust arm is often above the range of low beam car headlights and a reflective material may not work.

A recently introduced solution for this problem is the Indicator glove, which has a panel of blinking LED lights on the back, controlled with a simple finger switch. Although this might seem like gadgetry gone too far, the gloves really do command greater attention from motorists, who give more room. The gloves are well-made, too. Available in full and fingerless models. Information from:

Goude Design Group, Business & Technology Centre, Bessemer Drive, Sevenage, Herts SG1 2YF England.
E-mail: post@goude.demon.co.uk.
Web: www.indicatorglove.com

Water Bottle/Hydration System

It is important to drink plenty of fluids when cycling. Vigorous riding dehydrates the body, and by the time you feel thirsty your blood will have thickened up to 10 percent, elevating your heart rate. At this stage, no matter how much you drink, it takes several hours if not an entire day for the body to rehydrate. Drink before you get thirsty. The rule of thumb is to consume one water bottle an hour, drinking every 15 minutes.

The classic water bottle is a handy means for drinking on the fly. Insulated models will keep a drink cold or warm. One difficulty, especially in dusty or muddy off-road conditions, is that a water bottle can become dirty and anything but hygenic. An alternative are hydration systems, which consist of a bladder inside a bum pack or back pack. Depending on model selected, these can have three or four times more capacity than a large water bottle, and drinking is via a tube with a bite valve. The backpack models typically include additional storage space, with special compartments for tools, maps, personals such as wallet and keys, and so on.

I'm told on reasonable authority that for use in a water bottle "pure" spring water purchased from a store may not be as good as ordinary tap water, which usually contains chemicals. The reason is that with exposure to heat, the pure stuff is quicker to cook and develop bacteria. Personally, I drink tap water when I have to, but not otherwise.

One can carry only so much water, and on long rides away from civilization this can be a problem. We used to drink freely from springs, streams and lakes. The level of general pollution today means that drinking from open water sources, even in high mountains and remote locations, carries a risk of imbibing giardia and other unpleasant organisms. One alternative is to use a portable water filter. Basic models can keep out larger critters such as giardia. This level of protection may be adequate if the water in an area is not too bad. If you are in a country where there are viruses and other nasty itsy-bitsy things, then a filter with stage three micro-filteration is needed, and I'm told that even then, the water should also be treated with iodine. This is not good for you, because the iodine kills the friendly bacteria in your digestive system. In areas where the water is fairly clean, I rely on an old-fashioned method: a pot for boiling water clean.

There are many patent drinks, variously containing glucose and/or salts. I find that a little honey in plain water is good for a lift on a long ride. Caffeine will also give a momentary blast.

Wheel Discs

Wheel discs – smooth covers over the spokes – are standard in HPV racing. Everyone knows that spokes churn the air like an eggbeater, increasing turbulence and drag. If you want to go fast, you use discs.

In UCI-sanctioned events, wheel discs are allowed only if the disc is an integral part of the wheel structure. This means heavy weight and big money. In UCI races, only the rich go fast. In the real world, there are far cheaper options. Simple and effective is to make your own discs out of light cardboard or plastic and tape. Leave a hole for the valve and cover it with tape.

WRAP

Do not be afraid to spend money on accessories, as the return on investment will probably be excellent. But also be aware that many people have climbed aboard some beat-up old bike outfitted catch-as-catch-can, and traversed entire continents. You can always improvise; the virtue of purpose designed equipment is usually that it is very much better.

JENKINSON

FITTING AND GEARING

Setting up your bike for comfort and efficiency • Positioning the saddle, handlebars, and controls • Ensuring that the gearing setup is right

NJOYING A BIKE AND BEING ABLE TO GET THE most out of it requires a good fit: the right frame size and crank length, with correct placement of the handlebars, saddle, controls, and shoe cleats if used. If you are buying a bike, sort out the size business straightaway. You might be one of those lucky people who fits a common size without a hitch. However, if you have specific requirements, then knowing what they are can eliminate a lot of bikes that would be a waste of time for you to consider.

The various formulae and methods given herein for determining riding position have historic precedent. As you go about setting up a bike to suit you, keep in mind that any change in position may at first feel odd. Unless something is clearly out of whack, give any new arrangement a fair trial of at least 50 miles of riding before making alterations. On the other hand, everyone is a little different, and some variation from the norm may be in order. Just make changes gradually.

For how to adjust various components, look up Adjustment under the relevant heading in the Maintenance and Repair sections.

FITTING

Frame

From a practical point of view, frame sizes come in categories: extra-small, small, medium, large, and extra-large. Diamond-pattern frames with a level top tube have precise sizes, based on the distance between the seat lug and the center of the bottom bracket axle.

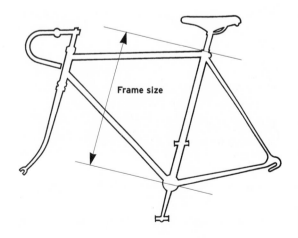

Frame size

Most frames, however, are the mountain bike type, where designs vary and a common reference point for measurement or sizing is not available. Knowing the seat lug to bottom bracket axle distance does not help in the case of a frame which has a steeply sloping top tube and a long seat post. Nevertheless, manufacturers continue to describe frame sizes in inches, and to make absolutely sure that this is meaningless, they use different ways of measuring; 16-inch according to one maker may be 18-inch by another.

The starting point in sizing a bike to a rider is that person's individual anatomy, with principal reference to height, and leg and arm lengths. More and more bike shops have fitting machines, and this can be a brilliant way of establishing your optimum bike configuration and riding position, which of course will be different for road, off-road or utility riding. Some of these fitting devices have impressive bells and whistles in the form of various meters, lights, and other instruments; others hook into a computer; and yet others are simply run by someone with a lot of experience at fitting people and bikes. Whatever, you hop aboard and saddle position, handlebars, etc. are adjusted until you are comfortable and pedalling efficiently. You then know almost everything – saddle height, crank length, stem length, handlebar width and rake, and so on. A bonus with more sophisticated units is that individual problems may be detected, such as legs of unequal length, or a need for extra float (degree of twist without release) with a clip-in pedal. Great stuff, but let's go through how it is done by eyeball.

• Road

First, establish your general size by finding a diamond frame (level top tube) bike that you can comfortably straddle with your feet flat on the ground. If the top tube digs into your crotch, you can be sure sooner or later of a nasty slam where it hurts the most. There should be an inch to spare, more if you are 5ft. 10in. or taller. Another method for determining diamond frame size is to measure your inseam length from crotch to floor

in bare feet six inches apart and multiply by 0.65. Either way, as a double-check, when the saddle height is correctly set (see below), four to five inches of seat post should be exposed.

In the case of a frame with a sloping top tube, there is no fixed reference point for precise measurement. Moreover, the sizes will usually be general – small, medium, and large. You're looking for the one that most approximates your diamond frame size. In borderline cases, go for the smaller size.

By and large, novices are prone to select a frame which is too large. An oversize frame feels a bit more secure and steady, and can have a slightly easier ride, as small frames tend to be stiffer than large frames. However, small frames weigh a little less and are more maneuverable. Once you become an experienced rider, you'll find that a little extra stiffness is useful.

A frame for a touring bike can be slightly larger in size. One reason is that the bottom bracket might be lower, so that the bike is easier to mount and dismount, and more stable when loaded. (In contrast, a bike for criterium racing may have a slightly higher bottom bracket, to increase pedal clearance when cornering.) A more important factor for a touring bike is ensuring there is sufficient room for mounting panniers without fouling the rider's heel on the pedal stroke. This can all get a little bit tricky, because providing space for panniers is better done by relaxing the frame angles and extending the stays, than by increasing the frame size. As for stiffness, it should be inherent in the materials used for the frame.

Women at 5ft. 5in. or less should seek a frame proportioned for a female. In comparison to men, women have longer legs and shorter arms and torsos. On a frame right for their leg length, many women will need a shorter stem for correct positioning of the handlebars. In large frame sizes this works well in most cases, but in small frame sizes the space can become cramped. It's better to shorten the top tube, and this is done by steepening the seat tube – hence a proportioned frame. See Chapter 7, Some Advice On Selecting A Bike, for more information.

• Mountain and Off-road

Mountain bikes are more difficult to size, because the bottom bracket height tends to vary more. Nonetheless, when you straddle the bike with your feet flat on the ground, there should be no less than four inches of clear daylight between your crotch and the top tube. After this, keep on downsizing until you find the smallest size that still provides enough saddle height and handlebar reach. Note that your riding position on a mountain bike is different than on a road bike (see below). Check that on the pedal stroke your knees do not foul the handlebars.

Why so small? One prime reason is safety and comfort. Once you start going over rough terrain and moving the bike around underneath you, lots of room is essential. This isn't just off-road. On one run home from the office I miscalculated a tight spot and drove a pedal down into a sidewalk, launching bike and self into the air with a car right alongside. The bike bucked and twisted violently and the top tube gave me a monster whack on the thigh that I felt for a week, but at least I was able to sort matters out for a safe landing. Had the top tube been a couple of inches closer to my privates, I'd have been put out of commission and possibly gone underneath the car.

Another prime reason for a small frame is simple fun and convenience. Small frames are lighter, stiffer, and more maneuverable. Riding a fast, deft, easily handled bike makes just about everything more enjoyable. This is true both on- and off-road.

If you are in doubt about frame size, then do some test rides. Over the years I've tested many brilliant bikes, and the ones I liked best all had a common characteristic: they fit. It's possible to get by on a bike which is not quite right, in fact not even be aware that something is amiss, but the moment you switch to a bike which *is* right, the difference is evident. Something clicks, the bike goes when and where you want, and feels comfortable and natural. Instead of being something that you are on, it is part of you.

• Recumbent

Some recumbents are made with frames in various sizes, such as small, medium, and large, others feature sliding seats or bottom brackets to allow for variations in leg length. I'm afraid there are no fixed rules for sizing recumbents, and when considering a machine for purchase it is vital that you take enough test rides to know you are comfortable with it.

So far, I think I've figured out the following with regard to efficiency and comfort when sizing and setting up recumbents. For machines where the bottom bracket is lower than the rider's hip line and the back is more upright, most people seem to like a position which gives complete leg extension when the pedal is as far away from the rider as it can get. In other words, with the heel on the pedal, the leg is straight at the bottom of the crank stroke. This is more or less equivalent to a 1.09 formula setting (see below) of saddle height on an upright bike, and from a biomechanical point of view, generates more power and places less stress on the legs. My completely subjective observation is that riders of recumbents where the bottom bracket is lower than the hip line tend to use fairly slow pedalling cadences, even when racing. The pattern of foot movement is quite distinctly push-push-push.

Once the bottom bracket elevates to the same plane as the hips, I believe that the balance of the body changes. It is of course still possible to brace one's back and thrust against the pedals, but in general, the rider is more cradled, and less as if sitting in a chair. The change is similar in some ways to what happens when you get well forward on a regular upright bike, place more weight on the arms, and the legs dangle. In both cases, the change of balance or weight distribution seems to encourage using faster pedalling cadences. My own experience with recumbents is that a rapid cadence, tightly maintained through precise use of the gears, produces optimum performance. For this sort of thing, a riding position with slightly less than complete leg extension at the bottom of the stroke seems best.

A point to watch with recumbents is the inclination of the seat back, and the position of the head rest, if there is one. I've spent many hours and chewed through countless bits of foam experimenting with different possibilities, and what's good seems to be a function of the riding conditions, and one's own fitness. In traffic, there is a natural tendency to want to be upright and more able to see, and this position is better for generating the kind of thrust power often needed in stop-and-go riding. Out on the road, or howling around the place, a slightly more inclined position seems better for maintaining a rapid pedalling cadence. Provided one has managed to get the seat position just about exactly right, the two different riding positions are almost equivalent to the rear-of-saddle, front-of-saddle positions one can use with a regular upright bike.

Saddle

Going back to an upright bike, the position of the saddle determines the fitting of the rest of the machine. For most riders the correct fore-to-aft position is with the nose of the saddle 1.75 to 2.5 inches behind a vertical line through the bottom bracket axle. Classically, the precise position is determined as follows: when comfortably seated on the saddle with feet on the pedals and cranks parallel to the ground (3 o'clock and 9 o'clock), a plumb line (weight and string) from the center of the forward knee should pass right through the pedal spindle. Thus, the taller the person, the further back the saddle.

The plumb line/kneecap method applies only to upright bikes and is not gospel; it serves only to establish a neutral position where the work done by the fore and aft muscle groups in the leg are evenly balanced. According to your riding style and technique, there are many variations. Touring riders often use a slightly rearward saddle position together with handlebars set on the high side. They are interested in comfort and steady power over long distances. Some climbers claim that a rearward position gives greater leverage in big gears. It's worth noting, though, that the

same effect can be achieved by simply shifting back in the saddle. Time trial riders and cyclists who like to spin the cranks rapidly often prefer a more forward position. As a rough rule of thumb, the more you like to crouch over the bars and spin, the more forward the saddle, and the more you like to sit tall, the further back the saddle. Experiment and see. Be sure to combine any changes in fore and aft saddle position with an appropriate adjustment in handlebar position (see below).

• Saddle Height

For saddle height, the rough rule of thumb is that while sitting on the bike with your heel on the pedal at its lowest point, your leg should be almost straight. This means that when riding with the ball of your foot on the pedal, your leg is almost but not quite fully extended at the bottom of the stroke.

Most saddles are set too low. A sound method for setting saddle height is to measure inside leg length from crotch bone to floor without shoes, and multiply this by 1.09. Example: 32 inches x 1.09 = 34.88 inches. Set saddle so that distance **A** from top of saddle to center of pedal spindle in down position with crank parallel to seat tube is 34.88 inches.

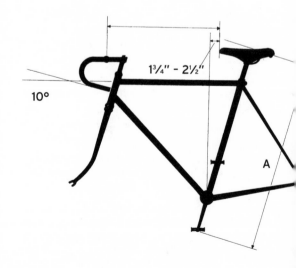

The 1.09 method was put together by experts. They found that an alteration in saddle height of four percent of inside leg measurement from the 1.09 setting affected power output by approximately five percent. Therefore, once you've set the saddle height by this formula, leave it alone for a while before making changes.

The exception to this rule is off-road riding, where a lower saddle height gives more room for the bike to move around underneath you. A lower position is also useful for hairy, steep descents, because it's easier to slide off the back of the saddle and put your weight to the rear, over the back wheel.

Some folks like a lower saddle position for town riding, so that when stopped, they can remain seated without pointing a toe like a ballerina. Careful. A low saddle position is harder on the knees, and stop-and-go traffic can call for higher peak efforts than steady riding. You're better off riding with the correct position and coming out of the saddle when necessary.

In fact, if you've got troublesome knees, a higher saddle position may help. Set the saddle by the 1.09 method and a bit more, then go for a ride with a friend. Ask your companion to observe if your hips are rocking from side to side as you pedal. If so, lower the saddle bit by bit until your hips remain even.

• Saddle Tilt

The horizontal tilt of the saddle, the height of the front relative to the rear, is crucial. Use a straightedge to set it dead level, and if you experience pain or discomfort, lower the nose a degree or two. Don't go too far, or else you will slide forward and place too much weight on your arms. However, riders using elbow rest bars and a forward saddle position may want a slight downward tilt.

The kind of saddle makes a difference. Padded anatomic saddles have a tendency to bounce the rider forward, and one recourse is to tilt the nose up a degree or two. Don't be afraid to make changes and experiment. With time you'll work out what is right for you.

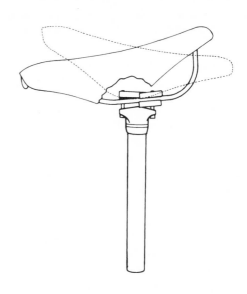

Handlebars and Stem

• Road

Drop bar width should equal shoulder width. The size range is 38 to 42 cm, with 44 cm sometimes available. Wider bars won't hurt, but bars too narrow for your shoulders will constrict breathing. The depth of the drop, or hooks, depends on your hand size. Measure your hands by grasping a tubular object and placing your fist on a table with the tube horizontal. A fist height of 2.75 inch is shallow, 2.75 to 3.5 inch is medium, and over 3.5 inch is large.

Handlebar height is set with the stem and for conventional use should be from one to three inches below the saddle. Lower if you have long arms and torso, or like fierce riding; higher if you have short arms and torso, or like relaxed riding. Position the bottom of the hooks level with the ground, or slightly slanted and pointing toward the rear hub.

The stem should position the bars so that the distance between the nose of the saddle and the rear edge of the center of the handlebars equals the distance from your elbow to your outstretched fingertips. When you are riding with your hands on the drops, your view of the front hub should be obscured by the handlebars. Your back should be straight, or nearly so, and your arms bent fairly close to 90°.

• Mountain

Flat bars range from 21 to 24 inches in width, and should equal shoulder width. Wider bars increase control at slow speeds, narrower bars quicken steering and are better for racing and shooting gaps in traffic. Flat bars are easy to trim with a hacksaw or pipe cutter, but before you do this, move the controls inboard and try out the new position. If you use bar ends, leave a little bit extra at each end.

Mountain bike bars are variously flat, swept back up to 11°, or combine both backward sweep and upward rise. These variations are for arm and wrist comfort, and it's a question of what you like – try and see.

Bar ends are great. They increase the number of riding positions, which promotes comfort through variety. They provide leverage for climbing, and also a longer, lower position for speed. Set them more upright if you are a beginning or relaxed rider, more pointing forward if you are a speedo. Models which curve inward are less likely to snag, but weigh a little more than straight models.

Mountain bike stems come in a wide range of sizes, from around 50 to 150 cm, with rise ranging from -5° through to 25°. The stem should place the handlebar about an inch below the top of the saddle. When you sit on the bike with your back at an angle of about 45°, your arms should be slightly bent.

Hybrid or cross bikes are apt to be supplied with short, high stems providing an upright riding position. This is OK if you're just starting out, but plan on switching to a longer stem with less rise, so as to get the 45° position. This allows your arms to carry some of your weight and to act as shock absorbers, thereby relieving your posterior, and makes more efficient use of the leg muscles.

Brake Levers

• Road

On drop bars, the tip of the brake lever should just touch a straightedge (or table top) laid along the bar end. In most cases this will be at about 3 o'clock on the hooks. This is a racing setup, where a lot of riding is done with hands on the hooks. Tourists and town riders more often ride in an upright position with their hands on the brake hoods. In such cases, for comfort and a secure grip when braking hard, the levers can be set higher, at around 2 o'clock. If you want, have the bar ends raked 10° from horizontal; for Sunday racing, rotating the bars slightly will bring the hoods back to 3 o'clock.

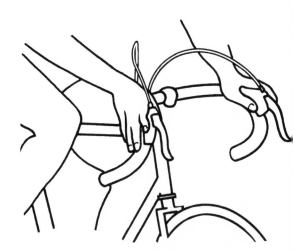

• Mountain

Brake levers should be set between 30° and 45° below horizontal to prevent damaged fingers in the event of a fall. Tighten the mounting bolt firmly enough to hold the brake lever in place, but still loose enough to move if the bike takes a tumble. Your wrists should be straight, and two fingers (usually index and middle) should extend around the lever. Almost all levers have adjustable travel; set the distance of the lever from the grip so that your brake fingers go around it easily.

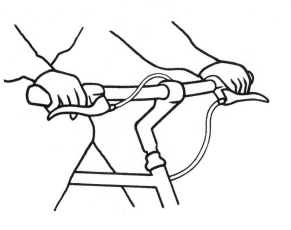

Cranks

Cranks on Ashtabula and cotterless cranksets are usually 165 mm long. Cranks for cotterless cranksets range in length from 160 to 180 mm. In theory, for road bikes the correct crank length is determined by your inseam leg length:

Inseam Length	Crank Length
29 inches or less	165 mm
29-32 inches	170 mm
32-34 inches	172.5 mm
34 inches and more	175 mm

The idea, of course, is that a tall person with long legs will find it difficult to twiddle short cranks, and a short person will not enjoy stretching all over creation to spin long cranks. Beyond this, longer cranks are held to produce more power through greater leverage. For this reason, mountain bikes are usually supplied with cranks 5 mm longer than on an equivalent size road bike. There's been a tendency for some roadies to head in this direction, too. If you're a physics fan, your gut should be tickling something is not right here, and you're right: there is no free lunch.

Using a longer crank is like changing gear, and bikes already have gears. I use 170 mm cranks on all my bikes, road, mountain and recumbent, because that's what I am used to, and can spin

best. For more torque when needed, I downshift. For more speed, I push harder – and from a physiological point of view, shorter cranks are better for this. The longer the crank and the more you contort your leg, particularly when muscling hard, the worse it is for your body. It's like having a low saddle. If you have dodgy knees this is a real consideration, and be advised that problems in this area may take years to develop, after which point a full fix is by the board. See gearing, below, for more on this topic.

Another factor in favor of short cranks is clearance when cornering or going over rough ground. Long cranks on a criterium racer with a high bottom bracket are OK, but on a touring bike with a low bottom bracket they will make the machine prone to ground when cornering. On the other side, when weaving around or over obstacles, mountain bikers often use part strokes, to keep the pedals clear of obstacles and to avoid becoming stuck in the power-dead TDC (6 o'clock/ 12 o'clock) crank position. Long cranks and wider bars provide (or feel like they do) better control at slow speeds. You can find plenty of opinions on this business of crank length, there's room for personal preference, and my two cent's worth is: short people should use 165 mm cranks, most people 170 mm, and a few tall people 175 mm.

• Unequal Legs

Some people have different length legs. The result when riding a bike can be inexplicable back, hip, and leg pains. If a qualified orthopedist or sports physician confirms that your legs are different in length, you can either use pedals of different heights, or shims underneath the shoe cleat on the short leg side.

Cleats/Toe Clips and Straps

Cleats are metal or plastic devices fastened to the soles of your shoes, that hold your foot down on the pedal. They are essential for fast, efficient pedalling, and a vital aid for safety.

Old-fashioned cleats have a slot which fits over the rear side of a cage pedal. The shoe is held down with a toe clip and strap. To tighten up, or release, you reach down and pull on the strap or release the buckle. The classic result of an unexpected stop with tight straps is a slow, teetering, undignified topple to the ground. One of my all-time best recoveries was when this happened to me while on my classic Evans road bike, near the Tower of London. I had the good luck to be wearing a large backpack, and perhaps because I am averse to scratching the bike, I somehow managed to twist and land on the pack and then roll into an upside-down position, bike in mid-air and wheels spinning like the flailing legs of an overturned beetle. The bike never touched the ground. A large crowd of slack-jawed tourists watched as I deftly detached from the pedals, sprang upright, remounted and sped on my way.

Aside from classic bikes, the only use for toe clips and straps is if you must or want to wear shoes that cannot mount clip-in cleats. In that case, make sure that the toe clip size (S, M, L) corresponds to your shoe size. To avoid scratching fancy shoes, either fit toe clip pads or mask the clips with tape.

Clip-in pedals are far superior. There's no strap or clip to bind or chafe the foot and cause numbness or blistering. Release is a simple matter of twisting the foot. Most important of all, the cleat mechanism is designed so that the foot can rotate or pivot a few degrees to either side before release takes effect. This is called float, and is for the saving of your knees. In the course of each crank rotation, the foot twists from side-to-side – a little in some cases, a lot in others. If the foot is locked rigidly to the pedal and the knee joint is twisted even just a little, damage can result.

When first fitting clip-in cleats, set the mounting screws just semi-tight, so that when the cleat is engaged with the pedal, you can still adjust the position by twisting and tapping your foot. Another reason for this is that when tightened hard, most cleats make an impression on the shoe sole. This can make later adjustments tricky, because the cleat will tend to home on a particular spot. For an easier life at cleat replacement time, lube mounting screws with grease or treat with an anti-seize product.

Position the ball or widest part of your foot right over the pedal axle. Your natural foot position may be dead parallel, pigeon-toed or duck-footed; to see, walk around with wet feet or in sand. Position the cleats accordingly, set the release mechanism as low (easy) as possible, and go out for a ride, experimenting with different positions until you are comfortable. In terms of lateral (in-and-out) placement, you want to be as close as possible to the cranks without bumping them.

If you start with semi-tight mounting bolts, you may not be able to disengage from the pedals without moving the cleats. Tighten the bolts a little until you can. Once you're happy with the position, snug the cleats right down. Another trick that sometimes works is, once the cleats are in the position you like, you stay on the bike while a friend tightens the mounting bolts. Note that cleats for Time A.T.A.C. pedals have no lateral or rotational adjustment; all you need to set is fore-and-aft placement. Put the cleat with the imprinted stars on the right sole for more float range, on the left sole for less.

SPD cleats are available in two types: multi-direction with vertical release, and single plane, with side only release. As far as I'm concerned, vertical release is for the birds. If I run into a rough patch while riding, I want to stay together with the bike, not suffer an unwanted release and loss of control. If a riding situation is one where I might need to bail out instantly, I ride with open pedals.

GEARING

Gearing is an important topic, but it is one that you can learn about and apply as you go along. So if you find your eyes glazing over while reading this section, pack it in and come back later. Production bikes are fairly well spec'ed for gear ratios, so with most new bikes you can ride out of the shop and be OK for a while. As your interest in cycling deepens or you develop particular requirements, you can get more technical and make the gearing changes you need. A point to watch, however, is that some bikes are sold with fixed chainsets and freewheels, where the chainrings and sprockets are held in place with rivets. An economy for manufacturers, perhaps, but you cannot do a thing with these. If you want to change the gearing, you will probably have to replace the whole transmission, crankset, freewheel, derailleurs, chain and all, and at today's prices for components, you would be better off buying a new bike. From your point of view, a bike with riveted chainset and freewheel is a false economy, big time.

What Gears Do

When I bought my first derailleur gear bike I was surprised to find that the gear ratios, instead of each having a separate range as on a car, had considerable overlap. One gear wasn't much different from the other. The reason is that in pedalling there is a cadence rate (number of crank revolutions per minute) which is the most efficient — quick enough to avoid fatigue from pressing too strongly on the pedals (pain in the legs), but not so fast that the rider becomes starved for oxygen (panting). Optimum cadence for general riders is typically 65 to 85 rpm, while racers can run to 120 to 130 rpm and up. The ideal rate is widely held to be 100 rpm. Although one can honk a big gear up a hill, or twiddle a small gear into an incandescent blur in sprint, for long term efficiency and comfort, you need to stay within 10 percent of optimum cadence rate. The primary function of bicycle gears is to keep you within this zone.

Road racing bikes usually have close ratio gears, with each ratio near in size to the next, while touring and mountain bikes usually have wide ratio gears, with greater differences between each ratio. The reason for this is that touring and mountain bikes encounter more varied conditions, frequently pack heavy loads up steep grades, and are more likely to be used by novice riders. You need to be fairly proficient and fit in order to comfortably use close ratio gears.

Gears and Inches

Strictly speaking, a gear ratio is the number of teeth (T) on the front chainring divided by the number of teeth on the rear sprocket (or cog). Thus, 60T front to 15T rear is a ratio of 4:1 – the rear wheel revolves four times for every revolution of the cranks. Since bicycle wheels are in different sizes, gear ratios are calculated as a single number by the formula:

$$\frac{\text{Number of teeth on front chainring}}{\text{Number of teeth on back sprocket}} \times \text{wheel diameter} = \text{gear ratio}$$

Gear ratio numbers are expressed in inches, as in 90-inch gear. This is an arbitrary reference, as gear inch number is not a measurement of how far a wheel will travel for each rotation of the cranks. The system is derived from the high wheel bicycle, where a gear of 60 meant that the driving wheel had a diameter of 60 inches. Thus, for one rotation of the cranks, a modern bicycle with a 60-inch gear will go the same distance as a high wheel bike with a 60-inch diameter driving wheel. If you want to know how far a wheel will travel per crank rotation, add pi to the gear inch formula:

$$\frac{\text{Number of teeth on front chainring}}{\text{Number of teeth on back sprocket}} \times 3.14 \times \text{wheel diameter} = \text{distance}$$

In general, 100 inches is the top range and is hard to push, 90 inches is more common, 80 inches is the usual speed gear, 70 and 60 inches are the most often used, 50 and 40 inches are for hills, and 30 inches right down to 15 inches are for steep terrain and/or heavy loads. Much depends on the kind of bike involved. For example, my classic racing mountain bike has a gear range of 28

NUMBER OF TEETH ON SPROCKET

NUMBER OF TEETH ON CHAIN RING

Chain ring \ Sprocket	9	10	11	12	13	14	15	16	17	18	19	20	21	22	23	24	25	26	27	28	29	30	31	32	33	34	35	36	37	38
60	173.3	156.0	141.8	130.0	120.0	111.4	104.0	97.5	91.8	86.7	82.1	78.0	74.3	70.9	67.8	65.0	62.4	60.0	57.8	55.7	53.8	52.0	50.3	48.8	47.3	45.9	44.6	43.3	42.2	41.1
59	170.4	153.4	139.5	127.8	118.0	109.6	102.3	95.9	90.2	85.2	80.7	76.7	73.0	69.7	66.7	63.9	61.4	59.0	56.8	54.8	52.9	51.1	49.5	47.9	46.5	45.1	43.8	42.6	41.5	40.4
58	167.6	150.8	137.1	125.7	116.0	107.7	100.5	94.3	88.7	83.8	79.4	75.4	71.8	68.5	65.6	62.8	60.3	58.0	55.9	53.9	52.0	50.3	48.6	47.1	45.7	44.4	43.1	41.9	40.8	39.7
57	164.7	148.2	134.7	123.5	114.0	105.9	98.8	92.6	87.2	82.3	78.0	74.1	70.6	67.4	64.4	61.8	59.3	57.0	54.9	52.9	51.1	49.4	47.8	46.3	44.9	43.6	42.3	41.2	40.1	39.0
56	161.8	145.6	132.4	121.3	112.0	104.0	97.1	91.0	85.6	80.9	76.6	72.8	69.3	66.2	63.3	60.7	58.2	56.0	53.9	52.0	50.2	48.5	47.0	45.5	44.1	42.8	41.6	40.4	39.4	38.3
55	158.9	143.0	130.0	119.2	110.0	102.1	95.3	89.4	84.1	79.4	75.3	71.5	68.1	65.0	62.2	59.6	57.2	55.0	53.0	51.1	49.3	47.7	46.1	44.7	43.3	42.1	40.9	39.7	38.6	37.6
54	156.0	140.4	127.6	117.0	108.0	100.3	93.6	87.8	82.6	78.0	73.9	70.2	66.9	63.8	61.0	58.5	56.2	54.0	52.0	50.1	48.4	46.8	45.3	43.9	42.5	41.3	40.1	39.0	37.9	36.9
53	153.1	137.8	125.3	114.8	106.0	98.4	91.9	86.1	81.1	76.6	72.5	68.9	65.6	62.6	59.9	57.4	55.1	53.0	51.0	49.2	47.5	45.9	44.5	43.1	41.8	40.5	39.4	38.3	37.2	36.3
52	150.2	135.2	122.9	112.7	104.0	96.6	90.1	84.5	79.5	75.1	71.2	67.6	64.4	61.5	58.8	56.3	54.1	52.0	50.1	48.3	46.6	45.1	43.6	42.3	41.0	39.8	38.6	37.6	36.5	35.6
51	147.3	132.6	120.5	110.5	102.0	94.7	88.4	82.9	78.0	73.7	69.8	66.3	63.1	60.3	57.7	55.3	53.0	51.0	49.1	47.4	45.7	44.2	42.8	41.4	40.2	39.0	37.9	36.8	35.8	34.9
50	144.4	130.0	118.2	108.3	100.0	92.9	86.7	81.3	76.5	72.2	68.4	65.0	61.9	59.1	56.5	54.2	52.0	50.0	48.1	46.4	44.8	43.3	41.9	40.6	39.4	38.2	37.1	36.1	35.1	34.2
49	141.6	127.4	115.8	106.2	98.0	91.0	84.9	79.6	74.9	70.8	67.1	63.7	60.7	57.9	55.4	53.1	51.0	49.0	47.2	45.5	43.9	42.5	41.1	39.8	38.6	37.5	36.4	35.4	34.4	33.5
48	138.7	124.8	113.5	104.0	96.0	89.1	83.2	78.0	73.4	69.3	65.7	62.4	59.4	56.7	54.3	52.0	49.9	48.0	46.2	44.6	43.0	41.6	40.3	39.0	37.8	36.7	35.7	34.7	33.7	32.8
47	135.8	122.2	111.1	101.8	94.0	87.3	81.5	76.4	71.9	67.9	64.3	61.1	58.2	55.5	53.1	50.9	48.9	47.0	45.3	43.6	42.1	40.7	39.4	38.2	37.0	35.9	34.9	33.9	33.0	32.2
46	132.9	119.6	108.7	99.7	92.0	85.4	79.7	74.8	70.4	66.4	62.9	59.8	57.0	54.4	52.0	49.8	47.8	46.0	44.3	42.7	41.2	39.9	38.6	37.4	36.2	35.2	34.2	33.2	32.3	31.5
45	130.0	117.0	106.4	97.5	90.0	83.6	78.0	73.1	68.8	65.0	61.6	58.5	55.7	53.2	50.9	48.8	46.8	45.0	43.3	41.8	40.3	39.0	37.7	36.6	35.5	34.4	33.4	32.5	31.6	30.8
44	127.1	114.4	104.0	95.3	88.0	81.7	76.3	71.5	67.3	63.6	60.2	57.2	54.5	52.0	49.7	47.7	45.8	44.0	42.4	40.9	39.4	38.1	36.9	35.8	34.7	33.6	32.7	31.8	30.9	30.1
43	124.2	111.8	101.6	93.2	86.0	79.9	74.5	69.9	65.8	62.1	58.8	55.9	53.2	50.8	48.6	46.6	44.7	43.0	41.4	39.9	38.6	37.3	36.1	34.9	33.9	32.9	31.9	31.1	30.2	29.4
42	121.3	109.2	99.3	91.0	84.0	78.0	72.8	68.3	64.2	60.7	57.5	54.6	52.0	49.6	47.5	45.5	43.7	42.0	40.4	39.0	37.7	36.4	35.2	34.1	33.1	32.1	31.2	30.3	29.5	28.7
41	118.4	106.6	96.9	88.8	82.0	76.1	71.1	66.6	62.7	59.2	56.1	53.3	50.8	48.5	46.3	44.4	42.6	41.0	39.5	38.1	36.8	35.5	34.4	33.3	32.3	31.4	30.5	29.6	28.8	28.1
40	115.6	104.0	94.5	86.7	80.0	74.3	69.3	65.0	61.2	57.8	54.7	52.0	49.5	47.3	45.2	43.3	41.6	40.0	38.5	37.1	35.9	34.7	33.5	32.5	31.5	30.6	29.7	28.9	28.1	27.4
39	112.7	101.4	92.2	84.5	78.0	72.4	67.6	63.4	59.6	56.3	53.4	50.7	48.3	46.1	44.1	42.3	40.6	39.0	37.6	36.2	35.0	33.8	32.7	31.7	30.7	29.8	29.0	28.2	27.4	26.7
38	109.8	98.8	89.8	82.3	76.0	70.6	65.9	61.8	58.1	54.9	52.0	49.4	47.0	44.9	43.0	41.2	39.5	38.0	36.6	35.3	34.1	32.9	31.9	30.9	29.9	29.1	28.2	27.4	26.7	26.0
37	106.9	96.2	87.5	80.2	74.0	68.7	64.1	60.1	56.6	53.4	50.6	48.1	45.8	43.7	41.8	40.1	38.5	37.0	35.6	34.4	33.2	32.1	31.0	30.1	29.2	28.3	27.5	26.7	26.0	25.3
36	104.0	93.6	85.1	78.0	72.0	66.9	62.4	58.5	55.1	52.0	49.3	46.8	44.6	42.5	40.7	39.0	37.4	36.0	34.7	33.4	32.3	31.2	30.2	29.3	28.4	27.5	26.7	26.0	25.3	24.6
35	101.1	91.0	82.7	75.8	70.0	65.0	60.7	56.9	53.5	50.6	47.9	45.5	43.3	41.4	39.6	37.9	36.4	35.0	33.7	32.5	31.4	30.3	29.4	28.4	27.6	26.8	26.0	25.3	24.6	23.9
34	98.2	88.4	80.4	73.7	68.0	63.1	58.9	55.3	52.0	49.1	46.5	44.2	42.1	40.2	38.4	36.8	35.4	34.0	32.7	31.6	30.5	29.5	28.5	27.6	26.8	26.0	25.3	24.6	23.9	23.3
33	95.3	85.8	78.0	71.5	66.0	61.3	57.2	53.6	50.5	47.7	45.2	42.9	40.9	39.0	37.3	35.8	34.3	33.0	31.8	30.6	29.6	28.6	27.7	26.8	26.0	25.2	24.5	23.8	23.2	22.6
32	92.4	83.2	75.6	69.3	64.0	59.4	55.5	52.0	48.9	46.2	43.8	41.6	39.6	37.8	36.2	34.7	33.3	32.0	30.8	29.7	28.7	27.7	26.8	26.0	25.2	24.5	23.8	23.1	22.5	21.9
31	89.6	80.6	73.3	67.2	62.0	57.6	53.7	50.4	47.4	44.8	42.4	40.3	38.4	36.6	35.0	33.6	32.2	31.0	29.9	28.8	27.8	26.9	26.0	25.2	24.4	23.7	23.0	22.4	21.8	21.2
30	86.7	78.0	70.9	65.0	60.0	55.7	52.0	48.8	45.9	43.3	41.1	39.0	37.1	35.5	33.9	32.5	31.2	30.0	28.9	27.9	26.9	26.0	25.2	24.4	23.6	22.9	22.3	21.7	21.1	20.5
29	83.8	75.4	68.5	62.8	58.0	53.9	50.3	47.1	44.4	41.9	39.7	37.7	35.9	34.3	32.8	31.4	30.2	29.0	27.9	26.9	26.0	25.1	24.3	23.6	22.8	22.2	21.5	20.9	20.4	19.8
28	80.9	72.8	66.2	60.7	56.0	52.0	48.5	45.5	42.8	40.4	38.3	36.4	34.7	33.1	31.7	30.3	29.1	28.0	27.0	26.0	25.1	24.3	23.5	22.8	22.1	21.4	20.8	20.2	19.7	19.2
27	78.0	70.2	63.8	58.5	54.0	50.1	46.8	43.9	41.3	39.0	36.9	35.1	33.4	31.9	30.5	29.3	28.1	27.0	26.0	25.1	24.2	23.4	22.6	21.9	21.3	20.6	20.1	19.5	19.0	18.5
26	75.1	67.6	61.5	56.3	52.0	48.3	45.1	42.3	39.8	37.6	35.6	33.8	32.2	30.7	29.4	28.2	27.0	26.0	25.0	24.1	23.3	22.5	21.8	21.1	20.5	19.9	19.3	18.8	18.3	17.8
25	72.2	65.0	59.1	54.2	50.0	46.4	43.3	40.6	38.2	36.1	34.2	32.5	31.0	29.5	28.3	27.1	26.0	25.0	24.1	23.2	22.4	21.7	21.0	20.3	19.7	19.1	18.6	18.1	17.6	17.1
24	69.3	62.4	56.7	52.0	48.0	44.6	41.6	39.0	36.7	34.7	32.8	31.2	29.7	28.4	27.1	26.0	25.0	24.0	23.1	22.3	21.5	20.8	20.1	19.5	18.9	18.4	17.8	17.3	16.9	16.4
23	66.4	59.8	54.4	49.8	46.0	42.7	39.9	37.4	35.2	33.2	31.5	29.9	28.5	27.2	26.0	24.9	23.9	23.0	22.1	21.4	20.6	19.9	19.3	18.7	18.1	17.6	17.1	16.6	16.2	15.7
22	63.6	57.2	52.0	47.7	44.0	40.9	38.1	35.8	33.6	31.8	30.1	28.6	27.2	26.0	24.9	23.8	22.9	22.0	21.2	20.4	19.7	19.1	18.5	17.9	17.3	16.8	16.3	15.9	15.5	15.1
21	60.7	54.6	49.6	45.5	42.0	39.0	36.4	34.1	32.1	30.3	28.7	27.3	26.0	24.8	23.7	22.8	21.8	21.0	20.2	19.5	18.8	18.2	17.6	17.1	16.5	16.1	15.6	15.2	14.8	14.4
20	57.8	52.0	47.3	43.3	40.0	37.1	34.7	32.5	30.6	28.9	27.4	26.0	24.8	23.6	22.6	21.7	20.8	20.0	19.3	18.6	17.9	17.3	16.8	16.3	15.8	15.3	14.9	14.4	14.1	13.7
19	54.9	49.4	44.9	41.2	38.0	35.3	32.9	30.9	29.1	27.4	26.0	24.7	23.5	22.5	21.5	20.6	19.8	19.0	18.3	17.6	17.0	16.5	15.9	15.4	15.0	14.5	14.1	13.7	13.4	13.0
18	52.0	46.8	42.5	39.0	36.0	33.4	31.2	29.3	27.5	26.0	24.6	23.4	22.3	21.3	20.3	19.5	18.7	18.0	17.3	16.7	16.1	15.6	15.1	14.6	14.2	13.8	13.4	13.0	12.6	12.3

GEAR RATIO CHART FOR 26-INCH WHEELS

NUMBER OF TEETH ON SPROCKET

NUMBER OF TEETH ON CHAIN RING (rows) × NUMBER OF TEETH ON SPROCKET (columns)

Chain Ring ↓ / Sprocket →	9	10	11	12	13	14	15	16	17	18	19	20	21	22	23	24	25	26	27	28	29	30	31	32	33	34	35	36	37	38
60	180.0	162.0	147.3	135.0	124.6	115.7	108.0	101.3	95.3	90.0	85.3	81.0	77.1	73.6	70.4	67.5	64.8	62.3	60.0	57.9	55.9	54.0	52.3	50.6	49.1	47.6	46.3	45.0	43.8	42.6
59	177.0	159.3	144.8	132.8	122.5	113.8	106.2	99.6	93.7	88.5	83.8	79.7	75.9	72.4	69.3	66.4	63.7	61.3	59.0	56.9	54.9	53.1	51.4	49.8	48.3	46.9	45.5	44.3	43.1	41.9
58	174.0	156.6	142.4	130.5	120.5	111.9	104.4	97.9	92.1	87.0	82.4	78.3	74.6	71.2	68.1	65.3	62.6	60.2	58.0	55.9	54.0	52.2	50.5	48.9	47.5	46.1	44.7	43.5	42.3	41.2
57	171.0	153.9	139.9	128.3	118.4	109.9	102.6	96.2	90.5	85.5	81.0	77.0	73.3	70.0	66.9	64.1	61.6	59.2	57.0	55.0	53.1	51.3	49.6	48.1	46.6	45.3	44.0	42.8	41.6	40.5
56	168.0	151.2	137.5	126.0	116.3	108.0	100.8	94.5	88.9	84.0	79.6	75.6	72.0	68.7	65.7	63.0	60.5	58.2	56.0	54.0	52.1	50.4	48.8	47.3	45.8	44.5	43.2	42.0	40.9	39.8
55	165.0	148.5	135.0	123.8	114.2	106.1	99.0	92.8	87.4	82.5	78.2	74.3	70.7	67.5	64.6	61.9	59.4	57.1	55.0	53.0	51.2	49.5	47.9	46.4	45.0	43.7	42.4	41.3	40.1	39.1
54	162.0	145.8	132.5	121.5	112.2	104.1	97.2	91.1	85.8	81.0	76.7	72.9	69.4	66.3	63.4	60.8	58.3	56.1	54.0	52.1	50.3	48.6	47.0	45.6	44.2	42.9	41.7	40.5	39.4	38.4
53	159.0	143.1	130.1	119.3	110.1	102.2	95.4	89.4	84.2	79.5	75.3	71.6	68.1	65.0	62.2	59.6	57.2	55.0	53.0	51.1	49.3	47.7	46.2	44.7	43.4	42.1	40.9	39.8	38.7	37.7
52	156.0	140.4	127.6	117.0	108.0	100.3	93.6	87.8	82.6	78.0	73.9	70.2	66.9	63.8	61.0	58.5	56.2	54.0	52.0	50.1	48.4	46.8	45.3	43.9	42.5	41.3	40.1	39.0	37.9	36.9
51	153.0	137.7	125.2	114.8	105.9	98.4	91.8	86.1	81.0	76.5	72.5	68.9	65.6	62.6	59.9	57.4	55.1	53.0	51.0	49.2	47.5	45.9	44.4	43.0	41.7	40.5	39.3	38.3	37.2	36.2
50	150.0	135.0	122.7	112.5	103.8	96.4	90.0	84.4	79.4	75.0	71.1	67.5	64.3	61.4	58.7	56.3	54.0	51.9	50.0	48.2	46.6	45.0	43.5	42.2	40.9	39.7	38.6	37.5	36.5	35.5
49	147.0	132.3	120.3	110.3	101.8	94.5	88.2	82.7	77.8	73.5	69.6	66.2	63.0	60.1	57.5	55.1	52.9	50.9	49.0	47.3	45.6	44.1	42.7	41.3	40.1	38.9	37.8	36.8	35.8	34.8
48	144.0	129.6	117.8	108.0	99.7	92.6	86.4	81.0	76.2	72.0	68.2	64.8	61.7	58.9	56.3	54.0	51.8	49.8	48.0	46.3	44.7	43.2	41.8	40.5	39.3	38.1	37.0	36.0	35.0	34.1
47	141.0	126.9	115.4	105.8	97.6	90.6	84.6	79.3	74.6	70.5	66.8	63.5	60.4	57.7	55.2	52.9	50.8	48.8	47.0	45.3	43.8	42.3	40.9	39.7	38.5	37.3	36.3	35.3	34.3	33.4
46	138.0	124.2	112.9	103.5	95.5	88.7	82.8	77.6	73.1	69.0	65.4	62.1	59.1	56.5	54.0	51.8	49.7	47.8	46.0	44.4	42.8	41.4	40.1	38.8	37.6	36.5	35.5	34.5	33.6	32.7
45	135.0	121.5	110.5	101.3	93.5	86.8	81.0	75.9	71.5	67.5	63.9	60.8	57.9	55.2	52.8	50.6	48.6	46.7	45.0	43.4	41.9	40.5	39.2	38.0	36.8	35.7	34.7	33.8	32.8	32.0
44	132.0	118.8	108.0	99.0	91.4	84.9	79.2	74.3	69.9	66.0	62.5	59.4	56.6	54.0	51.7	49.5	47.5	45.7	44.0	42.4	41.0	39.6	38.3	37.1	36.0	34.9	33.9	33.0	32.1	31.3
43	129.0	116.1	105.5	96.8	89.3	82.9	77.4	72.6	68.3	64.5	61.1	58.1	55.3	52.8	50.5	48.4	46.4	44.7	43.0	41.5	40.0	38.7	37.5	36.3	35.2	34.1	33.2	32.3	31.4	30.6
42	126.0	113.4	103.1	94.5	87.2	81.0	75.6	70.9	66.7	63.0	59.7	56.7	54.0	51.5	49.3	47.3	45.4	43.6	42.0	40.5	39.1	37.8	36.6	35.4	34.4	33.4	32.4	31.5	30.6	29.8
41	123.0	110.7	100.6	92.3	85.2	79.1	73.8	69.2	65.1	61.5	58.3	55.4	52.7	50.3	48.1	46.1	44.3	42.6	41.0	39.5	38.2	36.9	35.7	34.6	33.5	32.6	31.6	30.8	29.9	29.1
40	120.0	108.0	98.2	90.0	83.1	77.1	72.0	67.5	63.5	60.0	56.8	54.0	51.4	49.1	47.0	45.0	43.2	41.5	40.0	38.6	37.2	36.0	34.8	33.8	32.7	31.8	30.9	30.0	29.2	28.4
39	117.0	105.3	95.7	87.8	81.0	75.2	70.2	65.8	61.9	58.5	55.4	52.7	50.1	47.9	45.8	43.9	42.1	40.5	39.0	37.6	36.3	35.1	34.0	32.9	31.9	31.0	30.1	29.3	28.5	27.7
38	114.0	102.6	93.3	85.5	78.9	73.3	68.4	64.1	60.4	57.0	54.0	51.3	48.9	46.6	44.6	42.8	41.0	39.5	38.0	36.6	35.4	34.2	33.1	32.1	31.1	30.2	29.3	28.5	27.7	27.0
37	111.0	99.9	90.8	83.3	76.8	71.4	66.6	62.4	58.8	55.5	52.6	50.0	47.6	45.4	43.4	41.6	40.0	38.4	37.0	35.7	34.4	33.3	32.2	31.2	30.3	29.4	28.5	27.8	27.0	26.3
36	108.0	97.2	88.4	81.0	74.8	69.4	64.8	60.8	57.2	54.0	51.2	48.6	46.3	44.2	42.3	40.5	38.9	37.4	36.0	34.7	33.5	32.4	31.4	30.4	29.5	28.6	27.8	27.0	26.3	25.6
35	105.0	94.5	85.9	78.8	72.7	67.5	63.0	59.1	55.6	52.5	49.7	47.3	45.0	43.0	41.1	39.4	37.8	36.3	35.0	33.8	32.6	31.5	30.5	29.5	28.6	27.8	27.0	26.3	25.5	24.9
34	102.0	91.8	83.5	76.5	70.6	65.6	61.2	57.4	54.0	51.0	48.3	45.9	43.7	41.7	39.9	38.3	36.7	35.3	34.0	32.8	31.7	30.6	29.6	28.7	27.8	27.0	26.2	25.5	24.8	24.2
33	99.0	89.1	81.0	74.3	68.5	63.6	59.4	55.7	52.4	49.5	46.9	44.6	42.4	40.5	38.7	37.1	35.6	34.3	33.0	31.8	30.7	29.7	28.7	27.8	27.0	26.2	25.5	24.8	24.1	23.4
32	96.0	86.4	78.5	72.0	66.5	61.7	57.6	54.0	50.8	48.0	45.5	43.2	41.1	39.3	37.6	36.0	34.6	33.2	32.0	30.9	29.8	28.8	27.9	27.0	26.2	25.4	24.7	24.0	23.4	22.7
31	93.0	83.7	76.1	69.8	64.4	59.8	55.8	52.3	49.2	46.5	44.1	41.9	39.9	38.0	36.4	34.9	33.5	32.2	31.0	29.9	28.9	27.9	27.0	26.2	25.4	24.6	23.9	23.3	22.6	22.0
30	90.0	81.0	73.6	67.5	62.3	57.9	54.0	50.6	47.6	45.0	42.6	40.5	38.6	36.8	35.2	33.8	32.4	31.2	30.0	28.9	27.9	27.0	26.1	25.3	24.5	23.8	23.1	22.5	21.9	21.3
29	87.0	78.3	71.2	65.3	60.2	55.9	52.2	48.9	46.1	43.5	41.2	39.2	37.3	35.6	34.0	32.6	31.3	30.1	29.0	28.0	27.0	26.1	25.3	24.5	23.7	23.0	22.4	21.8	21.2	20.6
28	84.0	75.6	68.7	63.0	58.2	54.0	50.4	47.3	44.5	42.0	39.8	37.8	36.0	34.4	32.9	31.5	30.2	29.1	28.0	27.0	26.1	25.2	24.4	23.6	22.9	22.2	21.6	21.0	20.4	19.9
27	81.0	72.9	66.3	60.8	56.1	52.1	48.6	45.6	42.9	40.5	38.4	36.5	34.7	33.1	31.7	30.4	29.2	28.0	27.0	26.0	25.1	24.3	23.5	22.8	22.1	21.4	20.8	20.3	19.7	19.2
26	78.0	70.2	63.8	58.5	54.0	50.1	46.8	43.9	41.3	39.0	36.9	35.1	33.4	31.9	30.5	29.3	28.1	27.0	26.0	25.1	24.2	23.4	22.6	21.9	21.3	20.6	20.1	19.5	19.0	18.5
25	75.0	67.5	61.4	56.3	51.9	48.2	45.0	42.2	39.7	37.5	35.5	33.8	32.1	30.7	29.3	28.1	27.0	26.0	25.0	24.1	23.3	22.5	21.8	21.1	20.5	19.9	19.3	18.8	18.2	17.8
24	72.0	64.8	58.9	54.0	49.8	46.3	43.2	40.5	38.1	36.0	34.1	32.4	30.9	29.5	28.2	27.0	25.9	24.9	24.0	23.1	22.3	21.6	20.9	20.3	19.6	19.1	18.5	18.0	17.5	17.1
23	69.0	62.1	56.5	51.8	47.8	44.4	41.4	38.8	36.5	34.5	32.7	31.1	29.6	28.2	27.0	25.9	24.8	23.9	23.0	22.2	21.4	20.7	20.0	19.4	18.8	18.3	17.7	17.3	16.8	16.3
22	66.0	59.4	54.0	49.5	45.7	42.4	39.6	37.1	34.9	33.0	31.3	29.7	28.3	27.0	25.8	24.8	23.8	22.8	22.0	21.2	20.5	19.8	19.2	18.6	18.0	17.5	17.0	16.5	16.1	15.6
21	63.0	56.7	51.5	47.3	43.6	40.5	37.8	35.4	33.4	31.5	29.8	28.4	27.0	25.8	24.7	23.6	22.7	21.8	21.0	20.3	19.6	18.9	18.3	17.7	17.2	16.7	16.2	15.8	15.3	14.9
20	60.0	54.0	49.1	45.0	41.5	38.6	36.0	33.8	31.8	30.0	28.4	27.0	25.7	24.5	23.5	22.5	21.6	20.8	20.0	19.3	18.6	18.0	17.4	16.9	16.4	15.9	15.4	15.0	14.6	14.2
19	57.0	51.3	46.6	42.8	39.5	36.6	34.2	32.1	30.2	28.5	27.0	25.7	24.4	23.3	22.3	21.4	20.5	19.7	19.0	18.3	17.7	17.1	16.5	16.0	15.5	15.1	14.7	14.3	13.9	13.5
18	54.0	48.6	44.2	40.5	37.4	34.7	32.4	30.4	28.6	27.0	25.6	24.3	23.1	22.1	21.1	20.3	19.4	18.7	18.0	17.4	16.8	16.2	15.7	15.2	14.7	14.3	13.9	13.5	13.1	12.8

GEAR RATIO CHART FOR 27-INCH WHEELS

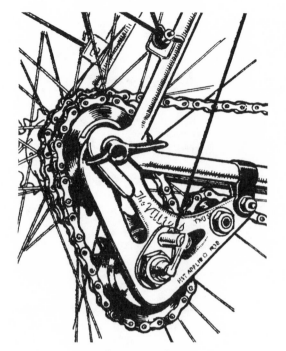

Villiers 2-speed gear

to 80 inches, my road racing bike is 47 to 108 inches, and my HPV goes from 30 to 144 inches. Same rider, but very different machines and operating conditions.

• Bottom Low

For touring and most mountain bikes this should be at least around the 20 inch mark. Many production road touring bikes only go down to around 30 inches. Mistake. It's a case of tortoise and hare. At low effort levels your muscles primarily burn fats, while high effort levels they use glucose. Most people have about a two hour supply of glucose, and once it's used up, replenishment takes a couple of days. The key to long distance riding is in staying within the fat burning zone of effort, and for steep climbs that means a walking pace gear as low as 15 inches.

For town bikes, a low of around 30 inches is OK for a bare machine. If any kind of loads or extra steep long climbs are involved, go lower. Road racing bikes can start with a bottom gear of 45 or 50 inches.

• Top High

If you are strong, gonzo, and ready to stand the world on its ear, I'd like you to read the following with special care. Many world champion riders like to use big gears. Most racers, however, gain speed by pedalling faster, not harder. For practical purposes, anything over 100 inches is an overdrive for more speed downhill. Fine if you are racing or into high speed thrills, but otherwise, consider that the hard work – and main need for gears – is going up the hill.

There is a vogue at the moment for fitting road racing bikes with ratios as high as 128 inches. This is going to be very bad news for some people. Consider: juvenile (under 16) racers are limited to a maximum gear of about 76 inches. This is to prevent injury to their legs and force the development of correct riding techniques. A 128-inch gear is too big for all but the most elite of elite riders, and if you have powerful leg muscles, can easily lead to damaged knees.

You probably know that if you are past 30 and take up running for the first time, you must take care not to damage your knees. The cartilage and other stuff to protect them and absorb shocks simply isn't there. Cycling is much the same. In a way, it's ironic. Cycling is a good universal form of exercise because people who are unfit and have only modest strength cannot generate enough force to do themselves any harm. People who are fit and strong, however, have enough power to hurt themselves if they strain too hard against big gears.

How hurt? Well, some years ago I blew out my already well worked over knees by pushing big gears, and wound up limping and moving around like I was made of glass. I don't like to complain, but it hurt and was inconvenient. It took me 18 months of very light spinning and never using a gear larger than 70 inches before I recovered mobility, and one knee is permanently slightly duff – push it too hard, and it starts to pack up.

So, if you are young and/or strong and raring to test how fast you can drive a bike, please, please heed my cautions and advice. Going for max with a bike is something like learning to be fast with guns. First you slowly – very slowly – learn how to do everything exactly right. Then whatever speed you have comes naturally. If you go at it the other way, and first push for speed, you may shoot yourself in the foot – or in the case of a bike, possibly blow out a knee. The way to gain speed on a bike is by learning to spin. Once you are well conditioned and have technique, maximum power efforts will be safer, and if big gears are your thing (they are for some people), then fine.

Gears The Hard Way

There are a number of factors to consider when working out the selection and placement of the gear ratios between high and low. Start with the fact that any derailleur system with 2, 3, or 4 front chainrings has fewer ratios than advertised. One reason for this is that you should not run the large front chainring to the large rear sprocket, or the small front chainring to the small rear sprocket, as this causes the chain to cut across at too sharp an angle, increasing wear and reducing efficiency. The problem is worse with a triple than a double, because with a triple the inner and outer chainrings are further apart. Running a triple with 7-, 8-, and 9-speed blocks, the no go combos are not just the extreme cogs, but at least 2 cogs on either side, and more often 3. That's 4 to 6 ratios gone. With a triple front, the middle ring often should not be used with the outer cogs, which is another 2 ratios gone, for a total of 6 to 8. Next, factor in duplicate gears – ratios in one chainring/cog combination that are identical or nearly so to another chainring/cog combination. The number of duplicate gears depends on the particular setup, but is often no less than 4 and can be 8 or more. The problem is worse with wide range triples. Our box of useless gear ratios is now quite brimming. A 14-speed double chainring system might well have only 8 usable ratios, and a 27-speed triple could fairly easily have only 14.

OK, we only have a few ratios to work with, so they have to be spent wisely. This is when you get into the matter of where you most need ratios, and the shift patterns you have to execute in order to obtain them.

For tourists, double or alpine shifts (simultaneous front and rear changes) were once a common method for moving through the gears at well spaced intervals. Touring riders have the time and energy for finesse, but a road racer running near the limit, or a mountain biker moving through varied terrain, needs a simple, one move gear change. That cannot be between front chainrings, because with a typical size difference of 10T (a 52/42 racing double, 52/40/30 road triple, or 42/32/22 mountain triple, to cite some common configurations), the magnitude of change is from 25 to 45 percent, well beyond the 10 percent maximum that will keep pedalling cadence in an optimum power band.

To obtain shorter steps between gear ratios, we have to move to the rear sprockets. Here, an important point is that changes with the smaller cogs have more impact than with the bigger cogs. If we switch a 13T cog for a 12T on block that starts with an 11T cog, the upshift doubles in magnitude from 9 to 18 percent. However, if we switch a 29T cog for a 28T after a 26T, the change is from 7.5 to 11.5 percent, despite there being a 3T difference.

In practical terms, what this means is that road racers should go for the classic "corncob," or a freewheel cluster where the small cogs progress in 1T increments, and only the last few cogs have 2T jumps. These days, a not uncommon 8-speed setup is 12-13-14-15-16-17-19-21T, paired with a 52/42 front. Mountain bikers should strive to keep their low- and mid-range ratios evenly spaced; if one or two of the high ratios involves a large jump or an alpine shift, that's not a big problem. Tourists are more or less in the same boat, with one difference: the mountain biker needs the right gear for power, the tourist needs it for efficiency. What both parties must remember is that the change between the small and middle chainrings will usually be greater than the difference between the middle and large rings. A 10T difference between small and middle rings is usually good for a jump of 30 to 45 percent. Cutting the jump to 10 percent requires a double shift, a simultaneous change of the rear sprocket.

After you've contemplated all this and wondered why we ever got started, there are more things to think about. One is rear derailleur capacity, which is a function of the difference between the large and small sprockets, and large and small chainrings. A 12-21T block has an 11T difference, and 52/42T chainrings have a 10T difference, for a total of 21T. The rear derailleur must have a capacity of 21T, an arm long enough to wrap 21T of chain. Competition derailleurs usually max at 28T but might catch 30T, and big 'un mountain bike and touring derailleurs might be able to wrap 40T.

At the front, derailleur capacity is a straightforward function of the difference in chainring sizes. Competition units are as little as 14T, mechs with deep cages for use with wide range triples are 26T or more.

Slipping back to the rear mech, maximum sprocket size is the largest sprocket the derailleur can manage. This is a function of the design of the mech, and not the amount of chain it can wrap. It's a useful titbit to know, because you don't want to base an ideal system on a bottom of 32T when the mech can only handle 30T. As a crude rule of thumb, the bigger the maximum sprocket size, the more mechanically complex – and therefore vulnerable – the derailleur.

Now we come to the cream pie: product liability laws dictate that derailleur gears on production bikes must be idiot proof, which means it must be possible to shift to any possible combination of gears, such as big ring to big sprocket, little ring to little sprocket. As a result, production bikes have more chain, and bigger derailleurs, than they need. If you make up your mind to watch what you are doing and avoid big/big and small/small combinations, you can use less chain and a lighter, more responsive derailleur. This can significantly reduce weight, give crisper performance, and improve reliability.

Gears For You (Hi, Frank!)

You can size a bicycle by taking a series of precise anatomical measurements and applying related formulae, or by simply climbing aboard and seeing if it fits. Similarly, gear ratios and shift patterns can be worked out on paper, or by simply going out and riding.

The function of the different gear ratios is to keep you churning away smoothly over a range of conditions and terrain. You also want to be able to shift easily to certain ratios. Ride for awhile and you should soon enough be able to identify four or

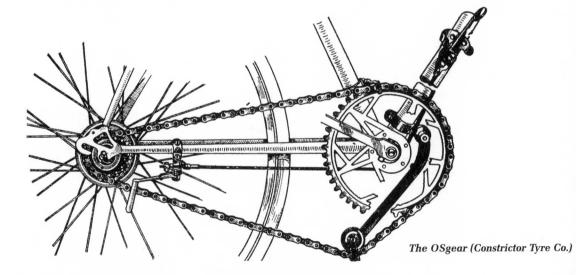

The OSgear (Constrictor Tyre Co.)

five recurring types of circumstances, each best met with a particular gear ratio. For example, for climbing shallow gradients and bucking headwinds, you might find that using the big chainring to a large cog still has you straining a bit. Try shifting to the middle chainring and running to a smaller cog, and you might luck onto a ratio more suitable for your needs. In a similar manner, you can work out the best ratios for other circumstances such as steep climbs, pulling out of corners, winding up some speed on slight downgrades, and so on. A useful aid for this process is the cadence function on a cycle computer.

Probably the best method is to start from scratch, with an estimate of the range of ratios you think would be good: say, 30 to 75 inches, and a combination of chainrings and sprockets to match, say 40/30T front and 14-24T rear. Now, suppose you find that when riding the 40T front to the 14T rear, you are frequently stymied. The gear is just OK on flat, smooth ground, but any slight upgrade forces you to move to the next sprocket up, say a 16T, and that one isn't right either, because it is too easy. Right, you swap the 14T for a 13T, which gives you a nice gear for slight downgrades, and the 16T for a 15T, and now you are smooth and have power on tap. You can work out the ratios involved, but they don't really matter; if you walked into a bike shop and asked for a 70-inch gear, you'd get a blank stare. You have to ask for a specific component such as a 15T sprocket, and might as well think that way to start with. Thus, most riders talk in terms of "I like 52/15," and "What a descent, 52/11 all the way!"

A pragmatic approach can be continued almost indefinitely. Once you find the ratios you like best, you can turn to the business of shifting patterns. For example, suppose you want to make the transition from your usual cruising gear to a slightly smaller and more powerful ratio with lightning speed. One way to do this is to have a half-step difference between the front chainrings, so that a shift at the front has half the value of a shift at the rear. (Remember: with larger rings, differences are less pronounced, so with, say, a 52/47T, the difference is 10 percent.) You use a rear sprocket which gives you a good cruising ratio when the chain is on the large ring, and simply shift to the small ring when you need a little more power. It's a very easy, quick shift, which is why a half-step front is a common racing setup.

Once you start riding, the areas in your gearing setup that need improvement will be clear enough. However, gear ratios and shift patterns are a complex subject, and it helps to know the whys and wherefores of half- and full-steps, crossovers, derailleur capacities, and all the rest. For the most illuminating course on the topic, consult guru of gears Frank "Gears to You" Berto's comprehensive book *Upgrading Your Bike* (Rodale).

WRAP

A bike is an extension of your body. It should fit like a glove, and move when you do. It is all right for cycling to hurt a bit because you are riding vigorously, or hardening yourself and extending your range. But the bike itself should be comfortable. If there are aches and pains that do not go away with a bit of riding and conditioning, then carefully review the fit of the bike.

In performance terms, a bike should work for you, not force you to try and keep up with the bike. In general, the key concept is moderation, and particularly in the vital area of gear ratios, you'll gain skill and strength more rapidly if you start out using modest-sized ratios and simple shifting patterns, and then change and upgrade in pace with your own development.

Riding Basics

How anyone, without help, can learn to ride a bike in 15 minutes or less • The basics of pedalling, shifting gears, braking, and bike handling and turning • Climbing and descending hills • Emergency braking

NYONE CAN RIDE A BICYCLE. BEING ABLE TO ride well is another matter, and here, technique counts more than anything else. Physical condition of course plays a part, as does innate strength and stamina, but skilled 60-year-old grandfathers and grandmothers can and do run rings around fit young adults. I cannot remember the number of times I've eventually reeled in some upstart who thought a burst of energy would leave me behind (or how often some slip on a battered old roadster has breezed by me like I was tied to a post . . .). Attention to the basics of technique will make your riding eas-ier and more enjoyable, and help realize your capacities and abilities. Riding well is part of the fun – and there is always room for improvement!

BALANCING

If you've not been on a bike before, get yourself a long 15 mm wrench for removing the pedals, the right size hex key or wrench for adjusting the saddle height, and head on out with your bike to a park or other traffic free area with a bit of sloping ground. Remove the pedals. The left (as you and the bike face in the same direction) side or port pedal has a left hand thread and unscrews by turning clockwise; the right side pedal has a normal right hand thread and unscrews by turning counter-clockwise. Lower the saddle until when seated you can easily touch the ground with your feet.

Sit on the bike and apply the brake levers. Try to move the bike. It should not move. That's how the brakes work. Now release the brake levers, give a little itty-bitty push with your feet, and apply the brakes again, not so fast this time. The bike should move just a short distance and stop. Do this as many times as you want, until you are sure you can stop the bike when you want to.

"(Left) The correct style. (Right) The incorrect."

Scout ahead for any wandering UFOs and now take off with a slightly stronger push, using both feet. As you bring your legs forward, instead of stopping, use them for another push, and then another, and then another, for as long as you like. See how far you can go before you need to push again.

Next, take off with your two-leg push, and then use only one leg for each successive push, alternating from side to side. You should be covering some distance now, gliding in fairly long scoots. Find some ground with a bit more slope, and see how far you can glide without touching your feet to the ground. All the way down the slope? Great! Put the pedals back on (the left side one has a small L stamped on the end of the axle or spindle, and screws on counter-clockwise), and do another run, this time just resting your feet on the pedals. Not bad, eh? OK, once more, and this time pedal gently, and see if you can steer out to flat ground or even just across the side of the gentle slope. Keep pedalling. Yes? You've done it, you've learned to ride a bicycle!

This method is cast iron infallible, 100 percent guaranteed to produce results with anyone who can stand up, young or old. It works fine for

The incorrect method! Do not allow anyone to help you balance.

blind people, too, many of whom really enjoy bike riding.

SHIFTING

Broadly, shifting is a matter of synchronizing pedal pressure and crank rotation with movement of the shift lever. Let your skill develop gradually. Back off if you start to get damaging "clunk" or "r-r-r-r-r-r" sounding shifts. These are caused by incorrect timing. The way to do things fast is to do them right. Slow down. Once you get the knack, smooth, split-second shifts will be second nature.

Hub Gears

To shift up to a higher (harder to pedal) gear, ease pressure on the pedals while continuing to rotate the cranks, move shift lever or twist grip to next gear, and resume full pedal pressure. Fast shifts can be made by maintaining pedal pressure, moving the shift selector, and then briefly pausing pedalling when you want the shift. If done too hard, this may damage gears.

Shifting in the other direction, down to a lower gear, is much the same, although you may need to make a more definite pause in pedalling. When coming to a stop and shifting across several gears at once, back-pedal a little.

Derailleur Gears

Shift derailleur gears only while pedalling. To see why, hang your bike up so that the rear wheel is off the ground, rotate the cranks, and manipulate the gear selectors so you can see how the derailleurs work. Shifting a derailleur without pedalling can result in a bent or broken chain or gear teeth. Before you start off on a bike, especially if it has been parked on the street, it's always worth doing a quick eyeball check that the chain, derailleur, and sprockets/rings are in alignment. Otherwise, under the pressure of a starting stroke, the works may jam and possibly be damaged.

As you spin the cranks and operate the gear

selectors, notice that the chain moves quickly and easily from a larger chainring (front) or sprocket (rear) to a smaller one. Three reasons: spring tension moves derailleur into the new position, the chain is dropping down, and the spring tension exerted by the arm of the rear derailleur is reduced.

Conversely, when moving the chain from a smaller chainring or sprocket to a larger one, you have to push the derailleur until it clicks into place in the new position. Climbing is a slower, more difficult process for a chain, because it is going up, and working against increased spring tension from the rear derailleur arm.

These mechanical factors affect how you use your gears in several ways. For example, when shifting you need to keep the cranks moving but ease pedal pressure. The exact amount depends on the kind of shift involved, and the design and quality of equipment. In a front changer downshift the chain is knocked off a larger chainring down onto a smaller chainring, and the derailleur moves itself. Since pedalling cadence increases, such shifts are usually fast. Operate the selector and you can usually dive straight into a more rapid cadence.

An upshift to a larger chainring, though, is mechanically slower, with a decrease in pedalling cadence, and it is usually necessary to have a longer pause in pedalling pressure, until matters have sorted through. There's also a difference in how you handle the shift selector. You need to push the changer against spring tension until it clicks into place in the new position. If you push too hard, soon, and/or fast, the works may gum up. For what you have to do, stroke is a more descriptive term than push. If you get it all right – the speed of the cranks, the amount of reduction in pedal pressure, and the stroke – then the shift will take place very quickly.

At the back, it's all much the same, but with one important difference: when the chain moves from a larger sprocket to a smaller one, the pedalling cadence decreases. So on an upshift, rather than diving with the chain, your fractional pause as you shift also has to include slowing your pedalling rate. Conversely, on a downshift, with the chain moving to a larger sprocket, you've got to pause pressure (not your spin) for a definite moment to let everything happen, and then lick into a faster cadence.

How does this all play out in real life? Perhaps some examples will help. You're blipping along in town, chain on middle ring to second smallest cog, when a traffic light forces you to make a very fast stop. There isn't the time to run the chain up to a large cog at the back, but while standing on the brakes you do just manage to tap the front changer and do the half stroke of the cranks needed to move the chain down to the little ring. This is a big change, probably a 10T difference good for somewhere in the region of 30 to 45 percent, and puts you in a gear low enough for a quick take off when the light changes to green.

You're riding along, middle ring, and up ahead spot a steep pitch. You decide to avoid any possible problems with shifting on the hill, and run the chain over to a large sprocket. Just as you hit the hill, you downshift to the small front ring. There's a moment when you are in too low a gear and have nothing to push against, but then you bite into the hill with your pedalling cadence running fast and easy, and no problems trying to make shifts under pressure.

You're in a drag race! Almost certainly you'll want to run on the middle ring and start with the largest cog, popping on down the block as you reach max pedalling cadence in each ratio.

You face a long, shallow climb, and want to keep moving. Middle ring, smallish sprocket, and as you ascend you steadily downshift, taking care to do so while your cranks are still moving quickly. Half way up the hill, middle ring and second largest sprocket, you realize you're going to need something lower. Single tap left selector for a front changer downshift, and at the same time, tap tap right selector for a double rear upshift that, however, puts you in exactly the gear you need.

You're in the 8th lap of a 10-lap circuit race and about to pull a jump on that leech who's been drafting you for the last 3 laps, taking a free ride on your slipstream and saving energy in the hope of pipping you on the sprint for the finish line, and you've picked your spot. Right alongside the stands there's a flat section, a welcome break after a longish shallow climb, and so far, both of you have been taking a breather of sorts by running the flat in an aerodynamic tuck cruise, in top gear. After the flat there's a short, stiff climb, and then a fast descent. Your plan, as you enter the straight, is to catch the big ring but hold the 15T rear third-from-last cog, and then instead of tucking, down-shift the front changer to the smaller ring and launch yourself out of the saddle in a full scale sprint. You'll carry the jump right up the hill. The leech will be taken by surprise, cross gears trying to catch up, and you'll crest the hill with enough daylight between you to last for the rest of the race.

You shift and jump all at once, launching your-self forward out of the saddle, your bike flexing underneath you with the power of your strokes, and the crowd, who understand perfectly well what you are doing, cheer loudly. You churn up the hill in a wild adrenaline rush, going as you have never gone before, and as you top out in tri-umph you glance back to find a grinning leech still right on your wheel.

He'd seen your chain stay on the 15T, and knew what was coming.

After all, he'd read the book, too.

• Back to Basics

Strive to keep your chain reasonably straight, by moving it across the rings and cogs more or less evenly. In terms of power efficiency, this is more important when you are pedalling slowly, usually in the lower gears. So as a rule of thumb, with a 3F/9R 27-speed set-up, when on the small ring and shifting up from the lowest gear (small front/large rear) you don't want to run the chain across more than 3 or 4 of the rear cogs before shifting to the middle ring at the front.

Modern derailleur controls are indexed; they have preset stops that center the chain over the selected sprocket or chainring. Gone are the days of listening for a rough riding chain, or contorting into peculiar riding positions in order to visually check rear chain alignment. Nevertheless, because gear control cables stretch with use, you need to ensure that the preset stops are accurately placed.

Usually, there is a knurled adjuster on the shift selector, right where the cable wire and housing enter the shift control unit.

Turning the adjuster changes the position of the wire relative to the housing, and thereby moves the derailleur up or down the block. The move-ment is slight, but a turn or two can make all the difference in terms of positive, crisp shifting and accurate alignment. Become familiar with using these cable adjusters. New cables stretch, some-what like new guitar strings, and need constant fiddling until they settle down. If you've got a new bike, learning how to adjust the cables is a high priority, and it's best to dive right in even at risk of sometimes getting it wrong. Once you've got the feel, you'll be able to do it easily even on the move. See Adjustment under the relevant component in Chapter 21, Bike Care, for more information.

PEDALLING

Ride with the ball of your foot on the pedal, not the arch. The ball, or widest part of your foot, should be right over the pedal spindle. The fun-damental technique for easy cycling is called ankling. This is where the foot pivots at the ankle with each revolution of the crank. Start at the top of the stroke (12 o'clock) with the heel slightly lower than the toes. Push with the ball of the foot and simultaneously pivot on the downstroke so that the foot levels out between 2 and 3 o'clock, and continue the motion so that at the bottom of the stroke the toes are lower than the heel. It's like cleaning the sole of your shoe of you-know-what. Lift on the backstroke.

At faster cadences you do not actually gain power lifting on the backstroke. You do the lifting bit to signal your muscles not to push back at the pedal as it comes up! It might seem kinda funny to suggest that you could work against yourself, but fast pedalling involves rapid expansion and contraction of large muscle groups – at 120 rpm, 2 per second – and the timing has to be right. If the muscles wait for a physical cue in the form of a change in resistance and/or direction, they'll run a half-beat behind. By "lifting" you lead your muscles into smooth, efficient movement and – very important – a cleaner burn that produces fewer energy sapping waste products. So especially if you're new to cycling (as opposed to being able to ride a bike), don't King Kong stomp on the pedals and try to bend the cranks; instead, regularly practice spinning as fast as you can. You're looking to develop a feather light touch, floating ahead of the pedals just a hair short of flying off them altogether. For this sort of thing, firm attachment to the pedals is essential: clip-in pedals, or at the minimum, toe clips and straps.

I prefer clip-in pedals over toe clips. Clip-in pedals hold tightly but release quickly on demand. With toe clips you've got to reach down to tighten or loosen the straps. If you use cleats as well for a firm grip on the pedal, you can get caught out. Fast stop for never-give-an-inch passive-aggressive Iron Daddy and baby stroller,

momentary realization that you should ha . . . kaclunk! However, this problem does not arise with smooth soled shoes, so toe clips are often a popular choice for utility riding.

For riding with toe clips, start with loose straps. Straddle the bike, slip a foot into a pedal at the 1 o'clock position, and snug the strap. Push off, using the downstroke to get you under way, and simultaneously, bring up the free foot, give the pedal a light tap to spin the toe clip around to the proper position, slip in foot, and tighten strap. The key is the deft, light tap to the pedal to bring the toe clip around so you can put your foot in. Single side cage pedals usually have a small, protruding lip on the bottom of the cage plate, which makes tapping the pedal around easier. Practice will soon make a smooth entry second nature. Try to avoid riding on the flat side of the pedal, as the toe clip and strap will be close to the ground and can easily scrape. Before stopping, reach down and loosen one strap so you can get your foot

back in easily when under way again. Do not worry about being trapped by toe clips. I've made zillions of emergency stops and have always been able to get my feet free. (This is of course assuming you are not using cleats as well.) On the other hand, in traffic do not tempt fate by riding with very tight straps. If you use soft soled shoes (bad, not enough support), or shoes fitted with cleats, keep the straps loose when conditions warrant.

With clip-in pedals, first check that the release tension is at a low setting. Straddle the bike, clip into one pedal by hooking the front of the cleat into the binding and pushing down, and then disengage by pushing your heel out to the side. Repeat several times until you are familiar with the procedure.

To ride, bring the pedal up to 1 o'clock, step in, push off, and as the other pedal comes around, put your foot on it and clip in. That's it.

To disengage, push down and to the side, leading with the heel. Train your exit reflexes by consciously disengaging one foot as you stop. After awhile, it will be second nature.

CADENCE

Optimum cadence, or crank rotations per minute, varies with the physical condition and technique of the individual rider, and the terrain and circumstances. I once read that in biomechanical terms the most efficient cyclist is an old rummy trundling along at a stately 55 rpm. That's quite true – on level ground, in dead calm air, at an utterly even rate. Once you throw in a bit of variety, a hill or two and some stopping and starting, the old soak's minuscule power output becomes, in modern idiom, seriously challenged.

Some of us can blast out surprising amounts of power, but only for a few seconds. On a steady basis, most people in reasonable shape can manage an average output of around one-tenth to one-eighth horsepower (hp). Faster cadences make the most efficient use of this limited power, which is about equivalent of that of a small garden weed trimmer.

If you are trundling at, say 50 rpm, and encounter a small upgrade, then adding power is a greater strain on the muscles. If you're doing 100 rpm to start with, there is more kinetic energy and momentum in the movement of your legs and the cranks, and it is easier to screw on more juice.

Most people gear too high and pedal too slowly. They don't think they are going anywhere or getting any exercise unless they are pushing against resistance. It is precisely this pushing which creates fatigue. It is much better to pedal against relatively little resistance. Especially when first starting with a bike, regularly try to pedal as rapidly as you possibly can without going into orbit. As a rule of thumb, if your legs are on fire, you are pushing too hard; if you are gasping for breath, you are spinning too fast. Maintaining a balance between these two extremes is the primary function of your gears; always shift up or down as necessary to keep a smooth cadence. Learn to shift just before you need the new gear. Do not wait for a hill to slow down your cadence; shift just before you hit it, and as needed while climbing.

Spinning at more than 85 rpm takes practice. The theoretical ideal is 100 rpm. Racers often do

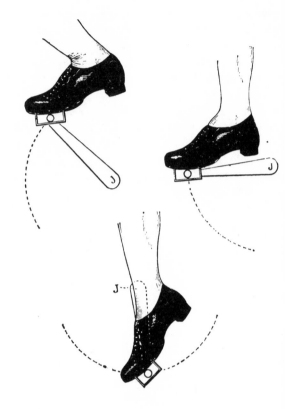

more, of course; tourists usually do about 75 rpm. I time most commuters at around 60 rpm, but couriers and other professional riders spin more briskly. It all depends on what's happening, too. On a hill, a racer can elect to change pace and honk up with slow, powerful strokes, because with only a 20 pound bike to worry about, they can get away with it. A heavily loaded tourist will need to maintain a rapid cadence, or else risk physical strain or even damage. This one reason why it is so important for tourists to have very low gears.

I've harped on this business of cadence and spinning several times in this book, and apologize if I've tested your patience. But it's really important. Work on your spin, think clean thoughts, and eventually your power will increase. At speeds that once had you straining and panting, you'll be gliding and comfortable.

BUMPS

When you come to bumps, pot holes, cables, etc., go light on the saddle and put most of your weight on the pedals and handlebars. This allows the bike to pivot underneath you, reducing shock for both you and the bike. Over washboard surfaces with lots of little bumps, use a higher gear than normal; pushing against the pedals will increase the amount of weight supported by your legs.

BRAKING

Try to be sparing in your use of the brakes. This will help you to anticipate riding conditions in advance and help to conserve energy. In traffic, I often back off well before a traffic signal, so that I hit the green rolling and have less work to do in order to resume pace.

Modern bicycle brakes are very effective!

Be careful of braking too hard and skidding, or pitching yourself in a forward fall over the bars. The front brake does most of the work, and the more rapidly you decelerate, the more work it can do. This is because more weight is transferred forward, increasing the coefficient of friction between the front tire and the road surface. At the same time, weight on the rear tire is reduced, making it more liable to skid. The technique for a rapid or panic stop is thus one of moving body weight to the rear while progressively increasing pressure on the front brake and simultaneously holding the pressure on the back brake just below the point where the wheel will lock up and skid. It is a coordinated sequence of events and can only be learned through regular practice.

Start with quick stops from low speeds and gradually increase velocity. Really throw your butt back as you hit the brakes, transferring most of your weight down to the pedals. This helps lower the center of gravity. Get to the point where you are stopping the bike just as fast as you can. At first, cue your stops with markers on the pavement or dirt. Then simulate emergency stops by having a friend prompt you at unexpected moments.

Once you master hard braking, keep your technique fresh and sharp with regular practice. Knowing is not enough. Your reflexes have to be kept in shape so that in a real emergency, you make the right moves without thinking. I start most rides with two or three very strong checks of the brakes, and usually finish with an all out, short as possible stop. Some people feel foolish doing this sort of thing – cowboy, or undignified. Fah. Better to burn some rubber and stay tight with your bike. It's also a dynamic check on the condition of your brakes.

On descents, safety-minded high bicycle riders lifted their legs over the handlebars, so that they would be thrown clear of the bike if they "came a cropper."

stantly test the brakes for more than you need, then you'll be able to detect any fade while there is still enough power left for a stop.

Always be able to stop. If you find yourself wondering if the brakes will work – say on a very steep pitch – find out at once. It is really and truly no fun to be aboard a runaway. Ride within your experience. If the descent is longer or steeper than you've made before, periodically stop and check for overheating. Careful of fingers! Things can get hot. I still remember, on one ride in the Catskill Mountains, I finally made it all the way up a particularly long and steep hill. Going back down, on a gravel road that did not allow much speed and required heavy braking, I stopped halfway to check, and the rims were so hot, I went over to a nearby stream and held the bike in mid-air so the wheels spun in the current. The rims steamed in the cool morning air. There was no sensation of danger, only beauty. You stay on top of your brakes that way, and you'll be OK.

Out on the other side, when you've got a clear road, don't be afraid to let your bike open right up and breathe. Past 20 mph you've got free speed control – air resistance. For speed, a racer will tuck into a full crouch, tighten in the elbows, and hold the pedals at 3 and 6 o'clock. If you sit bolt upright with arms and legs splayed apart, you'll find that air drag is often all you need to keep speed at a comfortable level. An important advantage in using this technique is that the mechanical brakes are kept fresh and ready.

TURNING

If you can ride a bicycle, then by definition you can turn it. Turning is how a bike stays upright. Underway, a bicycle is in a constant state of imbalance. A tendency to lean one way will be corrected

In slippery conditions, or when banked over hard in turn, favor the rear brake. The rear wheel does have a greater tendency to skid, but if it slips you may still be able to keep yourself upright, and at worst will land on your hip. If the front wheel washes away, you go down fast and hard, and possibly on your face.

If you have calliper brakes, then in wet conditions use gentle pressure on the levers to ride the blocks lightly against the rims, to wipe water off. Do this often, especially before junctions and such-like, and don't get caught napping; fully wet rims can increase stopping distance four to five times. Disc brakes are less prone to this problem, but nevertheless, make a habit of checking that your brakes are OK before you really need them.

Going down long hills avoid overheating the wheel rims or brake mechanisms by pumping the brakes. This is an on-off-on-off-on pattern which, among other things, can tell you if braking power starts to fade. With a steady application of the brakes, if there is gradual loss of power, then you may not learn about it until too late. If you con-by the rider, the bike will move through the center of balance, and then correct again. Most turning simply consists of taking advantage of a lean in the desired direction. Instead of correcting, the rider allows the lean to continue and thus effects a turn. The feeling is that the rider has changed balance and the bike has followed suit, and in that bicycle geometry is designed for a certain amount of self steering, the feeling is accurate enough. The rider does in fact change balance. This type of turn has two potential liabilities: it is slow, and it puts rider and bicycle weight in a single plane down to the point of tire contact with the ground.

In riding it is often necessary to turn – FAST! This can be done by hauling back on the handlebar end opposite to the direction in which you wish to go. The bike will move out from underneath you, you will start to fall, and then you will turn. Try to see it in your mind's eye: in a normal turn, you gradually topple to one side; in a haul handlebar turn, you snatch the bike out from underneath you, and immediately fall into a turn. In effect, you go one way, the bike goes another, and afterwards you catch up with each other. Like panic braking, this type of turn should be learned slowly, with lots of room for maneuvering.

Another type of turn consists of laying down the bike, while you remain relatively upright. The bike leans more than you do. This is useful when the road surface is rough and you want to lighten up on the bike, or when you've overcooked a corner and need some more turn, instanter. Keep your weight on the outside pedal and push down on the inside handlebar end. At the same time, pivot at the hips so that your upper body is more upright than the bike.

Yet another type of turn is the opposite: again pivoting at the hips, you lean your body into the

Pushing a rise

turn and keep the bike more upright. This is a standard technique for fast riding on shale and gravel, and is thought to lessen the chances of skidding. For me, it's pretty much a reflex. If I unexpectedly encounter a wet manhole cover or oil slick while riding, I automatically throw the bike up while keeping my weight down. I'm interested in preserving traction. Once the problem is past, I might go the other way, and press the bike back down to tighten the turn.

Get familiar with the extremes of turning and moving your bike around underneath you in an open area, where a mistake won't cost. Stay in practice, too. On morning rides I often include a quick spin through a big parking lot in my local park. It's littered with discarded food wrappers, broken glass, and other rubbish, which is a pity, but makes for a good dodge-em course.

CLIMBING

Climbing technique depends on the length and pitch of climb, the kind of bike, and the condition and nature of the rider. A racer may honk – stand up

out of the saddle and use body weight to help drive the cranks around. A heavily laden tourist is likely to drop into a low gear and twiddle – stay in the saddle while spinning the cranks lightly and rapidly.

Unless you know you can attack a hill and win, it is generally better to start a climb calmly and moderately, and increase the pace when you top out. On the other hand, slowing down too much can make a climb an eternal drag. You'll have to learn about pacing yourself for various kinds of terrain and climbs from experience, and if you get bogged down, do not hesitate to dismount and hoof it. Remember the turtle and the hare. You want something for the next hill.

Sort your gears out before you start a climb (see Shifting, above), because shifting can be more difficult if pedal pressure increases while cadence goes down. Tip: on very long climbs do not look at the top; concentrate on the immediate moment and surroundings, and on maintaining a steady rhythm. Let topping out be a pleasant surprise rather than relief at last. It's surprising how effective this trick is. If there is a long downgrade after the crest, keep your legs moving as you coast down, to prevent them from stiffening up.

Traffic: Fast Is Safe

Developing the knowledge, skills, and attitude for riding in traffic • Bike riding instruction • Understanding the road environment and motorists • Specific riding techniques • Cyclepaths • Crashes • Getting even

ALL CYCLISTS MUST KNOW HOW TO RIDE IN traffic, just as pedestrians have to know how to cross the street. Cycling in traffic is dangerous. Fear of being hit by a car is the principal deterrent to riding on streets and roads, and is an amply justified concern – nervousness when venturing into traffic indicates a sound mind. However, with time and experience you can learn to ride with a level of knowledge and skill that greatly reduces the risk of harm. The outcome of riding in traffic depends less on the situation than on what you do. Still, there is always an element of risk. Something can happen out of the blue, through no fault of your own, which wipes you off the face of the earth in a twinkling.

Taking a bath is also a risky affair. And people die unexpectedly in bed. The amount of traffic riding that suits you is entirely your decision. Although the basic principles are the same, there is a considerable difference between mixing it up with heavy weekday commuter traffic and cycling out to the park on Sunday. You must decide for yourself how much you want to bite off. I'll help you as far as I can, but the go/no go decision is yours.

The most important thing to understand about riding in traffic is the need for 100 percent attentiveness. Forget the stereotypes of happy-go-lucky laughing cyclists kicking their legs whee! into the air while sunshine breezes ruffle their hair. Riding in traffic, you must be alert at all times and know everything that is going on, from the size of the pebbles on the road to the debris which might fall on you from a construction project to the number and type of vehicles before and behind you – absolutely everything. Traffic riding requires total attention. There is no time for wool-gathering or pastoral pleasures.

Some people are just born inattentive. If you are one of these and a survivor, you've probably learned to steer clear of risky places and situations. Perhaps you prefer walking to cycling or driving a car. Great. I love people who have their own trails. But if you are spacey, then bike riding should be off-road, or on cycle paths. If you let your mind wander while you are riding in traffic, you may only survive as a statistic.

It's hardly all bad. Attentiveness has benefits. Total engagement is refreshing. I like physical and mental challenges, but spend a lot of time pushing a keyboard. For me, the change of pace provided by jamming quickly through traffic is often exhilarating. As they say, it takes your mind off your troubles. More to the point, once you gain experience you are still alert, but relaxed. Moving easy. Is crossing the street a megaproduction for you? In a more relaxed state, attentiveness is fun; you see more, notice more, feel more. Every once in awhile I give a ride a miss. I might be unhappy or worried, and perhaps not sharp enough. Or out of sorts and cross, and inclined to be too aggressive. But if I'm feeling good, it's hard to keep me off a bike and running with the joy of life. And if I'm marginal, I know from experience that a bike ride will probably chase the blues away and cheer me up.

Riding in traffic is pretty much a matter of dealing with the world as it is. Despite the risk, getting out and functioning is better than staying home and moldering in bed. Healthwise, you'll live longer, at least as a species; as an individual, you might draw a short straw. That's life. You ride not just for yourself, but for all of us – as we ride for you.

Before class goes any further, you need to know about two hazards: air pollution and harassment.

AIR POLLUTION

Inhaling car exhaust fumes and other pollutants is a serious health hazard for cyclists. Physical activity increases the effectiveness of the body's own natural defense systems against pollutants, so compared to motorists in the same locations, cyclists have lower blood levels of lead and carbon monoxide. You're better off riding a bike than in any other kind of vehicle, or walking. Fine, but as a cyclist you are nose-on to the primary source of air pollution – motor vehicles – and this cannot possibly be good for you.

What are you in for? It's difficult to say, exactly. A common statistic is that the average urbanite inhales the equivalent in particles and poisons of one to two packs of cigarettes a day. What's an average urbanite? Dunno. If it is someone who is 20 yards away from the road, then their exposure is much less than for someone in the thick of traffic. It depends on where the 20 yards is, too. Air pollution is more intense in areas with high buildings that restrict breezes and ventilation. Another common statistic is that urban air pollution causes 3 million deaths worldwide every year. A spectre of people dropping like flies is easy to visualize for a smoky, death-ridden place such as Mexico City, but what's the situation in New York City? Minneapolis? Seattle? Are people actually keeling over in the streets? Well, I've an answer of sorts for this question, and if at first you wonder if I've stripped my gears, stay on my wheel for a moment.

If you were a wolf, then on a cold winter's day with snow all over the land, even while moving at a run, you would be able to smell a rabbit buried several feet underneath the snow, 20 or so feet off the trail. I'm no wolf, but I used to do hard training rides in the local park early in the morning, before it opened at 7 a.m. and cars entered the road. On each outing I tried to shave a few seconds off my best time. If I was late and just one car entered the park on the road ahead of me, I felt the difference. Even after the car disappeared out of sight, the fumes hanging in the air made me feel dizzy, cut down the amount of oxygen I was getting, and slowed my time. Hypochondria? Prejudice? Nope: a recent study reported in *The British Medical Journal* found that in blindfold tests, athletes breathing a level of carbon monoxide matching that found in most cities reached exhaustion in half the time they could go when breathing clean air.

Motor vehicles contribute up to 85 percent of all air pollution in urban areas. They emit lead, unburned gasoline, nitrogen oxides, sulphur oxides, carbon monoxide, hydrocarbons, and grit. Worst for the cyclist are lead and carbon monoxide.

Up to 99 percent of the lead in the air comes from gasoline combustion. Hang on, isn't gasoline, or at least most gasoline, supposed to be lead-free? Yes, but we may still be looking at some nasty problems.

Lead is very dangerous. The list of possible damages is amazing, and ranges from headache, a string of severe disabilities including arthritis, gout, and heart disease, to simply shortening your life span. Lead damages the brain, liver, kidney, and central nervous system. But perhaps the worst is that lead makes you stupid. Researchers the world over have shown that children exposed to high lead levels are associated with low intelligence and verbal skills, bad hearing, and slow reaction times. It is estimated that one in three children in Europe is suffering damage from lead pollution. This is despite the fact that most European countries long ago acted to reduce or eliminate the levels of lead in gasoline.

We are not out of the woods yet, and an important reason for this has to do with a relatively recent change in our understanding of the toxic effects of pollution. Briefly, this is: it may take a large quantity to kill you dead, but only a little may do a lot of harm. Unfortunately, most safety standards were promulgated on the basis that a non-lethal dose, like a bullet which misses you, is harmless. Only with the passage of time has it become evident that cumulative long term effects, compounded by complex interactions between various kinds of pollutants, can be very damaging. So far as lead is concerned, all I can tell you is that the scientific literature is swelling with research reports of adverse effects at progressively lower levels of exposure. Bullets which missed us in the past may tag us after all.

In terms of immediate risk, a greater hazard for cyclists is carbon monoxide. Cars push millions of tons of the stuff into the air every year, accounting for 75 percent of the total. Carbon monoxide is a classic poison which interferes with the oxygen carrying capacity of the blood. Long before it kills, this action results in decreased alertness, headaches, vague dizziness, and nausea. Just the thing for riding in traffic. For bonuses, heart problems, memory loss, emphysema, and cancer. Whee.

On a broader canvas, emissions such as nitrogen oxides (46 percent from cars) and hydrocarbons (35 percent from cars) interact with sunlight to form hazardous photochemical oxidants. One of these is ozone, which in high levels can cause eye, nose, and throat irritation, and affect the respiratory system. Another is acid rain, a chemical pollution that is destroying forests and lakes across America and Europe – and so also livestock, wildlife, and fish.

Catalytic converters, air filters for cars, are effective against carbon monoxide, nitrogen oxides, and hydrocarbons. However, even with strict emission controls, the rapid growth in vehicle ownership means pollution levels are expected not to fall, but to continue to rise. Clean-up act or no, we have a major air pollution problem.

You don't have to be choking on fumes to be adversely effected by air pollution. It's not just a matter of your specific health. In your life, it matters plenty what the general weather is like: just right, too hot, too cold, pouring with rain, or not a drop of water in sight. On a global scale, transport accounts for one billion tons of carbon emissions, about one-sixth of the annual total. These carbon emissions have overwhelmed Earth's natural processes for fixing carbon dioxide, which has increased. The accumulation of carbon dioxide and other greenhouse gases over the 20th century has caused a steady rise in average temperatures, and if the trend continues, then in the 21st century and likely well within your life time, global warming is expected to bring about climate change and events of truly epic proportions. You may not know much about global warming, or think that it is a paper tiger, in which case I urge you to study up on the findings issued by Britain's Hadley Centre for Climate Change.

The problem in understanding and predicting the effects of global warming has always been having to deal with a huge number of variables. In 1998, the scientists at Hadley created a new computer simulation more suited for the job, and the results are bone deep scary – predictions by mid-century of major reductions in food production in Africa and the United States, and south-western Europe cooked into a virtual desert. Globally, the rise in average temperatures may seem relatively modest, but Earth's weather and climate are the result of a delicate balance of forces which, when upset, can trigger drastic changes on a regional basis. So for example, the warming effect of the Gulf Stream ocean current creates a temperate climate in Britain, a country that in fact is as far north as Newfoundland and southern Canada. When, as the Hadley scientists predict, the Gulf Stream current starts to change direction and go elsewhere, the effect on Britain's climate will be considerable. Air pollution is not just sinus tickle or a bad smell. It's wholesale change.

Dropping out of the global perspective and back aboard our humble, biochemical powered bicycle, as a cyclist you are better off with regard to air pollution than a motorist or pedestrian, but minimize your exposure when you can. Try to avoid traffic congested routes by travelling back streets and through parks, and when possible, avoid riding during the peak traffic rush hours, and on heavily used steep hills, which is where cars really pour out the junk. If you live in a city or industrial area, keep track of air pollution indexes, and when temperature inversions turn the air into toxic soup, stay out of town. If things are bad all the time, give consideration to moving to some place better. Quality of life matters.

Your chances of coping with pollutants are better if you take in an adequate amount of vitamin C. It reduces the toxicity of all sorts of things, including lead, carbon monoxide, and nitrogen dioxide. Our saber-toothed tiger-battling ancestors sometimes went a long time between meals, but they had higher levels of vitamin C from natural sources than we do, and a lot less pollutants to clear out. Some people feel the alleged benefits of vitamin C are a lot of hogwash. Others – some of them pretty smart – think the stuff is useful. I'm with the latter camp.

A well-balanced diet, with as much real, fresh food as possible, will help in equipping you to deal with pollutants. One nice thing about cycling is that your fuel is important, and this creates a predisposition for foods that are actually nutritious.

Cycling naturally makes you aware of air pollution. If you want to help in the fight for clean air, start by looking up one of the groups that has consistently been at the forefront of battle:

Friends of the Earth, 1025 Vermont Ave. NW, Washington, DC 20005 USA.
Tel: 877 843 8687. Fax: 202 783 0444.
E-mail: foe@foe.org. Web: www.foe.org.

Transport 2000, First Floor,
The Impact Centre, 12–18 Hoxton Street,
London N1 6NG England.
Tel: +44 020 7613 0743.
E-mail:
transport2000@transport2000.demon.co.uk.

A British group, which you might want to check out for additional information.

HARASSMENT

Motorists routinely harass cyclists. Sometimes it is unintentional, and sometimes it is deliberate.

The road environment contains many conflict points: junctions, cross streets, pedestrian crossings, and just plain space in which to move. While major junctions are typically regulated by signals or established right-of-way rules, most small scale conflicts are sorted out by the road users themselves. Confrontations are managed with controlled aggression: each road user indicates what they want to do, and at the same time, takes account of indications from other road users. One person says "I want to . . ." and another says "Fine, go ahead" or "No, wait, I'll go first."

In light traffic this sorting out of priorities and sequences usually goes smoothly enough, but in heavy traffic it routinely gets out of hand. Just as when the mouse population in a cage is intensified and the mice progressively become more frenetic, motorists in heavy traffic tend to become increasingly aggressive. The more dense the traffic and the more futile their efforts, the more angry and pushy they become. When there is a massive gridlock, motorists jockey vigorously and sometimes furiously for minute increments of space, looking for a tiny edge in a situation which in fact, is not going anywhere.

The aggressiveness of motorists is compounded by the fact that psychological factors such as ego, status, and territory are closely intertwined with motor vehicles. Driver personalities and attitudes are the main cause of so-called "accidents." Driving a car is a sexually-based expression of

power and potency. That this is directly related to risk taking is evident in insurance premium rates: higher for young males and/or powerful cars, lower for females and/or smaller cars, and experienced, accident free drivers. The common denominator here is degree of aggressiveness.

Traffic is an environment of regularized confrontation involving fundamental instincts and emotions – a sanctioned madhouse. Motorists are encouraged to prepare and gird for battle, to wear safety belts and use air bags, and have vehicles designed and armored for crash worthiness.

You ride into this wearing a shirt. You might be the reincarnations of Braveheart, Bruce Lee, and Captain Marvel all rolled into one, willing to go nose-to-nose with any motorist alive, but when you are on a bike you do not compete on even

terms and cannot go the full distance. If a confrontation with a car for space or right of way becomes tight, ultimately you must back off. You've too much to lose. A conflict that might not even scratch the paint on a car could put you in hospital or the morgue. More aggressive motorists know this perfectly well, and often do not hesitate to cut you up or otherwise take advantage of your vulnerability.

For beginning cyclists, the confrontational and competitive aspects of riding in traffic appear nothing short of insane. What's the sense of stacking up a bike against a car? What kind of contest is that? Novices tend to become frightened and to ride timidly, which makes matters even worse by giving aggressive motorists more openings to do the cyclist dirt.

At the intermediate stage of riding skill, cyclists know enough moves to feel victimized when a motorist is too aggressive, and may respond with flat out, total anger – cyclists' rage. If the first instinctive reaction to danger is to cower and hide, the second is to strike back. Often this is a great idea. Many motorists who endanger cyclists are simple bullies, and finding out they cannot always hide behind the protective shells of their cars can be a revelation which modulates their aggressiveness. But while fighting fire with fire is sometimes necessary and/or satisfying, it is more often counter-productive.

Continuous rage and conflict do not make for a nice day. In fact, they mess you up. If you ride with frustration and rage bubbling in your pot, and ready for trouble, you're going to find it. It is fundamental to understand that as a cyclist, you will get dumped on, and trying to send every load back will in the end soil you, too. Fear, frustration, and anger can accumulate, and then erupt in an incident where you are the one who is in a manic rage and completely out of control. This is not a good way to live, it is not a good way to fight, and it certainly is not a good way to ride a bike.

At least in traffic, a good deal of the art in riding well, and with satisfaction, comes through learning how to stay out of trouble in the first place. Most of the potential bad incidents can be spotted in advance and avoided, including the conscious and unconscious evils committed by motorists. Your own skill becomes a major element in making your journeys smooth and easy, and the worse conditions become, the greater the challenge. Real aces stay above the fray, slide on through, and move out ahead. The motorists are left behind, trapped in their cages.

That's fine, a creative, professional approach really does work, but there is one category of motorist for which there is no good answer: killers. There are motorists who deliberately mow down cyclists. It happens much more often than most people imagine.

Homicidal intent with a car is difficult to establish. Typically, when a cyclist dies at the hands of a motorist, the worst charge is negligence and the penalty is a fine and perhaps a temporary suspension of the motorist's driving license. Often there is no penalty at all. Killers know that if they off someone with a gun, or soak them in gasoline and set them alight, they are in trouble. If the instrument of murder is a car, it is called an accident.

It's one thing entirely to compete with a motorist, even an aggressive one, for space and territory, and quite another to find that someone in a car is trying to kill you. Perhaps you are a sporting type, more than willing to fend for yourself. Problem is, when you are under direct attack an immediate counter-move is usually impossible, because you are too busy trying to stay alive. If afterwards you manage to catch up the motorist and punish him or her, you may land in a lot of trouble.

Proving that a motorist made a deliberate attack is difficult, and in any case does not matter, because once the moment is past, if you assault a motorist, then you can face criminal charges and civil liabilities for damages which, by the way, your insurance, if any, is not likely to cover. Do not confuse life and justice! There are ways and means of retaliating against rogue motorists, and I'll discuss some of these later. Right now, I want to get just one thing across: there are outright

FEMALES - WARNING

Female cyclists are subject to harassment from motorists and passers-by. This ranges from insulting, lewd comments to outright assault, where a motorist will reach out and knock a moving female cyclist to the ground. I do not have statistics for this sort of thing, but on anecdotal evidence, it most definitely happens, and female cyclists must take warning.

I sometimes yearn for frontier ways. Out in Wyoming, the sister of a friend of mine who took up road riding found that motorists were taking swipes at her behind, making rude remarks ("ride on me honey"), and otherwise being a problem. She went home, slung a Dirty Harry 6-inch barrel .357 Magnum pistol in a rig over her shoulder and down her back where everyone could see it, and went out again. She has never been bothered since.

killers on the roads, motorists predisposed to murder you if they get the chance. You won't meet them every day, you might be lucky and never meet one at all, but they are there.

Why am I telling you these wonderful, cheerful things? It is much as if you were about to go swimming in the ocean, and I was briefing you on what to expect in the way of sharks and other hazards. The analogy is apt, because the patterns are similar. Sharks and cars alike have their ways of moving and doing things. Sharks are feared all out of proportion to the actual danger they represent. If sharks really wanted to dine on people, then there would be many more attacks than the relatively few that do happen. Heck, shark action is even a big vogue with amateur scuba divers. People with the right temperament who know what is going on can handle sharks comfortably. There are right moves and wrong moves for sharks – but sometimes they up and bite. You don't just go and have

a splash with them. You keep track of what's happening and what you are doing, and get gone when necessary. Cars are the same. There are right moves and wrong moves for riding in traffic, you can learn them and be happy – but sometimes cars just attack.

If you ride in traffic there is always a chance that you won't come back. Thousands of cyclists are killed every year. No matter how good you are, you might be one of them. If you cannot accept and deal with that possibility, then do not ride in traffic.

RIDING

There are many hazards for you to look out for when riding in traffic, but motor vehicles are your main concern. Theory says bikes have the same rights as other types of vehicles. The facts are otherwise.

Motor vehicles are inherently fast. They are designed to move at speeds well beyond those which are appropriate or safe for public roads. Their natural rapid gait means that for motorists, anything which obstructs forward progress – such as a slow moving bicycle – should not be there. They are wrong in the head, but it is essential to understand how they think, or rather, do not. As a cyclist, you are a relative nonentity. As often as not, motorists will cut you off, make turns in front of you, or ride on your tail when there is no room to pass. It never occurs to them to put on the brakes and give you room to maneuver, as they would for a car or truck.

In addition, many motorists are incompetent, under the influence of alcohol or drugs, or all of these things. Any cross section of drivers will find elderly, obese, and otherwise infirm people with the motion capacity of a frozen sloth. They may think or imagine otherwise, but the truth is that their control of a vehicle is marginal. If something untoward happens they are unlikely to react quickly enough, or correctly.

Finally, and by no means least, almost all motorists overrate their own abilities. Driving standards and training in the United States are low in comparison to those in countries such as Scandinavia and Germany. Few motorists are even aware of their limitations, much less prepared to admit to them. Rather tellingly, it is the very worst drivers – drunks, and people with histories of crashes – who are the most delusional about believing they are great.

In short, motorists are heedless, untrained idiots, and this means that in certain circumstances you must take charge and make them respect you. Riding successfully in traffic requires a blend of determination and knowing when to give in. For example, try never to block overtaking cars. But if it is unsafe for you to let them pass, then do not hesitate to take full possession of your lane so they can't pass. You have exactly the same right to use the street or highway as any motorist; possession of a faster vehicle does not entitle a motorist to forge ahead at the expense of your safety.

As a cyclist, it is extremely important for you to see yourself in positive terms, and not buy into stereotype images of bikes as second class to cars, or cyclists as nice but incompetent simpletons. These ideas are stupid. As a bike rider, you have absolutely nothing to apologize for. You are not blocking or in the way. If anything, you are owed a vote of thanks for using a minimum amount of energy, not polluting the environment, and not endangering lives. You need to ride with pride and conviction – and at the same time, be practical. Many motorists are outright maniacs. No matter how right you are, a confrontation with a motor vehicle where push comes to shove will see you the loser.

In order to assert your rightful place as a cyclist in the scheme of things, you need to know what is going on. I love the fact that anyone can ride a bike. Roll on democracy and independence for young and old and all the people that do not possess driving licenses or cars!

However, if you are going to ride a bike in traffic, then you must be able to do so according to law. Briefly, this requires that: you ride as well to the right as is consistent with safety; obey traffic signs and signals; give way to pedestrians; and signal turns and stops. Left turn is left arm held straight out to the side, right turn ditto right arm, and stop is arm pointing down.

Check if your state produces Bicycle Driver's Manual. Alternatively, ask for a copy of the Pennsylvania Bicycle Driver's Manual. This includes extensive extracts from *Street Smarts, Bicycling's Traffic Survival Guide*, by John S. Allen, with plenty of tips on how to handle intersections, bluff aggressive drivers, and other lore. From:

Patricia A. Marshall,
Asst. Pedestrian/Bicycle Coordinator, Bureau of Highway Safety & Traffic Engineering,
555 Walnut Street, 7th Floor, PO Box 2047, Harrisburg, PA 17105-2047 USA.
Tel: 717 705 1444. Fax: 717 783 8012.
E-mail: pmarsha@dot.state.pa.us.

KNOW YOUR ENEMY

Some motorists are considerate, but many, many are incompetent, oblivious, or emotionally immature and too aggressive. Some are outright killers. You've got to be able to suss out at a glance which motorists you can communicate and work with, and which ones may take a swipe at you if given the chance. A quick motorist-danger index is the car they drive. Big, powerful cars are a more arrogant, write-your-own-rules kind of territoriality than less assuming, waif-in-the-world economy cars. The most dangerous types are wannabe cheap muscle cars, and pepped-up small economy cars bearing TurboSuper logos and go-faster stripes. Another quick but not decisive clue is gender and age: males, especially young males, are more dangerous than females. The red flag danger combination is a young male driving a cheap muscle car.

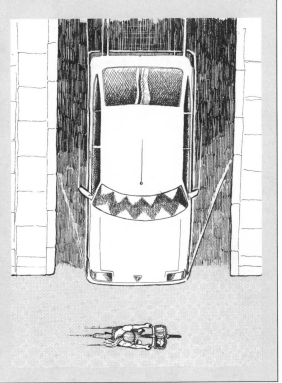

In addition, obtain a Motor Vehicle Operator's Manual for your state, and study the whole thing, from beginning to end. The purpose of this exercise is not just to learn what is expected of you, but also about other road users. I badmouth motorists a lot, but they have rights that deserve consideration, and you also need to understand the characteristics and problems of various kinds of vehicles. Communication and interchange between road users is a major dynamic of the road environment. You cannot fully participate in the game, much less assert your own status and rights, unless you understand what is happening, and know the rules.

How Important Are Rules?

Rules are relative to time and place. In New York City, motorists charge through red lights as a matter of course. I don't mean just nip the amber, either; a red light can be two or three minutes

gone, and cars sometimes still blast through. In NYC, you are not long for this world if you rely on the rules of the road for protection. Cyclists and pedestrians alike forge ahead where and when they can, regardless of rules. It is unusual, indeed completely extraordinary, to see a cyclist stop for a traffic signal.

You should ride by the rules whenever possible, for example stopping for a red light even when no one else is around. True, no harm would be done if you went on through, but you want adherence to the rules to be an ingrained reflex. The reason is, riding by the rules is faster, smoother, and safer, than riding with disregard for regulations. On the other hand, you should be aware that the rules were written to favor cars, not pedestrians or cyclists. There will be times when the best thing to do is break the rules. For example, it is often good to jump a light so you can get moving and be out of the way of faster vehicles. In countries like

Holland, early start green lights for cyclists are the norm.

When you break rules the reason has to be personal safety rather than convenience, and you need to use good judgment. For example, you are in heavy traffic, climbing a long hill in town, and up ahead two double parked trucks have created a tight one lane bottleneck. Ascending and descending vehicles are battling for priority, and you are moving too slowly to nip through. Should you jump up onto the sidewalk and ride there until you've cleared the obstruction? Yes, if the way is clear of pedestrians. No, if it involves a slalom around little old ladies and mothers pushing baby strollers.

Bend or break rules when necessary, but always be considerate of others. Take note of the fact that technically, you are supposed to observe traffic regulations, and can be subjected to penalties for dangerous riding, speeding, and riding under the influence of drugs or alcohol. You can be charged for traffic violations on a bicycle.

School

In the following section I give a long list of how-tos and things to be aware of when riding. However, some people learn more effectively from other people than from books. Cycling is dynamic, and often the quickest way to pick something up is to get on someone's wheel and do what they do. This is particularly true for bike handling skills. You might want to consider finding a more experienced riding companion who can lead you through some of the moves. Some cycle campaign groups can pair you with an experienced cyclist in your area who will keep you company on your first few rides, showing you the ins and outs of handling traffic, the local short cuts, and other useful lore. Check with your bike shop for your nearest campaign group.

The right of way

Another route is to go to school. Although "anyone can ride a bicycle," you've surely gathered by now that good cycling is a fairly evolved skill. Taking some lessons or a course can be a really good way to learn, or as a check on your habits and techniques. Scuba divers and skiers, even at very advanced levels, regularly take refresher courses. There is a nationwide program for cycling instruction known as Effective Cycling. Instructors are certified for both bike riding and teaching skills. Contact:

League of American Bicyclists, 1612 K Street NW, Suite 401, Washington, DC 20006-2082 USA.
Tel: 202 822 1333. Fax: 202 822 1334.
E-mail: bikeleague@bikeleague.org.
Web: www.bikeleague.org/advocacy/adec.html.

ROLLING

Hands by brake levers at all times. Always be prepared to stop. With modern brakes you should be able to exert all the braking force the tires will stand. If you are on a bike with poor brakes and must stop or die, try twisting the front wheel as you apply the brakes. So long as you are not going too fast, the bike will melt into the ground in a controlled crash as the wheel and forks buckle. I've had people question whether this technique works; yes, it does, but a better idea is a bike with decent brakes.

Keep your eyes constantly moving both fore and aft. When looking behind do not twist your head; duck it down. This is quicker and easier. Do this constantly. At any moment you might have to swerve to avoid an obstacle, and must know if you have the room to do so. A rearview mirror can be a great help.

Ride clearly and evenly. Save meandering for country lanes where you can see for a long way in both directions. Ride in a straight line. Signal all turns clearly. If on a wide street, make right turns from right lane and left turns from left lane.

Be decisive. If you tell other road users you are going to do something, do it. Part of the dynamic of road traffic is crispness; other road users, too, are looking to see matters sorted out and to have things happen. They are typically more responsive and cooperative if they see and experience you as a proper player in the game.

Being definite takes the form of a certain amount of aggressiveness. Do not let yourself be bulldozed into immobility by asking permission to do things. The odd good Samaritan may give you a break, but otherwise, you need to make and take your own breaks.

Be courteous. Give and take dialogue is the language of traffic. When a motorist gives you space or is otherwise helpful, give them a small thumbs-up. I do tell you to be definite, but courtesy is the key to speed. When every one tries to forge ahead at the same time, there is conflict, friction, and delay; when road users do each other small favors and otherwise lubricate progress, traffic moves more smoothly and quickly.

Communicate! Get in touch with other road users. Make eye contact. On a bike, you are part of the world around you, but motorists are ensconced and insulated inside little mini-territories. They blab on phones, pick their noses, scratch themselves, and otherwise behave as they would only do at home. You've got to reach through: eye contact and a smile or a gesture can make a motorist aware that you are not a minor problem to be ignored, but a human being with a rightful place in the scheme of things. Out of sight, out of mind! Intensely mistrust motorists who do not or will not look at you.

Always assume the worst. You can't see around the stopped bus? Assume that on the other side of it the entire cast of *101 Dalmatians* is prancing across the road. There is a car waiting to cross your lane? Assume it will – in four out of five bicycle/motor vehicle crashes, the motor vehicle committed a traffic violation. Always ride within a margin of control which allows you to stop or escape should absolutely everything go wrong.

Make noting bail-out possibilities a habit. Look for openings in traffic, driveways, streets, parking areas, front yards, even things such as ponds and streams, which you can duck into should the need arise. Try to plan where to go should you and the bike part company. In crashes, most often it is the bike which runs into something. The natural tendency in a collision situation is to try desperately to stop. Your interests may be better served by launching yourself over an obstacle, or swerving hard enough for a glancing collision.

While not exceeding a speed which gives you control, try to keep moving. Within reason, stay off your brakes. This will help you to look and plan ahead, and ride more smoothly and efficiently. Part of the danger from other vehicles in traffic comes from differences in velocity. Slipping into a lane of overtaking traffic in order to get around an obstacle such as a parked car is easier if you have some speed on, and have planned your move in advance.

Always be in a gear low enough to give you power and acceleration. Avoid becoming stuck in a dead high gear. To stay integrated with traffic requires that you be prepared to accelerate hard and quickly.

In heavy traffic or on a downgrade you may have the speed advantage. In that case you are better off out in the mainstream, or even out on what I call the high side, close to the center of the road. It's much safer overtaking cars there, than on the inside, where you may be squeezed into the gutter or against parked cars. Bear in mind that the high side is the territory of fast moving scooters and motor cycles, too. Be prepared to move over when necessary.

Do not tailgate! Car brakes are better than bike brakes. Leave plenty of room up front. Should matters unexpectedly tighten up, you want alternatives in the form of other places to go, not to have everything depend on your brakes, or worse, be hit by a following vehicle. This is where motorists accustomed to running bumper to bumper will try to pressure you from behind, even though you are moving at the same speed as the car in front of you. Maintain position, and if they give you the horn, mix them up by giving a friendly, cheerful wave. (My reflex is to give them the finger, but I've resolved to stop doing this. Too often this irks them into tailgating even more closely, which is the opposite of what I want.)

Be extra cautious at intersections where you already have right of way. Cars coming from the opposite direction and turning left will frequently cut straight across your path. Even if a stopped vehicle seems to be waiting for you to pass, don't trust it, for at the last moment it may leap forward. A good preemptive defense against this contingency is to ride through the intersection alongside a larger vehicle. Take care with this technique: if you enter an intersection *behind* a larger vehicle, a motorist waiting to make a cross turn may not be able to see you, and go just after the large vehicle passes through – catching you out.

Another problem at intersections are vehicles coming up from behind and then making a right turn across your path. This is perhaps the most frequent sin of motorists, and the essential defense tactic is again preemptive: take possession of your lane so that motorists cannot pull up alongside. If you are going straight ahead, it can help to signal your intention.

Observe lane discipline. On a three lane road where at a junction the inside lane becomes right turn only and you are proceeding ahead, you belong on the right side of the middle lane.

Often you will be riding next to parked cars. Beware of car doors opening in your path. Exhaust smoke, brake lights flashing, the profile of some-

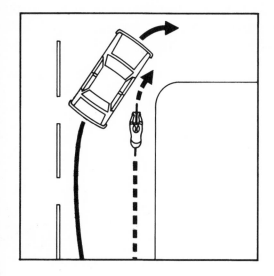

Low Side: car can turn across cyclist's path.

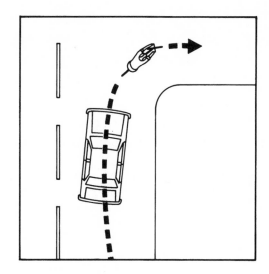

High Side: car must follow cyclist.

one sitting in a car, and faces in rearview mirrors are tips. Even if a motorist looks right at you and is seemingly waiting for you to pass, give him/her a wide berth. Believe it or not, the motorist may not consciously register your presence, and open the door in your face. The only safe way to deal with car doors is to keep clear of them. This brings us to an important crux of cyclist/motorist relations, your position on the road.

The law requires you to ride as far to the right side of the right lane as is consistent with safety. This is a very elastic and often abused definition. Cyclists have been charged for obstructing by riding too far to the left, and yet there have also been instances of opening car door/bike accidents where the cyclist was held to be at fault.

Always ride with enough maneuvering room for avoiding road litter and potholes. Never ride in

Low Side: hemmed in by vehicle A, the cyclist has no way of avoiding the opening door of vehicle B, and is invisible to the driver of vehicle C waiting at the junction.

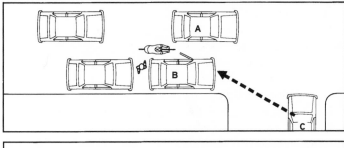

High Side: the cyclist is out of the way of the opening car door, and visible to the driver of vehicle C.

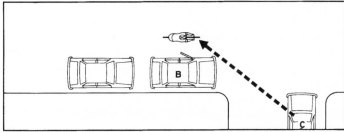

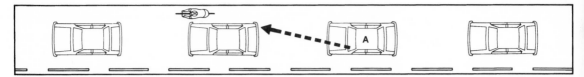

Low Side: with no room to spare, the cyclist cannot avoid pot holes or road litter, and is invisible to the driver of car A. If the driver is momentarily distracted, the cyclist may be hit.

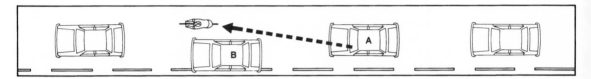

High Side: the cyclist has enough room to avoid holes and litter, and is visible to car A in time enough for the driver to allow extra room. The fact that car B has swung out also helps tell the driver of car A that the cyclist is there.

the gutter. Pass parked cars with space to spare should a door open. If the road or street is too narrow for overtaking vehicles to pass you with enough room, then ride bang out in the center of the lane. On a single lane road do not let them pass until it is safe for you to let them go by. On a two lane road, make them pass in the outer lane. This is where you will sometimes need to grit your teeth and hang in there. If you signal your moves and time them reasonably, capable motorists will understand what you are doing and make room. Mindless jerks will become frustrated and crowd you. *These are exactly the people you must control.* Do not be intimidated by impatient or stupid motorists. You are fully entitled to sufficient road space for safe passage.

On the other side, do not stand on your rights more than necessary. Let motorists pass whenever it is safe to do so.

Lane changing technique varies according to circumstances and what works for you. A common problem is a double parked car or other obstacle that narrows the road space, bunching traffic into a single line. If you are riding to one side of a steady stream of overtaking vehicles, joining the line takes good timing. You don't want to pull out and block a motorist for longer than necessary, or conversely, be boxed behind the obstacle by a selfish motorist who won't let you in. The trick is to pick a gap in the stream that gives you reasonable clearance, signal your move, and go. If the stream of traffic is irregular, you can leave the lane change until fairly late; if the stream is dense, make your move earlier.

Lane changing in thick, fast moving traffic can take muscle. John Forester, author of the comprehensive *Effective Cycling*, does not use hand signals. Instead, he establishes eyeball-to-eyeball contact with a particular motorist while positioning himself with the clear intention of moving right (or left). If the motorist makes room, Forester then changes lane. The method has a distinct advantage in that both hands stay on the handlebars and brakes, where they belong in heavy traffic. Another plus for this technique is the emphasis on communication.

Motorists sometimes understand body language better than signals. Glancing in the direction you want to go often gets the idea across. However, whenever possible, give a proper signal. At speed, I sometimes raise my arm somewhat slowly at first, then give a fully extended emphatic jab just before making my move.

The important general factor in relations with motorists is dialogue: here is what you want to do, here is what I want to do. Awareness is the key. Intensely distrust people who use mobile telephones while driving. Their attention is elsewhere, they are steering with one hand, and the fact that they are blase about this is their certification of stupidity. They do not know how to drive. Ditto drivers eating ice cream, guzzling drinks, lighting cigarettes, or otherwise not fully attending the business at hand.

If a car is waiting to join a stream of traffic in which you are riding and the driver is looking the other way, every alarm bell you've got should go off. Eyeball contact is no guarantee that a driver will do the right thing, but it does improve your chances.

Learn about other vehicles. An astounding number of people expect big buses and trucks to contravene basic laws of physics. They weigh an enormous amount and it is hard for them to change direction or stop. If you understand the problems of large vehicles there are many little courtesies you can extend that will be repaid in kind. Professional drivers appreciate craft.

Watch out for mopeds, scooters, and motor cycles, and know the differences between them. Motor cycle riders, for example, often have a good understanding of the problems of two wheel vehicles, and will cut you slack when you need it. All the same, they will want to keep on moving; let them roll on ahead as soon as is convenient.

Scooters, on the other hand, often must be dealt with firmly. All too many of the riders are adolescent hot shots with a big attitude and absolutely no sense. And if you want to identify a real hazard, watch out for pizza delivery bicycles!

Learn to read motorists. A harassed mother grinding along in an old wreck filled with screaming kids may well not have much of a grip on what's happening. A young buck in a heap with go faster stripes who keeps on charging ahead, only to pull up short, is someone to stay away from. If something goes wrong – doggie in the road or other surprise – young charger is likely to foul up. A big moving van, although awesome in size, may make better company, because the driver is likely to be more mature and sensible.

Taxicab drivers are a hazard for untrained cyclists. Cabbies drive every day, typically know exactly what is going on, and soon become accustomed to moving ahead at every opportunity. It's just something they do, and so long as you work within this framework by riding clearly and decisively, many cabbies will treat you decently enough. However, cabbies drive for a living. If you start to hesitate and dither, they will become impatient and shunt you in behind a bus, cut you off, or otherwise deal you out of the game.

Taxicabs are notorious for making sudden swerves and stops in order to pick up fares. It's sometimes irritating, but keep in mind that this is their business and that the driver needs to bring home the bacon.

The big problem from cabbies is crowding. They pass, and follow, way too close for safety, let alone comfort. How bad this problem will be depends on where you live. Where cabbies are properly trained – I don't know of a US city where this is the case – they can at least be tolerable. In a town like New York City, where licensing standards are abysmal and training does not exist, cabbies are a serious hazard.

Be aware of general conditions. Motorists are more aggressive in heavy traffic at peak travel periods, and also when under the influence of alcohol. Alcohol diminishes physical skill, mental judgment, and inhibition threshold. Drunks who cannot drive in a straight line imagine they possess wondrous skill and elan, and crucially, are much more inclined to try and prove it. A motorist does not have to be over the legal limit to become less skilled and more belligerent. There is no amount of alcohol which is safe.

Countries such as Finland have an absolute

prohibition on alcohol for motorists, even from medicine, and the penalties for infringement are severe. The result is a low accident rate, particularly of the drink related type. In America, drinking is a factor in 25 percent of accidents and many thousands of deaths a year. Be wary when out riding on Friday and Saturday nights.

Interpret local conditions. A street with an abundance of fast food outlets means you need to be extra watchful for opening car doors and people wandering onto the road while munching their pizza. On a fast section of road with limited access you can hold a little more to the right, to help ease overtaking traffic. Plan your routes according to your riding ability, sticking to slower, less travelled streets until you have built up your skill and speed.

Keep a lookout for sources of vehicles that could pull out in front of you. Look for side streets, building entrances, construction projects, taxicab ranks, driveways, and so on. Remember, the driver of a vehicle waiting to join the stream of traffic in which you are riding may not see you. They look at you, the image is flashed somewhere on their brain, but the message is not comprehended. You don't exist.

Bone up on different kinds of motorists and vehicles. Be cautious when you spot something like a sporty vehicle approaching a stop at speed. The driver is apt to ride the brakes out into the intersection, hoping they can dash across the road (or join the stream of traffic) without having to stop. In such a tightly timed sequence, the driver often fails to see a cyclist – or elects to deliberately cut them up.

Keep a weather eye on the road surface. Watch out for broken glass, stones, potholes, etc. Plenty of bumps are big enough to destroy a bike. Riding over obstacles, get off the saddle and keep your weight on the pedals and handlebars. As for holes, I still can't believe the size of some I've encountered. Always try to look as far ahead as possible. If you are caught out, jump.

A particular hazard are storm sewers, many are just the right size to swallow a bicycle wheel. This is one reason why you do not ride in the gutter.

Beware of slippery surfaces in wet weather. Newly wet streets can momentarily transform into ice rinks. There's a film of accumulated oil which mixes with the water to make everything extremely slippery until enough rain falls to wash the oil away. Remember, it's not just you who might have loss of control; first rain is always good for a rash of fender benders. Taxicabs especially. In first wet, keep clear of other vehicles.

Wet manhole covers and steel plates can put you down in a hurry. So can wet cobblestones, wet autumn leaves, loose gravel, and sand. Wet paint stripes, such as lane dividers, can be a particular hazard.

Ride with the traffic. Sometimes when there is no traffic coming the other way, it is better to ride in the opposite lane. As for riding against traffic on one way streets, you should not do it. It's OK for a short distance as a practical expedient, but not if it rattles oncoming motorists. In that case, get off and walk.

Pedestrians can be a nightmare. They don't think 200 pounds of bike and rider mean a thing, and will frequently jaywalk right in your path. On the other hand, there are cyclists who hurtle by pedestrians with nothing to spare. I understand their feelings, but they don't always make it – and any collision between a cyclist and a pedestrian will be painful. If a pedestrian hops out in front of you, it's OK to read them the riot act, but do not attempt to bring them into the real world by grazing their shirt buttons, or intimidating them with super horns.

Kids are as much of a hazard to the cyclist as to the motorist. Any child has the potential to suddenly race out into the street. When there are kids around, slow down.

Other cyclists. The fact that someone is riding a bike does not mean they are on your side. Like other categories of road users, many cyclists do stupid things. Stay clear of other riders unless you know them, or they obviously know what they are doing.

When you come up to a group of cyclists waiting at a traffic signal, take your place in the line. When overtaking another cyclist it is your responsibility to keep clear, and make sure you do; if your front wheel touches the other bike, you will go down like a shot. If a cyclist presses from behind, hold your line but let them by as soon as you can.

At night, lights and reflectors help make you visible to motorists. You need to light up like a starship. Even then, some motorists will not see you. If you use no lights at all, you will be invisible. I say no more. See Chapter 9, Accessories, for more information on lights and reflectors.

Sidewalks. The issue of whether cyclists should be allowed to cycle on sidewalks or be forced to stick to the streets and roads is a thorny one. In countries like the Netherlands, Denmark, and Germany, and in specific towns in Britain, pedestrians and cyclists have shared common paths for years with excellent safety records. Many factors make this so, but the most basic is that in a collision, a cyclist is likely to be hurt just as badly as a pedestrian. Both parties have an equal interest in avoiding conflict.

In America, sad to say, people are not up to speed on this one. There are more than a few cyclists who bomb along the sidewalks with selfish disregard for the safety and comfort of pedestrians. Fast food delivery riders seem to be the worst. The situation is made more difficult by the fact that many pedestrians are oblivious to the hazard. There have been plenty of accidents, and even a few fatalities.

In such circumstances, it is understandable that many people are enraged against cycling on sidewalks or in pedestrian areas, and want cyclists pushed out onto the streets and roads. This is the wrong way to handle the problem.

Fit adults can handle cycling on the roads. In fact, that's where most of them prefer to be, because you cannot ride very quickly on cyclepaths or sidewalks. Little kids, elderly folks, mothers-to-be, and just plain dreamers are not so capable, and are at far greater risk in traffic. It's the gentler souls – our kids, our parents and grand-parents – who need to use the sidewalks. For the most part, these people ride at a relaxed pace which is fine for mixing with pedestrians. Forcing them out onto the roads would be sending them to their deaths.

Yes, right now there are a good number of kids and louts who ride badly and inconsiderately on sidewalks and thereby terrorize and endanger pedestrians. Many a time I've wanted to throttle a cyclist who cut too close. However, this is a peo-ple problem, not a bike problem! Pushing a moron out into road traffic is exactly the wrong thing to do. The punishment should fit the crime. If some-one cuts up with a bike through ignorance or indifference, then take their bike away. No fine, no conversation, just bike gone. Give it back only after they have completed a cyclist education course in how to ride when around pedestrians. You make people behave responsibly by taking them into the fold and explaining what is required, not by banishing them to what may be terminal punishment.

Cycling on sidewalks is fine. It is often a far superior and safer alternative to riding on the road. However, you must always ride in such as way as to not upset or offend pedestrians. This applies even if you are on a cyclepath shared with pedestrians. Basically, this means two things: going at a moderate pace, and keeping in touch with people by giving them a smile or wink or some other indication to show you are aware of them, and intend to take care. With this, most pedestrians will relax. If not, and the vibes are bad, get off and walk. It's your responsibility to keep pedestrians happy, and if some of them are nervous nellies, then that's your draw.

FAST IS SAFE

Ride a bike and you'll live longer – provided you live! Make a wrong move in traffic, be in the wrong place at the wrong time, and you can wind up dead. In the 100 or so years that the car has been around, it has killed more people than all wars in the same period. For a cyclist, traffic is a war zone. The foremost priority in war is survival – and that means keeping out of no-win conflicts in the first place. The successful traffic cyclist is a guerrilla: aware, highly skilled, and always flexi-ble and elusive.

The hazards encountered in traffic can be made to work to your advantage. Riding fast promotes your own safety. This is because you must antici-pate and avoid the dangerous situations that would otherwise retard your journey. The best way to do this is to ride on the high side, out in the mainstream of traffic.

So long as you shift along quickly enough to keep pace with the other road users, riding the high side is safer than trying to stay out of the way by keeping to the low side, near the gutter. Riding the high side largely eliminates hazards such as road litter, opening car doors, cars overtaking and turning right across your path, and stray pedestri-ans stepping off the sidewalks. All of these are a greater danger than the risk of being struck from behind by a motorist. Furthermore, on the high side you are more visible to motorists than when on the low side.

Emotionally, riding the high side is more satis-factory than hiding in the gutter and waiting to be hit. Clear assertiveness diminishes rather than increases tension for the cyclist. The aim is to pass along smoothly, neither accelerating nor decelerating excessively. The mark of a good traf-fic rider is that he or she is in the right place at the right time. This skill is a function of awareness and a positive orientation, whereas tension is the negative outcome of worrying about finding yourself in the wrong place at the wrong time.

Riding a bike is a skill, and like skiing, or chess, has different levels and dimensions that you can constantly hone and improve. The basic technique for dealing with riding in traffic is to treat it as a game which you try to play with greater skill than anyone else. This helps to transform setbacks into challenges and above all keeps the initiative with you, where it belongs.

CYCLEPATHS

Cyclepaths are an inconsistent feature of the American landscape: abundant in some places, non-existent in others. In addition, they vary enormously in quality. Some are well planned and a pleasure to use, but many are badly designed and are more dangerous than the roads they are supposed to replace. How it is in your area is something for you to check out.

If you are lucky, you'll live in a town with a good network of cyclepaths which are entirely segregated from motor vehicles. These are not suitable for fast riding, but are wonderful for transport and just meandering along. If you are unlucky, the cyclepaths will run alongside roads and constantly intersect with driveways and cross streets. There will probably be obstacles such as signs and posts in the middle of the path. These kinds of cyclepaths are worse than nothing; you are a lot safer riding on the roads.

CRASHES

An accident is a surprise. It's not the same thing as crashing in a race because you pressed too hard. An accident is something you did not expect. When this happens, the problem is not so much knowing what to do, as being able to do it.

Most people react to an imminent crash with panic. They may freeze and do nothing, or blindly clamp down on the brakes and lose directional stability. This can make a bad situation fatal. For example, if a car is about to hit you from the side and you death grip the brakes, the rear wheel is likely to lock up and send you down in a slide, to be rolled up underneath the car. If at the moment of impact you instead try to get clear of the bike and make a dive for the hood of the car, you may slide along to the windscreen and perhaps even over the roof. Not fun, but the survival prospects are a lot better than if you are underneath the car.

Panic-induced muscular tension increases physical damage in a crash. A person who is able to relax and roll with a fall will suffer less injury than a person who tenses up and tries to save him- or herself. The ability to exercise the best of a series of bad options, and stay physically relaxed in a situation offering damage, can only be learned through experience and practice. If you do not know how to fall, try to have someone with training – fighting experts, skydivers, skiers – give you some pointers. Go to martial arts classes. Explain you don't want to learn how to kill anyone, just how to fall. It's a handy skill, you are likely to need it sometime.

Some people claim that bike accidents happen too fast for a rider to do anything. This is certainly sometimes the case. There will also be times when you have some choice in bail-out possibilities. If you want some useful practice in deciding which way to jump, try fast off-road riding with a mountain bike, particularly in sand, mud, and loose gravel. A few spills are inevitable, usually with little damage. This kind of play is even better on snow and ice. Careful though, frozen ground can be hard.

Keep your physical skills honed. Regularly practice the braking and turning techniques discussed in Chapter 11, Riding Basics. Keep your mind and emotions tuned, too. Think about what to do in various circumstances. If a car pulls up alongside you and then unexpectedly turns right, cutting you off, a sudden application of the brakes will simply pile you into the car. A rapid haul turn, however, might save you. If you do hit, then you and the car will be going more or less in the same direction.

Suppose a car pulls out in front of you from a side road or driveway. There may be enough room for a haul turn so that you hit the car a glancing blow. If not, then brake as hard as you can without skidding, and just before hitting the car launch yourself clear of the bike. You may be able to sail right over the car. Stay loose, tuck and roll! when you hit the road.

If you are hit from behind, DO NOT BRAKE. Try to get away by steering to the side.

HAVING IT BACK

You say all the right mantras, make all the right moves, give everything and everybody grace and consideration – and still, it happens. A motorist does you dirt, nearly kills you in fact, and you're mad clean through. What happens next depends on who and what you are. As the saying goes, different strokes for different folks.

One acceptable response is an explosive yell. It's the cycling equivalent of blowing a horn to signify potential or immediate danger. A good yell

can help you to release some of the adrenaline energy that danger generates. It can make a motorist just a touch uncomfortable, and is more effective if there are passengers in the vehicle. A lot of ruckus and commotion means that the motorist is doing something wrong, and the more passengers as audience, the greater the awareness of discord.

One of the most frequent sins of the motorist is to overtake a cyclist and then suddenly brake and turn right. The motorist knowingly creates trouble for the cyclist, and expects to get away with it through sheer greater size. If you are in a malicious mood, this can be a moment of opportunity. The cyclist is usually in the blind rear quarter of the vehicle and invisible to the motorist, who may be under some tension about the outcome of his or her misdeed. A well-timed yell can startle the motorist into a momentary loss of vehicle control. If there is a nearby obstruction, the motorist may hit it.

Another unsettling tactic in a situation where a motor vehicle is actively risking an accident is to hit it hard with the flat of your hand. This makes a tremendous bang, especially if done on the roof. You are allowed to slap a car as a warning. You may not do it as an act of revenge. The best time is when a vehicle enters the roadway from the right and cuts across your path in a left turn. By passing behind the vehicle you have the benefit of diverging trajectories, and with good timing you can give it a noisy bash on the flank.

Slap a vehicle only if you have a clear escape route. If you do this to a vehicle running alongside and crowding, the driver could panic and do something wrong, or lose their temper and swerve into you.

When crowded, one defense is to crowd back. At close quarters you know where you are to the inch. Few motorists are that good. If you call their hand by moving in tight, many motorists will back away. In heavy traffic this tactic can be used to brush motorists into giving you enough room.

A completely different but effective ploy against crowding is to wobble unsteadily, suggesting that you are not in good control and might do anything next. This works best when a vehicle is still behind you; the motorists' instinct is to shy away and stay clear.

What about really scrapping with motorists – damaging their vehicles, or getting into fights? Whoa – not recommended! An attack on a motorist or their vehicle is likely to produce greater polarization and make the motorist meaner and more willing to victimize cyclists. If you are tempted to tweak the tail of a motorist, think of the other cyclists who will also cross that motorist's path.

Think also of the basic odds. Some cyclists actively harass motorists. Sooner or later they get more than they bargained for. Remember, you could be playing with dynamite. Some motorists are armed with guns and other weapons. Some are outright homicidal. They will endanger or attack you for fun, or to satisfy angers and competitive emotions that are incomprehensibly stunted and malformed. Start razzing them, give them an opening, and they may literally try to kill you. It has happened to me more than once, with and without preliminaries. I don't mind a slanging match or exchanging choice insults, but mortal combat against a nutter armed with a car is too much.

As a cyclist, you are a quintessential guerrilla, out there completely on your own. You won't get any help, except possibly from other cyclists. If a motorist attacks you with a vehicle, even manages to bring you down, chances are the police will do nothing. I'm truly sorry to say this. Some police have personally been very helpful to me. Still, in a typical incident, I once saw a motorist jump out of a car and punch a cyclist to the ground. When the cyclist remounted and attempted to flee, the motorist leapt back into his car and ran the cyclist down. The bike was destroyed, the cyclist luckily was thrown clear and not severely injured. I calmed down the motorist and the police were called. Yet despite the presence of plenty of eyewitnesses who gave statements to the police, no charges were raised against the motorist. There have been many, many cases like this.

Steer clear of trouble whenever you can. Guard against unproductive blow-offs. Unless you are a regular tough customer used to hostile confronta-

tions, a run in with a motorist will probably set your adrenaline coursing and may make you irrational. Try to keep things in perspective. I've seen cyclists catch up to a motorist and then in a rage scream abuse and bash the vehicle – and more than once the car driver was a terrified little old lady who yes, had sinned, but had no real idea of what she had done.

Often, it is enough to simply have a firm word. For many motorists, the realization that the protective bubble of their car can be penetrated by a live, intent, and possibly angry human being can be quite a shock. A demand that amounts, in sum, to "Listen, you just nearly plastered me, don't do that" is most effective with women and least effective with cabbies and young macho males. If you confront a motorist and get an apology, then bury the hatchet at once. The whole idea is to get motorists to treat cyclists as people. The true guerrilla has a political objective!

DO NOT RIDE BY

If you see a cyclist and a motorist involved in an altercation, do not ride on by. Stop and observe.

In New York City, I've seen several cyclist/ motorist incidents where passing cyclists stopped and formed a small surrounding crowd. They were relaxed, and did not do or say much, but their presence had a decidedly calming effect and helped prevent more trouble.

My long time cycling friends agree that humor is the best ploy, as in "Nice one, buddy (or lady)!" and "What incredible driving!", said with patent irony. This makes your dissatisfaction known, but with the least amount of threat likely to provoke further polarization. If you can come up with a real joke or bit of misdirecting, this can help place conflict to one side, and give everyone a lit-

tle room in which to move and retreat or perhaps meet each other halfway. Whatever – in
my experience, the really hard riders, the
kind who can put blood on the pavement,
are rarely ruffled and usually leave matters
at a sardonic remark or two.

YOUR DECISION

Conflict is inherent in the traffic environment,
and owing to their vulnerability, cyclists suffer continuous threats to their lives. If the risk
of harm were only sporting, that would be
fine, but motorists routinely use their size and
power to abuse cyclists. Understandably,
many cyclists ache to strike back. It is human
and perfectly OK to be angry when a motorist
does you wrong, but it is not OK to use this as
an excuse for venting accumulated frustration
and rage. Moreover, any outright fight is not
likely to produce a good result, or even much
satisfaction. What's the percentage in beating
up jerks and emotional retards?

Wars never do anyone much good. Over
years of riding I've found the best squelch for
motorists is to leave them behind. Rage, and
sooner or later you will go down. Strive for
skill and grace and you may survive.

When push comes to shove, humor and misdirecting stand the best chance of defusing a
conflict, and will probably also do you the most
good. Humor helps you to manage an incident
on your terms rather than get caught up in a
degenerate scrap. Let aggressive motorists go on
to collect their own just deserts, because that is
exactly what happens to them.

URBAN COMMUTING

Travel and fitness exercise combined • Options in bikes • Researching routes • Mixed mode commuting • First rides • Special equipment • Security and parking

COMMUTING TO AND FROM WORK BY BIKE IS A great way to improve your life. It neatly combines travel and exercise while saving time and money, and most important, adds zest to your day. In the morning, instead of surrendering your existence to the vagaries of public transport or being trapped in a car, riding a bike puts you completely in charge, and brings you up to snuff, stimulated, awake, and aware. Employers note: bike riding employees are more vital and productive, more punctual, take fewer sick days, and work for longer periods of tenure. On the way home, you can have a vigorous ride to unwind from a hard day, or relax a bit and take the time to explore a new bit of territory. However you do it, whatever your style, commuting by bike makes part of the day exclusively yours. It's not always all roses, there are hazards and sometimes the weather can be rotten, but in balance you come out well ahead.

Cycle commuting is a specific activity and type of riding. You need to sort out the kind of bike to use and where it will be parked, the selection of equipment, and journey planning and routing.

The Bike

Many city streets are obstacle courses filled with bumps, potholes, uneven surfaces, steel plates which are slippery when wet, broken glass, bits of sharp metal, and other rubbish. In heavy traffic there often is not enough room for time in which to avoid obstacles. A machine for these

S.T.DADD.

conditions must be tough. Theft is a constant problem. An obviously expensive bicycle is more likely to be stolen, or stripped for parts. Finally, most regular commuters prefer a bike that requires a minimum of maintenance.

Roadster bikes with hub gears are low maintenance and fairly durable. The problems are brakes and weight. You'll need a new machine equipped with cantilever and/or hub brakes in order to have sufficient stopping power for safe riding in traffic. Traditional roadsters with long reach, wide arm calliper brakes are not good enough.

A roadster has a certain kind of relaxed style, and now and again I put one into commission – but only for local utility trips such as picking up timber and building supplies, fresh roasted coffee beans, and other errands. Riding a roadster more than a couple of miles or up lots of hills is a drag, because the work is double the effort required with a lightweight machine.

A bike for commuting needs to be light, tough, and versatile – a mountain bike is perfect. Moreover, it can be set up pretty much as you like: fleet and quick, or go anywhere, old boots tough. Some manufacturers produce city bikes, mountain bikes with 26-inch wheels, comprehensively equipped with fenders, lights, carrier rack, and kickstand. Great idea, but so far the machines are too heavy, because they are built of cheaper materials to sell at low price points. I'm sure this will change someday, and if you can find a fully-equipped city bike that does not make you grunt when you pick it up, then fine. Otherwise, first choice in my opinion is to pick out a good quality mountain bike, and then set it up to your liking. More on this in a moment.

What about hybrid bikes with 700C wheels? It's pretty much a question of personal taste and style. Larger wheels have less rolling resistance, a factor which can add up on long distance commutes.

They are strong enough in ordinary conditions, but hard knocks such as bouncing in and out of potholes and up onto sidewalks will strain them. A hybrid can go off-road and with a skilled rider tackle all sorts of rough obstacles, but it's a machine slanted towards smooth roads and swift passage. Another factor is fashion; hybrids have a more elegant appearance.

What about a road touring bike? Yes, yes, they are strongly built and can be fine for commuting. They are designed to carry things, and will capably ferry home the groceries, or a week's worth of work from the office. In performance terms touring bikes are steady and sure rather than responsive and quick. They are better for evenly paced long distance rides rather than sprinting through traffic. Frankly, it depends on what you like. If you dream of cycle touring and country lanes and far lands, then go ahead and get a bike of that kind; it's perfectly good for commuting and general transport. Scratching the itch of another possible use beyond the immediate job at hand is one of the secrets for success with a bike.

The same sort of thinking applies to a road sport bike, a machine set up for performance. A light, lithe bike is great if you live someplace

where the roads are well maintained. If you have to contend with mean streets, you'll be in a constant struggle to keep the bike from harm. My advice is first things first: set up a proper commuting bike, then later on acquire a good road sport model, which you can run lean and pure, as a fun riding machine.

A recumbent cycle, or even a fully faired HPV, can be great for commuting, but not for a rider new to traffic. There's a lot to learn and sort out when taking up regular cycle commuting, and adding the special requirements of recumbents to the mix could make for a stiff adventure. Don't misunderstand: I think recumbents are wonderful and use them all the time. My mainstay heavy traffic commuting machine for many years was a full bore HPV. All I'm saying is, first become familiar with bikes, heavy traffic, and commuting, then see what a recumbent might do for you.

A folding bike can be a good choice. It solves the security problem; you can take the bike inside at work, into restaurants and shops, etc. Another advantage is flexibility; if your plans change because it starts pouring rain, or you meet the love of your life, you're not stuck with a bike. A decent folder is no problem to manage in a taxicab, train, or bus. This relates to perhaps the most fruitful application for a folding bike, mixed mode transport, where you might ride a bike to the train station, whiz the bike into a bundle and hop on the train, and then from destination station ride the bike to your place of work. If the cycling portions are relatively short, you can use a very compact and easily managed folder such as a Brompton. If the riding distances are longer, you'll be happier with a more roadworthy machine such as a Bike Friday. See the entry on Folding Bikes in Chapter 6, Special Bikes and Trikes, for more information.

Going back to the mountain bike, exactly what you get is up to you. If you want a simple life, skip suspension, and go for fewer gears and sealed bearings on components such as hubs and bottom bracket. However, if you have your heart set on dual suspension and visions of playing in the woods leaping into the air or blasting down trails, then go for fancy with all the trimmings. A middle

ground is a hardtail with suspension forks, and I must admit these are very nice in traffic. Whatever, make sure the bike is lightweight and at least has V-brakes. Disc brakes are better. This means at least a middle range bike, which, if you are on a modest salary (say, a young school teacher) might run two to three weeks take home pay. If this is a daunting sum, consider borrowing, because the savings you will make by cycle commuting will more than cover the cost of credit. Alternatively, shop around for a used machine, and upgrade when you can afford to do so out of your savings.

Equipment and Accessories

Many mountain bike tires designed for off-road use run well enough on surfaced roads. The trick is to inflate the tire to a high pressure. The difficulty is that this can produce a harsh ride. Also, many gnarlies are designed with knobs on the side, so the tire will bite when it sinks into mud or soft dirt. Problem is, when you heel over hard on a smooth surface, the knobs can make the bike "walk" sideways in an alarming manner. I prefer to use a lighter 1.4- or 1.5-inch wide road tire coupled with a 22 mm rim in place of the usual 28 mm rim. This combination is swift and has good grip. I've had great success for years with the Specialized 1.4-inch Nimbus, which has a nice ride on pavement, yet can handle a bit of off-road riding in dry conditions. For more road performance, I've also set up several bikes with 1.25-inch Tioga City Slickers, which are quick but still a lot tougher than your average road tire. The Michelin Wildgripper is very strong. For weekend off-road rides, and town trips requiring bullet proof tires, you can have a second set of wheels shod with 1.9 or 2-inch gnarlies. These can also be reassuring for use when the weather and roads are really nasty.

Fenders are a necessity if you want to stay clean. Some people feel they are sissy and slow you down, but they make life easier and more enjoyable. In fact, I even use them a lot off-road. It's quite fun to blow through a mud bath or stream and emerge without a splattered face or wet behind. Many people use half length clip-on models. I prefer full length at the front, and bob-tail with a flap at the back. If you like, you can take fenders off when the weather is dry.

You'll need lights and reflectors – check these entries in Chapter 9, Accessories, – a Sam Brown belt or reflective vest, a helmet, and gloves. Wear cycling clothes if you can, they are more comfort-able, and change at work. You'll need some rain clothes, a basic tool kit, spare tube and puncture repair kit, a lock for in-case use, and last but by no means least, some means of carrying all this stuff.

If your bike is primarily a commuting and util-ity machine, then it makes sense to have a carrier rack. It adds flexibility – no problem picking up the laundry or extra groceries – and makes a good mounting point for lights. If your bike is first and foremost a sport machine, then a backpack is a good solution. An advantage of this method is that a backpack moves with you on and off the bike, so there is no time spent fumbling with panniers, etc.

Security

You need to organize secure parking. This is because there is no lock made that you can fully trust to protect your bike if you leave it on the street. One tactic is to keep three or even four locks at a regular parking spot in the hope of diverting thieves to easier game. Well, at today's prices three or four locks is a lot of money! More to the point, they won't protect your bike from vandalism, or from being stolen by simply cutting through the frame.

Best is someplace to park inside at work. Check around, there's usually a nook such as under the stairs that will do. If there is space available but your employer or head honcho is anti-bike, turn on the charm and delivery of impressive statistics about the productivity of bike riding workers (any campaign group will provide) and see if you can convert them. If not, I advise looking for another job. People are of course entitled to their opinions and feelings, but anti-bike is head way deep in the sand, which is not good for business. I'd look into employment elsewhere not just to be able to ride a bike, but also in the interest of job security.

Sometimes there just won't be any space for a bike. In that case, look afield. There might be a car parking garage nearby with odd bits of space where a bike could be slotted in. Perhaps a near-by business would be helpful. Do you regularly eat out at a nearby cafe? Perhaps they can help – or know someone who can. Try rousting out the local municipal authorities and explaining you need secure bike parking. They are supposed to be onto this sort of thing, and once in awhile they are. Whatever, keep after the problem and eventu-ally you should score.

Remember, you are not just feathering your own nest. Cycling really does make the world a better place. Just about everyone has to work for a living, and the largest area for increasing the use of bikes is in riding to and from work. Gaining parking, changing rooms, showers, and so on, are advances that really count.

Routes

Route planning and exploration is important. Bikes move in different ways than other vehicles and can go through alleys, parking lots, and other short cuts. Even if you know the territory over which you plan to commute, it is worth obtaining a map and giving it a good study. Local cycle cam-paign groups and bike shops sometimes have infor-mation on good cycle routes. Very often, things are not what you thought they were. Finding good routes is a matter of trial and error. Best are streets and roads where you can keep moving, but are not embroiled in the worst of the traffic. A good ride is more important than the fastest possible journey.

Start by drawing a straight line on the map between home and work. Pick out a trial route, bearing in mind whatever you know about the area. A direct path, for example, might crest three hills you could avoid by following a slightly longer route. Or perhaps there is a way to have a single sharp climb, followed by gentle down-grades for the rest of the journey.

For the first few trips allow twice the time you think you need. This gives a margin for problems, rest stops, and so on. Relate what you discover to the map. You'll usually find there are two or three other obvious options to check out. After a week or so you will probably have an optimum route down pat, but keep on exploring. You never know what you might find, and anyway, it is often practical as well as fun to vary your routes. For example, I live on a hill, so it is easy to run at speed in mainstream traffic when going down into town. On the return journey, especially if traffic is heavy, I'm likely to take advantage of a couple of "cyclists only" turnings and duck into quiet back streets.

Cycle routes and cyclepaths are a mixed blessing. Sometimes they are a good way of avoiding traffic. However, many cyclepaths are badly designed and dangerous. They tend to be littered with broken glass, cross traffic, and errant pedestrians. All too often they were only built to get bikes out of the way of cars, and pass through desolate areas which are tenable in broad daylight, but risk a mugging at night. Other cyclepaths route alongside heavily travelled streets or roads and are constantly crossed by traffic moving in and out of driveways, gas stations, shopping centers, and shops. These cyclepaths can be very dangerous, and you are usually better off out on the road. On the other hand, you might be lucky and have use of a cyclepath built by people who knew what they were doing. Lots of them are really lovely and in some places you can cover most of a journey without ever seeing a car.

Options which can reduce journey length or make for an interesting diversion are off-road trails, disused railroads, and canal towpaths.

What's going very much depends on where you live, of course. Generally speaking, trails that connect places will also be used by walkers and sometimes even horses. Be considerate of pedestrians, and if you meet a horse, stop. Horses are typically nervous of bikes.

Disused railroads and canal towpaths are a little known but sometimes valuable resource for cyclists. Railroads and canals were once a mainstay of transport and honeycombed the country. Many have been plowed under or paved over, but a few are still there. In some areas they have been reclaimed and rebuilt as paths for cyclists and pedestrians. If you are lucky, you might live someplace where it is possible to do long distance rides for 100 miles or more without ever meeting a car.

It's usually important to throttle down. Depending on where you are, there may be people fishing, boating, and walking, families and dogs, musicians, poets, and artists, people schmoozing, and peace in our time. Ride slow and don't upset anyone.

Fun and Games

Commuting by bike is a wonderful way to get to know an area. It's easy to divert and explore – a new road, a hidden courtyard, or whatever. I've lived and worked in various places, and each change of location has been accompanied by a galaxy of new things to see. I've found new restaurants, markets, shops, neighborhoods, farms, paths with stones trod by men in armor – the list of interesting things is endless.

Commuting can also be a dynamic challenge. You soon get to know some routes better than the back of your hand. You can plot every pothole and bump, the timing of traffic signals, and a thousand other details. If you want, you can elevate running that route to an art form, timing the lights and junctions so that you flow through the entire journey like silk. You can run hot, crowding the pace and chopping a little off your best time. This is really fun, because it is somewhat similar to inter-

val training, where you go very hard for a bit, relax a while, then hammer again. When you do this in traffic, one thing can lead to another: the jump that got you ahead on one portion of the run sets you up for yet another segment at greater speed, and so on. It's exciting, but the rules are, you're in traffic not on a race track, and if conditions force you to back off, do so. You'll get another chance.

Be civil to other cyclists. A certain amount of competitiveness is natural, in fact informal street racing is very common, but again, use common sense and don't push boundaries too hard. You are looking to get ahead by grace and skill rather than brute strength or ignoring rules. Incidentally, if you overtake another rider, make sure you maintain a pace that keeps you out ahead. It's thoroughly irritating when a cyclist puts on a burst to pass you and then slacks off and drops back into your face.

Pointers

Keep the weight down. It's tempting to take along every tool you think you might need, a full set of waterproof clothing, maps, food and water, and something for luck. Once the load gets up to a certain point you become a baggage laden tourist rather than a rider. It's also a nuisance coping with a forest of things when off the bike. Get the regular essentials down to what you can carry in a seat pack. Maintain your bike well, and a multi-tool, spare tube, puncture repair kit, and pump or inflator are all you need. Add a good waterproof but breathable cycling jacket and you're fairly well covered.

You may want to limit your cycle commuting journeys to fine weather at first, but once the bug takes hold, you'll find you want to use the bike whenever possible. When in doubt, ride. Rain can be unpleasant, but it's worse to miss a ride and discover that, after all, it only drizzled. If, as sometimes happens, the heavens cascade and you get soaked, it's not the end of the world – particularly if you have dry clothes available at the end of the journey. As for riding in winter, it's lots of fun – try it and see!

Cargo Cycles and Trailers

14

Shopping by bike • Cargo bikes and cycles • Using carrier cycles and pedicabs for the school run • Trailers for solo bicycles

SHOPPING FOR FOOD AND OTHER PROVISIONS, delivering children to and from school, and various other routine errands, constitute a major portion of all journeys. Most of these trips are under two miles, and are easy to do by bike, provided you have the right machine for the job. I suppose many people imagine that shopping by bike is a nice idea, but something of a trial. This is perhaps true if you try to cram a week's worth of groceries aboard a bike equipped with panniers. It's hard to keep the bike still as you load up, the extra weight makes the bike sway as you ride, and at home you again have to keep the bike upright while you root all the stuff out.

Set up right for the task, however, and shopping by bike is easier than any other method. There's no hassling with driving a car and parking, or trudging along with your fingers about to drop off from clutching a zillion plastic carrier bags.

I can roll out a bike, hitch up a trailer, and shoot down to the local supermarket faster than any car made, because I can use a short-cut over a pedestrian- and cyclist-only bridge. At the store I lock the bike right next to the door, and unhitch a trailer which I use as a shopping cart. The store has barcode scanners for customers, so the shopping goes straight into the trailer. After checkout, I hitch up, ride home, and then unhitch and wheel the trailer directly into the kitchen, where the booty is unloaded.

At no point have I ever lifted more than a single item. The bike and trailer have done all the work, literally collecting the goodies from the store shelves and transporting them straight into the kitchen.

If you like calling by a number of shops, a bike and trailer, or cargo cycle, is even better. You can go to more places greater distances apart, and your cargo carrier is right to hand every time you stop;

Gibbons Pentacycle or "Hen-and-chickens" once used for mail deliveries in Britain.

and it's also more fun. I can still feel my daughter nestling between my arms on the cross bar seat and hear her laughter while we whizzed down the back route to her primary school. Take it from me: using cycles for day-to-day activities is not just less expensive and easier. There's a real feel good factor. You're in touch with the little things that in the end are the true stuff of life.

There are two main options: a purpose built cycle, or a trailer.

Cargo Cycles

The traditional load-carrying delivery bike has a small front wheel, and a cage of stout metal tubing which can hold a box or large wicker basket. An enormous double kickstand ensures stability when parked even if the bike is fully loaded. Pashley makes a modern version, the Delibike, with hub gears and hub brakes. It's a splendidly functional machine, but is made of steel throughout and weighs a ton. It's more than solid enough to put a wonderful dent in a car.

For everyday use without a need to build up atomic legs, more specialized machines are better. One such is the Long John, which has the load

all you have to do is toss your purchases aboard.

Are you a parent doing a school run by car?

If you live in a city, you probably do not have very far to go, but this may be one of the most not fun activities of the day. The sudden influx of motor vehicles causes acute traffic congestion and flayed nerves. Steal a march and do it by bike! While your neighbors are stuck, you'll roll through. Depending on how many kids you have, there are many options, from a simple cross bar seat, to cycles made for handling two and even three children, plus shopping as well.

Using cycle transport for moving your kids around is typically more efficient and quicker,

Duplex "D" Model, 1937

platform low to the ground, between two wheels. Despite an odd appearance, this is a very effective bike and popular with delivery services. Another interesting extended wheelbase machine is the Reiko Transport Bike, which has a long, low front loading platform capable of supporting 80 kg. As well as cases of beer, one can of course also mount a child seat. The machine comes with cantilever brakes as standard, hub or disc as an option. Both the Long John and Reiko have a slim profile, and can slip along fairly easily in dense traffic.

For handling heavy loads or a mixed lot of kids and shopping, I particularly like the Christiania Trike from Denmark, a traditional rider rear/load box-front layout. The machine has been around for some time, and is well refined. It features hub or derailleur gears, hub brakes are standard, and there are lots of good detail touches, such as protective bumper rails for the front wheels, and built in brackets for twin headlights. The Christiania has a payload capacity of 100 kg and is very versatile. It can be set up to carry children in a stout box with a waterproof cover complete with windows, or hold a refrigerated box for vending ice cream, or carry livestock bound for market, to name but a few possibilities.

A machine high on my personal wish list is a quadricycle (four wheels) called the Pickup, made in Britain by Advanced Vehicle Design. This machine has a semi-recumbent forward riding position with a fairing for weather protection, and a large rear area which can mount a simple platform, a large open box, or a sleek fully enclosed van body. The model I like is a two passenger taxi with a folding top, which I reckon can hold as much shopping as I might ever want to do.

The Pickup weighs 35 kg, and can manage loads up to 180 kg. The chassis is articulated, so all four wheels stay on the ground even on rough terrain. There is optional electric power assist for use with heavy loads and gradients. Information from:

Advanced Vehicle Design, L&M Business Park, Norman Road, Broadheath, Altrincham, Cheshire WA14 4ES England.
Tel: +44 0161 928 5575. Fax: +44 0161 928 5585.
E-mail: bob@windcheetah.co.uk.
Web: www.windcheetah.co.uk.

Another machine on my wish list is the One Less Car, a tricycle developed and made in Bath, England, which has steep hills. To cope with these, there is electric assist, and yet the machine is not heavy. It is also cleverly designed, with a passenger seat which folds away in seconds to convert into a large cargo platform. The machine is mechanically refined yet simple, and easy to ride. Information from:

Cycles Maximus, 103 Walcot St.,
Bath BA1 5BW England.
Tel: +44 01225 319414. Fax: +44 01225 334494.
E-mail: sales@cyclesmaximus.com.
Web: www.cyclesmaximus.com.

If transporting very heavy loads on a regular basis is the task, then a sturdy quadricycle, the Brox, merits examination. Mechanical reliability and durability is a real issue when pedal-powered cargo cycles are in constant use by a variety of riders. The Brox has been around for a while and is well sorted out. It looks slick, too. Information from:

Brox, PO Box 12, Manchester M44 6DZ
England. Tel: +44 0161 775 4977. Fax: +44
0161 775 4881. E-mail: rjbrock@cwcom.net.
Web: www.brox.co.uk.

A US firm which has produced a wide range of cargo cycles for many years is:

Worksman Cycles, 94-15 100th Street,
Ozone Park, New York, NY 11416, USA.
Tel: 718 322 2000. Fax: 718 529 4803.
E-mail: cycles@worksman.com.
Web: www.worksman.com.

A new firm with a range of models is:

Lightfoot Cycles, 179 Leavens Road,
Darby, Montana 59829 USA.
Tel: 406 821 4750. Fax: 406 821 0963.
E-Mail: info@LightfootCycles.com.
Web: www.LightfootCycles.com.

• Parking

Finding space in which to keep a cargo/people carrier cycle may be a problem for some people. Pedal-powered vehicles are usually exempt from registration, or parking regulations, and can simply be parked on the street. The problem here is the risk of vandalism. Finding or devising off street parking is when you can start to get into some of the lifestyle changes that come with really using cycles. Could you share the cost of a big cargo carrier and a nearby garage with some of your neighbors? There could be a flexible rota for shopping trips. The garage could be used for all your bikes as well, which could make the cost entirely worthwhile. This solution to the problem

of bike storage is common in crowded cities such as Amsterdam.

Setting up a communal garage can take some doing, but in a way this is the point. We tend not to know our neighbors because we have no common ground. A bike culture is a social culture. A shared bike-storage unit could also be a workshop base, with shared tools – a nice economy.

Trailers

If space is tight, or if you are single and do not need to carry large loads, or want extra cargo capacity without the expense of another machine, a trailer can be a good solution. They are fine for shopping and errands, and some models can manage surprising loads. Most will attach and detach from a bike quickly, and a number are quite compact and easy to store.

For off-road riding the BoB Yak and Coz trailers are very popular. These have a single wheel and a narrow profile, so they follow in the track of the bike. This is also handy in crowded traffic. The quick release mounting is via the wheel axle, which reduces any adverse effect on bike handling. BoB trailers are also very good for touring.

For general use my favorite trailer for years has been and still is the Bike-Hod (address below, Two Plus Two). This is a two wheel, open frame design that looks a little like a golf cart. At 5.5 kg it is light, but it can carry up to 50 kg. Various bags and even a large wicker basket are available for mounting on the frame, and the Hod is then very handy for shopping because it can be trundled around just like a shopping cart. A big asset of the Hod is flexibility. With the open frame (and some long bungee cords), it is possible to carry a 4 x 8-foot sheet of plywood, or more famously, a full size cello. There's a quick release hitch to the seat post, and despite the high mounting, most riders forget that the trailer is there. Quite importantly, at least for me, when not in use the Hod takes up very little space in the bike room.

There are many other types of trailers, including ones specially designed for dogs, and big road transport carriers. A firm which handles just about everything is:

Two Plus Two, Cliffe Fair Place, Cliffe High Street, Lewes, Sussex BN7 2RD England.
Tel/Fax: +44 01273 480479.
E-mail: twoplustwo@pavilion.co.uk.
Web: www.twoplustwo.uk.com.

More

For more information on cargo bikes, trailers, and child carriers, an excellent source are issues of the annual publication *Encycleopedia*, available from:

The Overlook Press, 2568 Route 212, Woodstock, NY 12498, USA.
Tel: 485 679 6838 and 800 473 1312.
E-mail: overlook@netstep.net.
Web: www.overlookpress.com.

The website www.workbike.org is devoted to consolidating information on utility bikes of all kinds and has many links, and the site www.bikesatwork.com, has much useful information and ideas. See also the child carriers entry in Chapter 9, Accessories.

Mountain Biking!

Evolution of the mountain bike • Introduction to Britain • Kinds of mountain bikes • Selecting • Components • Riding techniques • Where to go • Respecting the countryside

THE MOUNTAIN BIKE CHANGED THE CYCLING world. There have always been bikes for hard work and rough use. Bikes were important in the development of wilderness areas such as the Australian Outback and Alaska, and most of the third world relies on heavy duty bikes

Rover, 1885

for personal transport and as cargo carriers. But these bikes were, and still are, very heavy. The crux of the success of the mountain bike is that it is both incredibly tough, yet lightweight and easy to ride. Other than for road racing or long distance road touring, if you are to have only one machine, then a mountain bike has to be a main contender. Nothing else on two wheels is so useful, so versatile, and so much fun.

Fun is how it all started. Mountain biking is an American innovation, born in Marin County, California, in the mid-1970s. It's a great story, told I think best of all by the first and perhaps greatest scribe of mountain biking, Charles Kelly, in *Richard's Mountain Bike Book* (Oxford Illustrated Press, 1988; Ballantine Books, 1988; Pan Books, 1990).

1976

It has been an unseasonably dry winter in northern California, and the three young men are sweating profusely as they push strangely modified bikes up the steep dirt road in the cool air. The subject of their breathless conversation is a detailed analysis of the condition of the road surface, which resembles an excavation site more than it does a road. On occasion one or another will stop and look searchingly back down the hill, perhaps kicking dirt into a small depression or rolling a rock to the side of the road.

These young men belong to the same adrenaline-driven breed that will always be found exploring the limits of human performance; in other circumstances they might be skiing off cliffs, jumping out of airplanes, or discovering America. In this instance they have developed their own unique athletic challenge, a race whose participation is limited to a few dozen local residents who know about it and have the unusual cycling equipment necessary to take part. The road they are on is the racecourse.

After more than half an hour of hard work, scrambling and pushing but hardly ever riding their bikes, the trio reaches the crest of the hill, where the road they are on intersects another equally rough dirt road. A small crowd of about fifteen other cyclists, similarly equipped and including a couple of high-energy women is gathered at the intersection. These people have come up by a slightly easier route that follows a properly surfaced road up part of the hill, but they have also had to ride a couple of miles of steep and rough road to arrive here. The three recent arrivals casually drop their bikes on the road, which has become a jumble of modified machinery.

Most of the crowd is in their twenties, but there are a few teenagers and one grizzled individual who claims to be fifty. All are wearing heavy shirts and jeans, and most are also wearing leather gloves and heavy boots. None is wearing a helmet.

Although the scene seems to be chaos, order begins to appear. One of the group takes out of his backpack a well-thumbed notebook and a pair of electronic stopwatches. Moving slowly through the crowd, he begins compiling a list of names. The notebook is the combined scoring system, archives, and publicity for the race, since it contains in addition to today's scoring all the previous race results and the telephone numbers of all the participants. Apparently races are not scheduled, they are spontaneously called together when the sun and moon have assumed appropriate aspects.

As names are taken the note-taker assigns a starting order based on the rider's previous performance and experience. Those racing for the first time are first on the list, followed by those with the slowest previous times. The current course record-holder is accorded the honor of starting last. Now starting times are assigned to the names on the list and a copy of the list is made. The watches are started simultaneously and the note-taker hands one copy of the list and one of the watches to an "official timer" whose appearance is undistinguished from the rest of the crowd. The timer takes a moment to tape a bottle cap over the reset switch on his watch, then he jumps on his bike and disappears down the hill.

For the next ten minutes the adrenaline content of the air builds while riders attend to their pre-race rituals. Some sit quietly eating oranges, some joke nervously or talk excitedly. Others make minute adjustments to their bikes, adjusting brakes, perhaps letting a little air out of the tires, or repeatedly shifting the gears, still undecided about which ratio to use for the start.

After an interval that is too short for some and too long for others the first name on the list is called. Up to the line steps a nervous young man who has by now tried every one of his gears without making a decision. He tries a few more last-second shifts as he rolls his bike to the line, which is a rough scratch inscribed in the road surface by the heel of the starter's boot. This is his first race, and he spends his last few seconds at the top of the hill asking questions about the course faster than anyone can answer, although answers are immaterial because he isn't listening anyway.

The starter props the young man up by holding his rear wheel, and as the rider stands on his pedals his legs are quivering. The starter intones, "Ten seconds . . . five . . ." Anticipating the start, the rider tries to explode off the line a second before the starter says, 'Go!' But the starter is used to this and he has a firm grip on the wheel, which he releases as he gives the signal. Thrown completely off-balance and draped over the handlebars by his premature jump, the novice wobbles off the line for a few yards before finding the throttle and accelerating to the top of a small rise 100 yards off and then disappearing from sight.

The sport going on here is so unusual and possibly even dangerous that it is unlikely to catch on with the public as a Sunday recreation, but the participants couldn't care less. They are here to thrill themselves, not a distant crowd, and in that respect this is a pure form of athletic endeavor untainted by any commercial connection.

The bicycles in use are as unique as the sport. They are all old balloon-tire frames dating from the thirties to the fifties; most of them were built by the Schwinn Company but a few other rugged and otherwise extinct species are represented. The standard set of modifications includes the addition of derailleur gearing systems (either 5-speed or 10-speed), front and rear drum brakes, motorcycle brake levers, wide motocross handlebars, handlebar-mounted shift levers, and the biggest knobby bicycle tires available mounted on heavy Schwinn S-2 steel rims. A few reactionaries cling to their 1- or 2-speed coaster brake models, but the majority have drum brakes and gears, and this looks to be the wave of the future.

The riders affectionately refer to their machines as "Clunkers," "Bombers," or "Cruisers," depending on the owner's local affiliation, and there are not more than 200 of the advanced models in northern California.

Certainly people have been riding old bikes on dirt roads in all parts of the world as long as there have been old bikes. These northern California riders have successfully crossed old news-boy-type bikes with the modern "10-speed," and the result is a hybrid that is perfectly adapted to the fire roads and trails of the Northern California hills. In the process of field testing their modifications the researchers have shattered every part to be found on a bicycle. Rims, hubs, handlebars, cranksets, seatposts, saddles, gears, chains, derailleurs, stems, pedals, and frames have all been ground to fragments along with some exterior portions of a number of clunking enthusiasts, who apparently will make any sacrifice in the name of science.

During the early experimental stage some rid-

ers recognized the steep dirt road now known as Repack as an ultimate field test for both bike and rider. This rarely used fire road loses 1,300 feet of elevation in less than 2 miles. In addition to its steepness, it features off-camber blind corners, deep erosion ruts, and a liberal sprinkling of fist-sized rocks. The name "Repack" stems from the coaster-brake era; after a fast trip down the hill the rider would heat the brakes to the point where all the grease in the hub turned to smoke, and it was time to repack the hub. . . .

In its history from 1976 to 1984, Repack saw no more than 200 individuals take part. In spite of this, the name has assumed legendary status among mountain bikers. This status may or may not be deserved, but it is certain that this unlikely event was the meeting place and testing site for the people who brought mountain biking to the world. Among the participants were course record-holder Gary Fisher, who helped put gears on Marin's "clunkers," and who is also responsible for some of the standard refinements by adding "thumb-shifters" and the quick-release seat clamp. Joe Breeze holds the second-fastest time, and his designs and framebuilding were the breakthrough that created the modern mountain bike. Tom Ritchey raced at Repack on a borrowed Schwinn Excelsior before he ever built a mountain bike; Tom's influence can still be seen in the designs of most mass-produced mountain bikes. Another early builder, Erik Koski, raced his designs there. For my part, I was the race organizer, scorer, and Keeper of the Records; in 1976 I had a frame built specifically for the purpose of racing there, the first custom mountain bike I know of. (This frame did not live up to my expectations, so I persuaded Joe Breeze to build me another one. Two (his and mine) turned into ten, the prototypes of the modern machine.) . . .

By 1979 several northern California builders were making major strides in off-road design, inspired by the feedback from each other's efforts. In addition to Joe Breeze, these included Erik Koski, Jeffrey Richman, Jeff Lindsay, and of course Tom Ritchey.

In 1979 Ritchey's frames became the first offered on the market commercially. Even at the staggering price of about $1,300 a copy, he could not keep up with the orders. About the same time Marin County brothers Don and Erik Koski designed the "Trailmaster," and shortly afterward Jeff Lindsay introduced his "Mountain Goat." In 1980 Specialized Bicycle Imports of San Jose, California, bought four of Ritchey's bikes and used them as the starting point for the design of the first mass-produced mountain bike, the Japanese-made Stumpjumper, which appeared in 1981. With the appearance of this and other mass-market bikes shortly afterward, the movement took off.

And how. The early Californian inventors only dimly foresaw that their creations would become the perfect transport in a different wilderness: the urban jungle. Bikes able to zoom down rocky trails could take on bumpy, potholed streets and come back laughing for more. Word spread like wildfire – hey, this machine is it! Sales soared through the roof and have flown high ever since;

currently, perhaps 80 to 90 percent of all lightweight bikes sold are mountain bikes.

Kelly was the founder of *Fat Tire Flyer*, the world's first mountain bike magazine, which was later absorbed into *Bicycling Magazine*. If you're interested in the early days of mountain biking, Kelly's *Mountain Bike Book* is both the best history and celebration; an evocative, unique, and wonderfully well-written chronicle of what it was like to have a dream and live it. The book is out of print, so you'll have to find a used copy, perhaps through one of the on-line services. A more recent book is *The Birth of Dirt* by Frank Berto (Van der Plas Publications, 1999), a tightly researched, technically focused historical record of who, when, and where in the origins of mountain biking. Berto convincingly shows how the mountain bike itself evolved as a dynamic outcome of activity, interest, and cross fertilization on many fronts. This is how I see it, too. First and foremost, and above all else, the folks in Marin gave us mountain biking – Ride to Live, Live to Ride! They deserve a great, big, wonderful statue, high up on Mt. Tam, to commemorate the birthplace of the mountain bike and enshrine their dreams and spirits forever.

MOUNTAIN BIKES IN BRITAIN

The story of how mountain bikes came to Britain is probably typical of how mountain biking spread throughout the world. In 1977, Richard Grant, a British journalist who later became a publisher of the magazines *BMX Action Bike* and *Bicycle Action*, was in northern California looking for interesting stories. Tipped to check out a new kind of bicycle to be found only in Fairfax, Marin County, Grant met Gary Fisher and Charles Kelly, went out on a couple of rides, and became a believer. He returned home with the first mountain bike in Britain, a genuine Marin County clunker, an old Schwinn Excelsior paperboy bike modified with derailleur gears. He still has the bike.

Around 1974 or 1975, yours truly, with no knowledge of events in Marin, but interested in off-road riding, fitted a stock roadster with low gears, chopped mudguards, and knobby speedway tires. The machine was a fair success for use on trails and bridlepaths, and open country, and I used it for off-road rides in Surrey and then on Dartmoor, where the family lived for a few years. In 1980, or perhaps very early 1981, I acquired a Murray Baja California from America, a machine that in prospect looked exciting, because it had derailleur gears and wide, knobby tires. However, it turned out to be a poser, an adult BMX chromefinished to a dazzling appearance, but gas pipe at the core and horribly heavy.

In 1981/82 I was back in London, as the founding publisher and editor of *Bicycle Magazine*, when I was contacted by a wealthy Greek shipping tycoon for advice on new and unusual bikes he could add to his collection, which he kept and ran on his own island. I steered him toward a Bob Jackson trike, and then inspired, said: "Hey, there's this new kind of lightweight, wide tire, go anywhere bike from California I saw at the New York bike show. Specialized are producing a batch. If I can get two, I'll buy one, but you pick up air freight for both, OK?" And that was how a few days later I acquired one of the first Stumpjumper bikes, serial T2C00 350, to be precise, in a lovely blue color.

The moment I rode the Stumpjumper, the Baja was abandoned to a neighbor's son. The Stumpjumper worked: it could ford streams, climb steep slopes, traverse rough ground – and also snap away from traffic lights. For months it hardly left my side, and because as editor of *Bicycle Magazine* I was constantly in touch with people in cycling, many riders, explorers, adventurers had their first mountain bike ride on my Stumpjumper.

In 1982, two riders fresh from a 6,000-mile jaunt from England to India, Tim Gartside and Peter Murphy, came to me saying they were thinking of doing a trans-Sahara ride, and what did I think about a bike? Try my Stumpjumper, I said, it's the perfect machine for the job. They did, and shortly thereafter, I

arranged for the purchase of three Ritchey MountainBikes. One arrived ahead of the others, a classy looking black and chrome model which we used for a cover photo and a feature story signalling the dawn of a new era in cycling.

The other Ritchey machines, blue and chrome, were from the first lot of Japanese built frames, and went to Tim and Pete, who in 1982-83 completed the world's first major mountain bike journey, an unassisted and unsupported north-south crossing of the Sahara Desert. You have to appreciate that "unsupported" meant just that. They rode from London through France, Spain, and Morocco down to the desert. They were constantly broke. On the crossing itself, at one point they carried 70

Fisher MountainBike, 1984

pounds of potatoes for 10-day rations. They couldn't afford anything else.

I parted company with *Bicycle Magazine* in 1983, and hooked up as a columnist and general contributor with *Bicycle Action*, published by Richard Grant and Nigel Thomas. Convinced that mountain bikes were the thing, Richard and I purchased 20 Ritchey Montare MountainBikes, the first commercial importation of mountain bikes into Britain. Our purpose, however, was to sparkplug rather than make money. We gave some of the bikes away, and sold others at cost, looking wherever possible to put the machines with key people in cycling, adventuring, and the media. I still have mine.

The Montares provided our swelling nuclear band of enthusiasts with what we needed – machines to ride. We started organizing rides and events, and through *Bicycle Action* magazine launched a race series, the Fat Tyre Five, starting with the first mountain bike race in Britain, at Eastway Cycle Circuit in London, June 1983.

Tim Gartside and I in particular, were sure that mountain bikes would take over the world, and proceeded to do all we could to help make it happen. We saw Wales as the place for mountain biking, the terrain was rugged and challenging, and because pony-trekking – dude ranch horse riding – had once been popular, many locals wanted to encourage tourism. Virtually every weekend would see us out sweet-talking farmers and landowners for permission to use their land, building mountain bike centers and opening rental businesses, and trailblazing routes in the Welsh hills.

They were wonderful times, possessed I imagine to some extent with some of the same spirit that prevailed (and still does) in Marin County. People did things together, helped each other, and I think above all laughed together. Our idea of a great time was a great ride. The dawning days of mountain biking in Britain were an energy; you rode, you worked, you built, you sweated – and people came, first a few, then more and more.

Manufacturers began producing bikes. At the forefront was Muddy Fox, who in addition to a range of affordable models, produced the Monarch,

a de lux gem of a machine which sold for a landmark £1,000 (about $1,600), in those days an amazing, mind-blowing fortune. The Muddy Fox crowd, riders all, were humorous and creative with their advertizing – the Monarch was shown standing, with no visible support, on the surface of a crystal Welsh lake – and such images helped spread the word. Suddenly, things took off.

Starting with the charismatic and most likeable Jacquie Phelan, three-time US NORBA mountain bike champion, who in 1985 played a seminal role in introducing mountain bikes to the annual Man vs. Horse vs. Mountain Bike race in Llanwrtyd Wells, Wales, front rank American mountain bike racers started coming over and participating in events. More and more manufacturers joined the fray. And at some point, where once we had been few and could identify each other even at a distance, we looked up and around, and there were more mountain bikes and riders than anyone could count. They'd sprung up everywhere. One day we were gathered around a flickering campfire alongside a rustic trail cabin, and the next day whole towns were lighting up with banners, race crews, and vehicles and TV cameras.

None of the original mountain bike pioneers in Britain got rich. What we did was what we had. There is a fundamental, almost absolute difference between pioneering, and successful commercial exploitation. As a case in point, in 1981 for sure, and possibly as early as 1978 or 1979, England already had its own, very highly developed off-road bicycle, the Range Rider by Geoff Apps. Unlike the California bikes, which were designed to go down, the Range Rider was designed to go up. It was lightweight, had a high bottom bracket, derailleur gears, hub brakes, steel-studded tires for extra traction, and could climb and maneuver like a goat. It was much more of a 4WD cycling equivalent than the Californian designs, and yet is comparatively unknown.

In Paris, France, in the 1950s, a group of motocross enthusiasts developed off-road bikes with many features of today's machines: reinforced frames, suspension forks, handlebar controls, and even disc brakes, adapted from mopeds.

Range Rider

It's a safe bet that there are still other places and times when individuals and groups devised their own technologies for riding dirt.

What made the mountain bike work was more than the advent of a lightweight off-road machine, because that had already happened. Mountain biking was a chemistry of love and luck – of energy, enthusiasm, and excitement mixing together in the right places and the right times, with magazines and books sounding the colors. The mountain bike was a specific technological development, of course, but the bug which bit all over the world was the actual activity of mountain biking. Saying exactly why it bit so rapidly and universally, is like trying to explain why you fall in love. All I really know is: one day a bike-mad Greek tycoon knocked on my door, and I got crazy lucky.

KINDS OF MOUNTAIN BIKES

Mountain bikes are not fettered by UCI regulations or other silly stipulations about how things should be. Mountain bike design is about innovation and development, and this will continue for a long time to come. At this writing, I see four broad kinds of mountain bikes: downhill, cross country, technical/trials, and freestyle.

• Downhill

Mountain bikes at the cutting edge have come full circle. The start of mountain biking, at least in California, was with racing down rocky, rutted fire roads and trails. The early Californian riders were famous for three-point, 75-foot sideways slides into corners, and speeds of 35–40 mph. Modern downhill mountain bikes are much faster, thanks almost entirely to suspension systems which iron out bumps and shocks, and help keep the tires on the ground for better control.

Flat out, full bore downhill racing machines typically have long travel suspension, ultrastrong frame and components, and beefy tires up to three inches wide. They are heavy and are not intended for riding up hills. Most often, they are used where there is some kind of uphill ferry service, such as a ski lift or motor vehicle.

Fast downhill riding is a specific sport, and should not be confused with cycling. It's thrilling, and so long as you use proper safety equipment, take the time to build up your ability and strength, and are not outright insane, you should survive. Make no mistake, though: if you tumble at 40 mph on a rocky trail, it's going to hurt. An essential point to take on board is that these days, when going for competition speeds, even very experienced, highly skilled riders are taking bone shattering spills. Sophisticated suspension systems have made the bikes so fast, riders are slipping over the edge of control before they know it's happening.

Wipe-outs do not win races. The big deal with fast downhilling is not speed, but control. You can learn this sort of thing only with time and experience, and if you are a novice rider, my advice is: start out with a hardtail, or even a straight bike without suspension. This way you will better learn some of the essential bike handling skills you need to know for effective and safe fast downhill riding.

Downhilling is plenty of fun. I've done my share of blasting, but get more enjoyment out of working a mountain and the terrain with control and grace. Bikes which are downhill oriented but not flat out racers are fine for this. Typically, suspension travel is less, and so is weight, so the bikes are usable for climbing. Ascending a course under your own steam is a good way of ensuring that you have the strength to descend it at speed.

• Cross country

Cross country is the largest category by far, and embraces everything from lightweight single speed models through to full suspension bikes. The basic premise of these go anywhere machines is that you ride, whether up the hill, down, or sideways. Weight is all important, and as for features, take your pick. The big decision area is suspension. Dual suspension bikes are becoming lighter and lighter, and hardtails are way outselling classic non-suspension models. Problems such as bobbing and other unwelcome traits are gradually being solved.

Well, if you are a beginner, here's my perhaps rather perverse advice: if you just want to mess around and have some fun here and there, then go on, get a bike with suspension. It's fun, and definitely more comfortable at times. If you're interested in really getting into mountain biking, then start out on a classic non-suspension bike, or at most, a hardtail. This will make you learn and build a stronger platform for the development of your bike handling skills. A bunny hop (tiny jump over an obstacle such as a log or small rock) is child's play with a dual suspension bike, harder on a straight bike when you are clipped to the pedals, and hardest of all on a straight bike with open pedals. Learn how to do it straight and open, and when you ride suspension – kangaroo!

If you are young and very fit, you might be interested in the latest mountain bike wrinkle – single speed. No derailleurs, no complications, no fancy stuff; just a very lightweight off-road bike which is to some extent, the equivalent of a fixed wheel road bike. To ride it, you've got to be good. On the other hand, with no frills and absolute minimum weight, performance can be surprising. It's a happening thing, lots of people are doing it for fun.

Pace RC-100, 1990.

• Technical/Trials

For a lot of people, developing precise bike handling skills and negotiating seemingly insurmountable obstacles are the interesting challenges in mountain biking. You don't have to be anywhere near a mountain for this; any city center or bit of wasteland will offer plenty of opportunities. Ready accessibility is one reason why so many people like this sort of riding. Spin out the door, and you're there.

You can ride technical on almost any mountain bike, but proper technical, or trials bikes, have a high bottom bracket, and are close coupled, for taut responsiveness and control. Competition trials courses are intricate mazes of problems and obstacles which riders try to ride clean, without dabbing, i.e. putting a foot down. Skilled riders can do the most amazing things: ride over cars, drop off cliffs, even scale walls. I've seen riders clamber up onto a 5-foot high log, 100 percent clean.

• Freestyle

Freestyle riding is a somewhat elastic category. Mostly, it's about whizzing around in a limited area, dipping and zooming, and looking to sharpen up tricks, such as blasting off a bump and laying the bike out flat, BMX style. Where trials riding is tight and precise, freestyle is fast and loose – but it still requires very good control, quick reflexes, and a high order of bike handling skills.

At the competition level, freestyle embraces short distance events such as a slalom, where several riders are released at once to run a marked downhill course through mounds of earth and sand. There's a mad scramble for the best line, and then whoop-de-do through the course. Big air and spills are frequent. It's over within seconds – and then the next lot are released.

Freestyle bikes are generally very compact. Saddles are set low, and pedals are typically open, to enable fast parting from the bike in a bail out. Some riders prefer no suspension, for maximum control. However, there's no doubt that suspension can be a bonus when settling back to earth after a big jump.

As with downhilling, it's wise to develop basics before trying to soar with the birds. You've heard the old saw "an inch is as good as a mile"? Same air at an inch as at 10 feet, but the landing can be real different! Get comfortable with air and learn how to bail out before you go high.

SELECTING A MOUNTAIN BIKE

The classifications given for kinds of mountain bikes are legitimate, but there's a lot of cross over. I see plenty of riders on freestyle bikes in traffic, who, despite being on heavy bikes and riding with low set saddles, capably screw on the juice when necessary. You can do a really hairy descent on a cross country bike. A technical machine capable of treading along the edge of a plank can quite easily manage a high street commute.

With mountain bikes, as with other kinds of cycles, the formula for success is to have a base purpose for the machine, and then add some capability in an area you think you might like to explore and develop. Obviously, much depends on your own inclinations, and the riding conditions you will encounter. A trials type bike with fat tractor tires will likely be a better mud plugger than a cross country model set up for fast trail running. If downhill appeals, a cross country model set up to favor stable handling on fast

descents may be your "Oh, I like this one" machine. On the other hand, if you need to do lots of climbing, a close coupled bike with good weight distribution may be the ticket.

Another point is that different riders suit different bikes. This is probably more the case with mountain bikes than any other kinds of cycles. Some people will swear a certain bike is the greatest thing ever made, others will say it's the worst – and they might both be right! Technical differences between bikes, sometimes at a fairly subtle level – a slight variation in top tube length, for example – that can produce what almost amount to rather different personalities. Some bikes are tractable, others are responsive and quick, and people like these things or not according to their own tastes and abilities.

The basic method for selecting a good mountain bike is to try for yourself and see what you like. When it works for you, go with it. Yes, it is quite possible that with time, your tastes and abilities will change, and you'll want something different. That's part of the fun. Some general guidelines:

Decide what you want the bike for. Are you going to ride all the time in town? Do you like belting down trails and gravel tracks? How about coming down really super steep slopes, butt well back off the saddle? Do you want to load up with camping gear and explore country roads and trails? Or do you like to go ripping through rolling terrain, zooming up and down like a roller coaster? Would you like to be able to skate over a 12-inch high log? Do you just want a strong, dependable bike?

Buy the quality you need. You don't need much of a hot shot machine if all you want is transportation. However, if you live where there are hills of consequence, then even a plain transportation bike should be of fairly good quality, to keep down weight. If you are going to go off-road, then buy the best – that's lightest – you can afford.

Buy a good name. Plenty of firms cashing in on the mountain bike act have advertising muscle and little else. Beware hot air. As said before, there are differences. Some brands steer for middle ground, a predictable, stable ride for 35+ middle high buyers. Other makes go for edge performance, with machines you ride all the time. Still other makers cover the range. For brand name and model recommendations, talk to people and look around. The people who know about mountain bikes are the people who ride them. This is just as true for a New York City courier as a Rockies trail blazer. Magazine bike tests have to be taken with liberal doses of salt, but if the consensus of opinion is that the new Muddy Morning Glory bike is the best thing ever, and it is selling like hotcakes, then it's probably a good bet. Tip: in any given year, there will be one or two models which are good value, and "sweet," with a riding chemistry that people just like. Don't stampede, but if you hear about a bike like this and one crosses your path, be ready to catch it.

Buy a small frame. The common tendency with frame size is to go too big. When you push a bike to the limit of what you can do (the bike usually still has a lot in reserve), you'll find that you want to be able to move the machine around underneath you quickly and easily. My advice is to ride the smallest frame that you can comfortably use. You'll grow into it.

Stem and handlebar reach, and saddle location. These are crucial variables in setting up a bike so that your riding position is well balanced and comfortable. Read or review the chapter on Fitting and Gears so that you understand the essentials. Often, a bike which feels marginal can be made just right with a few minor adjustments.

Components

Chapter 4, What Is A Good Bicycle?, covers most of the options in components. I just want to mention a few things pertinent to mountain bikes.

•Fenders

A mountain bike should be kept as simple as possible. If you ride a lot through mud, however, fenders can save a lot of bike cleaning and washing of clothes. Very few hard core racers go out in muddy conditions without using at least a Crud Catcher fastened to the down tube, and some sort of snap-on short fender for the rear wheel.

Equally, for wet urban riding, fenders can spare many a filthy soaking.

I like full length chromoplastic fenders, as they are light and durable. Only three bolts are needed for mounting, so removal can be done quickly. I position the fenders very high, to give plenty of clearance for mud build up on the tires. The rear fender is bob tailed, but I use a flap, held in position with a couple of spring wires. When the bike kicks up and stands on the rear wheel, the flap gives way, rather than breaking.

• Clip-in Pedals/Toe Clips

Most novices are taken aback at the idea of riding with feet firmly fastened to pedals. However, keeping your feet on the pedals actually enhances control and safety. At a tricky moment, stabbing your foot out to maintain balance can produce precisely the opposite result. What happens is the formation of a triangle, your out thrust leg is one side, the bike is another, and the yawning gap of ground between the two is the third. The more you try to gain control by placing weight on your leg, the less weight on the bike and therefore the less traction. The usual outcome is a rear wheel skid and a split triangle.

What you want to do is stay with the bike and move as a unit. The best way to do this is to get your feet onto the pedals and keep them there. If the bike slips, you are then able to go with it, rather than have it move out from under you.

Another reason for leeching firmly onto the pedals is safety. If you lose a pedal, bike control evaporates, and you're more vulnerable. Finally, and not at all least, with open pedals, sooner or later a crank will whip back around and bash you on the shin with the pedal. That one really hurts. It's really very much safer to ride with clip-in pedals, or at least toe clips and straps.

Riding

There's plenty to learn and know about how to ride mountain bikes, the topic is easily worth a book, and one of the best is *Mountain Bike! A Manual of Beginning to Advanced Technique*, by

William Nealy (Menasha Ridge Press, 1992). Nealy knows his stuff, he's a cartoonist with a fine sense of humor, and presents the art of mountain biking with a perfect blend of illustration, notes on fine points, and sympathetic understanding. Another great tome by Nealy is *The Mountain Bike Way of Knowledge* (Menasha Ridge Press, 1990). Try also *Dirt! The Philosophy, Technique, and Practice of Mountain Biking*, by John Howard (The Lyons Press, 1997), a good primer by a national champion and coach.

On a really fast take, here are some main pointers:

Balance on your pedals. This is why it is so important to stay connected to them. The basic control position is with the cranks level at 3 and 9 o'clock. This gives you a platform and pivot for maneuvering the bike via the handlebars. On steep descents, and going through mud, loose gravel, or other loose surface, get well back and keep the front wheel light. On climbs, stay far enough forward to keep the front wheel down, but not so far as to unweight the rear wheel and lose traction.

Use your gears afore ye needs them. Shift just before a hill, not on the slope when the transmission will be under pressure and sure to glitch. On descents, keep the chain up off the little (front) chainring; if the chain is slack, it can slap the chain stay and/or be sucked into the gap between the wheel and chain stay.

Good braking skills are essential. Careful of applying the front brake too hard and washing out the front wheel; this is a hard, fast fall. It's generally safer to brake hard at the rear. So long as you have a strong pedals/handlebar platform, you can sometimes steer better with back wheel locked up – but not on meadows!

Many mountain bike techniques involve locking a wheel and skidding in one way or another. These maneuvers are fine in loose dirt and places where nothing will be damaged. They are not OK in flower filled meadows, on most single track trails, or in wet weather.

Stay loose, but firm. If you death grip the handlebars, and choke up with maximum muscular tension, you'll be way too stiff to absorb bumps and shocks. If you go all slack, a chance stone or rut could tear the bars out of your hands. You want a middle ground, semi-tense and flexible.

Keep within your limits. You are learning skills. Practice things that are sometimes difficult to do, but not completely out of reach. Your body reflexes need to be conditioned, and once they are, the very best way to expand your limits is to follow a better rider. On one of my first rides, I'll never forget watching in astonishment as Richard Grant shot down a slope I would not have tried on my own in a million years. "Well, if he can do it, I can do it."

And oh yes!

The Great Outdoors

There is a lot of controversy over the use of mountain bikes in the countryside. In some places they are banned. My views on the subject are pretty simple. Anyone riding off the beaten track should have an idea of what is going on, and of how to behave with respect to fields under cultivation (stay off), livestock (stay clear), farm gates (leave as found), and horses and hikers (give wide berth). They should be self-sufficient, know where they are, and not be surprised that it becomes cold at night.

As far as mountain bikes themselves are concerned, they do less damage to terrain than a horse. Of course, if you come down through a mountain meadow, or a series of switch back turns on a single track trail, with the back wheel locked up and ploughing a deep furrow in the earth, then a lot of harm can be done. The furrow becomes a watercourse, erosion takes peace, and bang, no more meadow filled with pretty flowers, or no more trail.

Wilderness and the countryside have to be treated with care and respect, but should be used. I see mountain bikes as a great help for conservation and the environment. The more people who get outdoors and learn to love natural things, the better. Sure there are gonzo riders who headbang down trails, scaring the wits out of hikers and horseback riders. But the majority of mountain bikers enjoy and love the countryside just as much as anyone else, if not more.

Restrictions are a horrible fact of life. Prohibited. Not allowed. No swimming. No skiing. No, no, no. I hate this sort of thing, but I also have to admit, I've seen a lot of wonderful, beautiful places ruined and turned into rubbish heaps by thoughtless, wantonly destructive people. It's

criminal. The concern with preserving the countryside has good foundations, even if it does seem to attract an awful lot of busybody types who enjoy making up rules for other people.

I think a lot depends on how you go about your business. If you slip along quietly and don't make a lot of fuss, then most times things will be all right. If you are rowdy and toss beer cans all over the place, you're more likely to attract trouble. Talk to people: farmers, foresters, hunters, fishers, hikers. Try to hear what they are saying, whatever it is. Once they feel they are being heard, the process is much more likely to work in reverse, and once they know you have feelings and ideas, too, matters usually get a lot better.

Be Prepared

I was down on Dartmoor, in England's West Country, visiting a farmer friend, and we decided to go for a quick ride in a nearby field. I unshipped two bikes, away we went, only 200 yards or so and then – Dartmoor is famous for this – suddenly we were engulfed in a whiteout, cloud and mist so thick, we could not see more than a few yards. Back we went, but the road we'd started from was not there. It had to be there, that's where it was – but it wasn't.

It was only a ride in a field. I hadn't taken my compass, or ever ready survival kit, or anything. Now I, ocean sailor and wilderness traveller, was lost. My farmer friend, totally familiar with the area, was equally adrift. We quested and quartered back and forth, but could not find the road we'd started from. We looked at each other in rueful astonishment. It shouldn't be so – but we hadn't a clue.

Finally, knowing the basic topography of the area, we did what is often the sensible course in such a situation, and followed a stream downhill until we came to another road. A good long climb and we eventually made it back to our start point.

It was a chastening experience, and I hope instructive. When you are outdoors you must be self-sufficient and take care of yourself. It is important to think about what is going on and not take things for granted. As my tale indicates, you can get into difficulty only yards away from civi-

Food. At least a couple of granola bars. Better some fruit, too. Even more important, water.

Tool kit. Two spare tubes (some carry three), a puncture repair outfit, and a pump are essential. Allen keys and wrenches as required for your bike. Chain tool. Some of the multi-tools cover all these functions, but first make sure they work on your particular bike. A bit of tape, a few spare bolts, and some Zip ties.

First aid items. At least a few bandages.

Sufficient clothing, in layers, for the worst weather you might encounter.

A map.

lization. A particular point about mountain biking is that even on a short afternoon ride, you can cover a lot of ground. If the bike packs it in or you spill and are injured, far from anything, you could be in for some for real discomfort or even major trouble.

At the minimum, off-road riders should have:

A personal survival kit. Mine has a space blanket, pocket knife, waterproof matches, button thread for clothing repairs, game snares, or fishing line, a whistle, a signal mirror, a small flashlight, and a compass. Also a water filter straw and water purifying tablets, and a couple of energy bars. I include bug juice (repellent), a snake bite kit, and other items as required.

It sounds like a lot, but can pack down pretty tight. Lots of people like to use a small backpack. It leaves the bike free to move, and stays with you if you part company with the bike. Tools and spares can usually fit into a seat pack with room to spare.

When you go off-road, leave word with someone about where you are going and when you expect to return. At least a note. This is standard procedure for wilderness travellers of any kind. Even a general idea of where to start looking is better than having to ask "Which way did the guy go – north, south, east, or west?"

Mountain bikes open up the outdoors. It's your responsibility and joy to look after the place – and also yourself.

Lledr Valley.

Country Roads and Trails

Joy of touring • Touring bikes • Clubs and groups • Organized rides and holiday tours • Out on your own • Riding techniques • Dogs • Baggage • Using maps • Bicycle camping • Mixed-mode touring • Touring abroad

TOURING IS ONE OF THE REAL JOYS IN CYCLING. The only better way to see the countryside in detail is by walking. Touring by bike has the advantage of greater mobility and the means to carry baggage, yet you are always free to stop and explore an area or look at something.

Touring can be done in a tremendous variety of ways. You can go for an afternoon spin or spend a summer or more travelling thousands of miles. You can go as a self-contained unit with your own camping gear, or ultralight with only a credit card as baggage and stay in inns, guest houses, and hotels. You can count the miles travelled, or sink into the scenery (yeah!). Your journey can include transit by auto, bus, train, boat, and plane, so that you can hop from one interesting place to another. You can have a plan, or absolutely none at all. Touring is a call to adventure, beauty, and new sights and experiences.

There's a lot to touring, and plenty for you to think about. At the same time it can be quite simple. It's helpful to have a good bike and appropriate equipment and tools when headed for the sticks, but the main thing is to get out there. One of my greatest tours was on a battered 1935 BSA roadster whose vital parts shed like water. My only tool was a beer can opener. Part of the fun of touring is figuring it out and planning or not planning for yourself. Some people insist on careful preparation and planning; others heave map and compass into the bushes and go wherever fancy takes them. For some the fun and relaxation results from concentrated effort; for others it is through not thinking about anything. There is no "right" way to tour. Each to his or her own. Accordingly, this chapter simply tries to give basic information about touring. It is not a step-by-step guide. It's up to you to decide where, how,

"A merry heart goes all the way,
Your sad tires in a mile, a."
– SHAKESPEARE

and when you want to go, and what sort of equipment you expect to need.

You can take it as read that by touring, I mean both road touring and off-road touring. It does not have to be one or the other; I do a lot of rides which mix roads, trails, and pure cross country.

RESOURCES

Books

There are lots of bike touring books available. Best thing is to go to a book store or well stocked bike shop, or try Cyclosource at Adventure Cycling (address below) and see what strikes your fancy. Touring is an individual affair, and for books on this topic, the author's general attitude and approach can be more important than the absolute amount of information supplied. For some capsule reviews of touring books, check out *The Cyclists' Yellow Pages* (Adventure Cycling). Many touring books are regional – *Twenty Tours in Sullivan County*, and that sort of thing – and will only be found in local shops. Some books listed here are out of print, but are included because you might be able to find them used (try an on-line service).

Bike Touring, by Raymond Bridge, Sierra Club Books.

One of the best. It's enlightening, and full of detailed advice on bikes, equipment, planning, and enjoyment.

Bike Tripping, by Tom Cuthbertson, Ten Speed Press.

Good reading and a ride on the funny side.

The Bicycle Touring Book, by Tim and Glenda Wilhelm, Rodale Press.

A tome full of basic information.

The Bicycle USA Almanac, League of American Bicyclists.

An absolutely essential "where to go" annual with state-by-state information on climate, terrain, maps, contacts, etc.

The Cyclists' Yellow Pages, Adventure Cycling Association.

Annual compendium of useful information on all fronts, including international. Essential.

Clubs

One good way to get into touring is to join a club or group. You can go on planned tours, led by an experienced group leader, at a pace within your capacity, and with the benefit of lots of free friendly help and advice. Tours vary in character; some are fast and hard, others are slow and easy; some are self-contained, others use a sag wagon (motor vehicle) to carry baggage and spare parts for the bikes.

Adventure Cycling Association, P.O. Box 8308, Missoula, MT 59807, USA. Tel: 406 721 1776. Fax: 406 721 8754. E-mail: acabike@adv-cycling.org. Web: www.adv-cycling.org.

Born with the American Bicentennial in 1976, this organization has gone from strength to strength in helping and serving cyclists of all types. Membership includes discounts on equipment, maps, and accommodation, and a raft of literature including the essential reference annual, *The Cyclists' Yellow Pages*. Adventure Cycling is particularly big on touring, and have organized tours, route services, insurances, and just about anything else you might need or want. They're also super people. Get in touch with them if you want to tour anywhere in the Americas.

League of American Bicyclists, 1612 K St. NW, Suite 401, Washington, DC 20006, USA. Tel: 410 539 3399. Fax: 410 539 3496. E-mail: bikeleague@aol.com. Web: www.bikeleague.org.

A touring and general cycling activity organization for more than a century. They have variety of publications including the magazine *Bicycle USA*, all manner of tours and events, Effective Cycling instruction, and most everything else.

Well worth contacting.

American Youth Hostels, 733 15th Street, NW, Suite 840, Washington, DC 20005, USA. Tel: 202-783-6161. Fax: 202-783-6171. E-mail: hiayhserv@hiayh.org. Web: www.ditech.w1.com.

Good equipment and books. About 250 hostels, sometimes spartan but always serviceable. Tours in the United States and abroad. Inexpensive.

There are many other touring organizations, both private and public. The Adventure Cycling *Cyclists' Yellow Pages* and *Bicycle USA Almanac* both list local touring clubs.

Organized Rides and Holiday Tours

Mass Rides

A good way to get your feet wet is to go on a group (mass) day ride. These are popular throughout the country, and are in effect "cyclists' days"

where the organizers plan and map the routes, obtain permissions and cooperation from the police and other authorities, and arrange for food and drink, bike mechanics, sag wagons, and transport home. Big rides can see tens of thousands of cyclists swarming along the roads all at once and are an awful lot of fun. The focus is on enjoyment, and every effort is made to see that people have a good time. There's solid camaraderie and always a helping hand if you need it. With that many cyclists around, there are few problems with motorists. If you've never done a 50- or 60-mile run, a mass ride is an excellent way to do it. Check with any bike shop for the rides going in your area.

Resorts and Activity Centers

Many holiday resorts offer bike touring either based from the resort itself, or through surrounding areas with stops at selected inns and hotels. Tours are graded for different levels of rider ability and strength, and rental bikes and equipment are usually available. An advantage of riding out

S.T.DADD /94

of one place is that you can do a lot of exploring without having to range too far from home base.

If you are into mountain biking and off-road riding and live near ski country, check out what the ski resorts have on offer. Most now have trails and routes open for mountain bikes, ski lifts to ferry you and bike up the mountain, and food and accommodation and everything else you need. You can ride hairy downhill courses, slow and easy bunny slopes, or as you like out on touring trails. Better areas have races, events, and other cycle-related things to do. If you live in a town or city, check with your bike shop, as many do organized tours to nearby ski areas. If you are out of ski country, there might be other natural resources in your area that lend themselves to mountain biking, such as national parks, etc. Again, check with a bike shop.

Commercial Holiday Tours

Commercial tours vary in nature, and can be short and easy, or long trans-continental epics. Probably the most popular type are fully-supported tours, which come complete with cook, bike mechanic, and motor vehicle for carrying luggage, spare parts, and flaked out riders. Everything is provided, from bikes to cookies. In another type of setup, the tour operator only arranges accommodation; after breakfast you are given a map and lunch, and make your own way to the next rendezvous. This can be quite nice if you are not crazy about doing things on a schedule. You're free to stop for a swim, or charge down the road, as you like.

Quite often tours are organized around no more than an able tour leader and guide. Everyone brings their own bikes and equipment, and does their share of work. Obviously, how things go will depend on the group dynamics and ability of the guide. Tip: do more than your fair share of work. Here are a few established commercial firms:

Country Cycling Tours, 380 Lexington Avenue, New York, NY 10168, USA

Country Roads, P.O. Box 10279, State College, PA 16805, USA

Vermont Bicycle Touring, Box 711, Bristol, VT 05443, USA

There are many, many others. The spring issues of cycling magazines are loaded with ads for holiday tours. *The Cyclists' Yellow Pages* lists more tour operators than I care to count. Frankly, I have no hard information about any of them – but there's an easy test. When you contact a tour firm for their literature and prices, ask for the names of a few people in your area who have used the firm, and then get in touch and see what those folks say.

Solo

Where you go depends on your own temperament, interests, physical condition, and available equipment. If you favor back roads off the beaten track and camping, or pure cross country jaunts, you are going to have to deal with equipment for both you and the bike; touring on better roads and sleeping at guest houses and motels means less and lighter equipment. Limit your initial rides to 20–30 miles, and work up to longer hours and overnight stays as you become stronger and more experienced. A novice can do 60 miles in a day, but only on a one-time basis. Overlong daily distances will make a tour into a relentless grind. You're out there to have fun, not set endurance records. Balance hard runs with days of relaxation and shorter jaunts. One good trick is to establish your accommodation and ride within an area rather than from point to point. If you become tired, home base is not far away, and if you feel like riding until the morning star rises, you can do that too.

When you are on your own, you need to be more conscious of looking after yourself. As you surely are already aware, in most major cities you need to know which areas are safe. Some urban districts have high levels of crime and violence and should be avoided unless you are with a local.

A more important point is that American motorists are often poor drivers. Many do not even notice or think about cyclists, and worse, many are aggressive, and feel that cars take precedence over any other vehicles. In Europe, roads are often narrow, and motorists are accustomed to coexisting with cyclists. In America, roads frequently have a wide, hard shoulder marked off with a white line and motorists expect cyclists to use this space and stay out of the way of cars. Of course, not all roads have shoulders, and many are in poor condition. This can lead to problems. American motorists do not have the reflex of making room for a cyclist, and so may foul up if they encounter you in "their" space, and as well, have a low tolerance for frustration, which may result in aggression.

It is not appropriate to wind you up with horror stories about outright attacks on cyclists by motorists. Nevertheless, they happen. When you ride on roads, always be conscious of the one major hazard to cyclists: motorists. Never, ever, let your guard down.

Muggers and motorists aside, cyclists are in pretty good shape. Most people are pretty warm and friendly towards cyclists. In lots of places, they are even respected!

This is good, because if your touring takes you to strange territory, then it is important to keep in touch with locals and learn about things that might be important to you. In certain parts of the country, for example, you have to take care when riding at night, because snakes sometimes come onto the road to enjoy the radiant heat created by the daytime sun.

Don't let little snippets like this put you off. However you travel – cycle touring, hiking, motoring, canoeing, or whatever – you've got to look after yourself. Plenty of grandmothers and grandfathers have cycled across the US, on their own, without a single problem. It is a free country, and it's yours, too.

RIDING

I recommend taking the smallest, least-travelled roads practically possible. They are usually more interesting in terms of scenery, and have fewer cars. Motor vehicles in the country are a serious hazard, because the speed differences between cycles and cars are much greater. On fast dual lane roads the vehicles can run at 70 mph, often bunched so tightly together that the drivers' vision is limited to the vehicle they are following. When they come up on a cyclist there is no time to swing out and give room. This danger is acute at night.

On two lane highways many cars move fast, particularly if the driver is a regular who knows the road. When a car moving at 50–60 mph in a bend suddenly comes on top of a cycle moving at 10 mph, a bad situation can develop a lot faster than the many drivers who overrate themselves think is possible. There are fewer car/bike accidents in the countryside, but for cyclists, a far greater proportion of them are fatal.

The best bet for the cyclist are small roads that keep vehicle speeds down to about 30 mph, which gives more time and room to prevent serious crashes. Small roads meander and increase travel time, but are usually more interesting. When touring, the priority is what you see, not how far you go.

Depending on where you are, there may be alternatives to roads, such as trails, old railroads, cyclepaths, and so on. I have taken long tours that touched roads for only a mile or so. The scenery is usually fantastic, and the riding is often challenging and demanding. A mountain bike is the natural choice for this sort of thing, but I've done it many, many times on perfectly ordinary bikes.

Safe country riding is largely a matter of common sense. Most of the rules for traffic riding apply here also.

• Always carry identification, health insurance card or papers, written information on your particular medical or health requirements, and enough money to get you home should you or the bike pack it in.

• The cardinal rule is "what if?" Look and think ahead. Don't, for example, time your riding so that you and an overtaking car reach a curve at the same time. If a car – or worse still a truck – comes the other way there just isn't going to be enough room.

• Bear in mind the tremendous relative velocity of cars. In city traffic you can pretty much keep up, but in the country, cars will have up to 70 mph over your 5 to 15 mph. If you crest a hill and there is no oncoming traffic, move into the opposite lane for awhile. This avoids the hazard of drivers coming from behind who cannot see you over the brow of the hill.

• Try to have a place to duck into should everything go wrong. Where will you go if that tractor pulls out? If a car comes around the corner on your side of the road are you going to try for the ditch or a tree? You might wreck a bike going off into a field, but this is a lot better than colliding with a car. Think about this as much as you can and try to make it an automatic process. If an emergency does arise, instead of freezing in panic you might be able to save your life.

• Be particularly wary, when you have speed up, of people doing odd things. Whizzing down a hill you may be doing 40 mph, a fact that many motorists and pedestrians do not comprehend. They see a bicycle, and automatically class it as slow and unimportant, dismissing it from their minds (as you can be sure they would not do for a large truck), and step or drive out onto the road, or pass, or whatever. This capacity for visual recognition with no subsequent cognitive comprehension may seem bizarre, but I assure you it is so. Never trust other road users.

• If you have calliper rim brakes, then after running through puddles or wet grass, dry your brakes by applying them slightly as you ride. Running down steep hills do not apply the brakes steadily, which can cause overheating, but pump them on and off. This tells you if you have stopping power in reserve – which you always should.

• Run to the right, but leave room to maneuver in case you encounter road litter, potholes, or whatever.

• On two lane roads watch out for overtaking motorists coming towards you in your lane. They often do not see or just plain ignore a bicycle coming towards them. When this happens, claim your space by moving to the center of your lane; most oncoming motorists will return to their side of the road. Some will not and you must be prepared to make an emergency stop on the shoulder of the road.

• Beware the Hun in the Sun. At sunrise and sunset motorists with the sun in their eyes might not see you.

• Motorists may sometimes give you a hard time, riding on your tail and/or blaring their horns. This is certification of their stupidity and possible aggressiveness. Do not make matters worse by provoking them. However, if you are attacked, do whatever is necessary to defend yourself.

• Farm traffic is a law unto itself. Many farmers operate machinery on local public roads as if they were in the middle of a field. Make allowances. Like cabbies, farmers are working drivers.

• Watch for loose gravel, dirt, or sand, especially at driveway and side road entrances.

• Bridge gratings, cattle grids, railway tracks, etc., can all swallow up a bicycle wheel and send you flying. Cross railroad tracks at right angles.

• Give horses plenty of room. A bike is a strange phenomenon for many horses and, moreover, often it is the horse and not the rider who is in charge.

• A bike is very quiet, which means you may come upon animals by surprise. More than once I've suddenly found myself whizzing along in the middle of a herd of running, bounding deer. I'm not complaining.

Dogs

Dogs and other creatures of the field and air are a menace to the cyclist. I was once attacked by a determined and large goose. Dogs are the main problem, though, and you need to keep a constant lookout for old Towser. It is no fun to spend a month picking bits of gravel out of your legs and face because a dog knocked you off your bike. If you are bitten and the dog gets away, you will have to undergo a long and extremely painful series of rabies shots.

There are many theories about why dogs attack two wheeled vehicles. I think that the spokes make a noise that drives them nuts. In addition, dogs are prone to defend territory and chase fleeing prey. These natural characteristics are made worse by the fact that many dog owners cultivate aggressiveness in their pets, while others transgress through blinding ignorance. One couple expressed puzzlement after their dog chased and bit my riding companion. Every time the dog misbehaved, they said, they beat it until their arms hurt: why wouldn't it obey? With inept treatment like that, any dog will become irrational.

Understanding that old Poochie may not be directly at fault does not make being bitten or knocked off your bike more fun. Dogs are livestock, for which the owner is fully responsible. Except for dogs that are crazed by disease, they can be trained to leave cyclists alone. I like dogs very much and accept that some adjustment to their particular natures and quirks is necessary if they are to be around. I do not accept being knocked off my bike by some giant hound. If the owner will not control the dog, I will.

Most dogs attack according to a pattern. They circle to the rear of the cyclist and come up from

behind. Sometimes, if you already have speed up and are on level ground or a downgrade with a clear road ahead, you may be able to sprint and outrun a dog. More often this is not possible – you've been taken completely by surprise, there is an upgrade, or other traffic about – but in most cases there is still no serious problem. Nine times out of ten, dogs are normally friendly. All you have to do is stop, dismount, and face the dog directly. That's all. Simply stop. Often he will come up wagging his tail, wanting to make friends. Dogs enjoy excitement and action, but very few dogs relish a serious fight.

It is important to get the reflex of stopping if you are not going to outrun the dog. People do get bitten, but the majority of injuries happen because the cyclist panics, loses control of the bike, and crashes. Unless you are extraordinarily accomplished, it is difficult to ride a bike and deal with a dog at the same time. By stopping, you immediately increase your ability to control the situation.

The next priority is to clear off; dogs are territorial animals and are usually less interested in hurting you than in defending their patch of ground. Leave by walking away like "normal" (to the dog) people do, and nine times out of ten the dog will consider the job done.

The tenth time, when a dog won't let you move away and still threatens attack: the main thing when dealing with a vicious dog is to have confidence. As a human being you are one of the largest mammals on earth and a formidable contender in a fight. Suppress your fears and radiate the notion that any dog that messes with you will regret it for the rest of his days, if he lives that long. Point your arm at the dog and in firm, commanding tones say "Go Home," "Depart Ye Henceforth," or whatever articulation you can muster. Only the rarest of dogs will attack a human being who appears confident and obviously prepared to deal with matters. Continue to speak firmly, keep your bike between you and the dog, and slowly walk away.

If the dog attacks: one defense is an aerosol pepper spray made for exactly this purpose. These have a range of about 10 feet and are light enough to clip to the handlebars or your belt. Problem: they

don't always work. You have to be accurate and get the stuff into the dog's eyes, not always an easy trick when there is a lot of excitement and fast movement. Even when the spray is accurately directed, there have been plenty of instances where dogs (and people, too) have come back for more.

Well, there isn't a dog alive that will come back for another face full of water mixed with hot pepper sauce or powder. The solution can be sprayed from a water bottle or ex-container for detergent, shampoo, etc., all of which are easily carried on a bike. A big advantage of this method is that you can practice spraying until you are proficient. A two-hand squeeze produces a shotgun-like blast. Also, although a homemade chilli pepper solution will make a lasting impression on a dog and probably cure him forever of bothering cyclists, it won't do any permanent damage.

If you have no weapon and can't or won't climb a tree, get a stick or large rock. No? The bicycle pump. Ram it down the dog's throat. In any event, don't run, cower, or cover up, because the dog will only chew you to ribbons. *Attack*. A small dog can be scooped up by the rear legs and heaved away. A hard landing will almost certainly put other thoughts in the dog's mind.

With a big dog you are fighting for your life. If you are weaponless try to tangle the dog up in your bike. Use your legs to kick at the dog's stomach and genitals. If you have a pump or stick and the dog is moving too fast for you to ram it down his throat, hold the pump by both ends and offer it up to the dog horizontally. Often the dog will bite the stick/pump and hang on hard. Immediately lift the dog up and deliver a very solid kick to the genitals. If you have no pump or stick, throw rocks, or use a heavy rock as a club. One mountain biker beat off an attacking mountain lion this way. If worse comes to worst, and you are forced to the ground by the dog, ram your entire arm down his throat. He will choke and die. Better your arm than your throat.

Whoo! Not nice. Neither is the dog problem. There are millions and millions of dogs in America, and more than 800,000 people a year are bitten severely enough to require hospital treatment. Still more people receive lesser injuries or are simply given terrible frights. In America, dogs cause eight percent of all bicycle accidents. It is a rare cyclist who does not have a dog story to tell.

It is rightly said that there are no bad dogs, only bad dog owners. Properly trained attack and guard dogs rarely go out of control. It's careless and incompetent owners who are the real problem. If you are attacked or even just threatened by a dog, make every effort to identify the dog's owner. Ask in local homes, shops, gasoline stations, and so on. Report any attack to the local dog warden or police, whether you find the owner or not. This is a real responsibility, because the next cyclist or little child to come along might not be as lucky as you. Be as clear as possible about the appearance of the dog and any particular markings it has. If the dog has a previous history of trouble, the police might know about it. A dog which is a repeat offender could be put down. I've lived with and loved dogs all of my life and find this possibility distressing, but I like even less the prospect of sustaining serious personal injury or even death because a pet is out of control. Dog owners must face up to their responsibilities.

The law generally gives fair warning to owners of attack-prone dogs, and an opportunity to mend their ways. Anyone who truly loves a dog will take the trouble to see that it is able to get on in the world without coming to harm. If an owner does not know how to train and/or control a dog, professional help is available.

If you are bitten, however lightly, be sure to keep track of the dog and find its owner. If the dog cannot be certified as rabies-free and/or quarantined you will have to get a long series of painful rabies shots. Obtain immediate medical treatment. Notify the dog warden and police. Any damage you sustain as a result of a dog attack, hitting a dog, or seeking to avoid hitting a dog, while cycling in accord with legal requirements, is the full responsibility of the dog owner. If the owner is uncooperative, just find a lawyer. Unless you have done something completely stupid and wrong, the law is completely and absolutely on your side.

Technique

Cadence plays an extremely significant role in the technique of long distance touring. In short sprints you can drain your body's resources and strength, but on a long tour, energy output must not exceed your ability to replenish fuel and oxygen continuously, which makes it sound simple: just take it easy and have something in reserve. Not quite.

If you are interested in covering a lot of ground (not everybody is) and in feeling comfortable, then you must strive for a balance between energy output and the body's ability to synthesize and store energy. There is a pace that works best. Go too fast and the result will be fatigue and possibly strained muscles that will dog you throughout the tour. Go too slow and you will become sluggish and lethargic, and mistake this for genuine tiredness.

In combustive terms, if you go too quickly, you use up the body's supply of glucose, which takes a couple of days to replace. For long distance riding, you need to operate in the effort zone that burns fats.

A rough indicator of pace is respiration and heartbeat. You simply cannot sustain for long periods a level of effort that makes you pant hard, or causes your heart to hammer. The pace you can maintain depends on your physical condition, not on your strength. A simple test is to talk or whistle; hard climbs and exciting moments aside, when touring you should be able to converse or carry a tune.

Take it easy at first, sticking to the lower gears and not pushing hard against the pedals. This will help you find your own cadence and pace, and perhaps avoid excessive initial effort. Most people tend to lean into it hard the first day. The result is strained and sore muscles, and the next morning they can barely move. You'll go farther and faster if you take it easy at the start.

Riding position can make a tremendous difference. Going into the wind try to crouch. With a strong tail wind straighten up and get a free push. In Europe, many riders use homemade sails resembling kites strapped to their backs. These are effective even with a quartering wind. Position determines the muscle groups in use: hands high on the bars eases the back, stomach, arms, and hands; down positions do exactly the opposite and are the best for hill climbing.

EQUIPMENT

• Bike

Choice of bike depends on the kind of touring you do. Classic road touring bikes have wide range gears, mounting points for pannier racks and fenders, and cantilever or V-brakes, though you might get lucky and find a model with disc brakes. If you travel light, a road sport bike will be quicker, and if all you carry is a credit card, then you can fly along on a lightweight road racing bike. Of course if you want to be able to lope along and at the same time carry a fair bit of gear, and be comfortable, a recumbent or HPV is a strong contender. These machines were made for the

open road and are especially suitable for long distance rides.

For an all-around touring machine my personal first choice is a lightweight mountain bike. It's not as fast as a road bike, but it is tough and will stay together through thick and thin. Perhaps most important, it is versatile. I like to explore, and want a bike that can do it all.

Almost every large manufacturer now produces a model that is essentially a light mountain bike fitted out for touring. A common feature are multi-position handlebars, and these can be a real asset on long rides. Other conveniences are pannier racks and plenty of water bottle cages.

Another option is a hybrid with slightly larger 700C wheels. These have a little less rolling resistance, which could be useful if you want to do a lot of road miles. A hybrid can perform quite capably off-road, but must be eased over rough terrain.

If you want to mix transportation modes frequently, going by bus, train, plane, or car from one place to the next, you might find a portable folding bike the most convenient. Refer back to the section on folders in chapter six for details on various kinds of bikes.

Consider carefully how much you want to carry, and how. A very good option is to use a trailer, because then you do not need a special bike. See the Baggage entry below.

• Tires

On 700C wheels use 1.375-inch expedition grade tires for poor roads and/or very heavy loads. For more performance, use lighter 1.25-inch high pressure gumwalls, and if you really want to skim along, then use narrow profile, 1- or 1.125-inch high-pressure (100 psi) tires. Many shadings and variations are possible within each of the basic size categories – for example, narrow profile tires with amarid belts in the casings to help prevent punctures. But the general rule is: the narrower, harder, and lighter, the faster, and the more punctures.

With mountain bike 26-inch wheels, you can select tires for the kind of performance you need.

Lightweight 1.4-inch road tires will move nicely on the road, yet handle off-road in dry conditions. For more beef and better off-road traction, a standard 1.9 or 2-inch gnarly with a smooth center tread and knobs on the sides will deliver tolerable speed on pavement, yet still bite in dirt.

• Tool Kit

What you need depends on how far you go and how well you maintain your bike. The minimum day kit should include:

- Hex (Allen) keys
- Wrenches to fit your bike
- Screwdrivers, flat and cross tip (Phillips). (A multi-tool may cover the above, but check that it really works)
- Spare tube, puncture repair kit, including tire levers
- Chain tool and spare links
- Brake and gear cables, long (you can trim to proper size later)
- Amarid (Kevlar™) emergency spoke
- A few assorted nuts and bolts, some Zip ties, and a bit of tape
- Spoke key

For longer journeys add:

- A few spokes (tape them to one of the stays) and nipples
- Brake pads
- Headset, wheel hub, and bottom bracket spanners as required
- Freewheel remover
- Cotterless crank extractor
- Lubricants, including grease
- Any special gizmo or thing you might need, such as an air pump for a suspension cylinder, or hydraulic fluid for a brake. Don't forget things like small hex keys for shoe cleats, brake lever travel bolts, etc.

Sounds like a lot, but it can all be packed into a compact bundle. On group rides share one set of spare parts and major tools. Your lighting system should already include spare bulbs. Generator systems: have a bit of extra wire and tape.

Just a few essentials . . .

How many parts and tools to take will depend on how well you maintain your bike, the sorts of problems that might arise, and how self-sufficient you need to be. The more you work on your bike, the fewer tools you will need to take! The bike will be in shape, and you will know exactly which tools you might need. In the mechanics department, an ounce of prevention is worth many pounds weight off the bike.

I tend to go light, with a select number of proper tools, and a basic multi-tool. I'm wary of complex multi-tools, because they are often clever but impractical – there's that 10 mm socket you need, but it's cut into metal plate that is too large for the space occupied by the bolt you want to adjust. Multi-tools are fine for saving weight and contingency use, but before buying a particular model, try it out on your bike. No decent shop will refuse a request for this test,

indeed, they should be able to tell you which tool is best for your bike.

You should also carry a survival kit, and basic first aid items. See Chapter 15, Mountain Biking!, for details.

• Lights

See the lights entry in Chapter 9, Accessories, for detailed information. Generator lights are a good choice for touring because they are self-contained and inexpensive. You won't have the problem of a dead battery miles from anywhere. If you are going in for long distance touring, then a hub generator such as the excellent Schmidt Original will provide maximum performance with minimum drag.

Perhaps you are a morning person, riding in the summer, and likely to need lights only for short trips. Battery lights are good for this, and can be used for map reading, around a campsite, for repairs, and so on. The problem is that a battery light powerful enough to be of real use on the road is overkill for general use, and conversely, a general-use light probably will not be much help on a 12 mile downhill run on a winding road through a dark valley. For real light-up-the-road power, rechargeable battery systems with 10 W and 15 W lights are the answer, but these have a serious weight penalty, because in addition to a heavy battery, you will also have to carry a charger. You'll also need access to electric power for recharging. This not a problem if you stay in hostels or at campgrounds with conveniences, and is if you're out in the wilderness.

My take? If you are a nocturnal rider riding long distances, generator lights. Otherwise, you're better off rising early in the morning and running on free daylight. For very infrequent use, an ordinary flashlight with D-cell batteries will do surprisingly well for both lighting power and durability; tape or strap it to the handlebars.

Whether you go generator or battery, have LED blinker lights front and rear. I also recommend having a small, waterproof personal flashlight. If all the other lights go kaput, you'll still have something.

•Fenders

This is a matter of personal preference. I like fenders in the rain, or along dirt roads. They really do help keep everything clean. Best are the chromoplastic models.

• Pedals and Shoes

It's got to be clip-in pedals and sturdy touring shoes also good for walking. You'll spend a lot of time riding, and your feet need proper support.

• Baggage

An increasingly popular option for carrying baggage while touring is to use a trailer. There are many advantages. You don't need a special bike made for handling baggage, permanently fitted with carrier racks. Arrive at your destination, detach the trailer, and you have a regular lightweight bicycle – useful if you like vigorous riding as well as touring. With a trailer, the load is low down and will probably have less adverse effect on bike handling than if carried on the bike. The cost of a trailer may be less than the cost for a full set of carrier racks and panniers. Finally, in daily life a trailer is useful for routine activities such as shopping, while shopping with panniers is a nuisance. See chapter 14, Cargo Cycles and Trailers, for more information.

Loading a touring bike is an art. The cardinal principles are load low and evenly. Piling gear up in a high stack, or all in one place, creates tremendous instability. Bicycle carriers are designed to distribute loads properly. There are three basic kinds: handlebar bags, seat (wedge) packs, and panniers. People travelling light can get by with a wedge pack. These fasten to the seat and seat post and are available in various sizes, from little larger than a wallet to expanding models which will hold a lot of gear.

An alternative or supplement to the wedge pack is the handlebar bag. These give ready access for maps, food, cameras, and other things you need often. If you use a bag that hangs from the bars and protrudes forward, load it lightly, because heavy weight will have an adverse effect

on steering. If the bag rests on the bars – generally only possible with flat bars – weight is not a problem, and with the addition of a couple of elastic shock cords, it provides a platform for holding a rolled up jacket, bag of apples, or other odd items.

For panniers and carrier racks, weight should be well distributed front and rear, as low down as possible. In a nutshell, this means front and rear racks, with the front the low rider type which place the panniers alongside the wheel axle. Panniers come in one of two basic designs: single bag, which allows maximum cramming in of gear, and multibag, which separates gear into compartments for easy access. I personally prefer single bag, packing stuff into smaller bags which are color coded for easy identification. The bag within a bag method is flexible, and helps keep things dry in the event of a real soaking. Good panniers are very resistant to water, but few if any are completely waterproof.

Most panniers made today are quick on or off the bike, and some can be converted into backpacks. Some require special mounting hardware. Good brand names are Freedom, Karrimor, Carradice, Pakit, Altura, Trek, Topeak, Cannondale, and Eclipse. Ortlieb is a new brand that looks promising. I have used Altura, Freedom, Karrimor, and Eclipse with good results, but different models suit different uses. There are many more brands I've never had a chance to try. There's a lot of good stuff, and you really need to go to a bike shop and see what you like.

Panniers want the support of a stout carrier rack. There are two types: aluminium alloy and steel. Aluminium alloy racks are light and strong, and while breaks are rare, they have been known to happen. In such an instance special equipment is needed for a repair. Blackburn are the original alloy racks and are of excellent quality. Although the manufacturer would never recommend this, heavy duty Blackburn racks are strong enough to carry a passenger. Steel racks are less expensive and of course heavier than aluminium alloy racks, but have the advantage of being easy to repair with ordinary welding equipment – handy if you are far afield. Karrimor racks have been around for donkey's years and are proven performers.

When you load your bike, put heavy gear at the bottom of the bags, and light, bulky stuff like sleeping bags at the top. Give yourself a few shakedown trial runs. Panniers settle in, bits and pieces move, etc. After everything is sorted out and the rack bolts and screws have bedded in, use a sealant such as Loctite to hold them firmly in place.

• Maps

A compass is useful in conjunction with a map, and can itself guide you in the general direction you want to go without strict routing. Sometimes it is fun to dispose of maps altogether. Just go where fancy takes you, and ask directions along the way. You get to meet people, and often they can suggest interesting routes, scenic attractions, swimming holes, and the like. Fine, but have a map in reserve.

As well as keeping you on a desired route, maps have the vital function of keeping you off

main roads and out of industrial areas. Gas station maps are not detailed enough. Excellent are the widely available maps produced by the US Geological Service. They have contour maps for each state. If you know the exact area you'll be in, they also have local maps down to 1:24,000, a scale which shows walls, footpaths, tiny streams, etc. These are too detailed for any but the most local use, but are extremely interesting. Many map stores carry the USGS maps, or you can order them direct (for local maps ask first for free state index map):

East of the Mississippi: US Geologic Survey, Washington District Section, 1200 South Eads Street, Arlington, Virginia 22202 USA.

West of the Mississippi: US Geologic Survey, District Section Federal Center, Denver, Colorado 80225 USA.

Each state also produces a range of holiday and tourist maps, and I've rarely been in a town or area that did not have a variety of local maps for one purpose or another – fishing, hunting, bird watching, hiking, and so on – which are often useful for cyclists.

Working out a good selection of maps without becoming enshrouded in a blizzard of paper takes planning. The best method is to start at home, with large scale maps. Once you've established the main route, then for local navigation, small scale maps will show trails, buildings, private roads, small streams, and the like. If you are riding cross-country, then small scale maps are essential. The problem is that many maps may be needed to cover an area, and a selection for a long distance tour can be way too bulky and expensive. Hence, route planning for a cycle tour is something like sailing. You use large scale maps for a general notion of where you are, and a select number of small scale maps for areas you will explore in detail. I find that on most rides, just one map is the main one I need. Incidentally, it's very important to have a clear map case, so you can refer to the map at all times. There are all sorts of fancy models, but a Ziploc bag works perfectly well.

One indicator of my age is that I've used a sextant, but never a hand-held GPS unit, which as you probably know, works via satellite and can establish your geographical location down to a few yards. Basic models are fairly inexpensive, better models cost more. Sounds good? Well, humpf, grumpf, grumpf. Better you know where you are from the lay of the land, the sun in the sky, the moss on the trees, and dead reckoning. You're moving on your own steam, keep up the idea and make it your business to know where you are. If you rely on a GPS unit and it quits, you might be well and truly up the creek without a paddle. If you rely on yourself and become lost, you can usually get things back together again.

• Clothing

This is obviously a function of climate. There is real danger of hypothermia if you are lightly dressed while topping a high alpine pass in conditions of freezing rain; and equally, you can be fried cherry red if you ride unprotected under a blazing sun. The best guide for this sort of thing is simple experience gained on short excursions.

Shorts are pretty much universal except in winter. Proper cycling shorts have no seams through the crotch, and should be lined with terrycloth or other soft material for additional comfort. Some liners are removable for washing, and it then makes sense to have two liners, one for using, and one for the wash. Traditional racing shorts are lined with chamois, which is very comfortable, but after washing, the chamois must be rubbed with softening cream to prevent hardening. Since you're not supposed to use underpants with chamois liners, you wind up doing a lot of rubbing. Terrycloth liners are much more convenient. Sort out your shorts before you go; they are the one item that must work.

For an upper garment the common T-shirt is fine by itself in good weather, and a good undergarment when the temperature dips. If the sun is strong, it's a good idea to have long sleeves. Cycling jerseys are cut long to cover the kidneys when the rider is crouched over the bars, and usually have large pockets at the rear that will hold maps, food, gloves, and even a compact spare tire. Wash-and-wear synthetic garments provide a high convenience factor. However, they are often uncomfortable during sustained physical activity, and my own preference is for clothing made of cotton or wool. On the other hand, synthetics are effective at wicking away sweat, while cotton and wool can become soggy. It's very much a case of try for yourself and see.

Layers of clothing are more flexible and adaptable than a single garment. In cold weather, my

favorite standby is a down vest. It compacts into a small space for carrying, but puffs up into a well insulated garment that will protect the body core. For jackets and waterproof gear, see the discussion in Chapter 9, Accessories.

• Camping Gear

Personal experience and preference are the main basis for scope and choice of camping equipment. Some people need a prepared camp site with toilets, showers, and electric power. Others get by with a bivy sack and a candle. If you are unfamiliar with living outdoors, do some research before investing heavily in a lot of paraphernalia. Check out the following books:

Backcountry Bikepacking, by William Sanders. Excellent and definitive.

The Survival Handbook by Anthony Greenbank, Bell & Hyman.
Full of nitty gritty information on how to start a fire without a match, manufacture a compass, ward off frostbite, and other out there essentials.

The Survival Skills Handbook by Martyn Forrester, Sphere.
Another good all-around guide.

Bike Touring by Raymond Bridge, Sierra Club Books.
Has a good section on low impact camping.

I grew up in the forests of the Catskill Mountains in New York State, in a time when it was taken for granted that people could get along in the outdoors. People hunted, fished, and camped, without hauling along a lot of gear. Most of what was needed was already there: boughs for making shelters and beds, water to drink, fish and game to eat, and firewood without end. To this day I find the idea of a portable stove ridiculously synthetic; camping should be the evening caught trout grilling on an open fire.

But although the Catskill Mountains are still

reasonably remote, the water is no longer fit to drink, the rabbits and deer are diseased, and native fish are few. If you cut boughs or build an open fire, an angry forest ranger is likely to turn up and serve you with a summons.

It all changed gradually, as more and more people came to live in the area. It was not just the numbers – the Catskills were once mostly farming country, open and well-populated – it is how people live. Each household is a fountain of chemicals and sewage pouring into the water table. Tourists and louts leave streams littered with garbage and broken glass. Acid rain has killed all but a few genuine wild trout.

When we lived and played in the woods and took what was there we did not disturb things very much. No seasoned outdoors person uses anything but old, dead wood for fires, and none of us ever burned down a forest through carelessness. We certainly didn't pollute the entire water table, or kill all the fish. We burned or buried our rubbish – which was precious little anyhow – and as much as possible left things as we found them.

The old ways do not work anymore. There are just too many people. If all forage off the land, the cumulative effect is devastating to the environment. It's death by a thousand cuts; you do a few small things – a fish here, a branch there – and it does not seem possible they could have any effect. But done enough times, they accumulate, and significantly impact an environment already under major stress. So if you plan on camping, you must seek to make the minimum possible disturbance. This means, I'm afraid, being prepared to be self-sufficient in every respect. In some places, for example, fires will be permitted. In others they will not, and for a warm meal you will need to have a stove.

One saving grace is that camping, hiking, and for that matter, off-road riding, are popular activities, and so there is a lot of very good lightweight equipment for outdoor living. Just remember: for a cyclist, weight is not just important, it's everything.

•• Sleeping Bag

Some sort of shelter and a fire for warmth and cooking can always be improvised with a fair degree of success, but only the most skilled can keep warm in a bad bag. (If you are truly stuck and in genuine danger of freezing, build a fire and let it burn for awhile. Then shift the fire and sleep on the ground it has warmed. You can do this two or three times in a night, and be tolerably comfortable.) A poor bag weighs more, and if you freeze and can't sleep, this will give you ample time to brood on the economic and practical merits of having invested in something that would do the job in the first place. Get the best bag you can afford.

The best bags, pound-for-pound, are filled with down. Down has the greatest range (temperatures at which the bag will work), resiliency (bag packs small), recovery (gets loft back when unpacked), wicking properties (carries moisture away from body), and moral character. The less expensive, lighter (filled with 1.5-2.5 pounds of down) models are OK for warm weather. I suggest a multi-layered and/or openable bag that will also take a flannel insert. This gives optimum range and comfort.

When down becomes wet it turns into a useless soggy mess. One way to avoid this is to enclose the sleeping bag in a waterproof bivy sack. This increases the range of the bag, and should you lose or not want the tent, the bivy sack will get you through. Another approach is to treat the bag with Nikwax waterproofing products; these have given me good results.

Bags containing synthetic fillers tend to weigh more, and most are just awful when wet. I'm real prejudiced in favor of down,

but will admit that for warm season use, even a lightweight synthetic bag works perfectly well. Remember, you can always add another covering, wear more clothes, etc.

To stay dry, you need a ground sheet. Most versatile is triple purpose (rain cape, tent) poncho. For light weight, a sheet of thin plastic or even a large garbage bag will do. For repeated use, a tougher material is better.

For comfort, and also for warmth, you need a pad or mattress. Blow up air mattresses (avoid plastic ones) are comfortable but bulky. Ensolite pads are thin, but warm and comfortable. Self-inflating mats are luxurious but expensive.

•• Tent

Tents come in all shapes, sizes, and grades. Conditions and personal preference dictate choice. Tents are good for protection against bugs, rain, and to ensure privacy. If I'm establishing a base camp, I usually reckon it is worth hauling along a nice size tent, preferably a dome model with enough room to sit upright. If weight is the thing, then a slim, sleeping only tent is called for, and if the weather is likely to be good, then a minimalist bivy bag gives a good view of the stars. Plastic sheets can be rigged into a decent shelter with only a little effort and are extremely cheap and light. A poncho is just as good.

•• Cooking Stove

Cheapest are the solid fuel jobs such as the Hexamine, which will fold and actually fit into a

pocket. The flame on these cannot be controlled, which means no cooking inside a tent, and in windy conditions matters can get impossibly out of hand.

More tractable are gas stoves with disposable canisters. These burn clean and pack tidily, but the canisters have an annoying habit of running out when least expected; for regular use you will need to carry a refill. Gas stoves do not work when the temperature is below freezing. And I do not like the idea of discarding canisters.

Liquid fuel stoves variously use kerosene, meths, white gas, diesel, or gasoline. Some will run on only one type of fuel, others will digest the lot. Operating a liquid fuel stove can be something of an art. Some of the kerosene models I've used are especially interesting. First the burner must be preheated. Then you prick the jet with a wire to clear any possible obstruction, open a tap and, if all is well, the emerging kerosene vaporizes and ignites. If something is amiss, then the stove goes out and enshrouds you in a cloud of oily black smoke. Kerosene stoves are one of the few mechanical devices known to possess intelligence. They always wait for the key moment when your back is turned before malfunctioning and erupting in a ball of flame (although there is no particular danger, so long as you are within quick striking distance of the controls).

Meths stoves are simple and reliable. An excellent make is the Swedish Trangia, which comes complete with its own frying pan, two saucepans, handle, and kettle. The Trangia is clean and will cope with high winds. The snag is the cost and availability of meths. In fact, with kerosene, white gas, and meths you will always have to plan ahead, and ensure that you have an adequate supply. This can make your life miserable with, for example, a compulsory Saturday morning ride in a torrential downpour to make town before the shops close.

Gasoline is more easily available and is relatively cheap, but can blow you to kingdom come. So long as you are careful there should not be a problem, and many experienced tourists swear by the excellent performance and economy of stoves such as the Optimus. I think gasoline is fine if you use it all the time and are well in the habit of following the necessary precautions. For sometime use, white gas, meths, or kerosene stoves are better, as their quirks are merely inconvenient and amusing rather than fatal.

If you plan to camp a lot and want a good stove that performs when required, even under adverse conditions, you'll have to pay for it. Many models in bike and general camping shops are built according to a price, not to a standard of performance.

For my money, MSR stoves are among the best. Their XGK model is an expedition grade corker that will burn anything, anytime, anywhere. Their WhisperLite Internationale model will run on white gas, gasoline, or kerosene, and is lightweight and compact.

For utensils I prefer a steel pot, a steel frying pan that will serve as a lid for the pot (and simultaneously keep its own contents warm), and a steel cup that can also go on the fire. Avoid aluminium utensils, they are toxic. Skewers can be used on their own, or to form a grill, and are very compact.

•• Food

Dried lightweight foods are extremely convenient and palatable enough, but not to everyone – try at home before buying enough for a journey. I suggest carrying enough for emergencies only, however, and finding fresh food along the route. Stock up on supper and breakfast at about 4 o'clock. Mixtures of dried fruit, grains, dried milk, protein powders, yeast, etc., are nourishing, tasty, and easy to carry. Many health food shops have a dried fruit and nut mixture called trail food. Always have something more advanced than a candy bar in reserve, just in case you get stuck.

•• Mail Order and Shops

Most towns have camping and sports equipment stores, look for one operated by people personally involved in outdoor activities, so they can tell you what's good. This can save you a bundle. It's also fun to browse mail order catalogs, and quality can be excellent. Here are a few firms:

L. L. Bean, Freeport, ME 04033, USA.

Tel: 800 441 5713. Fax: 207 552 3080.
Web: www.lbean.com.

Not deadly cheap, but quality equipment which works.

Early Winters, P.O. Box 4333,
Portland, OR 97208-433, USA.
Tel: 800 821 1286. Fax: 800 821 1282. Web:
www.earlywinters.com.

Wide selection of high quality equipment.

Herter's, Route 1, Waseca, MN 56093, USA.
Tel: 800 449 3558. Fax: 800 515 6791.
Web: www.herters.com.

My favorite. Chest thumpers, and slanted towards hunting and fishing, but sound equipment at very low cost.

Recreational Equipment, Sumner, WA 98352
USA. Tel: 800 426 4840. Web: www.rei.com.
Excellent equipment at good prices.

Cyclosource, Adventure Cycling,
150 E. Pine St., Missoula, MT 59802 USA.
Tel: 800 721 8719. Fax: 406 721 8754.
Web: www.adventurecycling.org.

Limited selection, but geared expressly for touring.

• Please . . .

When you camp or otherwise hang out in the countryside, please be tidy. Never throw things away – nothing – not even a little plastic bottle neck ring into a lake. I've seen these stuck around trout. Litter is unpleasant, and dangerous for animals. Livestock and wild creatures can cut themselves on tins and glass, and choke to death on plastic bags. Take away all your rubbish and if you find extra, do yourself a favor and take away as much as you can of that as well. In a very real sense the countryside belongs to everybody. But the people who live and work there are getting increasingly fed up with the sloppy ways of tourists and outsiders. As a result, more and more real estate is being closed off. Do your bit to reverse this trend.

GETTING THERE

Other forms of locomotion complement bicycles very well. Most people live in cities, and unless you know the back routes and byways out of town, reaching a nice bit of countryside by bike can be a major undertaking. Mixing transportation modes means you can cover a lot of ground, and yet are able to explore interesting areas in detail.

• Cars

A bike with wheels off will fit in the trunk of many economy cars. Larger cars can easily take a couple of bikes in the trunk. Once you are up to four or five riders, things become crowded. For carrying several bikes you can buy or make a car rack. There are two types, rear end and top.

Rear end versions usually hold two or three bikes and are easy to load. The bikes tend to scratch each other, however, and collect a lot of road grit. It's also hard to get into the trunk. Top-mounted racks hold four to five bikes. The machines are kept clean and separate, and safe so long as you don't forget they are there, and drive into a garage or under a low bridge. It happens. Each bike must be firmly secured, which can be easy enough with a rack designed for bikes, and time consuming with a general-use rack that does not have hardware for bikes. When loading, it's important to take a belt and braces approach; at 60-70 mph the wind force on a roof-mounted bike is terrific. Guying, running straps from the side of the car to high points on the bike (like with a sailboat mast), is a good idea. At fuel and rest stops, check that the lashings are secure, and that the rack itself is firmly attached to the car. See also the car racks entry in chapter 9, Accessories.

• Airplanes

Airlines routinely handle bikes, and some will provide a special box for a bike. Some airlines carry bikes for free, others charge. This is often a flat fee for an item of sporting equipment – the same rationale applies to golf clubs, skis, and similar gear. If you are a member of a group such as Adventure Cycling, you might qualify for a discount with certain airlines. Sort out charges, etc., before you go. Always remember that airlines are run by people, if you are nice to them, they are more likely to be nice to you. The classic line is, "Chee, how can we solve this problem?"

Prepare the bike by removing the pedals and the rear derailleur if you have one, and loosen the stem so that the handlebars can be twisted parallel with front wheel. Protect the frame and crankset with a broken up cardboard box or a sheet of air bubble plastic. Deflate the tires to half pressure.

There are two schools of thought regarding the best method for shipping a bike: roll on, and boxed. A bare bike is in fact much easier for a baggage handler to manage. It can just be rolled along, and is light and easy to pick up. The difficulty is that if something goes wrong – a shift in cargo or whatever – the bike is vulnerable. Airlines force you to sign an indemnity release absolving them of any responsibility for damage to the bike, so the convenience of roll on has to be weighed against the prospect of a mangled bike. If you want to maximize protection for the bike, use a box or bike bag.

A large cardboard box can be obtained from any bike shop. It's far from proof positive against injury, and a common tactic is to line the sides of the box with thin sheets of hardboard, supported with struts made by rolling and taping lengths of cardboard. All in all, boxing up a bike is a fair production, and when you arrive at your destination, there is then the problem of what to do with the box. If you are returning home from a different airport you cannot take it along. If you are returning from the same airport then you may be able to check the box into storage, but this can prove expensive over a long holiday.

A more convenient solution is a bike bag. These come in two types: hard shell case, and fabric bag. Hard shell cases are usually made of fiberglass, are strong, cost a bomb, and are heavy enough to require castor wheels in order to be moved around. They are sensible only if strong protection is essential, and there is a place at your destination point to store the case.

Fabric bags are lightweight and fairly easy to manage, and at destination point, can be folded into a fairly compact package for storage. They are not great shakes as protection, and it is wise to line the bag with stiff cardboard or hardboard, and wrap the bike in bubble plastic and/or extra clothes. But for me at least, so far so good. I've travelled often using a stoutly made Carradice Pro Bag, always with success.

An alternative to airlines is to ship your bike via UPS, who will cover damages if the bike is packed properly in a box, within certain dimensions. You'll need a destination address.

• Buses

In a bus your bike lies flat on its side in a luggage compartment with a lot of other junk that can bang into it. Use a stout box or reinforced bag. If you know the bus and driver, and the vehicle is not crowded, then it may be feasible to simply slip the bike in as it is.

• Railroads

Trains are perfect for speeding you to a particular area, or for skipping over uninteresting sections on a long tour. In Europe, roll on is the norm, and you can load the bike into a luggage van yourself. No special preparation is necessary, other than labelling the bike with your name and destination station. In America, bikes must be checked as baggage, and a stout, strong box is a necessity. Stories of bikes reduced to scrap by railroad baggage handlers are legion. Don't use this method for any bike you really care about. Be sure to have insurance.

On local trains, conditions vary. In some places, bikes are prohibited; in others, you can take them aboard so long as you follow certain rules, such as using the last car of the train. This kind of thing can be fantastic, and whizz you clear out of town in 15-20 minutes. Find out the situation in your area by checking with bike shops, advocacy groups, etc.

• Another Way

A folding bike can be a very effective solution to the hassles and problems of travelling with a bike. The models with 20-inch wheels do quite well as bikes, yet can reduce to the size of a suitcase. For more information, see the section on folding bikes in chapter 6.

INTERNATIONAL TOURING

"Going foreign" with a bike is a particularly satisfying way of travelling, as it allows you to explore and savor a country to a degree not otherwise possible: In most places people admire and respect cyclists, and are exceptionally helpful and friendly.

For doing research, it is essential to obtain *The Cyclists' Yellow Pages*, produced annually by the Adventure Cycling Association. The international listings section is filled with information on organizations, web sites, books and guides, maps, and much more, for countries all over the world. What I am able to give you here is just a kind of taster skim.

The Americas

• Canada

Canada is a beautiful country. It's also huge. I suggest riding either in specific areas, or using mixed mode transport. Some Canadian cities, such as Toronto, are extremely advanced in providing for cyclists. Indeed, Canada is a double treat: full of natural wonders, and cities with fascinating transport and social engineering.

Organizations to contact are:

Canadian Cycling Association, 212A-1600 James Naismith Drive, Gloucester, Ontario, Canada K1B 5N4. Tel: 613 748 5629. Fax: 613 748 5692. E-mail:general@canadian-cycling.com. Web: www.canadian-cycling.com.

Tour du Canada, 145 King St. West, Suite 1000, Toronto, Ontario, Canada M5J IJ8. Tel: 416 484 8339. Fax: 416 484 1613. E-mail: sweep@cyclecanada.com. Web: www.cyclecanada.com.

For maps: Geomatics Canada, 615 Booth St., Room 703, Ottawa, Ontario, Canada K1A OE9. Tel: 613 995 4921. Fax: 613 947 7948. E-mail: topo.maps@nrcan.gc.ca. Web: www.geocan.nrcan.gc.ca/misc/contacte.html.

• Mexico

Mexico is beautiful, and in all honesty, that's all I know. I suspect it's one of those places where if you are in with the right people, everything is fine, and if you are a stranger in the wrong place, it might not be so fun. Check out:

Bicycling West, Inc., P.O. Box 15128, San Diego, CA 92175 USA. Tel: 619 583 3001. Web: www.rosaritoensenada.com.

Todo en Bicicleta, c/o Morales, Pirineos 239, Col Porteles, Mexico 13 DF.

Africa

Bicycles are a common form of transport for Africans, but their machines are of course extremely stout and sturdy, as there are often no roads. In Morocco, for example, south of the Atlas Mountains and into the Sahara Desert, the tracks for vehicles are like streambeds. Most of the locals simply cycle over the desert itself. In contrast, the roads in northern Morocco are quite negotiable, and there are not many cars. Similar varied conditions prevail throughout Africa.

Unless you run a local bike, parts are a problem, and in many areas so is thievery. Cyclists in Africa have been trapped in disease quarantine areas. There are wars, revolutions, famines, and other excitements for tourists. In many places life is less than cheap. Still, cycle touring can be good. I know a number of people who have toured Africa; they were all self-reliant, energetic, and able to get on well with people.

A highly entertaining read with useful snippets of information is *Bicycles Up Kilimanjaro* by Richard and Nicholas Crane, (Oxford Illustrated

Press). It's primarily about the Crane cousins' mountain bike ascent of Kilimanjaro, Africa's highest mountain, but the wry comments about reaching the place give a good picture of the kind of problems you might encounter.

Betina Selby is a long distance tourist who has chronicled a number of interesting journeys in India, Israel, Egypt, and other countries, and her books *Riding the Mountains Down, Riding to Jerusalem,* and *Riding the Desert Trail* (Chatto & Windus) all provide useful practical information. Finally, and by no means least, I've always liked the Lonely Planet guidebooks. They are intelligent, and respect people and culture. In travelling, how you interact with the people around you has a lot to do with how things go. Still, read the papers and stay out of the way of flash wars and other problems.

Asia and the Pacific

Much the same story as for Africa. Many people have cycled out that way, and most of them have a hair raising story or two to tell. There are organized tours, for India, Mongolia, China, etc., on a fairly frequent basis. Try the Cyclists' Touring Club (address below), and:

> China Passage, 168 State Street, Teaneck, NJ 07666, USA

> Cycling Association of People's Republic of China, 9 Tiyuguan Road, Beijing, China. Tel: 75 1313.

You can also just decide on an area, obtain the necessary visas and shots, grab a mountain bike, and catch the next plane out.

Europe

Europe is a common holiday destination for Americans, and cycle touring is an ideal way to see the place. In Europe, bikes are an accepted form of transport. Although the roads are sometimes narrow, European motorists are more used to coexisting with cyclists. In addition, many countries have extensive networks of cyclepaths. There are also comprehensive train services, it is easy to take or ship a bike by train, so you can leapfrog from one interesting area to another.

Years ago, American cyclists would often buy their bikes in Europe. It's the other way around now, with European cyclists going to America to buy bikes at better prices than they can find at home. Still, if you are interested in a particular machine, say, an HPV made in Germany, or a custom bike from one of the few old-time builders in England, then this can be a good way to focus a trip. Be sure to allow enough time to sort a new machine out before taking off on the main journey. Some builders and shops will help out with arrangements for bed and breakfast accomodation, touring information, and so on.

Britain

• Books

The CTC Route Guide to Cycling in Britain and Ireland, by Nick Crane and Christa Gausden, Penguin Books.

A classic containing much useful lore, and 365 routes which reach the furthest corners of Britain.

Cycle Touring in Britain and the Rest of Europe, by Peter Knottley, Constable.

Detailed chapters on tour preparation.

Weekend Cycling, by Christa Gausden, Oxford Illustrated Press

Meticulous, clear, and colorful.

For on-line UK book stores, try Bicycle Books (www.bikebook.demon.co.uk) or Cycling Bookshop (www.cycling.uk.com/books)

• Touring Clubs and Groups

First and foremost of the touring clubs is the Cyclists' Touring Club, the oldest national cycling organization in the world. Membership includes the *Cycle Touring Club Handbook*, a thick list of 3,000 recommended accommodation addresses, places to eat, people who can fix bikes, and CTC local information officers for Great Britain; a list

of overseas touring correspondents; information about touring areas, equipment, and travel by air, rail, and sea, including ferries, tunnels, and bridges; a catalog of books and maps; and a complete exposition of club services. The touring department has available a large library of comprehensive, personally researched tours complete with maps, and will also plan and suggest tours for routes and areas you request, as well as advise on cycle and personal equipment, maps, and travel books. CTC membership also includes various insurance services, and access to insurance policies at preferential rates. Other CTC services are too numerous to mention.

CTC District Associations each have rides throughout the year, mainly on Sundays but also during the week. There are also local, national, and foreign tours led by experienced members, numerous national competitions and rides, and an annual grand celebration, the York Rally.

Cyclists' Touring Club, Cotterell House, 69 Meadrow, Godalming, Surrey GU7 3HS England. Tel: +44 01483 417217. Fax: +44 01483 426994. E-mail: cycling@ctc.org.uk. Web: www.ctc.org.uk.

An essential organization for the economy minded is the Youth Hostels Association. The YHA has over 5,000 hostels in 64 countries, many in beautiful and historic areas. The hostels are sometimes spartan, but always serviceable. You provide your own sleeping bag, and help a bit with the chores. Inexpensive, and you can cook your own food. YHA stores sell camping and touring equipment, have a tourist service, and run guided tours.

Youth Hostels Association, Trevelyan House, 8 St Stephen's Hill, St Albans, Herts AL1 2DY England. Web: www.yha.org.uk.

A well known organizer of fun rides and tours is:

Bike Events, PO Box 75, Bath BA1 1BX England. Tel: +44 01225 480130.

General information on touring, brochures, accommodation lists, and so on can be obtained from tourist authorities:

British Tourist Authority, 64 St. James Street, London SWI 1NF England.
Web: www.visitbritain.com.
Scottish Tourist Board, 23 Ravelston Terrace, Edinburgh EH4 3EU Scotland.

Touring information and leads are obtainable from:

British Mountain Biking,
National Cycling Centre, Stuart Street, Manchester M11 4DQ England.
Tel: +44 0161 2302301. Fax: +44 0161 2310591.

• Riding

Riding conditions in Britain are for the most part good, but the number of cars per mile of road is very high, and it is important to stick to the smaller roads. On main through routes (A-class roads), vehicle speeds are high, yet the roads are usually narrow, often there is no room for a cyclist to manueuver. None. Instead of a shoulder where a cyclist might take shelter, there may be only a solid embankment of earth, rocks, and thorns. Smaller roads, B-class roads and under, help slow down the automobiles, and are more scenic. Single lane tracks are most interesting of all, but can be really cramped for space.

You ride on the left (port!) side of the road. This can be worrying in prospect, but in practice is not difficult. What you have to guard against are moments when your body reflexes might trigger a wrong move – the first time you face dazzling car headlamps at night, or when sprinting away from danger. When alarmed, your body automatically seeks safety – and it might be on the wrong side of the road. For the first couple of days ride cautiously and allow ample time to

think things through before making moves. Do not ride at night until you are well adapted to the changeover.

In Britain you are required by law to obey the rules of the road and all traffic regulations, and are expected to do so. Not all cyclists do, of course, but until you know local conventions and which rules you can break without causing offense, stay legal. At night, you must have front and rear lights, and reflectors. These various regulations can be, and sometimes are, enforced with fines. For your own comfort as well as safety, pick up a copy of the *Highway Code* at any (British) book shop to familiarize yourself with the rules of the road. At roundabouts, traffic from the right has priority.

The British are a nation of social drinkers, fond of frequenting pubs. Unfortunately, thanks to archaic laws, the pubs close at 11 p.m., and so around this time, and especially on Friday and Saturday nights, the roads fill up with inebriated drivers, and the accident rate soars. Do not be out on a bike at that time. Britain has a bad accident/cyclist fatality rate, ten times greater than countries such as Germany and the Netherlands.

An alternative to roads are bridlepaths (which cyclists are legally entitled to use) and footpaths (which they are not). Bridlepaths for horses honeycomb Britain and can carry you long distances. When you meet a horse, stop until it passes by. Footpaths are public rights of way for pedestrians, not bikes. There are people who don't like cyclists on footpaths, but for the most part it's a case of live and let live. You need to use common sense. In a popular area filled with Sunday strollers you should dismount and walk. Many times, however, no one else will be around and there will be no problem.

Another off-road option are canal towpaths. Some of these have NO CYCLING signs, but in fact, you may cycle on many of the 2,000 miles or so of towpaths administered by the British Waterways Board if you have a permit, which is free. Maps are shown on the BWB website and are also included in the National Cycle Pack (£5). Permits and information from: British Waterways, Customer Services, Willow Grange, Church Road, Watford WD1 3QA England. Web: www.britishwaterways.co.uk.

The canals and other inland waterways were Britain's first transport network and thread through many scenic and interesting areas. Quiet and calm, they are popular with strollers, fisherfolk, and others who enjoy a bit of peace. In this world, a bike is a high speed vehicle that can cause alarm; keep in tune with the environment by riding with studied, obvious consideration for others.

Yet another option is the 10,000-mile National Cycle Network of signposted cycle routes now being created by Sustrans. This network is a mixed bag of cyclepaths, canal towpaths, trails, and regular roads. In some places it is great; in others, it is mostly roads with cyclepath signs. Still, it is a wonderful start. Contact:

Sustrans, 35 King Street,
Bristol BS1 4DZ England.
Tel: +0117 929 0888. Fax: +44 0117 929 0124.
Web: www.sustrans.org.uk.

• Railways

Compared to other European countries, British railway services are inadequate and expensive. However, they still provide a wonderful means for getting around the country, especially for cyclists. In the past, you could put a bike aboard any train; now you have to ask in advance, and often pay a fee as well. Still, in most cases you can just roll a bike on, and then ride off from your destination station. It couldn't be easier.

• Maps

Excellent are the widely available Ordnance Survey (OS) maps. The OS has also produced a good series of cycle touring guide books with one day routes for various parts of Britain. OS 1:250,000 (about 4 miles to 1 inch) maps are good for general planning. Once you've established the main route, then for local navigation nothing can beat the OS 1:50,000 maps, which show individual buildings, private roads, churches, ancient ruins, telephone call boxes, and the like.

Ordnance Survey, Romsey Road,
Southampton S09 4DH England.
Tel: +44 08456 050505. Fax: +44 023 8079 2906.
E-mail: enquiries@ordsvy.gov.uk.
Web: www.ordsvy.gov.uk.

• Camping

Membership of the Camping Club of Great Britain and Ireland includes an International Camping Carnet, insurance services, a handbook on camping, and a guide to 1,500 sites in Great Britain and Ireland.

Camping Club of Great Britain and Ireland Ltd., 11 Lower Grosvenor Place, London SWI OEY England.

For camping equipment, Cotswold Essential Outdoor shops are the best I've found. Prices are not discounted, but all staff are outdoors people and the quality of service and especially advice is excellent. Shops in various locations and mail order catalog:

Cotswold Outdoor Ltd., P.O. Box 75, Cirencester GL7 5YR England. Tel: +44 01285 643434. Fax: +44 01285 650101. E-mail: sales@cotswold-outdoor.co.uk.

The Continent

The best single source of current information is the Cyclists' Touring Club. They have information sheets, pre-planned tours, maps, and insurance and travel services that make them unbeatable value for the tourist. They also conduct tours. So does the Youth Hostel Association, and membership includes a number of useful guides and handbooks (see addresses earlier in this chapter).

Then there are always the traditional aids to travel – the Michelin Guides and various sightseeing tomes. These can be very useful. One of the nicest things about cycle touring is that you are not obliged to make a plan and stick to a schedule. Even in crowded holiday areas you should not have much difficulty in finding accommodation if you just veer off the beaten track – which a bike makes easy.

Europe is a big place, with a lot of variety. Many folks try to do the whole thing at once, two days here, three days there, and so on. My advice is to pick one or two areas, and concentrate on those. There's always so much in the details – the foods, the flowers, the ways things are built. Rather than skim from country to country, let yourself go into an area with time to explore, and see what happens.

As to where – there's considerable variety. In the Netherlands, you can go everywhere on cyclepaths, and the riding is easy. Ditto Denmark. Germany is now a very cycle friendly country. Several countries share the Alps, which are truly amazing. Then there's the food in France, and

Italy, and . . . it goes on and on. You'll need to think about and follow your own star.

Continental railroads are comprehensive in coverage, easy to use, and inexpensive. Regulations vary from country to country; you should do a little research, but in most places, cyclists put their bikes aboard trains and ferries without hassle or difficulty.

• Books

Cycling in Europe, by Nicholas Crane, Pan Books.

Enticing and amusing with many useful pointers on designing and planning tours. Covers the best touring areas in 16 European countries, is full of all the information you need, and fun to read.

Adventure Cycling in Europe, by John Rakowski, Rodale Press.

Written by a 250,000-mile veteran; a gold mine of useful tips as well as a country by country information guide.

Cycle Touring in Britain and the Rest of Europe, by P. Knottley, Constable.

Covers 27 countries in a handy guide with chapters on preparation and planning, and also a country by country information guide.

• Riding

As in Britain, you are generally expected to observe traffic regulations. You are not allowed to use footpaths (but take cues from local riders), and must use a cyclepath when there is a round blue sign with a white bicycle in the center. At junctions, traffic from the right has priority unless a sign advises otherwise. In roundabouts, existing traffic must give way to traffic entering the roundabout – the opposite of the British rule. In general, don't rely heavily on right of way. European driving standards vary enormously; particularly in small villages and on back roads, locals tend to do as they please. Most European motorists respect cyclists and you should not have any untoward problems, but they have their crazies, too. Watch out for European motorcyclists; they're very good, but ride like the devil.

The pack-horse bridge at Allerford

SPORT and PLAY

Riding For Fitness

17

Nature of fitness • Fundamental principles of riding for fitness

THE BEST WAY TO GET FIT ON A BIKE IS TO RIDE. Broadly, if you are unfit or unwell, take it easy; if you are essentially healthy, then you can push harder. Either way, get out on the bike often enough, ride properly, and you'll be as fit as you can be within the parameters of your own physique.

Becoming more fit is essentially a matter of the pace you set, the frequency with which you increase the pace and for how long and how hard you do so, and technique. In a nutshell, the general pace you set is your fitness base, the times you go harder are for raising the fitness base, and technique will determine whether any of it works or not.

Training and conditioning can definitely improve elements such as strength and endurance. However, the nature and capacity of physical performance for any given individual is primarily determined by genetic potential – some people are naturally strong, others can go like blazes for short periods, others have long-term endurance, and so on. Within the context of your physical type and abilities, cycling will make you more fit. It is vital to understand, though, that for fitness, learning effective riding techniques is more important than stomping hard on the pedals.

Most thinking about rider performance tends to be mechanical in nature, and isolates things such as strength, the power part of the crank stroke, and so on. Yet cycling is motion, and in particular, the power element derives from spinning the cranks at a fair old rate – around 100 rpm for a rac-

The Open Road

ing cyclist moving at a rapid but not flat out pace. No matter how strong you are, you can only learn to spin at such speeds through conscious learning and practice. As it happens, this dovetails nicely with the basic physiology of cycling and exercise.

When you go out for a ride, you need to start with a warm up period, spinning the cranks rapidly but lightly, using very little pressure. To get a feel for this, find a downgrade and coast along with the bike in a gear just a little too low for the speed you are doing. Spin the cranks and if the gear is right, you'll only fan the air. Keep on spinning faster and faster, until you can just feel resistance on the pedals. That's technique. You get it by learning how to move lightly.

In the main portion of the ride, you maintain a smooth, fast cadence, but use a slightly higher gear with a little more bite. Now your muscles work as well as move. It's a combustive process, mixing oxygen with various body fuels, and needs to be paced to your particular physical condition. A crude measure of this is heart rate beats per minute. Your heart goes pitter patter when your muscles need more fuel and/or oxygen (or you get scared, and the body jump-starts to fight-or-flee readiness). The standard reference for maximum heart rate (MHR) is 220 minus your age. People who need to take it easy because they are frail or out of shape exercise at something like 55 percent of MHR, perhaps even less. People who are reasonably fit will fire along nicely at around 65 percent of MHR. Once you go past 85 percent of MHR, with the exception of the very superfit, you are burning shortterm glucose fuel, as opposed to longterm fat fuel. You have only about a two hour supply of glucose, and it takes a couple of days to replenish. If you redline, then you burn what is only actually stored in the muscles themselves; few people can do this for longer than 10 seconds. Again, building up a new fuel store is a matter of a day or two.

As you can see, if you are going to conduct your own fitness program, a heart rate monitor can be a handy tool. A good basic model with an automatic fitness level keyed program is the Cardiosport Autozone. See Chapter 9, Accessories, for more information.

Another way to monitor your exercise effort level is to whistle or sing. If you can carry a tune with reasonable ease while riding, you're probably running at somewhere around 60 to 65 percent of MHR.

Understand that all these figures are approximate! You might be an Olympic contender and not even breathing hard until up near 85 percent of MHR, or you might be in less great shape, and panting hard at 50 percent of MHR.

Right, you've run through the middle, exercise part of the ride, now you do the warm down. Same as warm up: you ride very lightly on the pedals, looking to have a good spin speed. During your exercise period, byproducts from combustion, including lactic acid, have built up in your muscles; the warm down is to clear them out. Do this, and you'll feel more refreshed and tip top as you should from exercise; don't, and you may be tired, laden, and possibly irritable. A good way to make sure you do a proper warm down is to again consciously practice pedalling technique. Dance on those pedals! How lightly can you press them?

How long should you ride? How often? This depends on who you are, your age, shape you're in, life circumstances, and lots of other variables. As a rule of thumb, you should seek to ride at least three days a week, for a minimum of 45 minutes each ride, better if it's an hour. If you ride every day, you'll get much more benefit, but at least one ride a week should be in the easy category, just out on the bike spinning lightly, no hard effort at all.

Once you are up and riding and have everything going well, then every third or fourth day, push harder on your ride. Don't push hard two rides in a row. It's very important to give your body a chance to recover.

Intervals

After you have built up some miles, you can try including intervals in your push rides. From cruise speed, launch into a hard effort – up in max territory, but not all out – and hold it for two minutes. Resume cruise, and when you begin to feel like you just might live, do another interval. Two is enough for your first time. Eventually you can do, say, five intervals, and if you want an experience that will make you wonder why on earth you ever thought about any of this, build up to five minute long intervals. These hurt.

After an intervals day, you must give your body two or three days to recover. Go easy on the next couple of rides. If you don't, you'll defeat the purpose of the process. Part of what you are doing is breaking down muscle, and then rebuilding it. For developing flexibility, on the rides after doing intervals, the warm up and warm down portions are especially important.

If you want to build power, climb. It's amazing what it can do for you. A monster hill may flatten you first time up. Keep at it. Come back again. You'll get better, and better, and one day take that hill proud.

If you really start to get into cycling as a fitness activity, seek out a sports coach or professional trainer. Competition level cyclists develop specific muscles and patterns of movement. Stretching of muscles, balanced exercise of other muscle groups, and massage are all vital.

It's out of print, but if you can scare up a copy of *Cycling for Fitness* by John Schubert (Ballantine), you'll have what I think is still the best book on this topic for the general cyclist.

It is easier to pace all-out intervals by roadside markers rather than a watch. Watch out for cars and critters.

Competition

Thrills and satisfaction of racing • Road racing: time trial; criterium, and stage races; track; cyclo cross • The Union Cycliste Internationale • Mountain biking: cross country; criterium; downhill; trials • Human-powered vehicles • Messenger races; cargo races

CYCLE RACING EVENTS RANGE FROM CLASSIC road racing, time trial, and track, to off-road cross country and downhill, to cargo carrying, messenger, and commuter races, to off the wall contests such as ice racing. There's something for every taste, and accessibility is usually built in: for most events you compete according to age, sex, and ability, so you start out on a fairly even basis. How you go from there will depend on your physique, how well you learn and train, and your particular mix of talent, dedication, grit, and genetic potential.

There's no cast iron rule for what makes a good bike racer. Some of the greatest bike riders in the world are lean and compact. The less weight to lug around, the better. Big people have fun, too – in sprint events, and on downhills they generally have the edge. What counts in the end is fitness –

and heart. Bike racing is an extremely rigorous sport. In skiing, running, football, and most other sports, when you are finished you drop. On a bike a lot of weight is supported by the machine and only a small amount of energy is required to maintain balance. It is quite possible to run your body to the finish and beyond, so that when you stop you are unable to stand on your feet. Any serious racer has to keep fit with a year round physical conditioning program.

The thing about racing is that the business is riding, pure and simple. It's all down to you and a bike. You are encouraged to start as a raw beginner. The clubs and training programs want as broad a base as possible, because only a few people can evolve into top-level competitors. On the face of it, this appears contradictory; after all, don't you race to win? Yes, you do! The basic expectation is that you will work hard and develop whatever potential you've got. One of the many rewards of racing is attaining a level of riding ability that is in another class. At some point, though, whether you are 545th in a field of 800 riders, a club champion, a national grade rider, or even a world record holder, winning is going to peak out. What you'll be left with is the real strong suite of racing life: wonderful days out, companionship, the thrill of competition, and the keen satisfaction of learning and doing better.

It's worth mentioning that there are many ways of participating in racing and competitions. I've done some competitive riding, but most of my time has been spent as a manager, mechanic, designer and builder, and event organizer. All these things are very satisfying, too.

I don't have the space for anything like a proper coverage of cycle sport. What follows is a brief overview, with references for books and places where you can obtain more information.

ORGANIZATIONS

To race in sanctioned events, you will have to belong to one or even two organizations, and possibly a club or group as well, depending on the type of event in which you compete. There's various kinds of licenses for domestic and international racing, for professionals, amateurs, and students, and for US citizens and foreigners. To sort it all out, get in touch with the umbrella organization USA Cycling, which covers the United States Cycling Federation (USCF), the National Off-Road Bicycle Association (NORBA), and various other racing groups.

USA Cycling License Desk,
Denver CO 80263-0889.
Tel 719 578 4581.
E-mail: membership@usacycling.org.
Web: www.usacycling.org.

Before spending what can be a good bit of money on licenses and other papers, it might be a good idea to check out the action in your area. Ask at your bike shop for local clubs, nearby races, etc. and see what's happening. There's plenty of informal competition, just for fun.

The Union Cycliste Internationale

The Union Cycliste Internationale (UCI) is the international governing body of cycle sport, to which national organizations such as the USCF are affiliated. Unfortunately, the UCI is autocratic in nature, and not at all responsive to the needs of cycle sport and competition riders.

One problem is technical: UCI regulations require that to be legal for sanctioned events, bikes must be made from tubes arranged in the classic diamond pattern used for racing bikes c. 1950. UCI rule amendments have banned monocoque frames, oval tubes, dropped top tubes, profile handlebars, disk wheels, and a host of other innovations, and require road, track, and cyclo cross bicycles to weigh at least 6.7 kg.

The UCI is anything but consistent in applying these regulations, however. The UCI has given approval, sometimes with glowing enthusiasm, to bicycles that clearly breach its own rules. Many bikes used in UCI events are technically illegal. This kind of capricious behavior and lack of accountability is bad for cycle sport and for the cycle industry. It is megalomania: the UCI is supreme, above all law and rules, even its own.

Ostensibly, UCI design restrictions on bicycles are to ensure riders compete on even terms as athletes, on machines which are safe. Otherwise, a UCI announcement asserts, "technology takes hold of the system" and leads to "uncontrollable costs, unequal access to technology, and wild innovations prepared in secret." Prototypes are developed which are unsafe, and "the bicycle looses (sic) its usability and removes itself from any understandable reality." Hence, "the UCI now intends to redefine its attitude towards technology by correction, stabilization and mediation as embodied in the following amendments to its Regulations."

This is pure hogwash. Competition improves the breed. Racing led to the successful development of the mountain bike, the evolution of suspension systems, and enormously improved brakes and gears. If the UCI had been in charge none of this would have happened. I do not imagine the late, great Tullio Campagnolo – famed for inventing quick release wheels and the parallelogram derailleur – would have approved of the UCI's position, either.

As far as it goes, the notion of a uniform bicycle is at odds with the very concept of cycling. Human beings are not all the same. In designing and building a bicycle, the idea is to create a synergy between rider and machine, which literally means different spokes for different folks. A short, wiry, 135 pound rider from the Andes can use one sort of bike, a tall, muscular 200 pound powerhouse needs quite another. It is grossly unfair to insist they ride the same bike.

The idea that a bike has to be a certain weight in order to be safe is truly ridiculous. Strength has to do with the nature of materials and how they are used. One could easily make a completely unsafe bike at double the UCI weight requirement.

As for escalating costs and riders competing on even terms, the UCI allows disc wheels only if the disc portion is part of the structure of the wheel; snap on discs are banned. As a result, only racers

with wealthy sponsors can afford disc wheels.

The UCI are notoriously abusive of riders, and, for example, banned a world champion from defending his title, because the man dared to criticize the UCI. They have done nothing effective about a really serious problem for cycle sport, the drugging of riders with performance enhancers. I believe that the majority of riders really would rather not abuse themselves, but do it to stay on even terms. It's not just a few cheats and sneaks. Top level riders have very high medical expenses and not just for massage! Souping up riders is institutionalized exploitation of a particularly vicious and cruel kind.

In 1997, the UCI went on record as claiming that cycle sport was drug free and clean as a whistle. In 1998, one of the world's greatest sporting events, the Tour de France, was wrecked by police raids for drugs. The French police were criticized for being heavy handed, but you'd better believe they had cause. The failure of the UCI to safeguard cycle sport and the interests of riders against drug taking is absolute. Ignorance is no excuse, and any other explanation could well be criminal.

The UCI's technical expertise is warped, they abuse riders and condone exploitation, but where they have a brain leak big time is in their understanding of the purpose and economics of bike racing. Ever since the record breaking runs of the first chain drive safety bicycles, manufacturers have supported cycle sport because racing victories help them to sell bikes. Today, more than ever, authentic design and manufacturing innovations are crucial to the ambitions and sales of bike manufacturers.

For example, let's look at the seemingly innocuous ban on top tubes with a height differential of more than 4 cm. Common on mountain bikes, a sloping top tube helps make the frame stronger, and the bike easier to handle. Used together with variable-length seat posts and an adjustable stem, a dropped top tube means that only three frame sizes – small, medium, and large – are required to fit the majority of riders. This is an enormous economy, for manufacture and for the expensive business of maintaining inventory, and results in better bike prices for you and me.

Or how about the ban on monocoque one piece frames? The use of composite materials has great potential for mass production of high quality frames at reduced costs. But composites do not work well when used as tubes; effective use of these materials requires new designs and shapes – all banned by the UCI.

Many national bike racing organizations, including the USCF, already ignore UCI regulations. Bicycle manufacturers eager to develop new ideas and markets and gain new sales cannot afford to allow the patently incompetent UCI to dictate the design of their bikes. European manufacturers are not happy with the parochial, ill-informed, and autocratic ways of the UCI, and American, Australian, and Asian organizations and manufacturers – who have the real economic clout – have already had it right to the teeth. There is increasing talk about having a cyclists' version of the Boston Tea Party, and chucking the UCI.

Cooler heads would like to preserve the UCI Creating a new organization for cycle sport would involve a long, drawn out series of damaging altercations and problems and a thorough mess for racing until the new governing body emerged. A change of top level management at the UCI would be an easier, less stressful solution.

As of this writing, departure of the UCI old guard does not appear to be immediately on the cards. However, time and tide wait for no man, let alone the UCI. Cycle sport is a major activity, and bikes are an important form of personal transport As consumers we cast votes through the kinds of bikes we buy. The UCI ban on recumbents retarded but did not prevent development of this genre The UCI disdain for mountain bikes did not make a jot of difference to their overwhelming success Modern bicycle design and manufacturing has completely outstripped the resources and capabilities of the UCI. From a manufacturer's point of view, the purpose of racing is to sell bikes. Sooner or later, the cycle industry will get its act together and pull the UCI back into line.

As for keeping cycle sport clean and preserving

fair athletic contests, I think riders should form their own union and start looking out for themselves. No one else is going to do the job properly.

ROAD RACING AND TRACK

• Books

Effective Cycling, by John Forester, MIT Press.

A massive work containing much information of value to the racer.

Bicycle Road Racing, by Edward Borysewicz with Ed Pavelka, Spingfield Books.

Highly readable and filled with tips from the man who led the United States team to nine medals in the 1984 Olympics.

Cycle Racing, by Frank Westell and Ken Evans, Springfield Books.

Out of print but still one of the best books on road racing, time trials, and training.

Cycle Racing: How to Train, Race and Win, by William Fotheringham, A&C Black.

A recent, well-reviewed release.

The Cyclist's Training Bible, by Joe Friel, Velopress.

Timely and acclaimed.

Bicycle Design, by Mike Burrows, Open Road.

If you want to know what is essential in making a bike go fast, there is nothing better and more clearly focused. Written by the designer of Chris Boardman's Olympic Gold Medal Windcheetah bicycle.

Time Trial

Individual or team rides against the clock over 10, 25, 50, and 100 mile courses, or rides for the greatest distance covered in 1, 12, or 24 hours. Pure riding ability and stamina count the most. It's hammer down and go as fast as you can. An increasingly popular variation are point-to-point races over fixed routes where you ride for the best time. Some of these are epic, such as the annual 3,000 mile Race Across America (RAAM).

The time trial or "race of truth" is a particularly British institution, the result of bans on mass-start road racing. At least in Britain time trials are run on public roads alongside regular vehicle traffic. In other types of races you can get hurt, but in time trials you can get dead. Every year, several well-known riders are killed by cars. In terms of fatalities, time trials are possibly more dangerous than hairy sports such as downhill mountain bike racing.

Nevertheless, time trials can be compelling and very beautiful. There's something about going in quest of a private mark that is particularly satisfying, possibly because it comes from inside you. In mass-start road racing the trick is actually to go as slowly as possible, but in a time trial the only thing is for you – emphasis you – to go as fast as you can.

Massed Start

Everybody starts together, first human over the finish line wins. The course can be 10 miles, or 2,600 miles, as in the Tour de France. Most single day events are between 50 to 100 miles for amateurs, and 80 to 180 miles for professionals. Races lasting 2 days or more are called stage races.

In road racing, riders are pitted against each other, and the resulting shenanigans are sometimes incredible. Intelligence, strategy, trickiness and psychology play an equal role with riding ability and strength. Teams work together to launch a strong teammate ahead of the pack to victory, and block opposition riders. In big races, bicycles collide and pedals jam into spokes.

The physics of road racing are that a group of riders can go faster than any single rider. This is done by drafting, riding in the slipstream of the rider in front, and woe to leeches who do not take their proper turn at the head of the bunch. Alliances are made and broken as riders seek to form or join breakaway groups to run ahead of the main pack. If a breakaway does occur, a team might deliberately sacrifice riders by sending them to the head of the pack, to drive the pack hard enough to reel back in the breakaway group. Meanwhile, the team's true lead rider is well back in the pack, conserving energy for the sprint to the finish line.

A type of road race that has increased sharply in popularity because it is easy for TV crews to film is the around the houses, or criterium. It is usually held on a closed circuit measuring less than 2 miles around, with sharp and narrow corners, over distances ranging from 25 to 62 miles. Precise riding is needed to cope with the corners and the dense pack of riders created by the narrowness of the streets or road. Criterium bikes tend to have stiff frames for quick handling, and a high bottom bracket so that pedalling can continue through the corners.

Triathlon

Mixed running, swimming, cycling events. The cycling portion is more or less a time trial, and I find it amusing that in an event that is patently athletic, there is no adherence to UCI style rules. Triathlon bikes are among the most futuristic of machines and are typically highly aerodynamic.

Cyclo Cross

Not actually a road event, but listed here because the bikes are usually drop handlebar, 700C wheel variations on road bikes. Cyclo cross is a mix of riding, and running while carrying the bike. Mounting and dismounting skills are prime. Cross country races are from point-to-point or around a course from 1 to 16 miles in length, run either as a time trial or with a massed start. The courses are rough, with steep climbs and descents, mud, thick woods, streams, and hurdles. It is a tough sport, physically very demanding, with plenty of spills. Many cyclo cross riders have crossed over to mountain bike racing, sometimes with excellent results.

Track

The machine common to a wide variety of track events is the greyhound of bikes: an ultralight frame with a short wheelbase; a fierce position with the saddle high and handlebars low; a single fixed wheel gear, with no brakes; and tyres bonded to the rims with shellac, to withstand the stresses of violent track maneuvers. There are no quick release hubs, gears, pumps, cables, etc., making these among the most lovely and functional of bikes.

- **Sprint.** Usually a 1,000 meter course with only the last 200 meters timed. Involves all kinds of tricky tactics and scheming. There are times when racers hold their bikes stock still while jockeying for position. Behind the leader and in his slipstream until the final dash is the favored winning position.
- **Pursuit.** Two riders or teams start on opposite sides of the track and try to catch each other.
- **Time Trials.** Against the clock, as in road racing.
- **Devil Take the Hindmost.** Last human over the line every 2 or 3 laps is out.
- **Paced Racing.** Motorcycles are used as pace setters for the riders, who stay as close as possible to the pacer's rear wheel so as to minimize wind resistance. Speeds up to 60 mph.
- **Madison.** Two person teams run in relays. Each team member runs one or two laps and then hands over to a teammate, literally throwing him or her by the seat of his trousers or by a hand sling. A very spectacular form of racing.

MOUNTAIN BIKE

Mountain bike racing is top banana in terms of money, glamor and color, and prizes. Get near the top of this game and you will be a very elite, very hard working athlete, and possibly also very rich. At the same time, mountain bike racing is uniquely, wonderfully accessible, with a very high level of participation for all comers, be they racers or just fans, of all riding abilities.

There are events all over the country on most weekends, and if you are interested in mountain biking, I urge you to give one of these a try. The event venues are off-road, away from the only true mortal hazard to cyclists, cars. There's a wonderful feeling of freedom in just being able to wheel around on your bike at an event, and most people do. It's not a case of drive in your car and sit by the side of the road watching bikes go by. At mountain bike events, people use their bikes, and you're part of the action.

A big world championship event is sensational. There will be an entire valley, park, or other major piece of real estate devoted exclusively to the event. The last one I went to featured a whole festival village set in a lovely valley, with tents and marquees for bike and component manufacturers, various clubs and organizations, and a range of restaurants, cafes, and other amusements.

The cross country course, a mixture of stream crossings, climbs, and heart stopping descents, wound around the valley sides and in and out of the village. This made it easy to walk or ride to various portions of the course and watch the competitors. The thing I liked best was that you could ride the course! Not at race times of course, but otherwise, people were free to see for themselves what a championship cross country course felt like. Moreover, although this was a world class event, over the weekend there were plenty of races for beginners, kids, and all categories and ages of riders.

Indeed, any major mountain bike meet will typically have any number of events going on at once: cross country, downhill, trials, freestyle, and short distance slalom.

• **Cross country.** To me, the premier mountain bike event. Mass start, and self-sufficient. Puncture, or have a mechanical problem, and you've got to fix it yourself. Course lengths vary. Most are circular and a few miles long, with several laps. This means a lot of different terrain can be included, yet spectators can (by riding or walking and taking short cuts) see all of the course. Recently, the UCI have implemented short distance criterium courses, because these work better for television.

Cross country racing is extremely competitive, and mixes elements of time trial and riding against the pack. It's usual for a course to include a lot of single track, so if you fall back in the pack, you've got a problem. Most winning riders seek to get out ahead and stay there, which makes setting an accurately judged pace important.

Some cross country races are point to point and may be as much of a mass ride as a race. On the big ones, hundreds and hundreds of riders may participate. The leaders are few and far gone, for most it is simply a great day out.

• **Downhill.** Zzwwoomm! Definitely the cutting edge for technology, though the fastest machines now look like motor bikes rather than bicycles. Well that's OK, but old uncle Richard is again going to advise: really good, fast downhill is a matter of active technique and control, not hanging on for dear life hoping the bike will pull you through. Even at the original Repack, the fastest riders kicked up the least dust, and the same is true today. Smooth is fast; scrubbing up clouds of dust and bounding through the air is slow.

Start out with a regular bike or at most, a hard tail. Learn how to make it behave and do what you need. Then try suspension. As for courses, I advise climbing them. You've got to look, look, and look again, trying out different lines and approaches. Keep in mind that while you have brakes, you are looking for a total approach, a ride that, even if composed of different parts, is a complete rhythm. I won lots of ski races by figuring out where going slow would set me up to run the next section without having to check and scrub.

Use plenty of safety equipment!

• **Trials.** A skill sport often involving a considerable amount of nerve. In simplified form, you ride a course with obstacles to surmount, tricky slopes to climb and descend, and whatever other challenges the organizers can devise, as much as possible without touching your feet to the ground.

• **Freestyle/Slalom.** More or less a kind of accelerated BMX dirt track racing. Lots of jumps and air, and of course spills. Short wired, with lots of quick heats, and very thrilling.

• Books

Look out! Bookstore shelves are groaning with mountain bike books as more and more publishers climb on the bandwagon. In many cases, the publisher whipped up a snazzy design, then dragooned some writers into supplying text. When buying books on mountain biking, be sure to read enough of the text to know the book has information or content you want, and is not just glitz.

Single Track Mind, by Paul Skilbeck, Velopress.

Provides a well balanced mix of training techniques, bike handling skills, nutrition, and other information.

The Mountain Bike Way of Knowledge and *Mountain Bike!*, by William Nealy, Menasha Ridge Press.

Both about general riding rather than racing, but are still what I would read first.

HUMAN-POWERED VEHICLES

Interested in the cutting edge of speed? In machines so radical, no one is quite sure how to define them? In practical vehicle competitions which can be won by the design of the machine rather than the performance of the rider? In a sport not too often featured on television, which is, ahem, not overcrowded? HPV racing may be for you. The organization to contact is:

Human Powered Vehicle Association, Jean Seay, PO Box 1307, San Luis Obispo, CA 93406-1307 USA. Tel: 805 545 9003. Fax: 805 545 9005.
E-mail: Jean Seay exec-vp@ihpva.org.
Web: www.ihpva.org.

The HPVA has chapters in various states, which organize regional races, tours, and other events. Once a year there is a national championship, with several days of speed trials, road races, tours, seminars and workshops, and other events.

People who become involved with HPVs tend to be independent, and various new groups, some affiliated with the HPVA, others not, are emerging to organize races, speed challenges, and other events. There are also many small clubs which are specific to an area, or to a project, perhaps at a university or college. Best bet for tracking these down is to check with the publication *Recumbent Cyclist News* (PO Box 2048,

Port Townsend, WA 98368, USA. Tel: 360 344 4079. E-mail: bob@recumbentcyclistnews.com. Web: www.recumbentcyclistnews.com.).

In Britain, the organization to contact is:

British Human Power Club, Dennis Turner, 7 West Bank, Abbot's Park, Chester CH1 4BD England. Tel: +44 01244 376665.
E-mail: recumbent_dennis@compuserve.com.
Web: www.bhpc.org.uk

The BHPC runs an annual series of races, and every six years hosts the annual European Championships. Race meetings are good places to meet enthusiasts and possibly try out machines. The racing is pretty informal, but can be sharp. The BHPC also organizes various touring weekends and other outings.

As for the European HPV Championships, held in various countries in different years, whatever kind of cyclist you are, if you have a chance to attend one of these, go! These events are really interesting, with machines from all over Europe and often the world, lots of races and seminars, and plenty of people to meet. The HPV movement is big enough to be going places, and to be technically very interesting, yet still small enough for you to take a very active part. My advice is get on board now, because just as mountain bikes exploded in the 1990s, HPVs in the 2000s will become increasingly important, both in transport and as a focus for competition. Why even that ornery old dog, the UCI, has been seen sniffing around HPV manufacturers!

COURIER AND CARGO RACES

Courier races are not always publicized, because technically, mass start races on public roads are illegal. Also, couriers are an independent lot who often just want to get on with it. Best way to find out what's happening is to talk to a courier, or to go along to a bike shop that has a lot to do with courier riders. There is an annual world courier races championship, held in various countries, for info get up on the Net, and follow links around. A start point is: www.wheelie serious.com/courier.

Couriers are working riders, their level of skill – and fitness – can be astonishing, and a courier race can really be quite something. Because couriers as a class are forced to largely look after themselves, they are individualistic and sometimes downright anarchistic. However, of any cycling group, they probably best appreciate the kind of political and economic changes we need for the benefit of all cyclists. If you get involved with this scene, expect a nitty gritty, practical working ethos – and also a capacity for hard fun.

As for cargo races, I know of only a few that have taken place, but expect there will be more. Cargo bikes are coming back on stream, and races and contests are a logical means for publicizing these machines.

Veteran and Classic

Fun of restoring and riding antique cycles and accessories
• Veteran and classic machines

ANTIQUE CYCLES ARE INTERESTING ITEMS TO collect and restore. Early models were largely blacksmiths' creations and bringing them up to snuff is a feasible home workshop project. The latter part of the 19th century was a heyday of innovation and experimentation in cycles, and many wonderful machines were produced.

You'll need some luck to turn up a good pre-1910 veteran bike. Most machines already on the market are expensive. At one auction two bidders got into a contest with each other and pushed a bike worth $1,600 to over $160,000. This has nothing to do with cycle collecting. Only a few of the people who love veteran cycles and actually restore and use them are wealthy, most want to have fun without having to pay ridiculous sums, and prefer to keep the lid on prices. If your interest in veteran cycles is sincere and you look for long enough, a machine might come your way at a reasonable figure.

Luck is more like it, though. You need to find an old wreck rotting in an old rubbish dump or in the junk shed of great-great uncle Fred the

bicycle dealer who unexpectedly kicked the bucket decades ago. What you find is usually a disheartening pile of rust, but it is surprising what elbow grease and rust remover can do.

By about 1910 cycle designs had fairly well settled down, and machines from then onwards can be had for sometimes surprisingly low sums. Many are elegant and of high quality. In particular, lightweight racing and touring bikes made to around

Thanet Silverlight

1960 and perhaps a little later, are now known as classics. Some makes with distinctive features are keenly sought and can command fairly high prices; others are more affordable. One thing I like about these bikes is that they are usable.

American paperboy bikes made from 1933 to the 1950s have become classics. Many had mock gasoline tanks and ornate decorations. In America and Canada there are still lots of old bikes in barns, attics, and the like, just waiting to be discovered. Hunting down one of these and fixing it up is more interesting and exciting than forking money over to an antique shop.

• Books

King of the Road, by Andrew Ritchie, Wildwood House.

An excellent history which traces cycling history in social terms – for example, how the bicycle changed the role of women.

On Your Bicycle, by Jim McGurn, Open Road.
A lovely book that covers the history of cycling and the significance of the bike in social, economic, political, and even moral terms.

The Bicycle, by Pryor Dodge, Flammarion.
Big, very lovely book with an abundance of beautiful pictures and accurate historical data.

Cycling History: Myths and Queries, by Derek Roberts, John Pinkerton.

I'm especially fond of this one. Derek Roberts, one of the most eminent cycle historians in the world, is incisive but fair. Obtainable through the Veteran Cycle Club (address below).

Collecting and Restoring Antique Bicycles, by G. D. Adams, Pedaling History Bicycle Museum, 3943 N. Buffalo Road, Orchard Park, NY 14127-1841, USA. Tel: 716 662 3853. Fax 716 662 4594. E-mail: bicyclemus@aol.com. Web members.aol.com/bicyclemus/bike_museum

Definitive information on hardware and restoration techniques.

Introductory Guide To Collecting the Classics, by James Hurd and Don Hemmings, Antique and Classic Bicycle News.

Includes information on clubs, shows and sales, and restoration methods.

For current periodicals, try:
Antique and Classic Bicycle News, PO Box 1049, Ann Arbor, MI 48106, USA.

John Lannis's Newsletter, P.O. Box 5600, Pittsburgh, PA 15207, USA.

• Organizations

The Wheelmen, 1708 School House Lane, Ambler, PA 19002, USA.
Devoted to old bikes. Events, rides, and publications.

The Veteran Cycle Club, Geoff Paine, 31 York Road, Croxley Green, Rickmansworth, Herts WD3 3EU England.

Events and rides. Publishes *The Boneshaker*, an engaging, well-finished quarterly with in depth articles and photographs, and also *News and Views*, a newsletter with short articles, letters, and for sale/wanted ads.

Working In Cycling

Expanding opportunities for working in the cycle industry and in cycle-related professions and services • Moving the Economy • Delivery Services • Courier work • Light goods • Pedicabs • Services for cyclists • Parking • Cycle Planning and Engineering • Bicycle sales • Training for mechanics

BIKES ARE GOOD BUSINESS. THROUGHOUT THE 21st century, bikes will continue to grow in importance as a staple foundation of sustainable transport. The pace of development is quicker in Europe than in America. Europe was settled when people walked and rode horses, and so the patterns of streets and spaces in cities, distances between places, number of small roads and tracks, and general layout of real estate, is favorable for bikes. In Europe it is easier to introduce provisions for cyclists and stimulate the use of bikes, and in some countries, up to 40 percent of all journeys to work are by bike. In America, a country where much of the real estate was and is defined by the automobile, average journey distances are double the European average, and less than one percent of all journeys to work are by bike.

You can see the supremacy of the automobile in American transport as a major hurdle – or as an opportunity. Never mind that cars present enough problems to make getting rid of them a matter of survival. A perhaps more important consideration is that living with cars is a pain in the butt. They are expensive, dangerous, time consuming, and most times do not work efficiently as transport. Bikes, on the other hand, are fun, healthy, inexpensive, and easy to look after, and very efficient. Introduce bikes, and you get two things: happier people and increased commercial vitality and prosperity. That's a pretty potent combination.

I've a gut feeling that America might one day become a leading country in terms of providing for cyclists and bikes as a staple of transport. Americans are builders. If they see something good, they go for it. And with a clean slate and a fresh start, they might come up with something pretty good.

It is often asked if men and women make history, or just happen to be around at the right time. I think pretty obviously you've got to be lucky and have the right conditions or circumstances, but I also think there's something else important: you've got to be right. There is a growing awareness that we must act to support the cause of life on Earth. Exploiting our world or fellow humans, no matter how successful, is self-defeating and in the end bitter. There are no pockets in a shroud. What we give is

what we get. If this is how you think, or perhaps only nebulously feel, and you are interested in a job, career, or opportunity connected to cycling, I think you are on the right track at the right time.

Hardly that long ago, working in cycling was very limited. You might be a mechanic or sales person in a bike shop, with slim possibilities for advancement. Perhaps a framebuilder. Or an employee in a factory with uncertain future prospects. Although some enterprising people did well enough, and there was a certain amount of glamor and sometimes even some money in cycle sport, the cycle industry was modest in size, and bikes were relatively unimportant in the scheme of things. There were no cycle transportation engineers or traffic planners. If you thought bikes were good, that they could and would make a better world, the most you could do was say so.

Today, the picture is different. The cycle industry itself has grown enormously and is humming with activity and change. All the spheres of major manufacturing and retailing are important — design, graphics, engineering, marketing, promotion, management, finance, and sales, to name just a few — and the room for advancement, very simply, is global. Even more growth is in prospect for cycle related services and industries. Because transport links virtually everything we do, there is huge range and scope for commercial activities connected to cycling. Then there's the whole busi-

ness of transportation engineering and planning.

A strong economic base for cycling is wonderful because there's more. Bikes are not just transportation from home to work, school, shopping, and so on. They can fundamentally change the economic and social organization of our society and the ways we live, and for the better. In taking up with bikes we are not talking, as it were, about returning to milking cows. Exactly the opposite. Bikes help develop our society and enrich our lives with more human contact, better communication, and greater commercial vitality. To me, the thrilling thing is not just that you can now earn a decent living working in cycling. It is that you can be paid for work actually building a better world. I cannot imagine a more fantastic or important change.

MOVING THE ECONOMY

In 1998 I was invited to a conference called *Moving the Economy*, in Toronto, Canada. Over a four day period, some 500 attendees and speakers participated in seminars and workshops ranging widely in scope, but linked by a pivotal idea defining and articulating the economic benefits of sustainable transport. The premise was straightforward: swell if something is green and better for us all, but to make it work and happen, it needs to be economically viable. In short, green has to pay

It does. The world's wealthiest cities have the best sustainable transport systems and spend the least per capita on transportation. Sustainable transport creates jobs, increases commerce, saves money, and revitalizes local economies. And – I particularly like this part – because transportation relates to just about everything we do, the range of possible activities is very wide.

Projects presented at *Moving the Economy* ranged from the design of train stations and pedestrian areas to the role of bikes in local agriculture to bicycle nappy delivery services to the global perspective of the World Bank on sustainable transport. Abstracts of the conference proceedings are available in printed form from:

Detour Publications, 500 University Ave., 8th Floor, Toronto, Ontario, Canada M5G 1V7. Tel: 416 392 1560. Fax: 416 392 0071. E-mail: detour@web.net. Web: www.detourpublications.com.

The conference proceedings are also published on the MTE web site: www.city.toronto.on.ca/mte. This is an indexed, searchable database of opportunities in sustainable transportation. On an ongoing basis, this site gathers and presents examples where sustainable transport policies, products, ventures, and technologies have worked. The purpose is to give useful information and resources which people can adapt and use in their own ventures and interest areas, be these back yard, business, government, or community. Crucially, the examples are all linked, so that from the MTE web site, you can find and go to all the other places and people that might be helpful.

Want to know what happens when bikes are provided to farmers in Nicaragua? How bikes help police forces? How to use bikes to promote locally grown produce for cities? What the latest word is in folding bikes? How to succeed with a new kind of bike? It's all there, and hats off to the *Moving the Economy* organizers for their initiative in getting this ball rolling. These folks are the better element, clean, green, and great singers, too (the group Toronto Song Cycles will stitch any

cyclist), but first and foremost they are showing what no one can ignore – green pays.

WHOA!

Before going any further, best to get a few points clear. The topic of working in cycling deserves not just a book, but several. While I might have some qualifications as a visionary enthusiast, I can't tell you how to design a bicycle, run a business, or apply for a job. What I'm good for, I hope, is whipping up some spirit and rattling off a few starter leads and ideas. The rest is up to you.

OPPORTUNITIES

Commercial viability is the bedrock for expanding the role of the bicycle. We've known all along that bikes are economical; the vital difference now is that bikes create wealth. Moreover, that wealth can be of a sort which is socially useful. The money involved in operating a delivery motor vehicle for a supermarket, for example, mostly goes outside the immediate community, to suppliers of fuels, and to the government as taxes which supposedly will be reinvested in the community. The money involved in running a fleet of delivery bicycles, however, primarily goes to local people, and in greater numbers than a single van driver. Moreover, a lot of it goes to those who have need of work: the young and energetic, and those still seeking education and training for jobs.

Delivery Services

Cycle delivery services are one of the most visible growth areas, and economically extremely strong. It is said that in London alone, more than $30 million a year is spent just on bicycle couriers. The figure for a town like New York City must be astronomical. There are many, many more possibilities in delivery services, from pizzas to nappies to pedicabs. If you are interested in starting a business in this area, then essential reading is:

Cycling for Profit: How to Make a Living With Your Bike, by Jim Gregory, Van der Plas Publications.

Gregory, co-owner of the firm Bikes At Work, shares lessons he has learned about things to do and pitfalls to avoid. The book is very much on the practical side, and I reproduce the table of contents to show the sort of things delivery services can involve:

1. Working as a Commercial Cyclist
2. Getting Started
3. Equipment
4. Communication Equipment
5. Insurance and Bonding
6. Marketing
7. How to Keep your Business in the Black
8. Hiring and Managing Employees
9. Jobs Requiring Only a Bicycle
   Pizza Delivery
   Airline Ticket Delivery
   Document/Small Pack Delivery
   Pharmaceutical delivery
10. Jobs Requiring a Cargo Bike or Trailer
    Grocery Delivery
    Newspaper Distribution
    Commercial Cargo Delivery
    Mail Delivery
    Furniture Moving
    Bicycle Transport
    Beverage Can Collecting
    Mobile Services
    Mobile Bicycle Repair
    Ice Cream Vending
    Pedicabbing
    Recycling Service

Gregory's book is particularly useful because he devotes considerable attention to the nuts and bolts of how to make a business work. Highly recommended.

Another source of information, fact sheets and booklets on delivery services is the Community Bicycle Network. Fact sheets include: *Put Bikes to Work for your Business!; The Bottom Line on Bicycle Delivery; Starting a Bicycle Delivery*

Service: A Sample Business Plan; Resources for Starting a Bicycle Delivery Business. Contact:

> Community Bicycle Network (CBN),
> 427 Bloor St. W., Box 6, Toronto, Ontario,
> Canada M5S IX7. Tel: 416 323-0897.
> Web: www.workbike.org/resources.

Cycle delivery books such as *Delivering the Goods By Bike*, on why bicycle delivery is an economically sensible option for businesses, with information for anyone considering starting a bike delivery business, and *Bikes Mean Business! A Primer on Starting a Bike-Related Business* which covers initial stages, and includes interviews with successful bike related business people, plus a comprehensive list of resources, are available from:

> Detour Publications, 500 University Ave.,
> 8th Floor, Toronto, Ontario, Canada M5G 1V7.
> Tel: 416 392 1560. Fax: 416 392 0071.
> E-mail: detour@web.net.

The internet mailing list workbike carries a constant stream of information on work bikes and business. To post to this list, send an email to workbike@ihpva.org. General information about the mailing list is available at the website www.ihpva.org/mailman/listinfo/workbike.

• Courier Work

Can you just hop on a bike and earn money riding as a courier? Possibly. Courier work is hard, demanding, and exhausting. Even if you are fit, it will take a month or more of daily riding before you are strong enough to handle a full day's work without finishing completely flat, ready only for bed. It's physically hard. On top of that, couriers as a class are not well-treated. They are freelancers, without employment benefits, and largely if not completely uninsured.

The courier scene is freewheeling, and part of the appeal of this line of work is a sort of gritty independence; couriers survive by dint of their own efforts. This anarchistic spirit is in some ways a liability; couriers have mixed feelings

about organizing and forming unions to better their employment conditions. Yet if it were me, this is exactly the area I would look at. Bicycle couriers are a vital part of the economy, the value of their contribution to communication and activity in financial markets alone is worth a mint, and if courier riders stand up all at once, they can demand and get the fair shake they deserve. Check out the:

International Federation of Bike Messenger Associations (IFBMA), PO Box 191443, San Francisco, CA 94119-1443 USA. Fax: 603 954 0473. E-mail: magpie@echo.com. Web: www.messengers.org.

A website with all sorts of interesting information and archives is Messengerville at www.wwonline. com/~jhendry/MAIN.HTM. For interest, try the websites of some of the UK delivery services and organizations:

Interaction: Web: members.aol.com/deltairter

London Cycle Messenger Association: E-mail: movingtarget@gn.apc.org

Security Despatch: E-mail: info@securitydespatch.co.uk Web: www.securitydespatch.co.uk

A mailing list on messengers can be joined by sending an e-mail to majordomo@cyclery.com with the words "info messengers" in the body of the message.

• Light Goods

Cycles can be very good at moving light goods, and making things better, even for motorists. In one innovative development in Germany, the town center and shopping districts have been pedestrianized. There are no cars at all. Motorists park in outlying car parks, where they are also assigned a locker. There is free transport to the town center, and quadricycles are used to deliver their shopping to the locker within one hour of purchase. People are encouraged to come to town, shop, and then have a nice meal or catch some entertainment. The early reports are that this arrangement has caused a strong increase in business. Makes sense. Think of the convenience of doing the weekly grocery shopping without having to lift or trundle any of the stuff. Especially if you've got some kids in tow. Also, once you get rid of cars in a shopping district, there's more room for customers, and shops can be more centrally located. If you've nothing to carry, it's easy to call by several shops.

In Britain, there are already a few pilot schemes using pedal-powered vehicles for grocery deliveries. I think it's the way to go, though one needs to separate the functions of delivering goods and providing pedicab services for customers. Hauling both a load of groceries and a customer is a fair old job, with only a single payoff. However, making three or four deliveries on one pass through an area can be worthwhile.

How do you get something like this going? Well, that depends on the kind of business, and that will depend on where it is. For example, big shopping malls would seem to be ideal for package delivery services to a single pickup point. I like the idea of getting cars out of the picture entirely, however, so let's talk about a delivery service in an urban area with limited car parking.

You need support, and first port of call are the stores and shops. Big stores have to provide expensive car parking facilities, and little shops are dying away as traffic congestion steadily worsens and parking becomes increasingly restricted. You can serve large centralized traders by consolidating deliveries to areas, and small dispersed traders with regular route runs.

Straight off, get the traders on your side with a simple message: you want to increase their business. They are also going to get the benefit of good publicity. Pedal-powered vehicles are an effective advertising medium. In a number of places, they just run around with billboards, like the old sandwich man. Anyway, you'll call your business something obviously benign and good, such as Green Machine, or Clean Planet Deliveries, and your vehicles will advertise the stores which use your service.

Next, get the police, municipal authorities, and any other outfit of similar ilk on your side. Simple message: you will provide employment. What's more, it will be of a particularly useful kind. A lot of those kids around the neighborhood, who need money as much as anyone else but have few ways to get it, can work part time. Plus, there will be increased social interaction. This is quite important, because one simple way to cut down on crime is to have more street activity.

You need all this support, because unless you are independently wealthy, you are going to need capital, possibly a loan from a bank, perhaps some kind of government support. The more successful your business, the more operating capital you will need. Politics, publicity, business management, finance, communications . . . plenty to sink your teeth into here . . . and as well, you've got to reach customers! One reason you make friends with the stores, the various social groups, and local media, is to do as much as possible to help drum up business. But it is fundamental to do your own grassroots work: knock on doors, talk to people, get them to know about what you're doing. You've got a rider, where does her family buy their stuff? What about their friends? Doing this kind of one-on-one contact is a tremendous amount of work, it might seem rather too personal and hardly relevant to sit down with old Mrs. Grundy and talk about the

days when the corner store had a faithful nag named Old Dobbin for deliveries, or whatever, but personal contact is the point. This is how you get the ball rolling. Personal service is your business asset. The whole thing works because people – your customers – know and like and support you, your ideas, and your people. When your drivers deliver to Mrs. Grundy, who has arthritis and can't get around, they bring along the papers and her medicine from the local pharmacy, and help put the groceries away – for which they get a useful tip. Help and ye shall be helped. Today the neighborhood, tomorrow a franchise system for the world!

A range of cargo and delivery cycles has been produced for many years by:

Worksman Cycles, 94-15 100th Street, Ozone Park, New York, NY 11416, USA. Tel: 718 322 2000. Fax: 718 529 4803. E-mail: cycles@worksman.com. Web: www.worksman.com.

For information on the quadricycles used in Germany, contact:

Advanced Vehicle Design, L&M Business Park, Norman Road, Broadheath, Altrincham, Cheshire WA14 4ES England. Tel: +44 0161 928 5575. Fax: +44 0161 928 5585. E-mail: bob@windcheetah.co.uk. Web: www.windcheetah.co.uk.

• Pedicabs

Running a pedicab on pure muscle is hard, hard work, and may not do nice things for your life span. This is one area where limited electric power assist can play a useful role, for extra help when starting off or climbing gradients.

Do pedicabs work? Of course they do. It's definitely a neighborhood and holiday area sort of thing, not competition for long distance trains, and requires real spade work. Where are the customers? Where do they need to go? When? What with light shopping, school runs, entertainment, and eating out, is there enough business? Again, can you get help? Will the movie house advertise your services? The school?

There's no question that neighborhoods need local transport, and that pedicabs can be useful. But to make it go, I think you've got to get right down to the level of where things are happening. It's a chicken-and-egg problem. The train and then the car helped drive apart what were once close knit neighborhoods. By increasing local mobility pedicabs can help bring communities back together. But the specific situation matters. For example, in my neighborhood, open air cafes and dining have become very trendy and popular. Where are the people coming from? And might there be more? Just over a bridge and down the road a short spell is London's largest street market. Could a pedicab shuttle service snag some more customers there? Also, because so many people come to the market on weekends, the tube (subway) train station is one-way: people can come out, but can't get back in. Pedicabs would be effective at shifting people and their shopping to nearby tube stations.

Or how about the school run? In rural America, centralization of schools has led to increased dependency on motor vehicles, but there are still plenty of places where small fry have only a mile or two to go to school, and hard working parents would welcome a pedicab bus service – provided you are obviously OK. Parents won't hand over their nearest and dearest without a firm assurance that your service is safe. You'll need to win friends, perhaps make presentations at the local schools, go along and talk to parents. Remember,

startup time on something like this seems like forever, but once you've got the idea in motion and machines going, it pretty well looks after itself.

One note: existing taxi services sometimes oppose pedicabs. Often this is in the form of a requirement for pedicab drivers to have the same qualifications as taxicab drivers. Add diplomacy to the list of attributes and skills you'll need.

One thing I'd like to see: pedicabs where the customers can pedal, too! Think of the fun we could have with those. Another item that appeals would be self-propelled tram vehicles. Instead of all the commuters straggling on board a train and hanging on to straps and looking miserable, everyone lays hold of a big bar and heaves it back and forth, arriving for work charged to the nines. Interesting thing is, a self-propelled tram could be lightweight; from a mechanical standpoint, at least, it would work.

CYCLE INDUSTRY

There is more growth and greater opportunities in providing cycle-related services than in directly manufacturing and selling bikes and accessories. The US population of 100 million bikes is already fairly large; the area for increase will be in bike usage. A broad demographic factor is that the percentage of middle age cyclists is becoming larger, while the number of younger cyclists is decreasing. Essentially, this will cause an increase in spending on quality bikes, and on services.

Cycle Related Services

Oh my! There's so much here. I think it is worth getting across that cyclists are spenders. In a given area, daily spending by cycle tourists is three times greater than for people travelling in cars. Cyclists are close down on the ground, they need food, accommodation, entertainment, and so on, and spread more money around than fast moving motorists.

Cyclists need food and more food, cafes, accommodation places, repair services, and

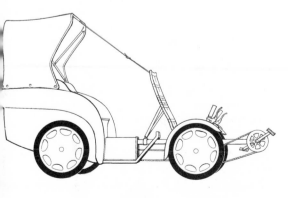

Pedicab

absolutely by no means least, entertainment. Can you tap into this? How would you do with, say, a little mobile repair service mounted on a delivery trike? Do you know how crazy cyclists are for ice cream? They go on a ride, become ravenous for ice cream and eat 36-mile's worth, then hit the saddle again to burn it off, but after 15 miles weaken again and have another . . . on a warm day, you can sell out an entire box trike long before sundown. Bad weather? No problem – sell hot soup.

Have you been thinking of a life in the country? How about running a road house for cyclists? Range of beds and bunks, nice parking for the bikes and some repair facilities, too, and some eats out of the garden. Like cooking? There are now some very successful restaurants surviving on the strength of hiking and walking trails. Entertainment? You've got some interesting possibilities here, because cyclists are doers, and up for more than flopping by the tube. Get 'em all in on a drumming session. Try interactive theatre. There are whole bunches of things that can happen, because bicycles and cycling are part and parcel of a new culture.

Where can you do this kind of stuff? Well, that depends. Many places, ski areas for example, are already gearing up for cyclists in a big way. There's work for mechanics, instructors, guides, and of course, cooks and cleaners. Trail building and maintenance, too. If you want your own business, you might be able to buy into an ongoing operation. There's a lot to be said for starting with some established turnover.

Some developments might be obviously set to deliver customers, say the construction of a new long distance cyclepath between two cities. Others might take a little bit of figuring and doing. For example, suppose there's a beautiful spot in the forest, 10 or so miles away from a ski area, with a range of cross country trails which make it easy for riders to reach you from the ski area, and to go there in the morning. It's in the middle of the woods, miles and miles from any road, and so you set up a place which is real woodsy and organic. The fact that there are no motor vehicles is part of the charm of it! (They park at the ski area.) You'll

need to hustle up business, get the ski area to help, bike shops in nearby towns to push you customers.

If you are interested in this sort of thing, start looking right now. An achingly lovely spot miles from anywhere but just the right distance from no less than three different towns for a lunch stop, a location just outside a major tourist city which would be a perfect accommodation place for incoming cycle visitors – these kinds of places could still be available for reasonable money. Start building now – perhaps start with a box trike, and root and grow as trade develops – and you could be in on the ground floor of a solid economic opportunity, and a lifestyle you really enjoy.

Sound too good to be true? I didn't say easy! New businesses and ventures are speculative, there's plenty to think about and even more to do, and that part you've got to pick up for yourself. The opportunity is there.

Country living is not the only route. The cycle commuting market is set to expand, and there is strong need for a variety of services. Prime among these is secure parking. A number of towns now have establishments which offer bike parking, changing rooms and showers, repair facilities, and shops. Again, you don't have to start with everything all at once.

Here's a free help the world, get rich quick scheme: arrange for the design and production of bicycle storage lockers that can be plunked down on the street. A unit that was, oh, truck size, could probably hold around 30 bikes in individual compartments. The unit should be designed and finished in such a way as to be an attractive piece of street furniture, with provision for flowers and decorations. Many communities want to promote bike usage. A modular, ready-to-use street parking facility is an item that would do a lot to solve the problem of where to keep a bike. It would not be suitable for expensive machines, but would be fine for utility bikes. Have a few compartments large enough for delivery box trikes, with access via swipe cards. The box trikes can be supplied and maintained by local shops, and card users would pay a modest rental.

REX·BRIT·IND·IMP

RRO·BONO·PVBLICO

For information on cycle parking, try:

Bicycle Parking Project, PO Box 7342,
Philadelphia, PA 19101 USA.
Tel: 215 222 1253.
E-mail: john-dowling@usa.net.

• Cycle Planning and Engineering

A new profession. Transportation engineering,
sometimes with a specialty in cycle planning, is
now a regular course of study at many universities
and colleges. There's great need for this sort of
expertise. Municipal areas everywhere are under
pressure from the government to increase cycle
usage. It will happen only when cycling is made
attractive and safer, and that means real engineering and planning, not just putting up a few signs

which say "Bike path." Funny thing is, thanks to
the Transportation Equity Act, there is funding
available, if you know what to do to get it. Find
out from:

Bikes Belong! 1368 Beacon St.,
Brookline, MA 02446-2800 USA.
Tel: 617 734 2800. Fax: 617 734 2810.
E-mail: mail@bikesbelong.org.
Web: www.bikesbelong.org.

Association of Pedestrian and Bicycle
Professionals, PO Box 23576,
Washington, DC 20026 USA.
E-mail: pedbike@aol.com.
Web: www.apbp.org.

A group with solid experience in making life
better for both cyclists and the community at
large, and also a tremendous list of links at a well
organized web site is:

Transportation Alternatives, 115 W. 30th St.,
New York, NY 10001-4010.
Tel: 212 629 3311. Fax: 212 629 8324.
E-mail: infor@transalt.org.
Web: www.transalt.org.

Expertise in promoting cycle usage can be
applied many ways. For example, you could pick
out three or four large firms in your area, do your
homework, and then march in and say: "Lucky
you, you've got the opportunity to hire me as your
cycle planning consultant, a remarkably astute
and worthwhile investment, because here's what
it will do for your productivity and profits . . ."
You then proceed to organize the whole thing,
from bike purchase programs to providing facilities to training for bike riding and route planning.

It is worth noting that many traffic engineering
ideas that are seen as radical in the US, have
already been in use for some time in other countries. Useful information can be obtained from:

Transport 2000, First Floor, The Impact
Centre, 12–18 Hoxton Street, London N1 6NG
England. Tel: +44 020 7613 0743.
E-mail: transport2000@transport2000.demon.co.uk

Cycling Campaign Network, 54–7 Allison Street, Digbeth, Birmingham B5 5TH England.

Sustrans, 35 King Street, Bristol BS1 4DZ England.
Tel: +44 0117 929 0888. Fax: +44 0117 929 0124.
Web: www.sustrans.org.uk.

Cyclists' Touring Club, Cotterell House, 69 Meadrow, Godalming, Surrey GU7 3HS England.
Tel: +44 01483 417217. Fax: +44 01483 426994.
E-mail:cycling@ctc.org.uk.
Web: www.ctc.org.uk.

Bicycle Sales

American cycle shops are possibly the best and most advanced in the world. There's a high level of professionalism; to succeed at retailing you need training in a wide range of skills. There's also payoff, because cycling is poor no more; the quality end of the market has grown, and retailers who target specific markets and employ modern methods can do well. On the other side, there's still room for different styles and starting off on the ground floor. I was walking along in lower Manhattan, New York City, and bumped into a pure street operation: an odd triangle of real estate, graced with a couple of wooden shacks and a melange of delivery bikes and pedicabs, plus a couple of snoozing dogs. It's a place that sells working bikes, there's not a speck of glitz in sight but it feels down home good.

• Modern Retailing

In terms of learning about modern retailing and marketing methods, you've got two routes: a broad based curriculum at a regular technical college or school, or more hands-on training programs offered or sponsored by cycle industry trade organizations. For information, contact:

National Bicycle Dealers Association, 777 West 19th St., Suite O, Costa Mesa, CA 92627-6130 USA. Tel 949 722 6909. Fax: 949 722 1747.
E-mail: bikeshops@aol.com.

Web: www.nbda.com.
CABDA - The Bicycle Dealer's Association,
2417 W. 183rd St., Homewood, IL 60430 USA.
Tel: 708 798 2004. Fax 708 798 2208.
Web: www.cabda.com.

• Mechanics

The traditional method for becoming a bike mechanic was to become fairly competent on a DIY basis, snag a low rung job in a bike shop, and then pick up the rest. This actually works fairly well. I've known many top mechanics who never had a lick of professional training, and some have gone far, to pro teams, and even beyond, to become managing directors of large distributorships or manufacturing firms. Two problems with this approach were, some people spent their lives making coffee and sweeping floors and never advanced anywhere, and some folks running repair shops did not know a wrench from a tire iron. Cycle trade industry organizations, anxious to establish benchmark standards for bike shops, have now instituted various training and certification schemes. Although if you are an ace mechanic you should not have difficulty obtaining work, it cannot possibly hurt to have accreditation.

General to advanced courses in bicycle repair are offered at the CABDA Service School in Elk Grove, IL (contact details above). A range of programs are available at:

Barnett Bicycle Institute, 2755 Ore Mill Dr., No. 14, Colorado Springs, CO 80903 USA. Tel 719 632 5173. Fax: 719 632 4607. E-mail: bbinstitute@juno.com. Web: www.bbinstitute.com.

• Strategies

Training to work in the cycle industry is not much use unless you land a job. It therefore makes sense to go after both at once.

Work-related education is a major growth area. In the US, there will soon be more students in employment than students in pure education. Job training is pretty much a continuous activity throughout most working careers.

Right. Whether your interest is in mechanics, sales, copy writing, or whatever, first do your homework and properly learn one end of a bike from the other, and what people do with them – there's no point to any of this unless you do in fact like bikes and bike people – and then go to a prospective employer and say: I want a solid future, give me a job which includes training, and I'll promise to work for you for a definite time period.

Not all of the cycle trade has entered the modern age, some possible employers will scoff, but others will bite. The thing is, an employee is an investment of time, energy, and considerable expense, and these days no employer treats the matter of hiring people lightly; when an employee is seen as a co-investor rather than someone riding along for what they can get, this can be very much more attractive for the employer. It also creates a win-win situation, because it is in your employer's interest for you to succeed – to make you an A student! Equally, you incur certain responsibilities, and it is in your interest to execute them properly and serve out the term of your apprenticeship, because otherwise you lose out. Both put in, both gain: the employer has an employee for a definite period, and you become employable.

• Company Bikes

The market for direct sales of bikes to businesses and companies is hugely undeveloped. Bikes are a perfect company perk, because they help make employees more punctual and productive, and qualify for tax breaks – a real win-win for any firm.

Bicycle Manufacture and Design

Bicycle manufacture has increasingly become a global business. Large holding companies and consortiums own major brands which were once primary national manufacturers. Firms of this size include a wide range of functions and employment possibilities.

The growth of large manufacturing firms has been balanced by the development of numerous smaller firms able to prosper by specializing. If you have a hankering to make bikes or components, understand from the get-go that competing with Asian manufacturers on price is a non-starter. You'll need to provide something others do not, and success will not necessarily be a blessing; once a market becomes evident, bigger fish may move in for a bite. Patent protection in this field is very difficult.

Are you interested in product design and engineering? Are you perhaps thinking of coming up with a new mechanism or device? Are you hoping that some bit of clever thinking or inspiration will launch you to a life on Easy Street? Well, it does happen – once in a long while!

Did you know that the pneumatic tire was first patented in 1845 by a Scottish engineer, long before John Boyd Dunlop began producing air-filled tires in 1888? Dunlop succeeded because he had strong commercial backers and was able to fend off a lawsuit for patent infringement, and because – as had not been the case in 1845 – thanks to the bicycle there was a market for the product.

The first thing to appreciate is that ideas and inventions are only rarely unique. The second is that even with a good idea or design, making the thing work requires a whole constellation of related elements and circumstances. It's not just that a lone crackpot working out of a shed might not get a hearing. I cannot count the number of times I have seen people with real position and influence champion good ideas that found no takers. Materials sourcing, production engineering, marketing – all these, and many more, must be in place before an idea can fly. One thing good designers learn is patience; if an idea is worthwhile, at some point it will get another turn at bat.

If you study design and design engineering, you possibly are aware that a great deal of what is taught and done in educational institutions is a total crock. Success in a design contest or with a school project is likely to have little if anything to do with the real world. Sometimes that sort of thing is an expedient necessity for certification. However, when you hit the real world, then at least as far as bikes and cycling are concerned, I've got two firm pieces of advice. One: try your idea out. Build working prototypes, no matter how crude, and use them. There is no substitute for what you learn by doing this. Two: ensure your idea is commercially viable. However green or nice or useful to civilization, it's got to pay, and very simply, that will happen only if people want it. Find out if they do.

Police Work and Social Services

Bicycle-mounted police are friendlier, have higher arrest rates, and are extremely cost effective. If you are in law enforcement and bikes are not part of the scene, be sure to get in touch with the:

International Police Mountain Bike Association (IPMBA), 28 East Ostend St., Baltimore, MD 21230 USA.
Tel: 410 685 2220.
E-mail: IPMBA@aol.com. Web: www.ipmba./org.

Bike Care

Benefits of bike care • Bike shops • Tools • Lubrication • General words • Bearings • Cleaning and polishing • Ride check • Wheel removal • Tires • Cables • Brakes • Derailleurs • Chain • Pedals • Cranks • Bottom bracket • Chainrings • Freehubs and freewheels • Wheel truing • Handlebars • Stem • Headset • Saddle

A BIKE IS AN EXTENSION OF YOUR BODY, AND how well you look after your bike affects how well you ride. There are degrees to this, of course. Utility bikes are designed for reliable operation with minimum care; high performance bikes like regular attention and fine tuning. A rider's nature makes a difference: some people are happy if their bikes just work; others really enjoy keeping their machines in perfect order.

A fair amount of latitude is possible in servicing bikes, hopefully you have chosen a machine suited to your level of skill and interest in maintenance. The more you ride, the more you'll appreciate that bikes are at their best when clean, lubricated, and precisely adjusted. A sensitivity for mechanics does not spring into being the moment you mount a bike. Let your awareness grow naturally, and don't feel bad if you sometimes miss or misunderstand something – we all do. Just learn. But just in case, let's have one thing straight: it is a sin to neglect a bike.

Once in awhile I like to have fun explaining about how rocks have feelings, or how trees talk to each other and are quite sentient and even sensible (check out the web site BikeReader.com). I'm practical about machines, and for exactly this reason, also emotional. Machines, and bicycles in particular, need regular lubrication and adjust-

ment to function. Without care, rust and deterioration set in, parts become dry and dirty and go out of kilter, and the bike slowly grinds itself to bits when it is ridden. This is abuse, just as much as physically or psychologically hurting a human being or other biological entity when there is no call to do so. A bike is made to work and be looked after. The design, materials, and quality may be anywhere from poor to remarkable, but in terms of maintenance – happiness for the bike – it is your duty to do at least what is reasonable and sensible, and better if you do more. Neglect, and

the bike may up and bite. "Old dependables" left out in the rain and never maintained sometimes make it for years, and then snap a chain and spill the rider underneath a truck, or let a brake cable go at the start of a long hill. Not looking after a bike is more than creating bad karma or missing out on the fun; it's a dumb risk.

If you are the sort of person who leaves tools outside to rust in the rain (rather than cleaning, lubricating, and storing them ready for the next job), that's your business, and I won't throw any rocks, not even my friendly ones. But maintenance for your bike is still essential; depending on how much and hard you ride, check your bike into a shop for servicing two to four times a year and tell them to do whatever needs doing. This should assure you of a safe, reliable bike, and will also save you money.

Even minor misalignment of a brake shoe can result in uneven wear and an early end to it's life. Replacement is not an idle expense. A filthy chain can grind an entire transmission to bits. Paying for regular maintenance will extend the life of your bike and cost less than the big time repair bills which neglect can cause.

Whether you leave maintenance entirely to a shop, or give your bike(s) as much unstinting personal TLC as possible, you will in any case need to have an ongoing relationship with a bike shop, as a source of components and accessories, advice, and servicing. How much work you do yourself, and how much you leave to the shop, depends on the kind of bike you have, and how far you want to go with maintenance.

Modern bikes can be mechanically fairly complex and require specific knowledge and tools for servicing. The specialized tools often required are usually expensive. It is not economic to equip a home workshop to deal with every aspect of maintenance for the sake of one bike. Moreover, there are many jobs which, even if you know how to do them, are better left to people with greater skill. Wheel building and truing is a good example. I have done these jobs often, to a standard which is decent but still short of the class of work produced by a professional. I do wheels when I have to, but otherwise, I go to a skilled pro. Investing in this kind of quality pays off; I have several sets of wheels, ten or even more years old, which are still running without a hitch.

Start with basic maintenance, and if you find that you enjoy it, you can gradually expand your skills and resources. You might work on friends' bikes, too. One of my treats is spending a warm Sunday afternoon in the garden working on bikes – sometimes just routine jobs with prosaic machines, other times experimenting with new ideas and exotic machines. If playing with mechanical bits is not your thing, fine, you've plenty of company, but at least keep your brakes and gears adjusted, and your bike clean. This will reduce wear and help when checking your bike into a shop for servicing. Ill-looked after, rusty bikes are difficult and time consuming to work on, which adds ouch! to labor charges. If your bike is in decent shape to start with, it will cost less to keep it that way.

Working with a Shop

If you have just purchased a bike, or are about to do so, hopefully this was/will be from a shop you can trust for maintenance. Of course you may have a used machine, or have purchased elsewhere, or have some other reason for establishing a new relationship with a shop. There are two basic ways of evaluating a shop: word of mouth reputation, and various certification programs run by industry trade organizations, and manufacturers such as Shimano.

Evidence of certification is a helpful indication that the shop is serious about what it is doing, but word of mouth is your best guide. Ask around, see what people say. Bikes are fine machines, tuning them up can be a craft verging on art, but they are not rocket science. Good bike shops look after their customers, and get repeat business, by doing good work. No one is perfect, you'll always hear a grumble or two about any shop, and someone is sure to complain of high expense, but if most people say, "Oh yeah, good work, bike runs fine," then it is worth a try.

Many shops post a menu of rates for various jobs, such as "Front wheel truing – $XX, parts extra." They may also give rates for complete bike jobs, such as a check and light tune-up, or complete overhaul and rebuild. The usual procedure for shop work is: you say what you want, someone examines your bike, and then a written estimate is drawn up that specifies the agreed work, parts, and cost. This is for the shop's protection as much as yours. When your relationship with the shop is more established you can leave matters on a more open basis, so that if they find something that needs doing but is not covered by the estimate, they are able to go ahead and do it. Get to this stage as soon as you can; it's a pain to collect your bike just before a dream tour or big ride and then discover that something vital was not done because it was not covered by the estimate. Make sure the shop understands that you do not want to get the last possible mile out of tires, cables, or other components; rather, every time the bike leaves the shop, it should be in shape for a good long roll.

Minor adjustments and fine points are best carried out by you. Only you know exactly where you like the brake lever to engage, for example. If you get new cable wires, they will stretch a little as they wear in, and need adjustment – a job not worth a trip to the bike shop, because you can do it in seconds.

Going hands-on with your bike and having a good ongoing relationship with a bike shop will make preventive maintenance – replacing parts

before they wear out and break – almost automatic. In turn, breakdowns and roadside repairs will be rare. You'll have more happy times with the bike, and you'll be more confident, because you'll know the bike is OK – and that you have done right by it.

Maintenance Information

In the rest of this section I cover some general things such as tools, lubricants, servicing bearings, and advice about procedures. The next section starts with basic jobs such as wheel removal, mending a puncture, adjusting and replacing cables, etc., and then takes a short tour through the highlights of a bike. I do not deal with all jobs much less all components. Wish I could! However, to do so would require an enormous book, far thicker than my publishers have agreed. It's not just that there are many different components. Even within a type, such as V-brakes, tolerances, settings, and procedures for various models vary. Another problem is that these days, bike technology is an evolving game, with a constant stream of new developments and innovations. At least in the book world, this means information can be out of date by the time it reaches print.

The best sources of up-to-date information for servicing particular components are manufacturer's own instructions, and magazine articles. The owner's manual for a bike should have all the information you need, but these handbooks are sometimes sketchy and hard to follow. In all likelihood, the components on your bike are name brand, and if you go to a shop and ask nicely, they might let you photocopy the instructions which come in the box when the component is sold separately. By and large, these instructions are good, and I wish bike makers would simply copy them into their owners' manuals.

Cycling magazines regularly carry well-illustrated maintenance articles covering current equipment, and most are very good. If you have access to a library, or can do a little research on magazine web sites, then some photocopying or selective purchase of back issues might be very productive.

By way of repair manuals, apart from very expensive workshop handbooks such as *Barnett's Manual* by John Barnett (VeloPress), there is nothing available that is comprehensive or inclusive of the very latest in gear, such as hydraulic disc brakes or electronic gear shifters. However, if you have a reasonably standard bike, or can cover the esoteric bits with manufacturer's instructions, then a proper manual can be very useful.

I quite like *Zinn and the Art of Mountain Bike Maintenance* by Lennard Zinn (VeloPress). This is an enjoyable read, and the instructions have a good level of detail. Zinn has another book out on road bikes which I haven't purchased yet, but it should be just as good. If you like color photos, then my *Bicycle Repair Manual* with Richard Grant (Dorling Kindersley) is a reasonably priced very basic guide to maintenance.

Another route is to go to school. Courses in bike maintenance are given by advocacy groups, riding schools, bike shops, and others. Most are directed towards beginners. If you want to go further, courses leading to accreditation as a bike mechanic are run by the Barnett Institute and CABDA. See Chapter 20, Working in Cycling, for more information.

TOOLS

You do not need many tools to work on a bicycle, but a number of them are specialized, and all should be of good quality. Studiously avoid the low class, cheap tools sold by supermarkets, chain stores, and even some bicycle shops that ought to know better. Cheap tools – often presented in collections sold on the basis of "Look how much you get for only $XX!"– are a false economy, for they are apt to bend or break under stress, or to fit poorly and thus risk causing damage. Quality tools which fit and work properly are a better long term value, because they last. Workshop tools for maintenance and servicing should be robust and strong; those you carry on the bike for ride repairs can be lighter in weight.

Multi-tools

A compact multi-tool is often sufficient for carrying on the bike, but before spending your money, check that all the parts of the tool work on your bicycle. That 4 mm hex (Allen) key so cleverly worked into the main body of a multi-tool – is it long enough to reach all the bolts on your bike? Does the tool give you enough leverage to actually turn the bolts?

A useful multi-tool, both on the road and in the workshop, is a fold-up hex wrench with 3, 4, 5, and 6 mm hex keys, and Phillips and straight blade (+/– for short) screwdrivers. Park Tools do a nice one, compact and good in the hand, with 4, 5, and 6 mm hex keys and +/– screwdrivers, and another all hex key model with 1.5, 2, 3, 4, 5, and 6 mm sizes. Minoura does several models of varying complexity, I like their basic Handy-10, with 2, 3, 4, 5, and 6 mm hex keys, +/– screwdrivers, and 8, 9, and 10 mm box wrenches.

You need a chain tool as part of your ride kit, and since good workshop models are large and strong, many people opt for a multi-tool which includes this function. The chain tool bit will usually be fiddly to use, but will serve in a pinch.

In more comprehensive multi-tools for the road or trail, the Minoura Handy Pocket-14 features 2, 3, 4, 5, and 6 mm hex keys, +/– screwdrivers, a chain tool, 8, 9, and 10 mm wrenches, with doubles of the 8 and 10 mm sizes, which is very useful. Particularly lightweight and compact is the alloy Ritchey CPR-13, with 3, 4, 5, 6, and 8 mm hex keys, +/− screwdrivers, 8, 9, and 10 mm box wrenches, a chain tool, 14/15 gauge spoke keys, and a bottle opener. The original multi-tool, the Cool Tool, is somewhat heavy but includes an adjustable wrench, tire lever, chain breaker, +/− screwdrivers, 4, 5, 6, 8, and 10 mm hex keys, and 14/15 gauge spoke keys, and works well. The Topeak Alien is a neat, complex affair with 2, 2.5, 3, 4, 5, 6, and 8 mm Allen keys, 8, 9, and 10 mm box wrenches, +/− screwdrivers, chain tool, and 14/15 gauge spoke keys, plus 2 tire levers, a knife, and a bottle opener. A similar collection of goodies is housed within the Park Micro Tool Box. I've never used the more intricate multi-tools because frankly, they are rather expensive, and in any case my preference is for simple models, augmented with a few select, purpose specific tools.

Workshop Tools

On workshop tools, you're in luck, because high class bicycle tools are produced by a number of firms. Good brands are Park, Wrench Force, and Var. Shimano do some nice tools, and then of course there's Campagnolo, famous for elite tools of truly esteemed quality. Both Park and Wrench Force produce complete kits, at various levels ranging from basic to "race mechanic", and these can be good value.

The number of tools you need depends on your ambitions. If you intend to stick to adjusting and replacing cables and brake blocks, then you will not need tools such as a crank puller. My list is more or less graduated from essential through to being able to do most things on a bike, in a pleasant and efficient manner. To this end, purpose-specific tools are invariably best, but I've also tried to indicate alternatives. Keep in mind that your bike will have particular requirements; for example, if it has a threadless headset, you won't need headset wrenches.

- **Air pump.** Best by a million miles is a floor pump.
- **Tire levers, plastic.** These are light and smooth, which helps reduce the risk of pinching and puncturing a tube.
- **Tube patches, glue, sandpaper, and chalk (or talcum powder).** Glueless patches will do for quick field repairs, but are not as strong. For your ride kit you should also have some material for temporarily patching cut or torn tire casings. A great item for this is a bit of FedX or other courier envelope; very light, and amazingly tough.
- **Screwdrivers:** straight blade 1/4 inch tip, 4 to 5 inch shank, and 1/8 inch tip, 2 to 3 inch shank; Phillips (X-tip) 2 to 3 inch shank. A long shank (6 to 8 or even 10 inches) Phillips is useful when adjusting derailleurs.
- **Set of metric open/box (ring) wrenches, 7, 8, 9, 10, 13, 14, 15, and 17 mm sizes.** Two very useful things to have are a long (10 inches or so) 10 mm box wrench for extra leverage, and a compact 10 mm box wrench with a slim box for slipping into tight places.
- **Set of hex (Allen) keys, 2.5, 3, 4, 5, 6, and 8 mm sizes.** Handiest by far are the ball end type. Extras of the 4, 5, and 6 mm sizes are sure to be useful.
- **Cable cutters/wire snips.** A truly essential tool for neatly cutting cable wires and housings. Pliers will make a mangled mess. Good models are Park, Wrench Force, and Shimano.

Cable cutters

- **8 inch- or 6 inch-adjustable end wrench.** It can be nice to have a small 4 inch one as well.
- **Pliers,** regular square end and needle nose.
- **Spoke key,** sized to the spoke nipples on your wheels.
- **Chain tool.** You can clean a chain without removing it from the bike, but if it ever breaks, a chain tool (and a couple of spare links) will be salvation. The Cyclo is an old standby, but the Park Chain Brute features a clever loop which permits inserting another tool for use as a lever.
- **Third hand tool,** for calliper brakes.
- **Pedal wrench, 15 mm.**
- **Thin hub cone wrenches, 13 x 14 mm and 15 x 16 mm.**
- **Headset wrenches, sized to your headset.** Not needed if yours is the threadless type.
- **Crank remover.** These range from compact models used in conjunction with a wrench, to self-contained models with a handle. A thin 14 mm socket can be used to tighten/loosen crankarm bolts, but check fit. Note that some crankarm bolts have a 8 mm hex key fitting.
- **Freewheel cassette cog lockring tool and chain whip.** You might have a now comparatively rare (at least on better bikes) thread on freewheel, in which case you will need a freewheel remover as per brand of freewheel, and a second chain whip.
- **Bottom bracket lock ring wrench and pin wrench, or if the unit is the cartridge type, splined tool as per brand of cartridge.**
- **Special tools as needed for your bike.** If you have suspension, you may need a small air pump/gauge as per the specific suspension component.
- **Stand or other means to hold the bike.** This will make a big difference to the comfort and speed with which you can work on a bike. A proper free standing workstand where you can walk around the bike is definitely best, but the better ones are darned expensive. This is the sort of item two or more people could share, at great benefit.

Park does an excellent stand which is rock steady, but folds as soon as you pick it up. Kestrel do a small tripod stand which holds a bike up the rear stays, allowing gear adjustments and removal of the rear wheel. They've also got a model which clamps into a workbench such as the B & D Workmate. Another alternative is a model which mounts to a wall, and folds down when not in use.

You might be able to knock something together. A bike can be lofted into the air using a couple of hooks on the handlebars and saddle, via rope running through pulleys attached to the ceiling or an overhead beam, and held with cam cleats or wrapped around a couple of nails. If you do this with a plaster ceiling, be sure that the pulleys or blocks are secured to a joist or other strong support, or else the whole thing may fall on your head. If you are working outside and there are a couple of handy trees or other supports, you can rig up a hoist on a beam. A hoist system can be supplemented with an arm to help hold the bike still. It does not have to be too fancy, a couple of screw-eyes and some elastic cord will do. Again, particulars will depend on your situation.

A self-contained, portable stand is far and away easiest and best, and if you go this route, check that the jaws will fit the tubing or other materials from which your bike is made. Never whomp the jaws down on the frame tubes with great force, as this could dent a tube. If the fit is not comfortable, use the seat post.

- **A bench vise** for holding small parts while you work on them, and for applying serious compression force or leverage when required. A small model will do.
- **Hammer.** Ballpeen is the usual sort. When a soft hammer is required, it is usually possible to use a block of wood or other material to prevent marring of surfaces.
- **Metal files.** It's useful to have a big one for shaping, and a couple of small ones for fiddly bits.
- **Hacksaw,** fine blade, and sharp knife.
- **Abrasive paper, fine,** and/or steel wool.
- **Channel lock pliers or vise grips** are perennial

favorites as all round problem solvers.

- **Set of metric sockets,** with a ratchet handle and various extension bars. Can be pleasing for speed.

From time to time you will need: electrician's tape, Zip ties in assorted sizes, cable wire caps, cable housing ferrules, and assorted nuts and bolts. And a good supply of rags.

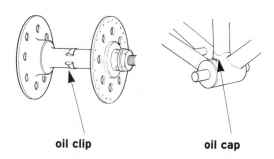

oil clip   **oil cap**

LUBRICATION

Two forms of lubricant are used for bikes: liquid and grease. Liquid is used for the chain, freewheel, derailleurs, brake pivot bolts, and gear changer mechanisms (B). (See below.) Grease is used for bearings at the headset, bottom bracket, wheels, pedals, and freewheel (A). Some freewheels and internal gear hubs use fluid; others use grease.

Some bearings use both grease and fluid, in particular, multi-speed hubs, and old-fashioned ultra-fancy racing bike hubs. You can tell these by the fact that the hub has a small cap or clip that seals a small hole. (Opposite column.) These need lubricating once a month: multi-speed internal

gear hubs a tablespoonful, regular hubs about half a teaspoonful, and coaster brake hubs 2 tablespoonfuls. Some bottom brackets are set up to use fluid as well as grease. A teaspoonful once a month. Use fluid wherever you find caps or clips. Too little is better than too much. If fluid leaks out of the sides of the bearings and dribbles all over your crankset or wheels, you are using too much.

Another variation you might encounter is a component with a grease gun nipple fitting. The thinking here is, rather than cleaning the part, a grease gun is used to inject fresh grease under pressure, displacing the old grease along with any dirt or water. It's very effective if done regularly.

The two basic types of lubricants are petrole-

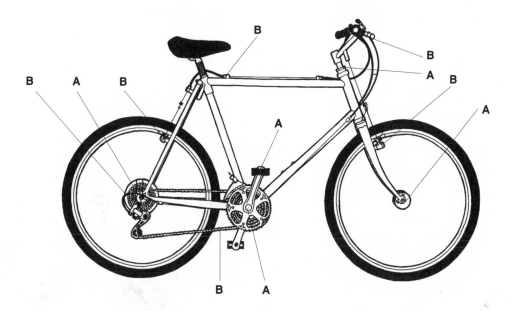

um-based (oil), and synthetic. Oil is a very good lubricant, but it has poor resistance to washing away by water, and attracts dirt, which is abrasive and accelerates wear. This means frequent thorough cleaning and lubricating of components, which is messy and time consuming. Synthetic lubricants perform as well or better, and are cleaner. This reduces wear and makes servicing easier. For a practical example, if you use oil for the chain, then once a month you should break it apart and remove it from the bike, soak and wash it clean in a solvent, dry it thoroughly with a heat gun or in an oven, oil it, and then remount it. If you use a synthetic lubricant, you need to clean the chain only every three to four months, and can do so without removing it from the bike. Indeed, if you ride in clean conditions and lubricate and wipe the chain regularly, you need never clean it.

A further advantage of synthetic lubricants is that there are a number of different kinds, each tailored to specific riding conditions. For example, wax lubricants go on wet, but set up dry, so that they are clean to the touch and attract the minimum amount of dirt. They are not durable, nor do they have much resistance to water, so fre-

quent application is required – but this is easy to do, as there is no mess to clean up. All you need to do is add more, wipe away any excess, and go back to the races. Wax lubricants are good for commuting and folding bikes.

Dry lubricants, like wax ones, go on wet but then become dry. These are middle-of-the-road in terms of lubricating power and durability, and will cover most kinds of riding conditions. Wet lubricants stay wet, and are formulated for durability, performance under stress, and resistance to washing away by water. They are good for machines such as off-road mountain bikes.

In oil-based greases, ordinary grease from a motorist's shop will work well enough, but lithium greases are less likely to be washed away by water. Campagnolo grease is quite expensive and while no one is quite sure if the stuff is truly superior, it is popular for use with very fine components. Lithium greases are typically lightweight and run freely, and are fine for racing, when maintenance is pretty well continuous. Ordinary riding is another story.

When lubricated with a lightweight oil-based grease, components with bearings are usually disassembled, cleaned thoroughly in solvent, packed with grease, and reassembled, every six months. With a good water- and dirt-resistant synthetic grease, the job can be left for up to three years if the bike is in moderate service (2,000 miles a year or less). High mileage bikes (5,000+ miles a year), bikes with heavy or hard riders, and bikes used regularly in wet, dirty conditions will need servicing annually. Note: these figures are advisory; any bearing which runs rough or tight needs immediate attention.

Petroleum oils and greases are cheap, readily available, and effective. You can probably find all you need for free in the rubbish at a gas station. Be sure to use a good quality motorists oil, SAE 30 is fine, although for the chain you can go up to SAE 90 with great results if you first heat the chain, so that the oil penetrates inside the rollers. The chain will then virtually shoot around by itself – until it becomes dirty and needs cleaning again.

Another approach is to split the difference, and use oil-based grease for the bearings, and a synthetic lubricant, preferably dry, for the lighter bits. Dry lubricants come in spray or liquid form and contain an exotic and sometimes secret blend of ingredients. You must lubricate more often – in regular service, weekly would not hurt, and as well, after any hard ride or thorough soaking – but with a spray applicator this job takes only a few seconds. So far as I know, all bike lubricant aerosols are air powered and do no harm to the environment. If you abhor waste, use the liquid form, which can be applied more precisely (and also fits more conveniently in a toolbox).

One excellent dry lubricant I've used for years is called Superspray. It has a high load tolerance and good resistance to abrasion and wear. It's not fond of water, but is easy to renew. I like it for convenience, and for the fact that it does not appear to have trouble mixing with other lubricants. This is useful when working on other peoples' bikes. I've also had good results with Tri-Flo products, which include both a waterproof grease and a general spray lubricant. Watch compatibility, though.

When I set up a bike for myself, I rationalize on one type and make of grease and liquid lubricant. This way, if I should ever mix the two types, no harm will be done. Two I've used a lot, with excellent results, are Pedros and Finish Line. Both offer complete ranges of products, including greases, cleaners and polishes, and several types of liquid lubricants so that you can set up a bike to your particular liking. I've also had excellent results with Phil Wood waterproof grease.

As a simple rule of thumb, mountain bikes headed for muddy boondocks should load for bear by using heavy duty wet lubricants such as Pedros Syn Lube ATB or Finish Line Cross-country; road racers will want to opt for lighter lubes such as Pedros Syn Lube Road or Finish Line Teflon Bicycle Lubricant; and folks in dry climates or who are happy to renew the lube when necessary, can have clean bikes by using Pedros Extra Dry, or better, Pedros Ice Wax or Finish Line KryTech Wax.

Some synthetic lubricants do not mix well with petroleum-based oil or grease. If you use a synthetic lubricant on a chain, best results will be obtained if you first clean off the old grease and grunge. This applies also to new chains, which come from the factory packed in grease.

Grip Shift gear changers require a special, silicon-based grease. Other greases, petroleum or synthetic, will gum up the works and may even damage plastic parts. A number of suspension forks also require silicon grease.

Never use ordinary household oils on any part of a bike, especially not inside hub gears, as these products often leave behind a sticky residue which can gum up the works like you wouldn't believe.

If you activate an old, petroleum lube era bike that has been out of use and resting for some time, be aware that because oil evaporates, the insides of the bike may be dry as a bone. Be sure to lubricate the bike before using it.

I read an enthusiastic review in *Bicycling Magazine* about a new product called ProLink Chain Lube, which will flush away all of the old sludge, grease, and dirt on a chain, and thereafter, lubricate and protect the chain, staying aboard and functioning despite repeated dirty rides and washings with water and even solvents such as Simple Green. If this is true, the reviewer's words "magic stuff" are apt. You might want to check it out:

Pro Gold Products.
Tel: 800-421-5823.
Web: www.progoldmfr.com.

GENERAL WORDS

There are a number of things to keep in mind when servicing bikes.

1. Do not use a great deal of force when assembling or disassembling parts. Bicycle components are frequently made of alloys for light weight. These are not as strong as steel and it is not hard to strip threads or damage parts. Always be sure that things fit. Be careful and delicate. Snug down bolts, nuts, and screws firmly, not with all your might.

2. Most parts tighten clockwise and come apart turning counter-clockwise. This is called a right hand thread. A left hand thread tightens counter-clockwise and loosens clockwise. Left hand threads are not often used. The left (port) side pedal and the right side bottom bracket cup and locknut are usually left hand threads.

3. When fitting together threaded parts hold them as perfectly aligned as you can, and turn one backwards (loosen) until you hear and feel a slight click. Then reverse and tighten. If this is new to you, practice on a nut and bolt until you have the feel of it perfectly. If you should cross thread a bolt, do not proceed regardless; it may not have a safe grip. Take the bike/component to a shop and have the thread cleaned or re-cut.

4. If you get stuck with a rust frozen bolt or nut, soak it in penetrating oil, give it a few taps to help the oil work in, and then try to undo it again with a tool that fits exactly. If this fails try a cold chisel and hammer. Go at this carefully since if you slip you may gouge a chunk out of your bicycle. If this method fails, hacksaw or file the nut or bolt off, or drill it out.

5. Be neat and organized when working on a bike. Lay parts out in the order in which they came apart or go together. Put tiny parts in boxes or jars. You might have to break for a meal or a visit to the shop, the cat might scatter your ball bearings, you might suddenly be involved in a rescue mission – anything could, and often does, happen. If the job is organized and secure at all times, you'll more easily be able to move with the flow of events.

6. Schedule your work. If your bike is in good shape, most jobs should be fairly predictable in length. Light tune-ups should be quick and efficient. I like to spread out bigger jobs, doing the wheels and hub bearings one time, the headset another, and so on. This helps preserve the sanctity of hammock time.

On bikes which have not been tended to for awhile, allow extra time, as there will be a tendency for one thing to lead to another. A simple brake shoe adjustment, for example, may see you overhauling the brake mechanism and installing a new cable. When someone asks me to "have a look" and the bike is likely far gone, I allow two hours.

7. There are a number of little nuts and bolts on your bike for racks, brake lever mounts, gear shift lever mounts, water bottle cages, and the like. These tend to get loose and need to be checked about once a month. One way to meet this problem is to let the nuts and bolts bed in first, e.g. ride the bike for a while, and then fix them in place with a product such as Loctite or Finish Line Threadlocker.

On the other side, there are some bolts, such as crank arm bolts, which you need to be sure can be undone. For these, a coating of grease will help prevent seizing or cold welding, and probably even better is a product such as Finish Line Ti-Prep Anti-Seize.

8. Solvents. Although gasoline is to be found sloshing around at a zillion gas stations and works a treat as a solvent and cleaner, no one will ever tell you to use it. The reason is that every once in a while someone gets blown to kingdom come. The gasoline itself is not so bad, but the vapor it gives off is very volatile. It is heavier than air, so it settles and pools on the ground, where it can then seep along to some unexpected spot to meet a careless match or appliance pilot light – Ka-Boom! A gallon of gasoline has about the same amount of energy as a stick of dynamite, and is much easier to detonate. It happens fairly often.

Kerosene can be used as a solvent, but it contains water. On a part that you can clean and wipe dry with a rag, no problem. A component such as a chain with lots of tiny bits is likely to be damaged, however, unless it is dried out in an oven or with a heat gun.

Easiest and kindest by far are citrus based degreasers, which are available from all of the lubricant manufacturers, work just fine, and are environmentally friendly.

9. Last, but by no means least, do not be afraid! The idea of mechanical things is that they go together and come apart. A feeling that something is delicate and might break if you mess with it is a symptom of uncertainty. Be neither brutish nor ineffectual. Get with it, get greasy, and stay with it until you know you've got it together.

SERVICING BEARINGS

Your bicycle has upwards of 200 ball bearings held in place by cups and cones, or contained within cartridges. The cone remains stationary while the cup, and whatever part is attached to it – in this example it would be a wheel – rides on the ball bearings and spins around. The distance between the cone and the cup is adjustable and must not be too tight (bind/grind) nor too loose (play/rattle).

dirt and water, and designed for the minimum of servicing, if any; often, they are simply replaced. This can backfire: although cartridge bearings are resistant to dirt and water, there is no such thing as a perfect seal, and – especially in these days of muddy off-road rides and cleaning with high pressure jet sprays – they can become contaminated. (If you use a jet spray, don't direct it at bearing seals.) Replacing a cartridge bearing usually calls for special tools, and there are too many different types and procedures to cover here.

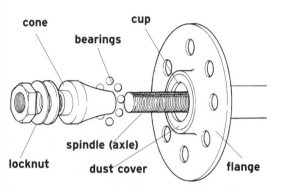

Cup and cone hub bearing

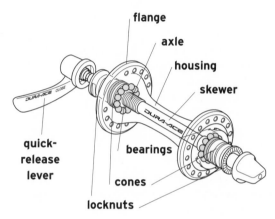

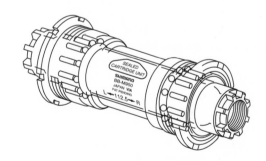

Sealed cartridge bearing

Sometimes the ball bearings are held in a clip called a race. Typically, this is positioned so that the balls are against the cup. Another type of bearing is a sealed unit known as a cassette or cartridge. These are held in place in various ways: press fit, glue, and with bearing retainers that serve the same function as a cone.

Cartridge bearings are usually sealed against

Standard Ball Bearings and Cone

A pedal is a good item to start with, because it is easy to handle. Work over newspaper or rag to catch any errant parts or ball bearings. Remove

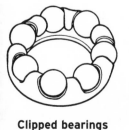

Clipped bearings

Cartridge bearings

dustcap A. Hold cone C still with a wrench, and undo locknut B. Use one hand to hold axle and pedal together and remove locknut and cone. Collect outer bearings, count, and place in jar. Withdraw axle, collect, count, and separately jar inner bearings. Keep apart, they may be different. Clean everything up, including inside of pedal. Check ball bearings for pitting, cracks, disorderly thoughts; cups and cones for uneven wear, pitting; axle for straightness.

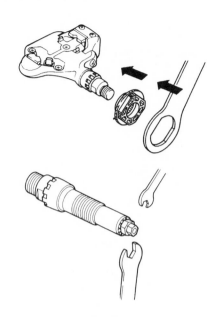

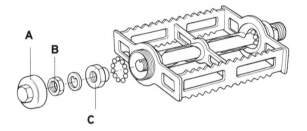

Clean hands. Pack grease into cups. Not too much, not too little. You want a line of grease sufficient for the bearings to nest in. Tip: obtain a wide bore syringe from a chemist. Toss away the needle, fill with grease, and you have a precision, dirt free grease gun. Hold pedal inner cup up, push bearings into inner cup (grease will hold), slide on axle, and hold in place. Turn pedal 180° and push outer bearings into cup. With a stiff grease, all the bearings can be placed before inserting the axle, this is a little less fiddly. Screw cone home and back off 1/4 turn. Secure with locknut. Check adjustment, replace dust cover. Coat pedal threads with a little grease before attaching to cranks.

A typical one-sided pedal needs a special tool to remove the lock bolt. (Opposite column.) Note: on the right pedal, the lock bolt has a left hand thread, and on the left pedal, a right hand thread. Once the axle unit is out, adjust bearings via a cone and locknut just like the old Lloytard, above. Be advised: if you take it apart for full servicing and it has loose ball bearings, getting it back together will be quite fiddly.

Bearing Adjustments

Bearing adjustments are a matter of measurement, feel, and circumstances. For example, when adjusting the bearings on a quick release hub, allowance must be made for the fact that when mounting the wheel onto the bike, closing the lever will also tighten the bearings. So will the final tightening of any bearing. It's always a good idea to check adjustment after all parts are in place. Generally, new bearings are set up tight, to allow for wear as they bed in. Bearings that are already broken in should be carefully set to the correct tolerance; too tight a setting risks damage. Basically, bearings should be adjusted as precisely as possible while still running smoothly. If, to attain this state the bearing adjustment has to be so wide that there is pronounced side to side play then something is wrong – there's dirt inside, the wrong number of bearings, damaged surfaces, or some other problem. Have a look and see!

CLEANING AND POLISHING

Keep your bike indoors. If it is left outside, or in a damp, open shed, condensation will cause rust

Use wax or polish to preserve the paint and make cleaning the bike easier. Bicycle polishes are OK for a finish in good condition to start with, but my personal preference is for a good quality car paste wax. Many top bike shops use ordinary furniture polish for bikes – it goes on quickly, and seems to do the job. Do not wax wheel rims; clean them with fine steel wool.

Wipe the bike clean once a week. If it needs a wash, ordinary soap (not detergent) and water will do, or you can use a product such as Finish Line Bike Wash, which works up a satisfying lather and leaves behind various anti-oxidants. A high pressure hose can be used to clean a very dirty machine, such as a mud encrusted mountain bike, but keep the spray away from the bearing seals, and be sure to lubricate the bike at once.

If I come in wet from a ride, I generally wipe down the bike, as this is an easy clean. If the bike has had a real soaking and you are putting it away for awhile, first ride it for a mile or two (or put it on a work stand and spin the various parts) to help drive water out of the bearings and other bits.

Out in Wales, after a day of riding we would pay local kids to ride our bikes through the river. We'd then lube them up and let the kids ride some more, before putting the machines away, appropriately enough, in an old stable.

RIDE CHECK

Before you whistle off on any bike, give it a quick once over. Make this a habit. You'll soon develop what is almost a sixth sense for when a bike might have a surprise for you.

- Check brake lever travel and that pads meet rim or disc accurately. Check that brake mechanisms and pads are firmly mounted. Apply front brake and push bike back and forth; clicking may indicate a loose headset or brake mechanism.
- Check tire pressure and examine casings for cuts or bruises. Spin wheels and check rims for truth. Check spokes for tightness. Check

wheels are firmly mounted and wheel hubs for play.
- Press test pedals and cranks for tightness, bottom bracket for play, chainrings for tightness.
- Check chain is lubed and moves easily.
- Check cables and housing have no damage.
- Check handlebars, stem, and saddle are snug.
- As you ride out, check that gears are shifting OK, and double check that brakes are OK.
- Go!

WHEEL REMOVE/INSTALL

With calliper brakes it is necessary to provide some slack so that the tire will clear the brake pads. Use one hand to compress the brake pads against the rim, and with the other, detach the cable guide tube (V-brake) or straddle wire (cantilever).

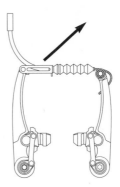

V-brake

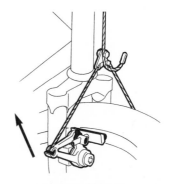

Cantilever brake

Quality side pull brakes have a built-in release mechanism. With hydraulic brakes it is usually possible to remove the shoe.

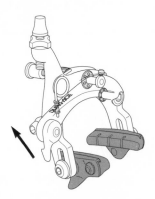

Side pull brake

Front Wheel

The wheel will be held by hex nuts, wing nuts, or a quick release (Q/R) lever:

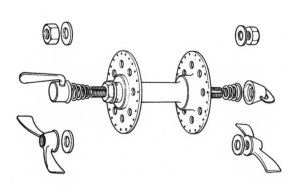

• Remove

Nuts: Undo both simultaneously (counterclockwise) and unwind a few turns.

Q/R: pull open the lever, hold the nut on the opposite side, and use the lever as a handle to unwind a few turns. This is necessary in order to clear the wheel retention tabs on the drop outs.

• Install

Nuts: Washers go outside drop outs. Slip axle onto drop outs and set nuts finger tight. Check that rim is centered between fork arms before tightening nuts firmly.

Q/R: slip axle onto drop outs, ensure lever is open position, hold nut with one hand and use other to wind lever down a little short of finger tight. Check that wheel is centered in fork arms. Close lever so that it points upward or to rear of bike. Use only firm force, not all your strength; too hard could put the bearings out of adjustment.

Rear Wheel

• Remove

Hub Gear: Shift to high gear, disconnect shift cable (sleeve A and locknut B). Undo nuts, note washers go outside drop outs.

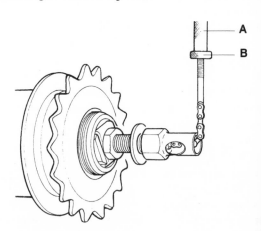

Derailleur Gear: run chain to smallest cog. Undo nuts or Q/R lever as for front wheel, hold back derailleur arm, and push wheel down and out.

• Install

Hub Gear: Work axle into drop outs, slipping chain over sprocket. Set nuts finger tight and pull back wheel so chain has half-inch up and down play. Check that this spacing remains the same through a full rotation of the chainring. If there is variation, fiddle best possible compromise. Center rim between chain stays and tighten nuts. Check chain tension again, reattach shift cable.

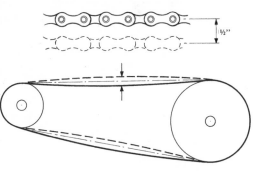

Q/R: ensure derailleur is in outer position, and Q/R lever is open. Partially insert wheel between stays and place chain on smallest cog. Continue inserting wheel, pulling back derailleur arm as you do so. Seat axle fully home in drop outs; rim should be centered between chain stays. Tighten nuts or Q/R as per front wheel.

TIRE PRESSURE

Tire pressure (psi) is important for performance, comfort, and durability. The recommended pressure for tires is often printed on the sidewall. Increase pressures for heavy riders/loads: for a 200 pound rider, 15–20 psi more with 40–70 psi tires, and 5–10 psi more with 90–120 psi tires.

Keep an eye on matters. Overinflation can blow a loose fitting tire off a rim. Hot weather over 80°F may require bleeding air from a tire to prevent overinflation. With wide mountain bike tires, pressure often is reduced in slippery conditions to improve traction. Again, careful: with too little psi, the casing can bang against the rim, pinching and puncturing the tube in a distinctive two hole pattern known as "snakebite." In the other direction, for road use mountain bike tires can be inflated hard for less rolling resistance, at cost of a stiff ride.

Ride with care for your tires. Most punctures are caused by picked up debris working into the casing as you ride. Keep an eye out for broken glass, etc., and if you go through some, stop and brush off the tire. Ruptures and tears can be caused by bashing into rocks or through sharp edged potholes. When you encounter such obstacles, lighten up in the saddle, or do a bunny hop.

• Pumping

Best is a proper track pump (with handles, that stands on the floor) with a built-in pressure gauge. Avoid gas station air pumps; despite a high psi, the volume of air in a bicycle tire is small, and overinflation can occur within a blink.

There are two kinds of tire valves, Schraeder, and Presta. On a Presta, undo the locknut A in order to add or remove air.

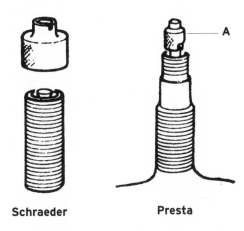

Schraeder   **Presta**

Remove dust cap. Schraeder: screw the hose onto the valve. Some pumps go directly on the valve and lock in place with a lever. Presta: undo locknut A, push pump on valve, and if there is no hose, hold the pump perpendicular to the valve while you pump. When finished, disengage pump with a sharp downward knock of the hand; wiggling it off may bend the valve. Close locknut A.

TIRE CHANGE

• Remove

Remove wheel. Deflate tire and remove valve stem locknut, if you have one. Go all around the tire pinching the casing walls together and working the beads (edges) away from the rim. Both beads should be down in the rim well; if necessary, raise the seat of the valve clear of the beads.

If the tire is a loose fit, it should be possible to work one bead over the rim with your hands. If not, use a tire lever, taking care not to pinch the tube when you insert it. If the tire is a tight fit, you will need 2 or even 3 levers. Make sure the beads are right down in the rim well.

Close valve locknut and with tender regard for same, lift valve out through valve hole. Remove tube. It should now be easy to work the other bead over the rim side.

• Install

Note that some tire tread patterns have a direction of travel, usually marked on the sidewall. If there is psi information, you might want to put this near the valve hole. Work one bead over the rim side. Partially inflate tube to prevent pinching, place tube inside tire, and insert valve stem through valve hole, making sure it is straight.

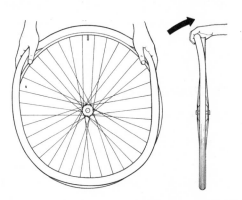

Deflate tube completely. Hold valve seat clear of rim and slip bead of tire over rim into well. Make sure it does not catch on the valve seat. Starting near you, go all around the tire pressing the bead over the rim with your thumbs, alternating hands between kneading the tire and maintaining a grip on progress so far. Eventually most of the tire will be on and your hands will be close together. Now decide the tire will go over, and give it the grand mal effort. It's a matter of feel and skill rather than strength, but a little talcum powder or a lick of spit can make the job easier. Sometimes it helps to reach over the tire.

If you have to use a tire lever, be very careful not to pinch the tube. When the tire is on, work it around with your hands and make sure it is even on all sides. Test inflate, and check again for even seating of the beads on the rim, and a straight valve stem.

Mending Punctures

Use patches, glue, and chalk. Glueless patches are convenient for field repairs, but are not as strong.

Remove tube from tire and note relative position of each; later, this will make locating the cause of the puncture easier. Inflate the tube and test the valve with a drop of spit. If valve is OK, locate puncture by sound, or by rotating the tube near your lips until you feel the stream of air. If necessary, immerse the tube in water and watch for bubbles. Mark puncture location, clean and dry tube, and then roughen an area around puncture larger than patch with sandpaper, or substitute. Clean hands, and apply a thin, even layer of glue over area. Set aside to dry until tacky – this is important, all the solvent must evaporate. Peel off the foil on the patch without touching the adhesive area exposed, and press it firmly on the puncture. Powder the chalk and sprinkle over cement around the patch.

Set tube aside to dry and meanwhile, check for cause of puncture. If the perforation was on the inside of the tube, it may have been caused by a protruding spoke. File spoke flush with nipple head. Check other spokes. If necessary, renew rim tape. Electrician's tape will do.

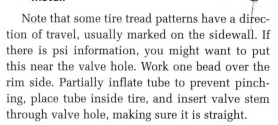

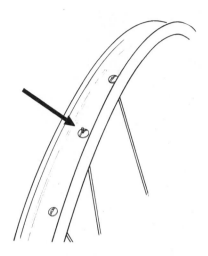

**File down protruding spokes flush
with nipple head**

If the puncture was near the rim edge, it may have been snakebite – the tire impacting against the rim and pinching the tube. Check for the other half of the bite, and in future use a little more air pressure or ride with less bang.

Slide a rag around inside the casing to feel for sharp objects. If you use your fingers, be careful. If nada, check the casing for a glass cut, this is a common cause of punctures. A small cut is no shakes, but a large cut or tear means a new tire.

For a get home repair, fit a reinforcing boot inside the casing to prevent the tube from blistering out. Best for this is a bit of FedX or other courier envelope, but a business card or money will do.

Back to the tube, remove the cellophane covering from the patch. Do not peel from side, the patch might lift, too. Compress the patch so the cellophane splits and peel from center. Install tube, pump up tire, put wheel back on bike, hook up brakes, and you're gone.

CABLES

Cable wires are used to control the brakes and gears, which are under spring tension – the brakes to open, the mechs to move over the smallest cog or

chainring. The cable wire, which pulls on the component to move it to a new position, is sheathed in a housing so that the cable run can be curved, and move with the handlebars. Cable wire length must be kept correct relative to the housing, and this is done via the barrel adjuster, which lengthens the cable housing, and the cable anchor bolt, which shortens the cable wire. Basically, you use the barrel adjuster for fine adjustments, and when it reaches the end of its travel, you screw it back home, reset the anchor bolt, and start over again.

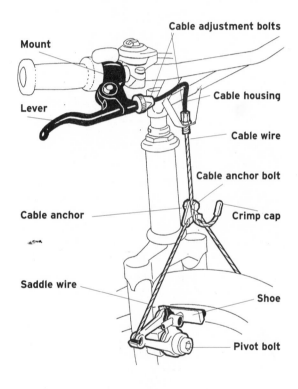

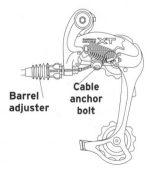

Cable barrel adjusters are usually next to the control lever, and depending on the type of components, at the brake or gear mech as well. Most are designed to be turned with the fingers, but some older types have a locknut which will need a wrench. Fiddle with yours until you know how they work.

The anchor bolt is usually on or near the component. One type has a hole in the shaft for the cable wire. Another type uses a slotted groove in a washer, or on the component itself, to pinch and hold the wire.

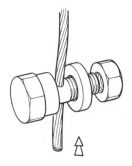

Adjustment

Screw barrel adjuster(s) home and reverse 1 turn. For brakes, secure the brake pads against the wheel rim. A third hand tool is good for this, but you can do it with string or elastic. Alternatively, slack off the brakes, as if removing the wheel.

For derailleurs, run chain to smallest cog (rear) or smallest chainring (front).

Use wrenches to undo the cable anchor bolt, and if it is the type with a hole in it, take care to hold the bolt still and turn only the nut, or else you may damage the wire. Move wire to new position, not too tight as you need a little clearance, and secure anchor bolt, using quite firm force. This is one part you don't want moving around.

Replacement

Maintain rather than repair wires and housings by replacing them before they break. For bikes in hard service this might be every 2 to 3 months, for average use bikes up to 2 years. Any obvious defect, such as a frayed wire or kinked housing, is immediate grounds for replacement.

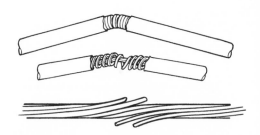

It is generally a good idea to replace both wire and housing, and to do the complete set; if one brake or mech wire has run its course, the other likely has, too. For a worthwhile upgrade that will in future spare having to replace the housing, consider using Nokon Trac-Pearls (see chapter 9 Accessories for more information). In any case, when securing replacements, take your bike or old cable to the store, as cables come in different shapes, lengths, and thicknesses. Indexed gears need special cables.

For cutting wires and housing it is essential to use proper wire cutters (see Tools). To prevent wire ends from fraying, use crimp caps, solder, or glue.

• Brakes

Screw home barrel adjuster. Release brake cable as for wheel removal. Undo cable anchor bolt and slide off wire, or pull wire out; if the end is frayed, use wire cutters (not pliers) to make a clean cut.

Slide housing off cable, or wire out of housing. If there are ferrules – little caps on the ends of the housing – keep track of where they go. Ditto any little donuts, these are used on bare wire sections to prevent the wire from marring the bike's finish.

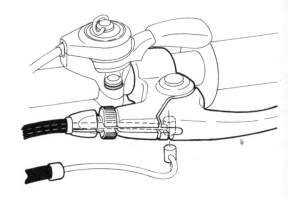

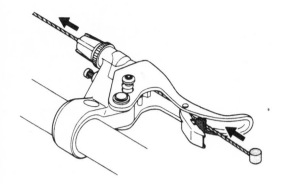

Depress brake lever. In most cases the wire can be disconnected by sliding it through a slot. If not, simply thread the cable back out of the brake lever.

Using the old housing as a guide, cut the new housing to size. Again, use proper wire cutters, or else there will be a squashed mess. Clean up any burrs with a file. Use a nail at the end to prick open the Teflon liner. If there is no liner, grease or otherwise lube the cable wire; if there is a liner, do not lube, as it is likely to gum up the works.

Thread wire through brake lever and/or brake lever mount. Place ferrules on housing as required and thread in cable wire. If it is sticky, try rotating it as you go, and do it in the right direction, or else it may unravel and really get stuck.

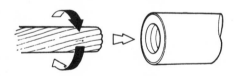

If you have more than one length of housing (likely with a rear brake), be sure to include any donuts or sheaths that are meant to be there. Once wire and housing(s) are united, connect wire to brake lever, if you've not already done so. Check that everything is firmly nested in place. Attach cable wire to cable anchor bolt, place a crimp cap on the end to prevent fraying, and proceed as per Adjustment, above. For a fine touch, compress the brake lever hard several times to stretch the wire, and adjust again.

• Derailleurs

Run the chain to the smallest cog (rear) or chainring (front). Screw home barrel adjuster(s) and reverse back out 1 turn. Undo cable anchor bolt. What happens next depends on the kind of shift lever. Sometimes the wire will slide out through the shift lever. Shimano XTR (post '96) have a plastic cover which must be removed. Line up slots in barrel adjuster and locknut and remove wire.

Reassembly is simply the reverse. After securing the wire to the anchor bolt, cap the wire end to prevent fraying.

A Grip Shift unit must be disassembled. Slide out handlebar grip. Undo screw A. Pull outer section away from main body until head of cable is exposed. Be careful not to lose the spring. Note how the cable is arranged; on some rear derailleur models, the cable loops around the housing tube; on others it is held by a 2.5 mm hex screw. Remove cable. It's sometimes easiest to cut it. Clean insides with rag and cotton swabs, and lubricate with non-lithium, Grip Shift approved grease.

Reassembly: thread cable wire through hole. Hex screw: feed wire directly through barrel adjuster. Replace hex screw. Non-hex screw: wire loops under and around housing tube, and then through a guide before exiting via barrel adjuster.

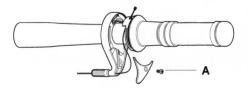

Rear shifters, line up highest gear number on grip with indicator marker. Front shifters, smallest number. Simultaneously slide grip and housing back together while pulling the cable snug. Check that cable is nested into track. Replace retention cover, and check that everything is OK by rotating grip and listening for clicks. If fine, thread cable through housing(s) and stops, being sure to include any necessary ferrules, donuts, or sheathing. Attach wire to cable anchor bolt, cap crimp wire end, and adjust mech.

•Hydraulic Systems

Hydraulic brake systems use fluid and are essentially the same as cable systems, except in reverse: pulling the lever compresses the fluid, creating pressure which operates the brake mechanism.

To maintain correct brake lever travel, there is a fluid volume adjusting screw – the equivalent of a cable barrel adjuster – usually located on the brake lever mount. When this screw has been used up, it is time to top up the system with fluid and/or adjust the brake pads. You'll need the manufacturer's instructions for this, as it is important to use the right kind of fluid, and avoid getting air into the system. Air will cause sponginess, and must be bled out; again, as per manufacturer's instructions.

BRAKES

With calliper rim brakes, before making brake shoe adjustments, check that the wheel rim is true by spinning it and seeing that the rim, not the tire, stays about the same distance from the brake shoe all the way around the wheel. If there is more than 3 mm of side to side or up and down play, the wheel should be trued before any brake adjustments are attempted. Check also that the wheel is reasonably centered between the fork arms or stays, and that the rim is free from major dents, scratches, and bulges. If the wheel does not center when mounted properly in the drop outs, take the bike to a shop to have the frame alignment checked, and if the rim is banged up beyond repair get a new one. Finally, check that the brake mechanism itself is properly mounted and adjusted (see below).

It will be helpful if you can obtain the manufacturer's instructions for your brakes. There are a lot of different kinds of brakes, and even within types – V-brakes, for example – adjustment tolerances and procedures vary from model to model.

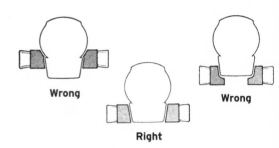

Wrong   Wrong

Right

In general, brake shoes must strike the rim squarely, with at least 1 mm of clearance between the top of the shoe and the tire. It is also important, especially with cantilever brakes, that the shoe strikes high enough so that there is no risk of it sliding underneath the rim. Test with a hard squeeze of the brake lever, because under heavy braking the shoe can compress slightly and extend its arc: if it rubs the tire the result will be damage and perhaps even a spectacular blow out; and if the shoe should slip underneath the rim and tangle in the spokes, both you and the bike may be wrecked. Brake shoes wear out steadily – some high performance models last for only a few hard rides, or one race – and can also be put out of adjustment by a chance knock; make a habit of checking them often.

Some shoes must be toed in so that the front leading edge of the shoe contacts the rim before the back of the shoe. Because of twist and play in the brake mechanism, under actual braking the shoe is flush with the rim. With old time side and center pull models, and cantilever brakes, the gap can be as large as 6 mm; try 3 mm and adjust as needed. (See below for instructions.) Stronger designs such as the V-brake should not need any toe in, but if need arises, try 1 mm to start.

Periodically inspect brake shoes and clean out any embedded grit or particles. If the shoes have become hardened or filled with very fine particles, clean them with block-mounted sandpaper. Or: simply insert sandpaper between shoe and rim, lightly apply brake, and rock wheel back and forth.

Brake Shoe Adjustment/Replacement

The kind of brake shoes you use have a big effect on braking performance. Shoes are available in various sizes and designs, and in a range of materials. There are models for all weather conditions, for optimum performance in wet conditions, racing, and so on. There are even dual compound models. Note that ceramic rims require special shoes. Nowadays, most original equipment brake shoes are quite good, and as well, some brake designs require the use of a specific brake shoe. However, the products of specialist brake shoe firms are excellent, at times even amazing, and quite honestly, this is an area where I would go along to the bike shop and ask: "Hey, what's good?"

• Side pull and Center pull

Loosen nut A, adjust brake shoe to meet rim, and tighten. You'll find that the brake shoe tends to twist slightly when you tighten the nut back down. Initially set the shoe askew, so that tightening the bolt brings it into perfect position. Do not use too much force; brake bolt threads sometimes strip easily.

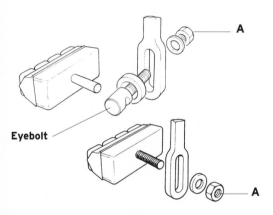

Eyebolt

A

A

With a quality side pull brake there should be no problem in adjusting the shoe to meet the rim properly. If there is, and a mild fix such as facing the shoe or fitting a bevelled washer (see below)

does not put matters right, take the bike along to a shop and see what they say.

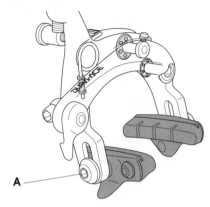

A

With a long arm side or center pull brake, if the shoe does not meet the rim properly, try reshaping it with a razor or block mounted sandpaper for a better fit, or find or make a tapered washer to tilt the shoe in the right direction. If neither of these does the trick, you can try bending the yoke with an adjustable end wrench. Caution: alloy fatigues easily. Slight, gentle bending is usually all right, but hard or protracted bending can make the alloy brittle and prone to break.

• Cantilever

Loosen nut A. The eyebolt usually has a hex fitting at C to help hold it still. Getting it all right may take some fiddling. If the !@§! thing has a tendency to slip, try roughening the parts with emery paper or a file. Some types, such as illustrated, have a bevelled washer to assist setting toe in. Loosen nut A and rotate B as required.

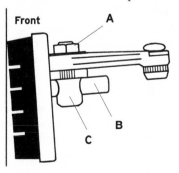

Front **A**

B

C

You'll notice that the brake shoe can be moved in and out and tilted up and down as well as rotated. Ha. You are now into territory that has sent some mechanics crying to their mothers, because several things have to be got right at once.

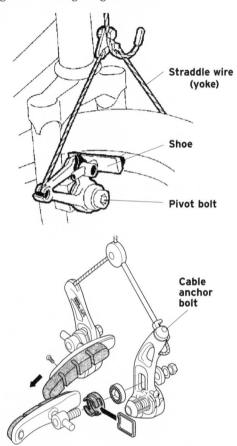

Straddle wire (yoke)

Shoe

Pivot bolt

Cable anchor bolt

First check straddle wire or yoke cable length. Ideally, when the brake is on, the straddle wire should form an angle of 90° with the brake arm. However, if it is the type with a cable anchor bolt at the end of the cable wire I advise keeping it at a fairly generous length. If it is short, and the anchor bolt unweighs, the straddle wire can catch on the tire – instant, absolute brakes. For this reason, as a safety, have 2 to 3 inches of cable wire protruding out of the cable anchor bolt. If it does slip, perhaps it will only move down the wire and stay clear of the tire. Keep your anchor bolts tight!

• V-Brake

There are two basic types of V-brakes: ordinary where the movement of the brake shoe describes an arc, and parallel-linked, where the shoe moves in a straight line. Each has particular servicing techniques. Most V-brakes have brake shoes with threaded posts, but a few models use shoes with unthreaded posts, and have different adjustment and servicing procedures.

•• Cable and Shoe Adjustment

Turn home barrel adjuster on the brake lever and reverse 1 turn.

Loosen cable anchor bolt CB and set distance A between the end of the cable guide/link and the cable anchor bolt to between 39 mm and 55 mm – the exact setting depends on the spec for your particular unit. There must be enough room for the yoke arms to travel, while keeping the shoes as close to the arms as possible. When the shoes contact the rim, the arms should be nearly parallel – about the same as a finger V-signal with your finger ends 1 cm apart. Do not make the setting too tight, or else as the shoes wear, the two arms may start to hit each other and render the brake ineffective or even useless.

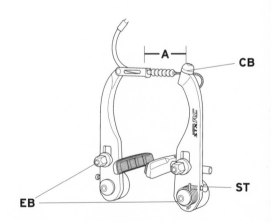

A

CB

ST

EB

Wrap string or tape around the yoke arms to keep them in position, and loosen the brake shoe eyebolts EB. Set the shoes against the rim, ensuring that there is at least 1 mm of clearance between the shoe and the top of the rim, and tighten eyebolts. No toe in should be required. Note: unthreaded brake shoe posts sometimes go out of adjustment no matter how carefully you tighten them. For a fix, try roughening the contact surfaces on the arms, posts, and washers with a file. Or try using an extra long wrench, just a touch viciously.

Use the cable barrel adjuster to set the brake shoes for 1 to 1.5 mm of clearance from the rim on either side. Check that the yoke arms operate in balance so that the shoes hit the rim at the same time. Adjust if necessary with the spring tension screws ST; clockwise to increase clearance, counter-clockwise to decrease. Finally, depress the brake lever hard several times to check that everything works OK.

• Parallel-link Models, Threaded Seat Posts

Hold the shoes against the rim and check that the distance A between the end of the cable-guide tube and the cable anchor bolt CB is 39mm or more.

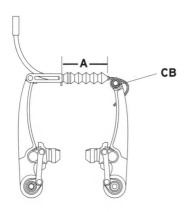

If it is not, wrap string or tape around the arms to hold them in position (if the arm return springs are the vertical type, flip them off their retention pins), and loosen bolt CB. Adjust the shoe offset (distance between shoe and brake-fixing link) as necessary to produce a distance A of 39 mm or more by changing over the 3 mm and 6 mm washers on the brake shoe eyebolt:

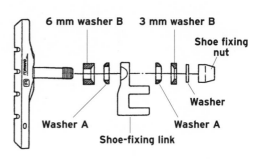

The convex (rounded out) washers go flat side against the shoe-fixing link, the different size concave (dished) fit over the convex washers. Position the washers in such a way as to allow angular adjustment of the shoe – that is, so that the shoe is flat against the side of the rim, with at least 1 mm of clearance between shoe and top of the rim.

Secure cable anchor bolt CB, free arms and re-hook return springs, and proceed as non-link unit.

• Replace Shoes

Removable shoes are held with a cotter pin which you remove with pliers. Slide out the old shoe and slide in the new, noting markings 'R' and 'L' for left and right, replace cotter pin and double check that shoe is secure.

One piece shoes, threaded, are easy: note how washers are positioned on the post, then undo the shoe fixing nut and remove old shoe. Placing the washers as they were before, install the new shoe.

Disassemble/Replace/Install Brake Unit

• Side Pull

Cheap side pulls mount to the frame via a pivot bolt; undo nut A to remove. Take apart by unhooking spring and undoing nuts B & C. Keep track of washers, all are needed. Clean bolt (polish with steel wool if corroded), grease, and reassemble. Turn nut B home, reverse one-quarter turn, and secure with locknut C. When mounting unit on bike, it may take several tries to get it centered over rim.

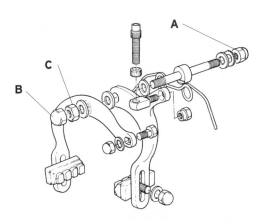

Quality side pulls also mount to the frame; undo hex bolt A to remove. Most models are double action, with two pivot bolts. Unhook spring, careful it's strong, and undo pivot bolts. Clean everything up, grease, and reassemble. Center unit over rim via adjusting screw S.

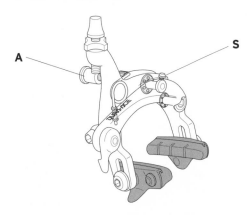

• Cantilever and V-brake

Disconnect cable anchor bolt (see above). Undo pivot bolt(s) (see previous illustrations) and before removing brake body, note the position of any washers, and which of three holes on the frame boss receives the stopper pin or spring protruding from the brake body. This washer business is important; some brake models have pivot cartridge bearings and the washers prevent binding.

Keep everything in order – right and left side springs are likely to be different – and clean the lot. Check that the bosses (also called spigots) are smooth, and if necessary, give them a polish with a mild abrasive or at most, a touch of fine steel wool. Some bosses are replaceable. Lubricate with waterproof grease and fit each brake unit, placing the stopper pin into original hole. Some folks use Loctite or thread adhesive to ensure that the mounting bolts stay in place. I prefer to check them regularly. Important: mounting bolts should be firm tight, not screwed down hard; overtightening can damage a boss.

If installing a new brake or set of springs, start with the center hole and if necessary, experiment to find the best position; the brakes should spring back easily, but operate without undue effort. A light setting is OK for a clean living road bike, a machine used off-road in winter mud and ice may need a strong spring return setting. Fine tune and balance units via the spring tension adjustment bolts.

• Disc Brakes

Disc brakes are a calliper design. As with rim brakes, brake lever travel is adjusted through the barrel adjuster and cable anchor bolt. Most units have a fixed pad which can be adjusted with a bolt. Set it near, but not rubbing on, the disc, Use the barrel adjuster/anchor bolt to position the other pad, and you should be away. Pads usually snap in and out. Note: NEVER press brake lever when wheel is removed.

• Hydraulic Brakes

A big advantage of hydraulic rim brakes is that they are simple. They mount to the boss via an adaptor, and remove via a quick-release lever. To replace a pad, pull off the old, and push on the new. For bleeding the system, obtain manufacturer's instructions. Note: NEVER press brake lever if any part of system is open.

DERAILLEURS (MECHS)

Place the bike on a work stand or hang it with the wheels clear of the ground so you can rotate the cranks. There are two basic adjustments: in and out travel of the mechs, and with indexed systems, centering the chain over the cogs (rear) and chainrings (front).

• Rear

Turn cranks and run mech back and forth across cogs, checking that jockey roller stays clear of cogs. To adjust, first loosen mounting bolt MB, then use screw at rear of mech, right behind the drop out, to change angle of mech.

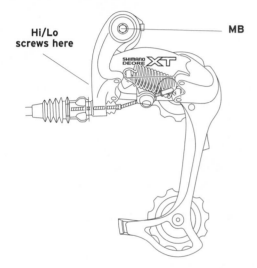

Hi/Lo screws here   MB

Shift chain to largest chainring and smallest cog. Turn the cable barrel adjuster(s) home, and if there is a lot of slack, take it up with the anchor bolt. Look on the mech for the high (outward) and low (inward) movement limit screws. They may be marked H and L, or cleverly disguised. To find, wiggle the mech around and see what it hits when moving outward and inward.

Turn the H screw so that when viewed from behind, the jockey wheel lines up with the small cog. Check that chain drops easily onto smallest cog when shifted. Adjust one-quarter turn at a time.

Shift chain to small front chainring and up to largest cog – gently, because if L limit screw is loose, mech could hit spokes. Set L screw so chain climbs easily onto largest cog, but is clear of wheel.

Indexed shifting is regulated by cable tension. Shift to large chainring/small cog, and then click

up one cog. If nothing happens, tighten the cable with the barrel adjuster until the chain moves up to the second cog. Tune until the chain whizzes back and forth between cogs with ease.

Shift to the middle chainring, and go through the same drill with the middle cogs, and again with the small chainring and largest cogs. Keep fiddling until you've got the best overall performance.

• Front

The unit shown has a braze on mounting bolt. Others use a band, or bottom bracket mounting. Whatever, use the mounting bolt to position the mech so that the bottom edge of the outer cage is 1-3 mm above the big chainring, and exactly parallel with it.

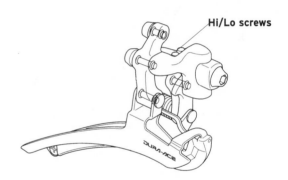

Hi/Lo screws

Ye front mech, too, has Hi/Lo limit screws, usually right on top of the unit. Create slack in the cable with barrel adjuster, run chain to largest rear cog. Shift back and forth between smallest and middle chainrings, twiddling Lo limit so chain settles happily on small ring without diving over it. Run chain to smallest rear sprocket, shift back and forth between middle and large rings, and you know what to do.

Place chain on small ring. If the cable has slack, take it up with the cable anchor bolt so that mech responds to shift lever, but leave enough play for easy action on the middle to small ring shift. Use barrel adjuster to fine tune.

Happy? Take the bike out for a ride, it will perform a little differently on the road or trail.

• Disassembly

The tension and jockey rollers have bushings; periodically remove, clean, and lube with light grease or chain lube. The mounting and cage pivot bolts should also be serviced, but have lotsa springs and tricky bits such as circlips, so proceed with caution.

CHAIN

• Lubrication

See section on lubrication for a run down on lubricants. Best by far is a synthetic dry or wet, and easiest method is simply to apply, work in to help float up grunge, and then wipe clean with a rag. Do this often and in most cases it will never be necessary to remove and clean the chain.

• Remove/Install

Chains need to be replaced every 500-2000 miles, depending on conditions of use. Do it sooner rather than later, as a worn chain will chew away at the rest of the transmission, and you'll have to replace the lot. A chain should measure exactly 12 inches from rivet edge to rivet edge. If it is more than 1/16 inch over, replace it. Bike shops have a special tool for measuring chains. A crude check is to lift the chain away from the chainring; if the chain clears the teeth, it is time for replacement.

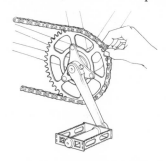

Hub gear bikes use a wide chain held with a master link. Pry it off with a screwdriver.

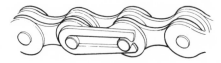

Derailleur gear bikes use narrow chain. Some types have a master link; check yours to see. All, however, can be broken and joined with a chain tool.

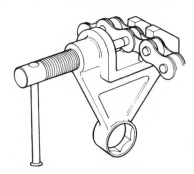

Place links over back teeth of a chain tool and drive out rivet. Be sure point of tool centers exactly on rivet and DO NOT drive it all the way out. Go only as far as outside plate. Stop often and check progress. Once rivet is near plate, free chain by twisting it. To replace the chain, reverse chain in tool, and again, be careful how far you go. Stop when the rivet is just proud of the far plate. The link will be tight. Free it by laying the chain in the spreader slot of the tool and giving the rivet a tweak – just 1/4 turn or less.

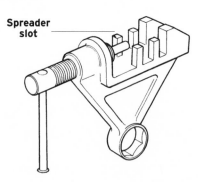

Spreader slot

Great Ideas #17 – Practice with some old chain first. It's an easy knack after a few times.

Shimano chains: you can break/join as described, but you are supposed to drive the rivet all the way out and then for joining, use a special Shimano (surprise!) sub-pin. Line up chain ends, insert sub-pin pointed end first, use chain tool to push until butt end is same as others, break off other end with pliers.

• Cleaning

Obtain a good biodegradable, non-toxic, citrus-based solvent, pour it into a jar and toss in the chain, and soak/shake until clean. If you use kerosene, be aware that it contains water, so to prevent rust the chain will have to be dried in an oven, or with a heat gun. Forget gasoline, although very effective, it is dangerous.

Another method which does not require removing the chain is to use a cleaner brush bath. This is a gimcrack with various brushes which fits over the chain. You fill it with solvent, then run the chain around until it is clean. It works, but then itself needs cleaning. I prefer the jar method, but if the idea of brush bath appeals, try it and see.

• Length

If you are installing an old chain, length will probably be OK. If not, or if it is a new chain and you do not have the old one as a guide, you want enough length so that with chain over large chainring and large cog, derailleur cage arm points straight down at ground. Check that when chain is on small ring/cog, mech does not bite itself, and if so, shorten the chain. In any case, you should not ever ride large ring to large cog. Save extra links in bike kit.

PEDALS

The right side pedal has a right hand thread and screws on clockwise; the left pedal has a left hand thread and screws on counter-clockwise. You'll need a 15 mm wrench, or for some units, a 6 mm hex key. Lightly grease axle threads before installing.

• Setting Up Clip-In Pedals

If your shoes have a pre-cut cover over the cleat area, cut outline with a knife and remove with pliers. Some shoes have pre-tapped holes, others need an adapter. For latter, lift shoe liner, and place backing plate inside shoe with threaded plate on top. Don't use waterproof sticker yet.

Grease cleat bolts and fasten cleats loosely. The instructions or an arrow will indicate which way

is forward. Position so that cleat centers across the ball of your foot (big bulge behind large toe/widest part of foot). If you are pigeon toed or splay footed, set rotational position accordingly. A.T.A.C. pedals do not need lateral or rotational adjustment.

Tighten bolts enough to hold cleats when stepping in or out of pedals, and go for a ride. Fine tune the cleat position so that the rotational adjustment is comfortable and your feet are as close as possible to the bike without bumping the cranks. When all is well, tighten bolts firmly, and if needed, apply a waterproof sticker underneath liner.

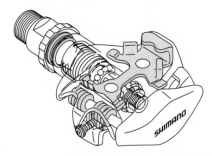

Tension adjustment screws are usually fore and aft on the pedal, and are usually 3 mm hex. Most click from setting to setting, and some have indicators. Set as you like, but make sure the screw stays in the plate. Most clip-in mechanisms are coated in grease. This is OK, but a chain lube may be better at keeping the works clear of dirt.

Pedals should be stripped, cleaned and lubed about once a year. See Servicing Bearings, above.

CRANKS

One piece cranks are part of the bottom bracket. Cottered cranks are held to the axle by a cotter pin; cotterless cranks by a 14 mm or 8 mm hex bolt.

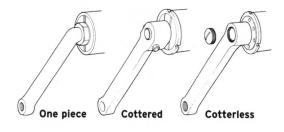

One piece   **Cottered**   **Cotterless**

Crank tightness check: with cranks level, press hard on both pedals, rotate cranks 180°, and press pedals again. If something clicks, probably one of the cranks is loose. For tightening a cotter pin, support the crank with a block of wood (else the bearings may be hurt). Tap the head of the pin with a soft hammer (or protect with piece of wood) and snug down nut. For removing, do the reverse: loosen nut but leave on to protect threads, tap with hammer until loose.

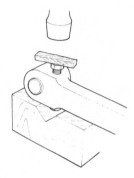

• Removing

To remove a cotterless crank, take out mounting bolt and washer and fit crank remover. Be sure to thread body fully into crank. Tighten bolt A. If the crank sticks, tap it lightly with a hammer, tighten bolt A a fraction, tap crank again, and so on until it comes free.

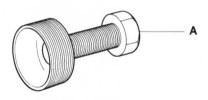

Crank remover

• Installing

Some folks say you should not grease the axle, but I'm not happy with this, because the crank is alloy and the axle is usually steel. Definitely do grease the bolt threads. Retighten every 25 miles for first 200 miles. Tighten very firmly, but if you are strong, not with all your might.

BOTTOM BRACKET

Most modern bottom brackets are sealed units and are run until they drop. Replacement requires special tools – it's a good job for a shop.

Older bikes use traditional ball bearings and cones, and are adjusted via the lockring C and cone D, which need special tools. Clean and regrease once a year, if bike is in hard service. Leave fixed cup F alone; inspect using a flashlight, and if replacement is needed, have a bike shop do it.

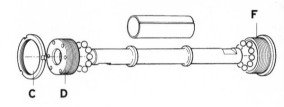

CHAINRINGS

Check periodically for damaged or worn teeth. Remove chain and with a strong light behind the chainwheel, rotate it, looking from the side for chipped teeth, and from above for bent teeth.

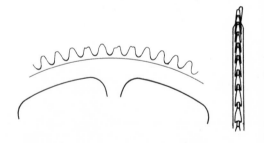

Shark's teeth mean it's replacement time.

Chainrings are usually held with hex bolts. Keep them tight. New bolts need to bed in, and until they do, can be escape prone; check often. Once they are seated, best to secure them with thread adhesive.

FREEHUBS AND FREEWHEELS

A freehub is part of the hub, and the cogs slide onto splines.

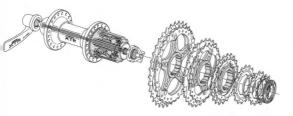

A freewheel threads onto the hub, and in most cases, the cogs thread onto the freewheel, although a spline design has also been used.

Periodically check the cogs for bent or chipped teeth. When replacement time comes, do all cogs at once, as there are many different kinds, with all sorts of special features, and you need a matched set to know they will get along with each other.

To get the cogs off a freehub, remove skewer, wrap chain whip around middle cog, to hold wheel in drive direction (clockwise). Fit special cassette lockring remover and undo (counter-clockwise) with a big wrench. If it is stuck, use the skewer to hold remover in place, but undo it the moment the lockring releases.

Lubricate by laying wheel flat and flowing chain lube into the gap between the fixed and moving parts. In some cases excess will flow out other side; be ready with rags to prevent a mess. Not all units can be lubricated this way; check manufacturer's instructions.

To remove a threaded freewheel from a hub, remove skewer/nuts and washers and fit free-

wheel remover. It must fit exactly. Hold in place with skewer (leave springs off) or nuts. Use a big wrench to break loose the freewheel, and the moment it does, release the skewer or nut, or else in spades. If it won't break, put the freewheel remover in a vise and turn the wheel.

To change cogs you need a bunch of special tools, and these days few people bother – they just buy another freewheel. Similarly, you won't find anyone who wants to take one of these apart. It's logical enough inside, but there are zillions of tiny ball bearings, and getting them to all stay in place while reassembling the freewheel is a real feat involving clever sophistry with bits of string. If your freewheel sticks up and does not cure with cleaning in solvent, get another.

Installing a threaded freewheel, grease the threads, and take care not to cross-thread. Snug with remover, but riding will wind tight. If you have got a freewheel with new thread-on cogs, then on your first ride, use your chain to tighten them in the order in which they were mounted.

WHEEL TRUING

The rim is laced in position by the spokes, which are tensioned via threaded nipples at the rim.

Truing a rim can take patience and skill. Check rim by holding a pencil or some-such at a fixed point such as a stay or brake arm and spinning wheel. If wobble is more than 1/2 inch, take wheel to a shop and ask if they can save it.

Remove tire. If you do not have a wheel truing stand, use the bike drop outs. First check that rim is structurally OK. If there are cracks or anything like that, again down to the shop. Pluck all the spokes and tighten any that are much more slack than others. Remember, on a rear wheel, spokes on either side sound different. Note: spokes tighten by turning counter-clockwise.

Hold a chalk or crayon at the outer edge of the rim and spin the wheel so that high (up and down) spots are marked. Working 1/4 turn at a time, tighten the spokes at the marks, and loosen them opposite the marks. Continue until wheel is round.

Next, hold chalk or crayon at side of rim so that side-to-side wobbles are marked. Working 1/4 to 1/3

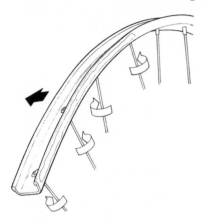

turn at a time, and in groups of 4 to 6 spokes, tighten up the spokes opposite the marks, and by the same amount, loosen the ones next to the marks. Tighten or loosen spokes in the center of the marks more than those on the edges. When you are finally successful, run your fingers around the rim well and check for protruding spoke ends. File protruders down.

Replacing spokes, or frozen nipples, is straightforward enough, but make sure you have exactly the right size. To replace spokes on the freewheel side of a hub, the freewheel has to be removed.

HANDLEBARS

Tighten or loosen handlebars via the binder bolt(s) B. Designs will vary, but function will be clear.

Handlebars take a lot of stress, and eventually wear out. Bikes used only on Sundays will be safe for a long time, but bars on hard used bikes should be replaced about every 3 years, or if they get bent in a crash. Never straighten out bent bars.

To install or remove handlebar grips, lubricate them with water.

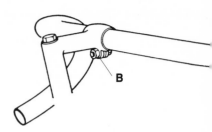

B

STEM

There are two kinds: quill and threadless. The quill type has a long bolt with a wedge which grips the inside of the steerer tube. It is used with conventional headsets, and can be lowered or raised (but not past the safety mark).

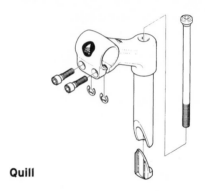

Quill

The threadless type has a clamp in place of the quill. The clamp secures both the stem, and the top race of the headset. It can be raised or lowered only with washers and spacers, so that the headset remains in adjustment.

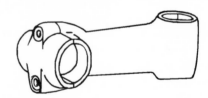

Threadless

To move or remove a quill stem, loosen the mounting bolt and then tap it with a hammer. Use a block of wood or similar to protect finish. At least once a year remove the stem and grease it to prevent corrosion.

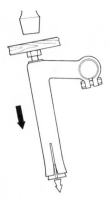

To remove a threadless stem, loosen the (horizontal clamping bolts. Secure fork to bike (it can stand on floor) and remove the adjusting bolt in the top cap. Pull cap and stem off steerer tube.

To change the height of a threadless stem, consult a bike shop. Washers have to be changed, the star nut inside probably has to be moved (special tool), and the steerer tube may need to be cut.

Whatever type of stem you have, keep it tight enough to be steady, but loose enough to give in a crash. And don't forget to lube it.

HEADSET

As with stems, there are threaded and threadless or unthreaded headsets. On a threaded headset, the top cup can be turned with a wrench, and is held in place with a locknut. Basically, it works like any classic cup and cone bearing.

On a threadless headset, the top cup and a tapered compression ring slide onto the steerer tube and are held in place by the stem via an adjusting bolt which grips a star nut rammed down into the steerer tube. Although the method is different, this, too, is a cup and cone job.

Fortunately, both types tend to utilize caged ball bearings, which makes working on them eas-

ier. To adjust a threaded headset, first ensure that you have wrenches of the right size, and don't use plumber's tools, because they may bend things out of shape. Loosen locknut A, turn down cone B, and resecure locknut A. It's easier to say than do, and will doubtless take a few tries. Tightening the locknut will effect the bearing adjustment, and the locknut must be good and tight.

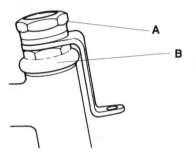

Adjusting a threadless headset is a breeze. Loosen the horizontal clamp bolts and tighten or loosen the adjusting bolt as required. Careful not to overtighten, or the headset may be damaged.

If your bike is in regular use, the headset should be cleaned and regreased once a year. It's not that bad a job, but take care that the fork does not fall out of the bike, and if you have loose ball bearings, that you get them all. Installing headset cups, or a new headset, are shop jobs.

SEAT POST AND SADDLE

Raise or lower the saddle by loosening the binder bolt on the frame (usually a hex bolt). Do not raise the seat post past the safety mark – the consequences could be ruinous. At least once a year remove the seat post, clean it up and the seat tube as well, and grease the lot.

To move the saddle forward or backwards, or to adjust the tilt, loosen the clamp which grips the saddle rails, held by one or more bolts. Fiddle with yours to see how it works, and have fun.

RENDEZVOUS

Done!

Dreams come true • Get rid of cars • Fighting the road lobby • Becoming involved in cycle activism

Everybody has dreams and here is one of mine: cars are banned from central areas of all metropolitan regions. Each city provides free bicycles (with adjustable seats and handlebars) scattered about to be used as needed. Because cities can buy enough bikes at a time to make special orders feasible, each city has a bike with a unique and readily identifiable frame design. All bolts and screws have left hand threads, like the light bulbs in subway stations, to discourage the stealing of parts for private use. There are repair centers throughout town, as well as special racks in which bikes in need of servicing can be left.

—Richard's Bicycle Book, *1972*

ONE! OH ALL RIGHT, STARTED. AS YOU MIGHT already know, a number of free bike programs in the Netherlands, United States, and elsewhere have fizzled, because the bikes were abused or stolen. However, in France, a scheme known as Plan Velo has been extremely successful. Instead of bikes being left around on the streets, or handed out willy-nilly to whomever, they are kept in various centers across town, and riders are registered and have smart cards for checking out machines. Riders are responsible for the bikes, which may be returned to any of the centers. The bikes are a unique design, to discourage theft, and also to provide space for graphics – the firm operating the scheme, Adshel, does outdoor advertising. They are now expanding to other countries.

Great. Making green pay is the route to go. Indeed, cyclists should be paid to ride their bikes, and public transport should be free! That would really put us out ahead.

We must get rid of cars. It's headline news when a big airliner crashes, for days and even weeks afterwards the papers and TV are filled with stories about the tragedy, the search for the black box, and the mourning of the bereaved.

Cars are currently killing people at the rate of 10 jumbo jet crashes a day.

That's only direct fatalities; an additional some three million lives are lost each year to air pollution, for which cars are the major source.

There's major environmental damage.

And to top it all off, cars don't even work; acute traffic congestion is chronic, at great cost to economic development.

Politicians are aware enough of the facts, but in the United States, few are bold enough to cross swords with the road lobby, or to do anything to alienate motorists. Ours is the most extravagant consumer economy in the world, Americans have been raised to equate cars with power and freedom, and often they are perfectly right. Motor vehicles are used for the majority of journeys in the US; in a lot of places, if you don't have a car, you're dead. Reason? There's no public transport, or if there is, it's so slow, you'll die of old age before you get anywhere. Why are things this way? The road lobby.

According to my uncle David, it used to be possible to ride on trams from the southernmost point in the US, Key West, Florida, all the way up to Maine and the Canadian border. A tram is a small, ground surface train or trolly which runs on rails, often just one car, perhaps three or four on a busy route, serving a community or city. The first ones were horse drawn, then they went electric. There used to be hundreds of tram companies. You could get free transfers between different lines, and so if you didn't mind an awful lot of stops, it was possible to go up or down the entire country for a few cents.

Tram services are common in Europe and work brilliantly. America has virtually none, because between about 1933 and 1955, General Motors and a group of allied companies bought all the electric tram companies and closed them. The tracks were torn up and paved over. This made more room for cars, buses, and trucks – and eliminated any possibility of competition.

The road lobby is a self-serving monopoly, and very unfriendly. Thanks to champions such as consumer advocate Ralph Nader, we are aware that auto makers value making a buck more than saving lives. A case in point was the infamous Ford Pinto, an economy car with a badly designed gas tank which could rupture and catch fire if the car was lightly struck from behind by another vehicle. The impact would also jam the doors closed, trapping the car's occupants in the fire. The Pinto was a death trap – and Ford knew it. They had their own tests and reports on the Pinto's defects, plus a cost benefit study which said it would be less expensive to deal with the cases where people were killed, than to fix the tank. Ford had decided to keep on making and selling the Pinto as it was.

The Pinto is one story among many. The road lobby is organized for just one purpose: making money. It's serious action: the ten largest companies in the world all produce oil or cars, and have turnovers bigger than the gross national product of most countries. There's a price, too: in creating a transport structure dominated by motor vehicles, the road lobby has killed more people than all the wars of the 20th century.

Can't make an omelette without breaking eggs? Fact is, cars have a fatal, self-defeating snag: they only work when used in limited numbers in open spaces. In cities and suburban areas, where most people live, cars take up too much room and obstruct each other to the point where they come to a standstill. The attempted solution of building more roads only attracts more cars and results in even worse congestion. In the City of Los Angeles, 70 percent of the real estate is devoted to cars. It's one huge motordrome, and yet during peak travel times even a short journey by car can take several hours.

Faced with severe traffic congestion, government and municipal authorities have typically reacted with punitive economic measures to reduce the use of cars: raising parking fees and penalties, and fuel taxes. Although gasoline in the US is ridiculously inexpensive – it costs less than bottled water – Americans are right to be sore about fuel price hikes.

Transport is an essential, not a taxable luxury. When the cost of transport is directly met by the consumer, then people who are poor and not so well off – more than half the population – proportionately pay more, and hence are less mobile. This is not fair. Raising the cost of motoring only makes the use of cars more elite, transport and social problems even worse, and restricts economic development.

We've got to get rid of cars, but imposing punitive costs on motorists will not help. It's undemocratic. There's also a backfire: the very expense of owning cars becomes an incentive for their use; people try for their money's worth. Sooner or later, the string runs out.

In Britain, the cost of gasoline at the pump is five times greater than in the US, thanks to high fuel taxes which are increased annually, at a rate deliberately set above the rate of inflation. This is supposedly to discourage the use of cars, for the benefit of the environment, but in fact is what the British call a nice little earner, because people have no choice but to pay. Thanks again to the road lobby, public transport in Britain has deteriorated terribly in recent years. Just as in America, in many places there is no practical alternative to using cars. Well, people in Britain finally got fed up with price hikes, there was a spontaneous blockade of fuel depots and deliveries to gasoline stations, and within a few days the country came to a standstill. Schools closed, hospitals were slowed down, and grocery store shelves emptied. Yet the protest had overwhelming widespread support. People knew they were being screwed. Finally, the government called out the army, and the demonstrators, having made their point, called off the blockade and went home. There were similar protests in other countries throughout Europe. None were because of any big conspiracy or plot. People simply reached the end of their tether.

What we need for transport is not higher taxes or more government controls, but real alternatives. It would be more productive to pay people for riding bikes! This would encourage people to use the method of local transport which is most efficient, costs the least, and does the most good for society. We would all enjoy better health, longer lives, and – bottom line – increased prosperity.

Is this a crazy idea that would only suddenly swell the ranks of welfare recipients with millions of deadbeat cyclists? Not at all. Remember – bikes pay.

Instead of handing out company cars and providing car parking spaces, employers ought to provide bikes and cycling allowances. People who cycle to work are more punctual, take fewer sick days, are more productive, and are less likely to change jobs. Providing financial incentives to employees for using bikes is both fair and practical. It pays for itself.

Car-free shopping areas enjoy greater commercial vitality. Cars use a lot of space and can bring only limited numbers of shoppers into an area. Holding back cars by harassing motorists with parking restrictions and traffic tickets does not do anything to improve business. Providing free cargo bikes – one for every household, or a pool of machines for each large building or block – surely would.

It would even make economic sense to pay people to ride bikes for fun. You can only go so far on a bike, there is no danger of people pedalling around the planet and draining the treasury dry. Thing is, people who cycle regularly are healthier. A ride a day keeps the doctor away. Preventative maintenance is cheaper than repair. Or: bicycles are way cheaper than hospital beds, and a lot

more fun to ride. US health care costs are crippling. Providing financial incentives for healthy exercise would cost less than what we are spending keeping couch potatoes alive.

The complement to free bikes and subsidized cycling as a staple of local transport is free public transport for longer journeys. Public transport should be publicly owned and supported through taxation on the commercial activity it generates, not by fare revenues. If public transport is made free, or at least inexpensive, then movement and – bottomline again – gross national product will be greater.

Those are some carrots. There is a stick, too. The only sure way to get rid of cars is to ban them. As long as people own cars, they will use them.

What's at stake here? Our freedom? That's a crock, and plenty of people know it. The US is a big place, with a lot of variety, and while cars are a mainstay of transport, some towns and communities have made progress in promoting sustainable transport. In places, people have started to move away from owning cars. In some towns, a bike is all you ever need.

There are many different ways in which to move when seeking a better world in terms of transport. Some people sneak out and destroy cars and roads. Others don suits and work in the corridors of power, striving to bring about legislative changes. Still others ignore politics of any kind and just get on with the physical building of cycling facilities.

All these different kinds of efforts are useful, each has their time and place. A lot is happening, much work is being done, and if you are interested in participating, my suggestion is that you look over the various possibilities and follow the line which suits you best.

Resources and Organizations

Alliance for a Paving Moratorium, PO Box 4347, Arcata, CA 95518 USA. Tel: 707 826-7775. Fax: 707 822-7007. E-mail: alliance@tidepool.com. Web: www.tidepool.com/alliance. Stuff cars! All about car free living. Publishes *Auto-Free Times*.

Bicycle News Agency.
Web: www.bikenews.org.
Advocacy issues from around the world.

Bicycle Parking Project, PO Box 7342,
Philadelphia, PA 19101 USA.
Tel: 215 222 1253.
E-mail: john-dowlin@usa.net.
Info on parking, and on equipment for securing bikes.

Bicycle Transportation, John Forester, MIT Press.
Classic handbook for cycle transportation engineers.

Bikes Belong! 1368 Beacon St.,
Brookline, MA 02446-2800 USA.
Tel: 617 734 2800. Fax: 617 734 2810.
E-mail: mail@bikesbelong.org.
Web: www.bikesbelong.org.
Assists in developing cycling facilities with funding under the Transportation Equity Act.

Bikes Not Bombs, 59 Amory St., No 103,
Roxbury, MA 02119-1011 USA.
Tel 617 442 0004. Fax: 617 445 2439.
E-mail: bnbrox@igc.apc.org.
Web: www.igc.org/bikesnotbombs.
Recycle donated bikes and ship to South America. Also work with urban youths.

Car Busters Resource Center, 44 rue Burdeau,
69001 Lyon, France.
Tel: 4 72 00 23 57. Fax: 4 78 28 57 78.
E-mail: carbusters@wanadoo.fr.
Web: www.antenna.nl/eyfa/cb.
Share information on international car free movement. Quarterly magazine.

Critical Mass.
Rides in various towns and communities. There's no central organization, for info on rides near you, ask around or hunt on the web.

Cyclists' Touring Club,
Cotterell House, 69 Meadrow, Godalming,

Surrey GU7 3HS England.
Tel: +44 01483 417217. Fax: +44 01483 426994.
E-mail: cycling@ctc.org.uk.
Web: www.ctc.org.uk.
Experienced touring and advocacy organization. Well informed, publishes much useful information.

Detour Publications, 500 University Ave.,
8th Floor, Toronto, Ontario, Canada M5G 1V7.
Tel: 416 392 1560. Fax: 416 392 0071.
E-mail: detour@web.net.
Web: www.detourpublications.com.
A rich source of information and books on a wide spectrum of activities in transport.

East Coast Greenway Alliance,
135 Main St., Wakefield, RI 02879 USA.
Tel/Fax: 401 789 4625.
E-mail: ecga@juno.com.
Web: www.greenway.org.
Working on a long distance, Key West, Florida to Canada, cycle trail which will be 80 percent off road.

Friends of the Earth, 1025 Vermont Ave. NW - Washington, DC 20005 USA.
Tel: 1 877 843-8687. Fax: 202 783 0444.
E-mail: foe@foe.org.
Web: www.for.org.
General environmental organization, much work and info on air pollution.

Institute for Transportation and Development Policy, 115 West 30th St., Suite 1205,
New York, NY 10001 USA.
Tel: 212 629 8001. Fax: 212 629 8033.
E-mail: mobility@igc.org.
Web: www.itdp.org.
Projects and policy advocacy. Publishes *Sustainable Transportation.*

International Bicycle Fund, 4887 Columbia Dr. S. No. R, Seattle, WA 98108-1919 USA.
Tel 206 767 0848.
E-mail: ibike@ibike.org.
Web: www.ibike.org.
Promotes bike transport, tours in Africa and Cuba.

International Mountain Bicycling Association (IMBA), PO Box 7578, Boulder, CO 80306-7578 USA. Tel: 303 545 9011. Fax: 303 545 9026. E-mail: infor@imba.com. Web: www.imba.com.

Promotes environmentally sound trail cycling. Publishes *IMBA Trail News* and various booklets on trail maintenance.

League of American Bicyclists, 1612 KJ St. NW, Suite 401, Washington, DC 20006 USA. Tel 202 822 1333. Fax: 202 822 1334. E-mail: bikeleague@bikeleague.org. Web: www.bikeleague.org.

National organization working through advocacy and education.

Rails to Trails Conservancy, 1100 17th St. NW, 10th Fl, Washington, DC 20036 USA. Tel 202 331 9696. Fax: 202 331 9680. E-mail: rtcmail@transact.org. Web: www.railtrails.org.

National organization with large membership, working to convert disused railroads into cycle paths.

Reclaim the Streets, PO Box 9656, London N4 4JY England. Tel: +44 020 7281 4621. E-mail: rts@gn.apc.org. Web: www.gn.apc.org/rts.

Home base for an organization which has spread world wide. Parties, events, and rides, to reclaim the streets for people.

Transport 2000, First Floor, The Impact center, 12–18 Hoxton Street, London N1 6NG Engand. Tel: +44 020 7613 0743. E-mail: transport2000@transport2000.demon.co.uk. Long term transport planning. International perspective.

Sustrans, 35 King Street, Bristol BS1 4DZ England. Tel: +44 0117 929 0888. Fax: +44 0117 929 0124. Web: www.sustrans.org.uk. Constructing a 10,000 mile cyclepath network in Britain. Veteran activists.

LAST MILES

Some people only want to ride their bikes, others are spoiling for a fight. There are many paths in cycle activism, what's best is a matter of time, circumstances, and your own inclinations. If you like, it's your ride. A few suggestions and pointers:

• Watch your back. Activists are typically created through radicalization. The sequence starts with innocence, advances to awareness and protest, as in signing petitions and going on demonstrations, and then when the police come and knock heads, to a shocked realization that crying "shame" is not enough, when issues and conflicts are deep rooted, they sometimes have to be forced.

Radicalization is a natural process, and unfortunately a highly visible one. The first place to look for hard core militant activists is among the ranks of protesters. If you think you might be inclined to be militant in a serious way, you might want to zero your profile.

• On the other side, do not be afraid to stand up for what is right. It can be all too easy to remain inert because making an effort seems futile. Groups such as Mothers Against Drunk Drivers (MADD) arose in reaction to a culture which condoned drunk driving and murder. Despite a worthy cause, MADD had to endure ridicule and abuse. They stuck to their guns, and while our attitudes and laws about drinking and cars still need improvement, drunk driving is no longer an approved sport.

• A common difficulty in doing what is right is the claim that this may be counter productive. Critical Mass rides are sometimes criticized on the grounds that filling the streets and roads with cyclists to obstruct traffic will alienate motorists. The point, however, is that cyclists *are* the traffic.

• Do not use activism and protest as a means to blow off steam or vent personal angers that were in fact generated elsewhere, and do not rush to judgment. One traditional method for subverting popular movements is to encourage hotheads.

Actions which are beyond immediate self-defense should have a clear political objective.

• Many worthy organizations have fallen into the hands of professional fund raisers. There is a practical relationship between the amount of money an organization has, and what it can accomplish. Slick solicitations which press obvious buttons can in the short term be more successful than sincere requests from real activists. If you get a load of literature which is obvious hype, make allowances; the original idea for the organization may still be a good one.

• The bicycle is an anarchist machine; it confers independent mobility at minimum expense or bother to anyone else. Bikes do not need licensing or regulation. People can just use them. This is exactly what drives bureaucrats, government agencies, politicians, and profiteers crazy. Always keep bikes free!

That's it. It's been a great ride, thanks very much for your company!

"Sweetheart turned her head to count the milestones which we passed."

Index